Russia and the Third World in the Post-Soviet Era

Russia and the Third World in the Post-Soviet Era

Edited by Mohiaddin Mesbahi

University Press of Florida

Gainesville/Tallahassee/Tampa/Boca Raton
Pensacola/Orlando/Miami/Jacksonville

Library of Congress Cataloging-in-Publication Data

Russia and the Third World in the post-Soviet era / edited by
  Mohiaddin Mesbahi.
      p.   cm.
    Includes bibliographical references and index.
    ISBN 0-8130-1270-8 (cloth).—ISBN 0-8130-1271-6 (pbk.)
    1. Developing countries—Foreign relations—Russia (Federation)
  2. Russia (Federation)—Foreign relations—Developing countries.
  I. Mesbahi, Mohiaddin.
  D888.R8R87   1994
  327.47017'24'09049—dc20   93-42807

The University Press of Florida is the scholarly publishing agency for the State
University System of Florida, comprised of Florida A & M University, Florida
Atlantic University, Florida International University, Florida State University,
University of Central Florida, University of Florida, University of North Florida,
University of South Florida, and University of West Florida

University Press of Florida
15 Northwest 15th Street
Gainesville, FL 32611

To Ali and Erfan

Contents

Preface

It was only a few years ago that the issue of Soviet involvement in the Third World occupied much of the literature of Soviet studies and the Cold War. The stunning collapse of the Soviet Union brought, among many other dramatic changes, a revolutionary transformation in relations between Russia, the new independent states of the former USSR, and the Third World. While significant changes had taken place in Moscow's relations with the developing world by the late 1980s, the abrupt collapse of the Soviet Union not only fundamentally altered the relationship but also raised critical questions concerning the place both of Russia (as the successor state of the USSR) and the Third World in the emerging post-Soviet world order. What will be the nature and scope of Russia's relations with the Third World in the long run, especially after the hype of continuous change has diminished? How will the Third World cope with the implications of the Soviet collapse? What will be the future of socialism in the Third World? Does the Third World even exist now that the second has disappeared? This volume has been designed to provide both the intellectual and policy frameworks for addressing these and other important questions concerning Russian–Third World relations.

The contributions to this volume (with a few exceptions) originated from papers delivered at the international conference on "The Transformation of the Former USSR and Its Implications for the Third World," organized by the editor and hosted by the Institute for Political and International Studies (IPIS) in Tehran, Iran, in March 1992. Co-sponsors of the conference were the Oriental Institute of the Russian

Academy of Science and the Department of International Relations of Florida International University. The three-day conference brought together more than fifty renowned scholars from the United States, Europe, China, Russia, the Muslim republics of the former USSR, and the Third World. Not only did the gathering generate considerable debate among the participating scholars, it also created a significant contribution to the policy debate on the subject.

The chapters in this book have been updated since the conference, although by design they were mostly written so as not to be acutely time-sensitive. While they reflect the rich diversity of the contributors' intellectual and cultural orientations, they are also unified under a central theme—continuity and change.

I would like to express special thanks to the IPIS for hosting and sponsoring the impressive international gathering that made this book possible. In this regard, the project is especially indebted to Abbas Maleki, Ahmad Hajihosseini, Sohrab Shahabi, and Ali Ghaderi, whose support was essential.

I am grateful to Irina Zviagelskaya of the Russian Academy of Sciences for assisting me in managing the contributions of the scholars from the former USSR. I would also like to express my appreciation to Provost James Mau, Dean Arthur Herriott, and Professor Ralph Clem of Florida International University for the support they rendered to the project. I am also grateful to Michael Senecal of the University Press of Florida for his useful editorial suggestions. Last but not least, I would like to thank Naisy Sarduy, my graduate assistant, whose help both in the organization of the conference and the preparation of the manuscript for this book was indispensable.

Introduction ━━━━━━━━━━━━━━━━━━━━━

Russia and the Third World after the Soviet Union:

Departure, Convergence, or a New Centaur?

Mohiaddin Mesbahi

The collapse of the USSR in December 1991 not only dramatically altered the relationship between the United States and Russia, it also transformed a large component of the international system—Russia's intricate relations with the Third World. Just as the Soviet reluctance to withdraw from Iranian Azerbaijan in 1946 helped ignite the sparks of the Cold War, the Soviet military intervention in Afghanistan gave official birth to a new Cold War in the early 1980s. Throughout the Cold War years, international high politics was occupied both by the relentless energy of the superpowers' rivalry in the Third World and by Third World sociopolitical and ideological dynamics, which often independently affected the system.

Many have referred to the post–World War II confrontations in the Third World as "wars on the periphery," implying that their impact on the "war at the core" between the United States and the Soviet Union was marginal. But the war at the core, which centered on the struggle over the balance of nuclear and conventional forces in Europe, was fought immediately after the end of World War II, and the situation in Europe remained largely stable, if tense, throughout the postwar era. Military and political demarcation lines in Europe had been clearly drawn; the key elements of the rivalry were maintained through religiously pursued policies of military buildup and through tight control over rival alliances. Meanwhile, the Third World, larger in area, population, and raw wealth than either the United States or the Soviet Union, was the seat of "hot wars"— regional conflicts, revolutions, and counterrevolutions. The bloody part of the Cold War was fought in the Third World, and the history of war and peace in the post–World War II era would be very different if the U.S.-Soviet rivalry had not been tested in so many Third World nations.

It is therefore not surprising that Sovietologists, whether sponsored by government or by universities and think tanks, have long been concerned with the issue of Soviet involvement in the Third World. Much of the controversy among policy makers and in academia over the nature and objectives of the Soviet system was affected by Soviet behavior in the Third World. Was the USSR a purposeful totalitarian entity that was driven to perpetuate its ideology through expansion, or was it simply a pragmatic power acting in response to the structural imperatives of the international system and the laws of balance of power?

The fact that Marxism became a global phenomenon—modified and adapted to the needs of Third World radicals—created a subjective connection between the Third World and the Soviet Union—a collective consciousness—that went beyond Moscow's intentions. Whether the revolutionaries of the Third World considered the Soviets committed ideologues or pragmatists, the existence of the Soviet Union allowed many Third World states and revolutionary movements to maneuver with a degree of flexibility incommensurate with their status in the international system. To use Kenneth Waltz's term, the "distribution of capability"[1] in the system did not explain the high degree of importance and relevance of the Third World to global politics. The physical and ideological presence of the Soviet Union in the system provided the space within which these states and movements operated.

Thus the collapse of the Soviet Union created not only a vacuum in global relations but also laid the foundation for the transformation of the Third World itself. What is the meaning of the Soviet collapse? How will the parts of the former Soviet Union fit into the evolving international system? Does the old "Second World" of the USSR and its satellites still exist, or are the former Soviet nations being transformed into Third World nations themselves? What will the Soviet collapse mean for the future of socialism in the Third World, and how will the so-called North-South conflict be affected? Finally, how will Russia, the successor to the USSR, and other republics of the new Commonwealth of Independent States (CIS) relate to the Third World?

This volume has been divided into four parts. In part 1 enduring theoretical and policy issues ranging from the nature of the Soviet collapse to the future of socialism in the developing world are discussed. In part 2 contrasting yet complementary views on the meaning of the Bolshevik revolution and the impact of the Soviet Union on the Third World are presented. The three essays in part 3 examine the significance of Russian/Soviet–Third World relations in the context of U.S.-Soviet relations and the political, ideolgical, and military implications of the Soviet collapse on U.S.-Third World relations. The essays in part 4 address past, present, and future relations between Russia and Africa, Asia, Latin America, and the Middle East.

The first essay in part 1, Vendulka Kubalkova's "A Requiem for the Soviet Union," is a comprehensive assessment of the international significance of the Soviet Union and the meaning and essence of its collapse. Kubalkova argues that the "ambivalent and controversial" nature of the Soviet Union was due in part to the geographical and ideological compartmentalization of the field of Soviet studies during the Soviet era, which diminished the pertinence of academic views of the Soviet Union and undermined the possibility of academic exchange between East and West and left and right. In order to evaluate the international significance of the Soviet Union's collapse and assess what might take its place, Kubalkova contends, a reassessment of its historic goals and aspirations needs to take place in an atmosphere free of ideological disputation.

The ideological bias of "mainstream" Sovietology undermined an otherwise useful and less politically loaded interaction with non-mainstream, "left" Sovietology, which, in spite of its own ideological handicaps, was keener and more consistent in its interpretations of the "systematic contradictions" of the Soviet system and the inevitability of its collapse than the unshakable, though elegant, "totalitarian model" of the mainstream. A more balanced study of the post-Soviet transition demands the abdication of the intellectual arrogance of both the right and the left and calls for an interdisciplinary approach and depoliticization of the field.

The second essay in part 1, "The 'Third Worldization' of Russia and Eastern Europe" by Andre Gunder Frank, provides an unconventional interpretation of the meaning of the collapse of the Soviet Union and Eastern Europe in relation to international politics.[2] Basing his thesis on the world system approach, Frank questions both Soviet and Western concepts of the existence of two rival world systems—capitalism and communism—as an "optical illusion" emanating from the notion that politics and ideology are the prime movers of historical events. "In the real world," he argues, contrary to what Mao, Lenin, Reagan, and Francis Fukuyama believed, "economics is in command." Forty years of socialist development have not changed the economic position either of the Soviet bloc or of Third World countries, Frank claims. There has been and will continue to be a dominant world system, capitalism (the First World), to which both the Second World and the Third World have been related; now that the Soviet Union has collapsed, the process of integration is gaining momentum. Socialist development has both objectively and subjectively failed to provide an alternative to the world capitalist model, especially for the Third World. Instead, in the "new" world order, which is as new as the old world order, the socialist countries of the Second World are joining the Third World, reinforcing an enduring center-periphery structure between nations. Notwithstanding the dramatic changes since 1989, both the East and the South were and remain in the Third World.

In the third essay in part 1, "The 'End of History' and the Third World: The Relevance of Ideology," Georgy Mirsky addresses one of the key theoretical discussions of the post-Soviet era, namely the "end of history" thesis put forward by Francis Fukuyama.[3] Mirsky criticizes both the Marxist-Leninist historical failure to grasp the importance of nationalism and religion and the idea that the Western capitalist model is a universal alternative to failed Soviet socialism. The mythology and passion of the goal of achieving "a just and egalitarian social organization" in the world will continue to generate violent revolutionary impulses, in spite of the collapse of Soviet communism and the triumph of Western liberalism. Ethnonationalism, religious militancy, and revivalism will either replace or, at times, complement the remnants of socialism, and as such those forces will provide the contradictory and driving dynamics of twenty-first-century politics and international relations. Mirsky supports his thesis by providing a succinct analysis of ethnonationalism in the former Soviet republics of Central Asia and argues that in a world in which the majority of people are not inhabitants of the West and that lacks the inertia of the Cold War arrangement, nationalism will be used as an ideology to articulate grievances, channel frustration, mobilize the masses, and implement political ambitions.

The final essay in part 1, "The Collapse of the USSR and the Future of the Socialist Model" by Elizabeth Kridl Valkenier, discusses the evolution of Soviet theory and practice toward the Third World and the implications of the collapse of the USSR for the future of the socialist model, especially in the Third World. Valkenier, who by the early 1980s had already discussed the changing nature of Soviet–Third World relations,[4] argues that socialism as exemplified by the USSR ceased to be credible to Third World leaders well before the actual collapse of the Soviet Union itself.[5]

Valkenier's careful analysis of the evolutionary stages of Soviet–Third World relations from the era of Khrushchev to the collapse of the USSR reveals a gradual yet definite change in the socialist aspect of Soviet behavior. "For the sake of cold economic efficiency," socialism gradually gave way to pragmatism while the rhetorical cover was maintained. Thus the post-Soviet phase of Russia's relations with the Third World does not constitute a radical break with the past. Valkenier provides interesting "model-scenarios" for the future relationship between Russia, the Commonwealth of Independent States (CIS), and the Third World, and argues that, in spite of the Soviet collapse, Marxism will continue to inform and affect Third World collective consciousness and especially international economic negotiations, though it will not serve as a source of strategic threat to the West. "The USSR's collapse and the choice of the CIS to hitch its fortunes to the Western market economies do not remove or alleviate old irritants in North-South economic relations," she concludes.

The two essays in part 2, "The USSR and the Third World: A Historical Perspective" by Yuri Krasin and "Russia's 'New Thinking' and the Third World" by Viktor Kremenyuk, provide interesting and contrasting views of the Soviet-Russian experience in the Third World. Krasin's essay on the historical significance of Russia's experience in the Third World provides a perspective characteristic of the architects of Gorbachev's "new thinking" in foreign policy. Krasin argues that the messianic impulse of the October Revolution, in spite of its periodic modifications, "remained invariable throughout seventy years." This excessive ideological emphasis led to "a selective approach" toward the Third World, emphasis on military aid, and, finally, to the failure of the socialist-oriented model of economic development in the developing world. Yet Krasin reminds his readers that it would be ahistorical to overlook the positive results of the Soviet Union's impact on the Third World's progress, including its contribution to national struggles for liberation. Questioning the validity of replacing the failed Soviet utopia with Western forms of government and society, Krasin argues for an "integral world"[6] of synthetic experiences and culture within which Russia could play the role of a bridge between the new East and the West.

Kremenyuk's essay on Russia's "new thinking" investigates the anatomy and essence of that new thinking within the context of Russia's historical interests and the future framework of Russian and CIS involvement in the Third World. Kremenyuk draws a geopolitical parallel between the experience of the Russian empire and the USSR in the Third World and argues that while both were initially bifurcated and hesitant, they both "joined the other great powers in active politics in the colonial periphery." Within the historical context of competition with the West, Kremenyuk analyzes the essence of new thinking as "a balance of virtue and necessity"—not the result of an abstract thinking influenced by Western achievements, but "a bitter necessity in order to avoid the complete collapse of the nation and consecutive chaos." In a post–Cold War world that has yet to create the just new world order promised by new thinking, Kremenyuk argues that the influence of Russia (and the CIS) will diminish in the old Third World while it will acquire a new and active role in the new one. Russia will play a "conciliatory and constructive role" in shaping the future of the former Soviet Islamic republics by becoming "the main sponsor and promoter of change" in Central Asia, thus overshadowing the "Islamic factor."

The essays in part 3, "The Dynamics of U.S.-Russian Interaction in the Third World during the Gorbachev Era and Beyond" by Alvin Z. Rubinstein, "America's Post–Cold War Military Policy in the Third World" by Mark Katz, and "The End of the Cold War and the 'New World Order': Implications for the Developing World" by Roger Kanet and James T. Alexander, deal with different aspects of the U.S. factor in Russian–Third World relations. Rubinstein's careful and detailed analysis provides a survey of the evolution of the Soviet Union's policy in the Third World from the end of World War II to the Gorbachev era. Rubinstein then examines the different periods and categories of the Gorbachev era, arguing that the most important hallmarks of the Gorbachev revolution were Gorbachev's "acceptance of linkage in U.S.-Soviet relations" and that there was a contradiction between the USSR's projection of power in the Third World and its attempt to improve relations with the United States.

Characterizing the U.S.-Soviet rivalry as "imperial" as opposed to "imperialist," Rubinstein argues that the primary considerations for both superpowers were political and strategic, not territorial or economic. The rivalry acknowledged the formal legitimacy of the nation-state system and the requirements of working within it; it was largely satisfied with patient and incremental change and gains; and it was informed by a utilitarian attitude toward disposable client states. Thus Rubinstein limits the role of ideology in shaping the rivalry: "The ideological residual may well be the result of a need to exaggerate an external enemy/threat in order to strengthen the leadership's domestic legitimacy." The future of Russia's involvement in the Third World, especially within its own periphery, will depend on whether the CIS can succeed. A successful CIS (meaning the emergence of truly independent states in the former USSR) will separate Russia from the Middle East: "Russia will no longer be a Middle East power." However, an ephemeral CIS, Rubinstein contends, might pave the way for the resurgence of a new Russian expansion and a return to "familiar great power politics" in the Central Asian and Middle Eastern heartland.

Katz's essay on America's military policy in the Third World provides an analytical framework to study the U.S. reaction to the collapse of Russia's influence in the Third World and the areas of continuous American interest in the region. He rejects the notion that the United States plans to expand its influence in the Third World after the Soviet collapse and argues that to a large extent, America's former interventionism was a function of perceived communist expansion, whether real or imagined. In the absence of a Soviet global threat and in view of the improbability of Russia's return to past policies, there is no longer a strategic motivation for U.S. intervention: "The Third World was primarily important for the United States only in the context of the Cold War."

Furthermore, an expansionist U.S. policy scenario ignores the pivotal role of the domestic factor, especially American public opinion, in restraining policy makers from large-scale intervention. Katz identifies four vital considerations that might prompt America's unlikely intervention in the Third World: proliferation of nuclear weapons, prevention of regional hegemony, maintenance of Western access to the world's sea lines of communication, and the maintenance of Western access to oil. Yet Katz cautions that these interests and the interpretation of threats to them are subject to modifications and flexibilities that deprive them of being considered an automatic blueprint for a

U.S. interventionist policy. "The American public is not likely to regard most of the Third World as having sufficiently vital significance for the U.S. to justify costly intervention," and, whatever security interests there are, they "can be effectively pursued by the U.S. through means other than direct intervention."

Roger Kanet and James T. Alexander's essay on the end of the Cold War and the new world order introduces a systematic analysis of not only U.S. and Soviet policy during the Gorbachev era but, more significantly, devotes considerable space to the discussion of the meaning and the essence of America's call for a new world order. Arguing against conventional wisdom that considered the new world order as a mere political slogan borne out of a temporary need for the United States to develop a coalition against Iraq, "the concept," Kanet and Alexander maintain, "does have concrete meaning. It is a reformulation of the basic historical principles that underlay U.S. policy throughout the twentieth century." While the Cold War and intense competition with the USSR "often required compromising ideals," the absence of the Soviet threat has provided a different, and flexible, context, "a new level of consciousness"—exactly what American political philosopher Louis Hartz recommended in 1955.

Yet this new level of consciousness is but "a new example of extending the concept of America's 'manifest destiny' to the outside world"—a vision of a *Pax* Americana that "includes aspects of idealism and self interest." The collapse of the USSR and the challenge of the Persian Gulf War provided the simultaneous context for the conceptualization of the new world order as a framework of a new U.S. foreign policy that envisioned an expanded U.S. global influence tied to international legality and uniformity, the promotion of peace, democracy, and the free market economy, the strengthening of American competitiveness, the protection of the United States from traditional threats, and the meeting of humanitarian needs. In the absence of the Soviet alternative, the United States can more directly use its instrumentality, especially economic aid, to persuade the Third World to comply with the requirements of democratic reform and the free market. Kanet and Alexander remind us, however, of the present obstacles and uncertainties facing the long-term relevance of the new world order vision. The present U.S. economic crisis, the financial burden of unpopular foreign aid, and the uncertainty of the role that Germany, Japan, and China will play in the developing world are among the key uncertainties contributing to its dubious future.

The first essay in part 4 is Stephen Neil MacFarlane's "Russia, Africa, and the End of the Cold War," which addresses three major themes, including the consequences of the collapse of Soviet influence for African politics and security, the influence of the evolving situation in the USSR on Africa's role in the world economy, and the future of Russia's role in Africa.

The restructuring of formerly Soviet foreign policy was the key to the end of the Cold War in Africa and to the resolution of major regional conflicts such as the civil war in Angola. MacFarlane argues that the end of the superpower competition meant a reduction in the flow of resources to military establishments in African states and may have some effect in reducing the influence of the military in the domestic politics of those states. The end of the Cold War may also lead to the emergence of regional powers to play a more active role in management of regional security. While the UN's role in African conflict management seems promising, MacFarlane points to some underlying dynamics, such as the UN's diminishing financial capabilities to respond to the African needs and the regional alarm over the perceived hegemony of the United States in the Security Council, as constraining elements.

MacFarlane draws a rather bleak economic picture for Africa, claiming that the Soviet collapse erodes the market position of African mineral exports, removes a major rationale for foreign assistance, and may also lead to a lessening of foreign investment. MacFarlane's analysis argues against the tendency in current Western circles to write Russia off from Third World involvement in general, and, more specifically, from involvement in Africa. Instead, he argues that Russia's interests in Africa predated the October 1917 revolution and are influenced by the geopolitical reality of being both an Atlantic and Pacific power and by the Russian appreciation of the strategic significance of the Red Sea and the Indian Ocean's sea lines of communication. "Normalcy," not withdrawal, will be the hallmark of Russian foreign policy in Africa, MacFarlane concludes.

The discussion of Russia's policy in the Asia-Pacific region is the subject of Gennady Chufrin's essay, "Russia and the Asia-Pacific Region: Toward a New Doctrine." Arguing that Russia's post-Soviet policy will be "Eurasian," Chufrin rejects the idea that Russian foreign policy will become regionalized and believes that in spite of Russia's current decline, the nation remains a global power. While the end of the Cold War has removed the hegemonic, imperial tendencies of the superpower confrontation, it has not guaranteed a conflict-free or noncompetitive world order. Rather, it has resulted in a competitive world that now includes two of Russia's powerful Eastern neighbors, Japan and China, as prime players.

The essay focuses on the development of Russia's Asia-Pacific doctrine and analyzes Moscow's relations with China, Japan, and the two Koreas in addition to relations with the Southeast Asian states. Fear of a triangular alliance between Washington, Tokyo, and Seoul and of Sino-U.S. strategic cooperation were critical factors that led to the new thinking in Moscow's Asian policy and the normalization of relations with China in 1989. In discussing the growing trade relations between China and Russia, Chufrin maintains that the full utilization of the normalization will depend on the ability of Moscow and Beijing to resolve border issues that are a key factor in creating zones of economic cooperation in the border region. Normalization of relations with Japan will be equally critical for Russian foreign policy in Asia. Though the resolution of territorial disputes can act as a prerequisite and catalyst of normalization, Chufrin maintains that Russian-Japanese relations may not dramatically improve even if the territorial dispute is resolved, because the structural incompatibility between the Russian economy (especially its Far Eastern sector) and Japan's economy will diminish the potential for utilization of Russian business opportunities. The study warns that while Russia should continue its political normalization and expansion of economic relations with South Korea, it should avoid the further isolation of North Korea, especially in view of Pyongyang's nuclear ambitions.

Anatoly Glinkin provides an overview of Russia's policy toward Cuba and Central America and presents a framework for the analysis of the post-Soviet period in those regions in "Moscow, Cuba, and Central America." Glinkin claims that the Nicaraguan revolution was a watershed in Soviet relations with Central America. The "imperial mentality" of the Brezhnev era saw the development of a Havana-Managua axis supported by Moscow as a "magnetic force" attracting or influencing other Central American countries that in one way or another were engulfed in internal sociopolitical conflicts and transformations. Ironically, the Soviet desire to make inroads in Central

America was tamed by the contradictory desire to prevent Nicaragua from becoming a second Cuba in U.S.-Soviet relations. Gorbachev's new thinking in foreign policy, though it provided a new atmosphere for a more serious exploration of conflict resolution—especially in support of the Contadora initiative—did not drastically change Moscow's immediate policy; indeed, Soviet aid to Nicaragua increased substantially under Gorbachev, and superpower competition and mistrust still dominated. Glinkin argues that the Soviet relationship with Cuba was one of the most challenging and delicate foreign policy issues facing Gorbachev. Moscow's decisions had to be made within a framework of contradictory and legitimate concerns—the significance of the Cuban factor in improving relations with Washington and the unwillingness of Havana to engage in domestic reforms on the one hand, and thirty years of strategic and economic cooperation and the considerable political cost associated with leaving a long-term Third World ally on its own on the other. These two contradictory tendencies characterized Cuban-Soviet relations during the Gorbachev era. Glinkin details the dramatic changes in the relationship between Cuba and Russia after the Soviet collapse, including Cuba's attempt to establish political and economic ties with CIS states such as Kazakhstan, the Ukraine, and Latvia and renegotiating economic, political, and military agreements with Russia. Russia under Yeltsin, however, cannot and will not abandon Cuba completely. Major economic interests, such as the nuclear power plant, and residual political and military interests remain.

Moscow's relations with the two South American giants is the subject of the essay by Aldo Vacs, "Moscow's Relations with Argentina and Brazil: End or Renewal?" Vacs's essay addresses both political and economic aspects of relations between the USSR and Argentina and Brazil during the Gorbachev era and after the Soviet collapse and provides a dynamic analytical framework to investigate the relationship in the context of changes in Soviet domestic and foreign policy and the coincidence of the Soviet transformation with the political and economic changes in Argentina and Brazil.

Perestroika had a generally positive impact on the reduction of tension in Latin America and opened the possibility of finding innovative ways of enhancing political and economic relations. The crisis of reform in the USSR and the internal shift both in Argentina and Brazil toward a neoliberal economic model and pro-West foreign policies by early 1990, however, dealt a heavy blow to a relatively stable, promising political and economic relationship with Moscow and brought the relationship to an impasse. Vacs's analysis provides a mixed picture. The collapse of the USSR and the ensuing economic crisis in Russia and the other former Soviet republics meant that Russia and the CIS would not be able to sustain the huge trade deficits with Argentina and Brazil that the Soviet government condoned until 1985 for political-strategic reasons. Most likely, the CIS will try to satisfy its domestic needs through other markets, especially in Canada, the United States, and the European Community, that offer the best prices, quality, and credit. Although relations with Russia will remain cordial and new diplomatic initiatives have led to the establishment of diplomatic ties with the republics, the end of the Cold War might also diminish the ability of the Latin American countries to achieve independent foreign policies, thereby forcing them to make political and strategic concessions to the United States and other Western nations that would have been rejected in the 1970s and 1980s.

In "Russia and the Middle East: Continuity and Change" Irina Zviagelskaya and Vitaly Naumkin provide a general overview of Russia's prospects and challenges in the Middle East in the post-Soviet period. Zviagelskaya and Naumkin identify major trends and dilemmas facing Moscow's leadership in the face of the new geopolitical realities of the Soviet southern periphery. Dividing the region into two "operative theaters"—Arab-Israeli and the Persian Gulf—allows Zviagelskaya and Naumkin to identify specific challenges that each theater presents separately to post-Soviet Russia. Between the two fundamental driving forces of Soviet policy in the Middle East, ideological designs and geopolitical imperatives, the authors give primacy to the "desire to establish a military and political presence in the vital parts of the region." While this geopolitical imperative motivated the rivalry between the superpowers in the Middle East in winning allies and clients, under Gorbachev this rivalry was subordinated to the requirements of the new détente in U.S.-Soviet relations. It was this U.S. factor that became the key parameter of Soviet attitudes toward regional conflicts such as the Arab-Israeli conflict and the Iran-Iraq War. Zviagelskaya and Naumkin also believe that Washington's positive change of attitude toward Moscow, especially since 1988, was a critical factor in the promotion of superpower détente in the region.

Perhaps more than any other region of the Third World, the collapse of the USSR has transformed the Middle East. The geopolitical and cultural addition of the Central Asian republics to the Middle East has opened an entirely different context for Moscow's policy in the future. Yet the study points to some critical elements of continuity, especially in the area of Russia's historical preoccupation with a security threat from the South and the continuous importance of domestic factors. The possibility of a threat emanating from the now unstable South—the soft underbelly—is intertwined with a growing concern over the Islamic factor and Russia's Muslim minority. Economic imperatives, a rather subordinate variable in the past, are now acquiring a special importance as Russia and the other republics look into the oil-rich states of the Middle East for trade and investment. Common interests with the United States, especially in the area of Arab-Israeli peace, do not "eliminate the asymmetry" of interests and policies, some with potential for tension, such as arms sales to the region.

Yuri V. Gankovsky's essay, "The Dynamics of Russia-Afghan Relations: A View from Moscow," argues that the Soviet intervention in Afghanistan was perhaps the most controversial event in the history of Soviet foreign policy, one with enormous international and domestic implications. The essay provides an overview of the relationship between the two countries both before and after the October Revolution. This historical survey will be particularly relevant as pre-1917 historical trends have acquired new significance in the post-Soviet period. Gankovsky then provides an analysis of the socioeconomic development of Afghanistan to set the stage for the discussion of the Soviet intervention. The author analyzes different aspects of the decision to intervene, particularly the opposition of Soviet generals and the inability of academic advisers to influence the decision.

The collapse of the Soviet Union and the pro-Moscow regime in Kabul and the emergence of the independent states of Tajikistan and Uzbekistan on the Afghanistan border will not be the end of Russia's interests in Afghanistan, for "if events in Afghanistan have negative repercussions on the situation in the republics of Central Asia, Russia will not be able to remain impartial. Ten million Russians live within these republics." Deployment of Russian troops on the border with Afghanistan in September and October 1992 was a clear indication of this uneasy continuity.

The final essay in this volume, "The Collapse of the USSR and the Northern Tier States" by Shireen T. Hunter, deals with Iran, Pakistan, and Turkey. Few other countries in the world have been affected so thoroughly by the disintegration of the USSR as Turkey and Iran. These countries were subjected to big-power rivalries even before October 1917, as the Russian and British empires fought over the region. The contiguity of these countries to the border of the former Soviet Union made them subjects of Cold War rivalry up to the collapse of the Soviet Union.

The emergence of newly independent Muslim states in Central Asia and Azerbaijan, with the intertwined ethno-territorial and religious complexities, puts their future relations with Russia at the top of Russia's concerns and is a major source of Western attention. Hunter's study provides a comprehensive pyramid-shaped model in which the place of the Northern Tier states in both the Cold War and post–Cold War international system have been analyzed. This conceptual approach promises to be flexible as it allows the incorporation of the unpredictable and constantly changing political situation since the collapse of the USSR into a broader, more manageable analytical framework, allowing a certain degree of predictability. Among the key systemic ramifications of the Soviet collapse and the emergence of the post–Cold War system is the perceived potential of Islam "as an alternative both to defunct socialism and to the seemingly victorious Western liberal democracy." The Northern Tier countries, especially Iran and Turkey, will be particularly affected by the Islamic factor. Hunter maintains that among these countries, Turkey, "as a secular state with a Muslim population and close ties with the West and Israel," will be the principal beneficiary of the collapse of the Soviet Union, and able to expand her influence both in the Caucasus and Central Asia. Iran in contrast, because of "its espousal of militant Islam" and its perceived threat to the interest of Russia and the West in the Caucasus and Central Asia, will be the continuous target of pressure and containment.

The remarkable and intriguing ambiguity of the Soviet experience has greatly influenced post-Soviet Russia's global role and its relations with the Third World. The nature of Moscow's relations with the Third World has irreversibly changed, yet the consensus emerging from this volume points to a certain element of presence and continuity. Russia and the new states of the former Soviet Union will continue to have an uneven relationship with Third World states. While Moscow remains more selective in its involvement in a region such as Latin

America, it will remain fully engaged in other regions, such as the Middle East, Southwest Asia, and, to a certain degree, Africa.

The long-term orientation of Russia's policy toward the Third World, however, will depend on the interdependent dynamics of its domestic evolution and its foreign policy requirements. In this context, three broad scenarios can be envisioned.

Russia's enormous economic and scientific potential and its apparent ideological commitment to democracy and a market economy points to a westward direction that ideally will lead to Russia's membership in the special club of the industrialized world: this is the "1 + 7 formula." In this case, departure from the Third World seems to be the logical outcome.

Yet the collapse of the Russian economy and the ensuing political crisis has led to considerable doubts about the ideology of the reform. Combined with the economic underdevelopment of Russia's infrastructure, another scenario, namely Russia's "Third Worldization" or "Latinamericanization," may eventually lead not to departure from the Third World, but to gradual convergence with that region. The implications of such a convergence are significant, because Russia, with its still enormous military potential—even in the absence of its messianic ideology—will join the North-South conflict.

The ambiguity of the nature of the Soviet system and its objective conditions of uneven socioeconomic development and its undeniable geopolitical weight and military power may lead to a third and more practical Russian alternative, a "double-faced" centaur that will have the simultaneous potential to be both in the First World and in the Third World. Russia's unique geopolitical and geocultural characteristics as a Eurasian entity will be more fitting to this contradictory yet more realistic scenario.

Notes

1. Even the actions of the most powerful Third World states, individually or collectively, should not have been so detrimental to the changes in the structure or dynamics of the international system, if only the "distribution of capability" was the deciding factor in shaping the opportunities and constraints of states and alliances in the hierarchy of the international system. The ideological factor both at the state and the systemic level played a considerable role in shaping the post–World War II dynamics of international relations, a factor

that structural realism tends either to relegate to unit level analysis or ignore altogether. For a structural realist perspective, see Kenneth Waltz, *Theory of International Politics* (New York: Random House, 1979).

2. See for example, Andre Gunder Frank, "Long Live Transideological Enterprise!: The Socialist Economics in the Capitalist Division of Labor," *Review* 1, no. 1 (Summer 1977); *The European Challenge: From Transatlantic Alliance to Pan-European Extent for Peace and Jobs* (Nottingham: Spokesman, 1983); and "The Socialist Countries in the World Economy: The East-South Dimension," in Helio Basso, ed., *Theory and Practice of Liberation and the End of the 20th Century* (Brussels: Bruylant, 1988).

3. Francis Fukuyama, "The End of History," *National Interest* (Summer 1989). Fukuyama further develops his "Hegelian" interpretation of the end of history and the eventual triumph of Western political and economic liberalism in *The End of History and the Last Man* (New York: Free Press, 1992).

4. See, for example, Elizabeth K. Valkenier, *The Soviet Union and the Third World: An Economic Bind* (New York: Praeger, 1985). Another useful work is Ellen Brun and Jacques Hersh, *Soviet–Third World Relations in a Capitalist World* (New York: St. Martin's, 1990).

5. A somewhat critical assessment of Moscow–Third World relations by Soviet authors began to surface in a more sophisticated analysis of Third World economic models and development that appeared in the mid-1970s and early 1980s. See, for example, Evgenii Primakov, "Strany sotsialistocheskoi orientatsii" (Countries of socialist orientation), *Mirovaya ekonomika i mezhdunarodnye otnosheniya*, no. 7 (July 1981). For a more open Soviet critique, see Alexi Kova, *Nasional'no-osvoboditel'noe dvizhenie: teoriya i praktika* (The national liberation movement: theory and practice) (Moscow: Nauka, 1989).

6. The concept of the "integral world" was a key theoretical foundation of Gorbachev's "new political thinking" in international relations, which was discussed in writings and speeches of Soviet "new thinkers" in the late 1980s. See Mikhail Gorbachev, *Perestroika: New Thinking for Our Country and the World* (New York: Harper and Row, 1987). For an earlier Soviet reflection leading to the elaboration of Gorbachev's "new thinking," see Georgi Shakhnazarov, *Gradushchij miroporiadok* (The coming world order) (Moscow, 1981); "Mirovoe soobschchestvo upravliaemo" (Governability of the world society), *Pravda,* 15 January 1988; and "Governability of the World," *International Affairs* (Moscow), 3 March 1988.

Part 1 ━━━━━━━━━━━━━━━━━━━━━━━━━━━━

The Soviet Collapse,
the World Order,
and Shifting Paradigms

━━━━━━━━━━━━━━━━━━━━━━━━━━━━

Chapter 1

A Requiem for the Soviet Union

Vendulka Kubalkova

There is a strange crowd in the dimly lit mortuary. Standing around the table with the draped corpse are theologians and priests, members of political parties, medical doctors—dermatologists, radiologists, pathologists, even veterinarians—biologists, policemen and detectives, statesmen and diplomats. They are of different ethnic origin, they speak different languages.

The room is filled with voices arguing about the deceased and the cause of death. One fellow claims loudly that the deceased was a Satan and proudly points to the stake through his heart. "Let's forget him, let's have a party to celebrate!" Not everybody is cheering: the deceased, some say, was not a bad guy and did a lot of good when he could in his youth. Alas, he got too big-headed and forgot his station in life, became exhausted and overextended. That was the cause of death. The real villain, they say, is also in the room and should be put away for murder. An old man in an army uniform with medals on his chest and a black band of mourning on his sleeve, eyes full of tears, kneels and whispers a prayer. "You have it wrong," says a sharp-eyed woman wearing a lot of jewelry. The remains are not those of a human. It is even unclear whether the corpse is animal, mineral, or vegetable. It might have been a freak mutation, or an alien being or perhaps a dinosaur that survived too long.

Standing aside quietly are a group of medical doctors dropping technical terms in their conversation. They look subdued and embarrassed: they not only lost a patient but never even reached a diagnosis. Despite their efforts at a post-mortem, they find even fixing the time of death difficult. As for causes. . . There are different symptoms—the emaciated body, the decomposing flesh. "The cause of death," says one doctor, "was a highly infectious disease."

But then the crowd turns in shock. From another corner of

19

> the room, a man in a three-piece suit is shouting. "Fools! Can't you see it's not dead at all. This is just another trick!" Two attendants take him quickly away.
>
> But not everyone is upset. An old man in a blue robe and pointed cap chuckles to himself and mutters, "My greatest illusion yet. They all think they see a body."
>
> Whoever or whatever it is on the table, may he rest in peace, *requiescat in pace*. There is however something seriously wrong with the gathering in the mortuary.

In this century no phenomenon of world politics has been the subject of so much disagreement across the world as the Soviet Union. Throughout the seventy years of its existence, the nature and the role of the USSR in the global sense—the exact nature of the East-West conflict, the relationship of the USSR to the Third World and to North-South issues, and Soviet strength, aspirations, and objectives—have been among the most ambiguous and controversial features of world politics. The spectrum and range of interpretations of the Soviet Union was seldom appreciated in its entirety, nor was its absurd diversity fully comprehended.

This is because international political thinking has been divided and compartmentalized, geographically and ideologically, a situation exacerbated in the West by the division of those who studied the phenomenon into a multitude of separate academic disciplines. Specialized expertise was achieved but at the price of tunnel vision and a loss of context. Ideological considerations skewed the range of acceptable views and research agendas. Intellectuals of the West and of the East stopped communicating, regarding each other as propagandists, ideologues, or fools, which meant there was little meaningful academic interchange between them. Soviet and Western leftist writers were ignored by their Western mainstream academic counterparts; in effect so was the Soviet Union itself, in a variety of academic fields. Findings from other disciplines about the Soviet Union were uncritically accepted in place of analysis.

Views on every aspect of the Soviet Union differed so sharply so that it could be regarded as an example of "incommensurable" discourses.[1] Paradoxically, no matter how ambiguous the Soviet Union was, it served as a prime meridian upon which the geographical and intellectual maps of the political and ideological worlds were based.

The confusion continues. Does the collapse of the Soviet Union really mean that—as we are sometimes told—there is no longer left and right, and that both communism and socialism are extinct? Will the terms "West" and "East," created by the presence of the Soviet Union, be abandoned? Are there any defining features that justify the continuing designation of the former Soviet bloc or its parts as the "Second World"? And, if the East was previously regarded as part of the rich North, now that the Eastern economy has collapsed, how will the former East see itself in relation to the Third and Fourth Worlds and to the poor South? Will it adopt the rhetoric of global inequality and poverty? Is the Soviet Union going to become a "new Third World"? Where will the countries of the Second World fit in a world which is projected, by the year 2020, to consist of one billion rich people, and five billion poor and starving? In 2020, who will be the East, the West, the North, and the South, the left and the right?

It seems to me that we need to reexamine our views of the Soviet Union if we are to clarify our view of the world without it. This short chapter can only raise some of the issues that are addressed in more detail elsewhere in this volume. Its purpose is not to provide a comprehensive critique of mainstream Western Sovietology, but to place it in the context of explanations of the Soviet Union traditionally not regarded as important or relevant. The chapter will sketch the traditional Cold War dichotomies of East-West and left-right before the collapse of the Soviet Union, focusing on four specific controversies: (1) the Soviet Union and socialism; (2) the Soviet Union and communism; (3) the Soviet Union and the East-West conflict; and (4) the Soviet Union and the Third World.

The Controversy about the Soviet Union and Socialism

Controversy attended the Soviet Union from its birth. The 1917 Great October Revolution from which it emerged was presented by its leaders as the historical moment at which, in Engels's words, the history of mankind would begin and prehistory would end as socialism replaced capitalism. His and Karl Marx's understanding of both capitalism and socialism was limited to the social conditions brought by nineteenth-century European industrialization. They saw socialism as a more humane, moral, and efficient socioeconomic and political system.

Even at the time of the revolution, there was controversy: was Russia a suitable venue for the events that were expected to bring about a speedy and more or less simultaneous worldwide collapse of capitalism? According to classical Marxism, the official doctrine of the socialist movement in the nineteenth century, semi-capitalist, semi-feudal Russia was not the right place. But according to Marxism-Leninism, into which Marxism metamorphosed under the Russian Bolsheviks, it was. The first Bolshevik government implemented as best as it could the sketchy directions of classical Marxists for the termination of capitalism. The Bolsheviks abolished private property, declared all nations and ethnic groups equal, and disassociated the new (though hopefully temporary) state's foreign policy from that of their czarist predecessors. They regarded the Bolshevik state as temporary, since the collapse of the state system was an inevitable consequence of the imminent collapse of the capitalist socioeconomic system.

The Bolshevik theory of imperialism offered an explanation of why the Russian revolution could be seen as a part of the world revolutionary process. This theory remains one of the lasting intellectual contributions of Russian Marxism. It marked the start of a tradition of viewing the world not in terms of individual states but from the perspective of transnational and/or subnational social forces. This view is in marked contrast to the dominant Western perception of world affairs propagated in the academic field of international politics, which presumed a world ranked hierarchically into the great, medium, and small states on the basis of their politico-strategic power. The theory of imperialism adds a second dimension, or an overlay on this perspective, when it identifies beneath the surface of interstate relations other factors and forces that are portrayed as more important than states. The theory of imperialism identifies unequal and uneven development of capitalism, inequality, and exploitation, thus giving rise to the non-statist perspective of International Political Economy, in one of the approaches of which the world is seen in terms of centers and cores, semi-peripheries, and peripheries. Wars are interpreted not as consequences of human nature or games that states play but as an inevitable feature of capitalism. In this reading, the foreign policy of states becomes "ideologized": each state is seen as driven not by the simple pursuit of power but by the imperatives of its mode of economic production, exchange, and distribution, whether capitalist or not.

According to the theory of imperialism not only was each society split into oppressed and oppressor classes, as Marx and Engels postulated, but the world itself was split into two groups of nations, the exploited and the exploiters. The Great October Revolution was allegedly made on behalf of both the exploited classes and nations.

Neither Lenin nor his colleagues anticipated the Third World. With the exception of the German theorist of imperialism, Rosa Luxemburg,[2] who foresaw the possibility of a growing gap between the poor and rich parts of the world, these theorists argued that global inequality would only be temporary, since the spark of the revolution lit in the "second world" (the exploited countries) would ignite revolution in the "first world," destroy capitalism, and "begin history." The October Revolution was portrayed[3] as a milestone not only in Russian politics but also in world history.

The reception of the USSR by the socialist movement was mixed: not only was Russia seen as the wrong site to build socialism, but, in the view of many leftist thinkers, the Stalinist policies that soon appeared deflected the USSR from the one true course, and may even have betrayed the revolution. The Left disagreed on the next steps in the revolutionary process and the relationship of the October Revolution to the cause of worldwide socialism and the world's oppressed. At the heart of this disagreement were questions of the primacy of the consolidation and development of the USSR vis-à-vis the world revolution and of the appropriateness of the Soviet model of development. Differing answers to these questions split the world socialist movement: European and North American social democracy and socialism diverged from Soviet-style socialism led by the "communist parties" of the Comintern, which sought to subordinate the world revolution to the requirements for the survival of the USSR and the goal of "socialism in one country."

The split has continued to paralyze the socialist movement. It produced the separation of what became called "Western Marxism" from Soviet Marxism-Leninism. The forced exile of Trotsky, one of Lenin's colleagues and Stalin's unsuccessful competitor for Lenin's mantle, produced an inadvertent endorsement of the split by one of the revolution's architects. According to Trotsky (and Trotskyists ever since), the Soviet experiment would inevitably be "deformed" and doomed unless supported by a worldwide socialist revolution. The major agency in this deformation process was, according to Trotsky, the Stalinist party from which Trotsky had been expelled. Insofar as most non-Soviet Marxists shared the Trotskyist view that the Soviet Union was somehow lacking, weak, and of very uncertain future and duration, the Western Left was influenced by Trotskyism in its attitude toward the USSR, and Trotskyism became the dominant Western form of Marxism in the Anglo-American world.[4]

For those who gave their lives for the creation of the first socialist bastion, including Lenin himself, the 1991 collapse of the Soviet Union would have been a historical tragedy and a set-back for socialism. On the other hand, those with allegiance to the theories of imperialism in their many contemporary guises might regret that the Soviet Union ever was. To them there is nothing new in the recent developments, and the world is again at a point Bukharin and Lenin described before the revolution, except that this time, without the USSR as a complicating factor, the revolution just might turn out right.

The term "socialism" itself has apparently been in use since 1827 to describe a movement that can claim ancestry and support in early Christianity, if not before.[5] It was not invented for the Soviet Union; thus, the meaningful question is not whether socialism died in 1991 but what role the Soviet Union played in relation to the socialist ideal. Similarly, there is a good chance that as in the seating of the French parliament in the eighteenth century, there will continue to be left and right even without the Soviet Union. As Kolakowski put it, "The Left draws the dividing line between the Left and the Right, while the Right fights this division systematically—and in vain." "The Left" or "on the left" are notoriously imprecise terms, characterized by a certain ideological and moral attitude and not by a single defined political movement, party, or group of parties. If at all definable, it is an attitude of negation toward, or permanent revision of, the existing world and a quest for change, set out in its ideal.[6]

Left and Soviet "Sovietology"

Focusing on the USSR's socioeconomic nature, Marxists had four principal ways of viewing the country:[7] (1) that it was socialist; (2) that it was originally socialist but at some point became deformed; (3) that it might have shed some features of capitalism but was neither capitalist nor socialist, that is, it was quasi-capitalist; or (4) that it was capitalist.

As for the first position, apart from Moscow-oriented Western and Third World communist parties, which continued to view the USSR as a true socialist model and an heir to classical Marxism, this view was taken seriously only in the Soviet Union. Even there it was abandoned in the Gorbachev years, as he permitted the view that it was an example of "deformed" socialism. Gorbachev talked about "barracks socialism" deformations but never accepted the Trotskyist notion that the Communist party itself was responsible for the deformations.

The position at the opposite extreme, that of the USSR as state capitalist, was a position theoretically substantiated in the works of Charles Bettleheim and adopted by the Chinese Communist party and pro-Chinese communist parties across the world. It was weakened when some Chinese admitted during the Gorbachev years the possibility that the USSR still had some socialist features. In this view, the renegade Soviet Union defected from the socialist path to capitalism not under Stalin (as the Trotskyists maintained) but under Khrushchev. Thus its present disintegration represents a further and particularly painful step in its transformation from state capitalism to another of capitalism's forms.

The most common leftist views of the Soviet Union have been the two in-between positions, namely, as a socialism manqué and deformed (though at different points its deformations were not regarded as incorrigible) along the neo-Trotskyist lines of group two. Either that or (group three) that Soviet society failed to shed its class structure and developed into a new class formation, or returned to a long-defunct one such as an Asiatic mode of production with slave labor deployed in the implementation of giant state projects. The first two positions viewed the USSR as socialist albeit deformed. The third and forth positions regarded the Soviet system as having failed to move away from capitalism and either as having recreated a specific form of capitalism in Russia or led to a throwback but equally exploitative class formation. A third possibility was that it was a hybrid system, highly volatile, unstable, and doomed.[8]

Listing these positions now that the Soviet Union is no longer is worthwhile if for no other reason than to show that to none of these positions would the disintegration of the Soviet Union have come as a surprise. Many of them insisted for years that the demise of the Soviet system was forthcoming.

Western Sovietology

The understanding of the USSR by Western academics and other observers was significantly different from that of both Soviet and leftist thinkers. This was hardly surprising: the differing views reflected very different concerns and political attitudes. Western thinking on the USSR—Sovietology—could be defined largely through these differing concerns. It is widely acknowledged now that Sovietology was a product of the Cold War. Its fate and development proceeded in lockstep with the Cold War: launched as an academic enterprise in the countries most involved in the Cold War (the United States and the United Kingdom), it depended (certainly in financial terms) on the exigencies of the Cold War, and their highs and lows, the beginning and the end of both the Cold War and of Sovietology, coincided. Mainstream Sovietology was noticeably partisan; it stood on the side of the West and the Right, against the East and the Left. This orientation has had major consequences for the intellectual integrity and prowess of the field and its exponents.

As the pioneer Sovietologist John Hazard has pointed out, the beginnings of serious academic study of the USSR in the West were slow: by the time the Soviet Union had divided the world's socialists into warring groups, there was still relatively little interest in it in the West. The Soviet government was not recognized in the United States until 1933, and at that time "those who concerned themselves with things 'soviet' . . . were looked upon with suspicion by their fellow countrymen." The Second World War forced the development of the field.[9] Modern Sovietology, however, was constituted in the late 1940s and early 1950s with the appearance of the Cold War perception of the "Soviet threat." Lacking that perception, Soviet studies would have developed into an ordinary field of "comparative studies," like the studies of Latin America, Asia, or France. With the Cold War, however, the Soviet Union became a prime national security issue for the United States and a subject of central importance to every field of international studies. Sovietology encompassed all aspects of study of the Soviet Union. Its history, domestic politics, foreign policy, economics, literature, and other areas were ruled off-limits to nonexperts as too specialized. Sovietologists were a privileged academic elite with close access to American decision makers. Compared to other area studies, the field, isolated and overindulged, was exempted from the self-corrective mechanisms normally associated with academic life. This point does not need belaboring. All major universities established well-endowed research institutes such as other area studies did not have. The grants and awards made by major foundations to projects with a Soviet component further proves this point.[10]

Enjoying a degree of proximity to U.S. policy makers and focusing on a topic of the highest political and public relevance, Sovietology lived, as one observer put it, in a "ghetto."[11] The perceived uniqueness of its subject matter, the peculiarities of the Soviet system, the paucity or unreliability of data, and other factors have insulated Sovietology from the larger debates and issues of the social sciences. The conceptual armory in use in comparative political study, comparative foreign policy, and other area studies was regarded for a long time as inapplicable. Finally in the détente years, when contacts with other social sciences were begun and some limited borrowings from other social sciences were accepted, little intellectual benefit was gained. As one observer put it, the discarded fashions of Western scholarship became the *dernier cri* of Soviet and communist studies. The concept of pluralism, for example, faced with an onslaught in the field where it developed, transformed itself into group theory in Soviet studies, where it showed signs of replacing the dominant but somewhat discredited totalitarian model. The behavioral approach made a tardy appearance in Soviet and Communist studies in the 1970s. Studies of political culture, political socialization, mass participation, and public opinion were all undertaken. Development studies also enjoyed a passing vogue, and a later import, policy analysis, drew heavily on the bureaucratic or administrative model of politics.[12]

Many Sovietologists in the United States became nationally known media personalities, but left thinkers were notably absent from their ranks. Behind the ideological barricades, Sovietology maintained its unusual epistemological uniformity at the cost of skewing its own philosophical/epistemological base. Trotskyist, neo-Trotskyist, Hegelian, Weberian, Chinese, and other Marxist or left-inspired approaches were shut out. Sovietology also excluded Soviet views of the Soviet Union, except as caricatures.

This uniformity was so prevalent that throughout the entire Cold War Sovietologists maintained a high degree of consensus.[13] And thus throughout its several stages the field of Sovietology was characterized by a persisting contrast between the ambivalent nature of the USSR, the consensual nature of Sovietology's main approaches, a low level of controversy and the relatively low theoretical or explanatory quality of its end product. The Sovietologists' comfortable consensus failed periodic challenges not from within the field but from events in the USSR, events that more often than not arrived unforeseen, "out of the blue," and received no satisfactory explanation.

The orthodox Sovietology of the early years of the Cold War, now referred to also as "traditionalist" Sovietology, was based on a consensus in regard to the "totalitarian"[14] explanation of the USSR, an interpretation that was either explicit or implied in the Western political histories of the USSR that characterized that stage of Sovietology. It was at this first stage, when the Cold War was at its coldest, that Sovietology flourished and some of the best historical analyses were written.

The détente years of the Cold War brought a marked decline in Sovietology both in intellectual and financial terms: the field suffered an enormous drop in government and private funding and a consequent decline in recruitment to the field. According to one estimate, by 1985 the USSR had three times more experts on the United States than the latter had on the Soviet Union.

The diversified and liberalized version of Sovietology of the détente years (which shattered the previous consensus but remained significantly under "totalitarian" influence) produced debate on the correct approach to the study of Soviet politics, a debate manifested by a plethora of models and theories. But even under the new Sovietology consensus reappeared. Consistent with the harmonious liberal spirit of "détente Sovietology," the consensus essentially inclined towards a convergence thesis that stressed the growing similarities in patterns of economic and social control and foreign policy behavior in East and West. In contrast to the "totalitarian" approach, the unique features of the USSR, and its ideology in particular, were thus perceived as diminishing in importance. But not even détente Sovietology[15] moved out of the confines of the ghetto. To the historical descriptive method of the earlier stage of Sovietological endeavor were now added models of the essentially positivist behavioralist era, of vintage fifties and sixties thinking. Theoretical as against descriptive thinking on the USSR has however never prevailed, and the influences of other social sciences have been disappointingly selective, inconsistent, and much delayed.[16]

Consensus characterized even the closing era of Sovietology, the Gorbachev years. The final consensus, immediately preceding the demise of the USSR, was based on a somewhat lopsided convergence theory admixed with the greatly stressed declinism concept popularized by Samuel Huntington. The declinist or convergence view rested on an understanding of Soviet foreign policy as an expression of problem-ridden Soviet domestic politics rather than on the traditional communist-expansionist explanation, a diagnosis characteristic of the earlier "traditional" Sovietology.

Stephen Fortescue has sorted the approaches of détente Sovietology into two groups: the "vanguard party"[17] models and the "pluralist models."[18] In both of these groups of approaches the Soviet Union was no longer seen as totalitarian but was instead characterized by an incipient pluralism, whether its society was still dominated by the Communist party (as in one or another variant of "vanguard party" Sovietological models) or was competing for power and influence with the Communist party (as in the various "plurality models" of the Soviet Union).[19]

When the subject matter of Sovietology disintegrated in front of the Sovietologists, they were methodologically and factually unprepared for the transfer of power away from the Kremlin and the Communist party, the main features of the USSR with which Sovietologists had concerned themselves. Unsurprisingly, given this record of consensus and failure, the field has become an easy target for ridicule; collections of misguided predictions made by leading Sovietologists are now considered amusing reading.[20]

The Consensus about the Soviet Union and Communism

How was the Soviet Union explained by the Western mainstream academics and other guards at our intellectual gates? Did they, like the leftists, perceive the end of the Soviet Union in sight? Was there an overlap between the continuum of socialist and capitalist interpretations of the Left and where on the Western Sovietological continuum of totalitarian, vanguard party and pluralist models?

The overlap between the leftist and Sovietological theories was minor and superficial. Western Marxist theory fits loosely into the group of "vanguard theories," variants of Trotskyism according to which a privileged stratum of rulers controls the means of production and thereby dominates the working class. Variations turned on the question of whether the ruling stratum was or was not a class. Western Sovietology, in turn, might fit (even more uncomfortably) into one of two categories of left analysis: one which regards the USSR as capitalist (détente Sovietologists who saw the Soviet Union converging on capitalism), or that category which regarded the USSR as the heir of the Marxist dream. The Sovietological totalitarian approach was based on a caricature of this Soviet self-assessment: in this view the USSR was not a harbinger of a more just and equitable world but a rapacious, cruel, satanic oppressor. Soviet propaganda, official statements, and scholarship returned the compliment when they identified the United States as a demon.

The Cold War's left and right, argued Holsti, had much in common, however far apart the endpoints might seem to be. As Holsti has shown, the left-right continuum is not linear but circular, the extremes bending back like a key ring to lie parallel, though separate and opposed.

Holsti identified extensive structural similarities between the radical left and right.[21] They both share a penchant, he says, for "integrated, scientific" theories that explain everything, and for a Manichaean view of international affairs as a fight to the death between the forces of good and evil, with "freedom and justice" ("us") on one side and "aggression and repression" ("them") on the other. Both left and right see domestic and foreign policy as indivisible. They see world conflict and wars as linked to a single source, ultimately derived from the other side's "malignant institutions" (rather than from aspects of our human nature or the structure of the international system). These institutions are perceived as inherently expansionist, violent, static, autonomous, and elitist, and they are in command of powerful armed forces. Both analyses conclude that world peace requires a total triumph of "our" point of view. This triumph is assured because of fundamental flaws in the antagonist's essential nature. Because of the evil nature of "them," any means to victory is justified, a belief that produces seemingly unlikely alliances.[22]

At the core of the radical right analysis characteristic of Western "totalitarian" Sovietology was a set of assumptions about international communism and its implacable drive to world power. The nature of that movement was alleged to have been discovered in the theory of "protracted conflict," which postulated a multifaceted, long-range war against the "Free World."[23] The communist system was driven by its adherence to an immutable set of dogmas, a secular religion extrapolated from the corpus of Bolshevik utterances and writing. While aware of the transnational importance of communist ideology, such an analysis saw the state as the key unit, and the balance or imbalance of strategic power was the perennial focus of policy concern. The preferred value was that of "freedom," defined in individualistic terms. This was the essence of totalitarian Sovietology. The term "communism" to describe the Soviet system was used as a synonym for "Soviet," "socialist," "Marxist" and the Left. Détente Sovietologists went to an opposite extreme when their theory of convergence denied the existence of special features for the Soviet Union.

In retrospect, the crucial question is whether any Western Sovietologists of either school foresaw the end or recognized the terminal weaknesses of the Soviet system. For the totalitarian school of Sovietologists, its nature was seen as virtually immutable and indestructible, except by force from outside (or, as George Kennan argued, the prolonged frustration of its expansionist drive). True, writers on totalitarianism usually included in the small print a theoretical recognition that one day the system would die, in the sense that all things ultimately die, but the emphasis was always on its invulnerability, capacity to control, to manipulate, to atomize, and to crush. The second scenario, of the more liberal détente Sovietology, anticipated a slow and incremental convergence of the Soviet system with ours. When the USSR collapsed, détente Sovietologists could not accommodate the development. As Karatnycky put it, they were in Moscow talking to the wrong people, "wired" into wrong sources of information.[24]

The Controversy about the Soviet Union and the East West Conflict

The engagement of the Left and the Right in a mirror-image confrontation was the essence of the Cold War. The radical left, starting from Leninist theories, always argued the central (negative) significance of capitalist imperialism. International injustice and exploitation were seen as the consequence of global corporate capitalism—its internal contradictions, its rapacious propensity for accumulation, its single minded pursuit of profit. Class was the central unit of analysis, albeit states enacted its imperatives and drives. Class formation on a global scale was, because of its reflection of changing modes of production, the analytical level at which to proceed. The balance and imbalance of socioeconomic productivity, the crisis of capitalism and its aggressive consequences, were the abiding preoccupation, and the preferred value was "equality," suitably defined in collectivist terms.

The conventional Western wisdom that the Soviet Union was the cause of the Cold War was attacked, not from the ranks of Sovietologists, but from the academic discipline of American history. Perhaps not deliberately, revisionist Left historians paralleled and echoed Soviet views of the state of the Cold War, a point not perhaps recognized in the West but fully appreciated by the Soviets. These revisionists were viewed by the Soviets as advocates of the USSR who supported the Soviet view of the Cold War.[25]

The first "revisionism" was inspired by the philosophy of the New Left, and a cadre of American historians (William Appleman Williams, Gar Alperovitz, Gabriel Kolko, and others)[26] challenged the conventional wisdom of the 1950s and 1960s by offering a revision of the popular belief that the USSR was responsible for starting and fueling the Cold War. Some referred to events as far back as the end of the nineteenth century to support their argument that U.S. imperialism needed an "image of threat" in order to function. The revisionist U.S. historians often did not deal with the USSR at all: Williams's *The Tragedy of American Diplomacy* contained only about fifteen lines referring to the Soviet Union.

When the Soviets invaded Afghanistan, a second generation of Marxist "revisionists" added to the earlier inculpation of the United States the exculpation of the USSR: the Soviet Union was not only weak and incapable of confronting the U.S. superpower, it was also post-revolutionary or post-capitalist in nature and therefore inherently less aggressive in nature than the United States. Fred Halliday tried to revise the conventional wisdom by arguing that the end of the détente years of the 1970s was not brought about by the invasion of Afghanistan but by the U.S. decision to modernize NATO. The invasion of Afghanistan, went the argument, was just as much as the earlier invasions of Hungary and Czechoslovakia an example of the "nervous reflexes of the frightened superpower."[27]

These views were articulated in a debate provoked by an article by E. P. Thompson, one of the doyens of British Marxism and the peace movement. Thompson endorsed the convergence thesis when he argued that the Soviet Union was exhibiting isomorphism with the other superpower. Attacking the traditional Marxist-inspired socioeconomic analysis, he argued that in an age dominated by two "exterminist" superpowers caught up in the "deadly symmetry of over-kill," "It means rather little to peer into the entrails of two differing modes of production, searching for auguries as to the future, if we are so inattentive as to overlook what these modes produce, namely the means of war."[28]

The responses to E. P. Thompson were a rich range of countertheses, all seeking to explain why it was not the Soviet Union but the United States or capitalism that was responsible for the Cold War. One could identify several distinctive foci of these explanations.[29]

On what could be called a "micro" level, U.S. revisionist historians explained the need for the Cold War from the dynamic of American society. Intrastate theories of the Cold War blamed domestic factors for the major powers' foreign policy involvements. Foreign policies were seen as designed to resolve internal tensions or as reflections of shifts in internal power structures. An example of this view is the work of Alan Wolfe, which explains U.S. foreign policy via reference to American domestic politics.[30] In this reading a stepped-up Cold War was required for the resolution of U.S. domestic troubles, and the Soviet invasion of Afghanistan provided a sufficient excuse for the required heightening of tensions.[31]

U.S. imperialist theories of the Cold War offered much the same conclusion when, in a mirror image of "Soviet threat" theories, they postulated aggressiveness and belligerence in the workings of the capitalist social system, which required confrontation and military production for its survival. Into this category fitted Ernst Mandel's *Late Capitalism* and *The Second Slump*,[32] as well as works by Harry Braverman and Michel Aglietta.[33] When Mary Kaldor argued that the arms race was a race of technologies and equated modes of technology with modes of warfare, she concluded that the Soviet military establishment was always essentially defensive and conservative, while the U.S. establishment was aggressive.[34]

Other left authors chose to concentrate on the ubiquitous intracapitalist contradictions that derived from the defective capitalist socioeconomic system. West-West theories of the Cold War singled out the conflict between the richer capitalist states as holding the clue to the "New Cold War." The idea of a "Soviet threat," they argued, was the only operative ideological instrumentality and the binding agent of the major capitalist states. Thus Andre Gunder Frank saw the Soviet threat as "an instrument to blackmail Western Europe into accepting U.S. economic conditions and to prevent Europe from liberating itself economically from the United States."[35] Noam Chomsky, with a similar understanding, stressed that it was not the USSR but Europe and Japan that have always been the United States' "real rivals."[36] Mary Kaldor described the conflict between the West and the East as a "ritual" designed to mask tensions between the Western nations.[37] D. and R. Smith described the Cold War as a means by which the United States could reestablish hegemony over its allies and "offset capitalist rivalries."[38] Related arms race theories of the Cold War, such as Thompson's "exterminism," blamed the New Cold War on the stockpiling of nuclear weapons.

The macro- aspect was apparent in a variety of leftist North-South theories of the Cold War that saw the states as protagonists in worldwide class conflict. Theories of dominance and dependence,[39] derived from theories of imperialism, identified the rich countries' attempts to control and exploit the poor populations of the Third World as the root of the secondary problem of East-West conflict. Thus, these theories argued, policies actually aimed at defeating the revolt of the Third World were pursued in the name of combating the Soviet Union.[40]

Theories of the Cold War based on class conflict perceived the global ebb and flow of social revolution at times as the expression of revolutionary activities in the Third World, at times as class conflict within major capitalist states, or, less frequently, as the confrontations of states. Mike Davis described the Cold War as "an age of violent, protracted transition from the lightning-rod conductor of all the historical tensions between opposite international class forces," emphasizing that the bipolar confrontation was not in itself the dominant dynamic of the world politics. That was instead the process of "permanent revolution arising from the uneven and combined development of capitalism."[41] In a grand theory of Cold War, allegedly improving Wallerstein's portrayal of the world as uniformly capitalist,[42] Halliday argued that the world was based on coexisting but contradictory structures that were pre-capitalist, capitalist, and post-capitalist. The main contradiction, the crisis of capitalism, was seen as complemented by the "great contest" between the United States and the USSR. Halliday borrowed the notion from Isaac Deutscher, the student of Trotsky. The "great contest" of the Cold War has now concluded along the lines predicted by Trotsky.[43]

The first wave of "revisionism" initially caused quite a stir. The second wave ceased to be revisionism with Gorbachev's ascent to power in 1985. Then, the conventional wisdom implicitly recognized the validity of the revisionist argument by embracing its important parts. Convinced by Gorbachev's admission of weakness and his acknowledgment of the need for a radical restructuring of Soviet society, mainstream analysts accepted the notion of Soviet decline that had been expounded for at least a decade by the Left. Again substantially anticipated by the revisionists, mainstream understanding of Soviet foreign policy was revised, and the traditionally assumed expansionist communist drive was seen to have waned. Instead, Soviet foreign policies were understood as motivated primarily by the urgent demands of domestic reform and the need to extricate the USSR from costly foreign policy involvements in order to allow a focus on domestic reform.

The Controversy about the Soviet Union and the Third World

It is in regard to the role of the Soviet Union in the Third World that the controversies that I have surveyed so far are not simply of interest to the historian of ideas but are directly relevant to contemporary issues. Those Western analysts who saw the Soviet Union as an aggressor in the Third World requiring to be countered by the United States, or who saw superpower competition underlying much of the regional Third World conflict, expect a significant waning of the North-South tension in the aftermath of the Cold War. This assumption may be implied or spelled out. For example, in one liberal scenario[44] the world is portrayed as split into the core and the periphery, terms borrowed without their *dependencia* content from the Left theories of dependency. The core will include among its members the great powers acting in a newly found post–Cold War harmony based on a shared commitment to liberal capitalism and political democracy. Russia is expected to be a part of this interdependent gathering in which the old rules of power politics, balance of power, and alliance making will no longer apply. The world's periphery, not yet harmonious, will continue to be the field of power politics; however, without the great powers playing out their differences in the Third World (for there will be no differences), the Third World conflict will significantly diminish. The end of the USSR in this scenario is seen to have significantly contributed to the diminishing of tensions even in the Third World and to world peace.

Leftists paint a totally different picture. If for no other reason than the greater accuracy of their past assessments, we should not dismiss their views this time. Their position is worth restating. One realizes, of course, that a correct prediction does not necessarily validate a theory any more than an inaccurate prediction necessarily invalidates another one. However, given two theories—correct or incorrect—one might be prudent to listen to the "one that got it right."

No one on the Western Left regarded the East-West Cold War conflict as in any way overshadowing the more fundamental problem of inequality that underpinned the North-South issue. The demise of the USSR and the end of the Cold War, in this view, will produce results opposite to those predicted by many authors in this book. The leftist authors do not foresee any less conflict in world politics, including in the Third World. The Left differs also in its prognosis for the former Soviet Union: the former Soviet Union, or most of it, will now become what it always was destined to be, a part of the Third World. Ravaged by the Soviet version of socialism, it will become deindustrialized and marginalized in relation to the world capitalist economy. This will finally put to rest the spurious portrayal of the Soviet bloc, initiated by Stalin and emulated in the West, as a Second World freestanding between the first and the third. The Second World (or its constituent parts) and the third will now merge to face the first together. The contentious issue will be growing inequality and poverty, now also experienced by the former Soviet Union, in contrast with the affluence of the rich North and the different explanations of how this lopsided world development has come about. The Third World, now joined by the former Second World, will carry on in the socialist, collectivist tradition. There will be fresh attempts to devise new socialist models of development.

It is worth reiterating that to the Left the issue of the East-West conflict was always secondary and subordinate to the more important, continuing, and deepening problem of North-South relations. Since the Soviet Union was not seen as socialist, the East-West conflict lacked the socioeconomic substance found in North-South relations. Both Soviet official doctrine and leftist thinkers claimed to develop the tradition of theories of imperialism. Soviet theory, however, differed from dependency and world-system theories in its insistence on the socialist identity of the Soviet Union. The very existence of the USSR was seen by the Soviets as offsetting the gloomy effects of the capitalist exploitation portrayed in the dependency theories. The Soviets always asked that the center-periphery issue be seen within the context of East-West relations; the Soviet Union offered its economic model, aid, and the protective umbrella of nuclear deterrence, and claimed to be ready and willing to assist national liberation movements. And for many years, at the height of its prowess, it did. In the view of the Left, since the Soviet Union was not socialist, it did not do nearly enough to advance Third World revolutionary liberation movements, but the little that it did was perceived by the Left as, on the whole, positive. Now we are back to two worlds, with the term "socialism" no longer tarnished by its association with the Soviet superpower.

Gorbachev was aware of the Left's concerns. It is interesting to note how diligently he sought to restore the socialist vision of the Soviet Union. Gorbachev was widely welcomed in the West (including by many liberal Sovietologists) as a nonsocialist liberal, and his Marxist socialist pronouncements were almost totally ignored. It passed virtually unnoticed that in order to save the image of the USSR as a socialist state, a goal to which he remained committed till the end, Gorbachev was as concerned with Soviet domestic economic troubles as he was with the role of the USSR in the world.[45] Few observers have noticed that he sought to preserve the Soviet role in the world by redefining, indeed abolishing, old-style interstate politics.[46] In order that the Soviet socialist superpower could attempt to recapture its status in international politics, Gorbachev even abandoned the theory of imperialism upon which the existence of the Soviet state was based. When, in 1986, he declared that "peaceful coexistence of states of different socio-economic systems [that is, the East-West Cold War conflict] was no longer a form of class struggle" he removed class struggle from interstate politics and undid the fusion between the two made by Bukharin and Lenin. The Soviet Union pledged itself not to act out its socialist designs through interstate politics; therefore the Cold War could end.

The priorities outlined in the annals of historical materialism were to be reordered. While the collapse of capitalism as a socioeconomic system was once supposed to lead to the collapse of the states system, Gorbachev reversed the order. In the nuclear age, he argued, the state and class levels, which had been fused together by Lenin, were to be separated, since nuclear annihilation could no longer be risked. International politics was to be "de-ideologized," the locus of class conflict returned from international to domestic politics, and Soviet

Marxism-Leninism reoriented toward its pre-Leninist form. On closer reading, it becomes obvious that Gorbachev's proposed solution was to do what none of the Soviets or leftists had managed to do thus far. He sought to redefine the rhetoric of socialism, abandoning nineteenth-century clichés about industrial capitalists, the proletariat, class struggle, and exploitation, and replacing them with the more relevant issues of the late twentieth and twenty-first centuries—what Gorbachev called the global problems of humanity, including environmental issues, global poverty and inequality, the nuclear threat, and so on. Gorbachev's Gramscian-inspired antihegemonic strategy for the crippled Soviet superpower was to rely neither on military nor economic competition with the United States, strategies that were no longer within the Soviet reach. Gorbachev's first step was to dispel the image of the Soviet threat, to end the Cold War, and to revise the meaning of the term "superpower" from its military connotation to a moral position of global leadership from which the USSR could assist in solving the problems of humanity. It was not a bad parting shot.

Neither this aspect of the "new thinking" nor the epoch-making abandonment of the theory of imperialism was seriously considered in the West. Instead, most Western Sovietologists misled all by concurring with the Western public's prima facie view of Gorbachev: as a good man—not Marxist, or communist, or socialist, but a liberal. Most observers failed to comment on this final Sovietological mistake when the Soviet Union itself disintegrated. It was the Soviet version of socialism and the Soviet state, not socialism or a socialist state, that collapsed. Just as the Left historically failed to do, Gorbachev did not grasp the ethnic issues that contributed to the dissolution of the USSR. Any future socialist ideology will have to take full acount of ethnicity and religion as new "identities" and place them among its central concerns.

Western scholarship has kept a splendidly detailed historical record of Moscow's activities in every corner of the Third World and has provided examples of masterly historical-empirical analyses of Soviet–Third World relations. That is not, however, what has been lacking. Rather, explanatory frameworks with a reasonably good record of predictive success have been in short supply. It is striking to see how difficult Sovietology has found it to define what the Soviet Union was doing in the Third World and for what purpose, and what effect, if any, its involvement in the Third World has had.

Among the motley of suggested answers are those consistent with the Sovietological schools described in this essay and supplemented by the contributions of Western theorists of international relations: namely, that the Soviet Union entered the Third World (1) to pursue its goal of world communism (the totalitarian model and some ex-Soviet or neocommunist views); (2) to fulfill its imperialist ambitions (the explanation of classical power realism and détente Sovietologists); or (3) to counterbalance the U.S. presence (structural realism). It has finally collapsed because of (1) economic failure, (2) political failure, (3) obsolete ideology, (4) imperial overstretch, (5) failure to handle ethnic and religious issues, (6) the changed meaning of power, (5) world interdependence, (6) U.S. containment and military policies, or (7) relentless worldwide cravings for democracy.

A survey of the Left's answers adds to the list and postulates some scenarios not included in the new conventional wisdom. For example, it is easy to see that Hillel Ticktin is justified in doubting that any Russian leader will ever see a capitalist reform through to full completion, since "Latinamericanization," the loss of great-power status, and permanent impoverishment of the population will inevitably follow.[47] It is easy to anticipate a left thinker who will argue that the "socialist underdevelopment" of the CIS (which is more serious than theorists of "capitalist underdevelopment" of the Third World ever imagined) is the result of the Cold War's breakneck arms race, and will blame U.S. imperialism for the possibly irreversibly damaged condition of the former Soviet Union. It is only a matter of time before *dependencia* theory will be mutatis mutandis extended to the former Soviet bloc, particularly since the rapid slide of most of the CIS into the ranks of the Third World seems to be unstoppable. The subject of this book, in other words, has an unfortunately prescient dimension.

Notes

Author's note: I would like to thank Henry Hamman for his linguistic assistance with the preparation of this paper.

1. In some modern theories of knowledge, theories are seen not only as describing but constituting reality. It is then argued that such theories refer to different, "incommensurable" realities. T. S. Kuhn, *The Structure of Scientific Revolutions* (Chicago and London: University of Chicago Press, 1970).

2. V. Kubalkova and A. A. Cruickshank, *Marxism and International Relations* (London and New York: Oxford University Press, 1989), chapter 3.

3. Martin Malia, "The Hunt for the True October," *Commentary* 92, no. 4 (October 1991): 21.

4. Perry Anderson, *In the Tracks of Historical Materialism* (London: Verso, 1983).

5. R. N. Berki, *Socialism* (London: J. M. Dent and Sons, 1975).

6. L. Kolakowski, *Marxism and Beyond* (London, 1971), 94.

7. For reviews of these positions, see A. Carlo, "The Socio-economic Nature of the USSR," *Telos,* no. 21 (Fall 1974); C. K. Chase-Dunn, ed., *Socialist States in the World System* (Beverly Hills, Calif.: Sage, 1982); Kubalkova and Cruickshank, *Marxism and International Relations,* 237; and Kubalkova and Cruickshank, "The 'New Cold War' in 'Critical International Relations Studies,' " *Review of International Studies* (1986): 12.

8. See, for example, F. Feher, A. Heller, and G. Markus, *Dictatorship over Needs* (Oxford: Blackwell, 1989). In that book the Soviet system is portrayed as neither socialist nor capitalist, but as a self-reproducing social order with universalist aspirations. Hillel Ticktin's group, in contrast, saw the volatility of a system which failed to establish itself as a mode of production and therefore was not going to last.

9. John N. Hazard, *Recollections of a Pioneering Sovietologist* (New York: Oceana Publications, 1987).

10. Academic fields are divided into narrow compartments, each with its own raison d'étre and its separate discourse. The social sciences as a whole, however, share some methodologies. Any field of social science normally engages in its own internal debates, which tend to correct excesses and make it difficult for any particular approach to become elevated into the unquestioned source of the truth. Hence scholars are granted the special "academic freedom" to underwrite the academic goal of the pursuit of knowledge.

11. For reviews of the literature of Sovietology see S. Fortescue, *The Communist Party and Soviet Science* (London: Macmillan, 1986); R. Amann, "Searching for an Appropriate Concept of Soviet Politics," *British Journal of Political Science* 16, no. 4 (1986); Stephen F. Cohen, *Rethinking the Soviet Experience: Politics and History since 1917* (New York: Oxford University Press, 1985); Archie Brown, ed., *Political Culture and Communist Studies* (London: Macmillan, 1984); and Margot Light, "Approaches to the Study of Soviet Foreign Policy," *Review of International Studies* 7 (1981).

12. Fortescue, *The Communist Party and Soviet Science.*

13. Amann, "Searching for an Appropriate Concept of Soviet Politics."

14. The proponents of the totalitarian model that dominated the Western view of the Soviet Union until the 1970s claimed that the party exerted total dominance over the Soviet political system by denying the legitimate existence

of any values other than its own repressive ones. See C. J. Friedrich and Z. K. Brzezinski, *Totalitarian Dictatorship and Autocracy* (New York: Praeger, 1956). For summaries of extensive literature see L. Shapiro, *Totalitarianism* (London: Pall Mall Press, 1972); T. H. Rigby, " 'Totalitarianism' and Change in Communist Systems," *Comparative Politics* 4, no. 3 (April 1972); L. Shapiro, *The Communist Party of the Soviet Union* (London: Eyre and Spotiswood, 1970); B. Meissner, "The Soviet Union and Its Area of Hegemony and Influence," in *Is Communism Changing?* ed. H. J. Veen et al. (Mainz: Mase and Koehler, 1981). For neo-totalitarianist or neo-traditionalist modifications of this approach, see K. Jowitt, "Neo-traditionalism: The Political Corruption of the Leninist Regime," *Soviet Studies* (October 1983); K. Simis, *USSR: Secrets of a Corrupt Society* (London: Dent, 1982); A. Yanov, *Detente after Brezhnev: The Domestic Roots of Soviet Foreign Policy* (Berkeley: University of California Institute of International Studies, 1977); and A. Shtromas, *Political Change and Social Development: The Case of the Soviet Union* (Frankfurt am Main: Lang, 1981). For a critique and an attempt to revise the totalitarian approach see W. Laqueur, "Is There Now, or Has There Ever Been Such a Thing as Totalitarianism?" *Commentary* 80, no. 4 (October 1985); Allen Kassof, "The Administered Society: Totalitarianism without Terror," *World Politics* 16, no. 4 (July 1964).

15. One of the most successful and best-known examples of "détente" Sovietology is the "government (bureaucratic) politics paradigm"; see G. T. Allison, *Essence of Decision: Explaining the Cuban Missile Crisis* (Boston: Little, Brown, 1971).

16. Amann, "Searching for an Appropriate Concept of Soviet Politics."

17. In the vanguard-party models, the functional and institutional groups that are recognized are not seen to have any genuinely autonomous role. See, for example, A. G. Meyer, *The Soviet Political System: An Interpretation* (New York: Random House, 1965); Meyer, "USSR, Incorporated," in *The Development of the USSR: An Exchange of Views*, ed. D. W. Treadgold (Seattle: University of Washington Press, 1964); Rigby, " 'Totalitarianism' and Change in Communist Systems"; Alec Nove, "Is There a Ruling Class in the USSR?" *Soviet Studies* (October 1975), and Nove, "The Class Nature of the Soviet Union Revisited," *Soviet Studies* (July 1983). For another summary of this approach see D. C. Lane, *The End of Soviet Inequality: Class, Status and Power under State Socialism* (London: Allen & Unwin, 1982).

18. The pluralist model, popular among U.S. Sovietologists in the détente years, denied the party any inherent dominance because of the counterbalancing power sectional groups hold in complex societies. Modern society is seen as increasingly segmented and specialized, with technocracy often its centerpiece. In this view the party as an actor was not more than the party apparatus, which was not homogeneous. Although the party might be granted special

status in the political system, it did not occupy the position of total control described in the totalitarian approach nor the dominant position perceived by the vanguard-party theorists. The pluralistic model claimed its origins in the theories of industrial society and especially the works of Comte de Saint-Simon, Emile Durkheim, and Max Weber. It was a variant of the approach propagated by Almond and Powell in their works on political development, which examined the transition from traditional to modern industrial society. Its most important outgrowth was the ill-fated notion of the convergence of the United States and the Soviet Union. See G. A. Almond and G. B. Powell, *Comparative Politics: A Developmental Approach* (Boston: Little, Brown, 1966). Another variant of this approach was "institutional pluralism"; see H. G. Skilling and F. Griffith, *Interest Groups in Soviet Politics* (Princeton, N.J.: Princeton University Press, 1971). For a survey of this literature, see A. H. Brown, "Problems of Interest Articulation and Group Influence in the Soviet Union," *Government and Opposition* (Spring 1972), and Brown, "Pluralism, Power and the Soviet Political System," in *Pluralism in the Soviet Union,* ed. Susan Solomon (London: Macmillan, 1983).

19. Fortescue, *The Communist Party and Soviet Science.*

20. Arch Puddington, "The Anti-Cold War Brigade," *Commentary* (August 1990); C. A. Montaner, "But the 'Nobel Bomber' Isn't Alone in His Anti-Red Idiocy," *Miami Herald,* September 24, 1992; Adrian Karatnycky, "Getting It All Wrong: The Fall of Sovietology," *Freedom Review* 23, no. 2 (1992); Owen Harries, "Communism, the Cold War and the Intellectuals," *Commentary* 92, no. 4 (October 1991).

21. Ole Holsti, "The Study of International Politics Makes Strange Bedfellows: Theories of the 'Old Right' and the 'New Left,' " *American Political Science Review,* quoted in Ralph Pettman, "The Radical Critique and Australian Foreign Policy," in *Independence and Alliance,* ed. P. J. Boyce and J. R. Angel (London: Allen and Unwin, 1983).

22. Holsti, "Strange Bedfellows," 58.

23. Ibid.

24. Adrian Karatnycky, "Getting It All Wrong," 34.

25. O. L. Stepanova, "Istoriki 'revizionisty' o vneshnej politike SShA" (The 'revisionist' historians on the foreign policy of the U.S.), *Voprosy Istorii,* no. 3 (1973): 105–6.

26. W. A. Williams, *The Tragedy of American Diplomacy,* revised edition (New York: Dell, 1962); Gabriel Kolko, *The Politics of Allied Diplomacy and the World Crisis of 1943–1945* (London, 1968); G. Alperovitz, *Atomic Diplomacy: Hiroshima and Potsdam* (New York: Simon and Schuster, 1965); Alperovitz, *Cold War Essays* (Garden City, N.Y.: Doubleday-Anchor, 1970); David Horowitz, *From Yalta to Vietnam: American Foreign Policy in the Cold War* (Harmondsworth: Penguin, 1967), published in the United States as *The*

Free World Colossus, 1965, 1970, 1971. For examples of the reviews of this extensive literature see Henry Pachter, "Revisionist Historians and the Cold War," *Dissent* 15 (Nov.–Dec. 1968): 505–81; Robert W. Tucker, *The Radical Left and American Foreign Policy* (Baltimore: Johns Hopkins University Press, 1971); and Robert Stover, "Responsibility for the Cold War—A Case Study in Historical Responsibility," *History and Theory* 11 (1972): 145–78.

27. Ralph Milliband, "Military Intervention and Socialist Internationalism," in *The Socialist Register 1980,* ed. R. Milliband and J. Saville (London: Sage, 1980), 20.

28. E. P. Thompson, "Notes on Exterminism, the Last Stage of Civilization," *New Left Review,* no. 121 (May–June 1980), reprinted in Thompson, et al., *Exterminism and Cold War* (London: New Left Books, 1982).

29. Based on a summary from Fred Halliday, *The Making of the Second Cold War* (London: Verso, 1983), 27, extended in Kubalkova and Cruickshank, "The 'New Cold War' in 'Critical International Relations Studies,'" 12.

30. Alan Wolfe, *The Rise and Fall of the "Soviet Threat"* (Washington, D.C.: Institute for Policy Studies, 1979).

31. "U.S. Foreign Policy in the 1980s," *Monthly Review,* no. 4 (1980): 7 (editorial).

32. Ernst Mandel, *Late Capitalism* (London: New Left Books, 1975); Mandel, *The Second Slump* (London: New Left Books, 1975).

33. For example, Harry Braverman, *Labor and Monopoly Capital* (New York: Monthly Review Press, 1975); Michel Aglietta, *A Theory of Capitalist Regulation: The U.S. Experience* (London: New Left Books, 1979).

34. Mary Kaldor, *The Baroque Arsenal* (New York: Hill & Wang, 1981); Mary Kaldor, "Military R & D: Cause or Consequence of the Arms Race?" *International Social Science Journal* 35 (1983): 43.

35. Quoted in Halliday, *The Making of the Second Cold War,* 27.

36. N. Chomsky, Jonathan Steele, and J. Gittings, *Superpowers in Collision* (London: Penguin, 1982), 20.

37. Mary Kaldor, *The Disintegrating West* (London: Allen Lane, 1978), 10.

38. D. Smith and R. Smith, "The New Cold War," *Capital and Class,* no. 12 (1980–81): 27.

39. Dependency theories are also known as *dependencia* theories to mark their Latin American origins. They describe situations in which the economies of Third World countries (called the periphery) are conditioned and subordinate to the economic development, expansion, and contraction of the economies of advanced capitalist states (called the center or the core). This dependent condition that inhibits balanced economic development in the periphery is explained differently by different authors in different historical circumstances,

but the explanations include domestic constraints and structures shaped to facilitate the exploitative patterns.

40. *Monthly Review,* no. 4 (1980): 2 (untitled editorial).

41. Mike Davis, "Nuclear Imperialism and Deterrence Extended," in E. P. Thompson, *Exterminism and Cold War* (London: New Left Books, 1982), 30. For surveys of Soviet literature, see R. J. Hill, *Soviet Politics, Political Science and Reform* (Oxford: Martin Robertson, 1980); and A. Brown, "Political Science in the Soviet Union: A New Stage of Development," *Soviet Studies* (July 1984).

42. M. Ougaard, "The Origins of the Second Cold War," *New Left Review* (Sept.–Oct. 1984): 62; and E. Hobsbawm, "Are We on the Edge of the World War?" *New Society,* January 19, 1984, p. 85.

43. Halliday, *The Making of the Second Cold War.*

44. James M. Goldgeier and Michael McFaul, "A Tale of Two Worlds: Core and Periphery in the Post–Cold War Era," *International Organization* 46, no. 2 (Spring 1992).

45. M. S. Gorbachev, *Perestroika: New Thinking for Our Country and the World* (New York: Harper and Row, 1987); and Gorbachev, "The Idea of Socialism Lives On . . . No Time for Stereotypes," *New York Times,* February 24, 1992, p. A13.

46. For this argument, see Kubalkova and Cruickshank, *Thinking New About "New Thinking"* (Berkeley: University of California Institute of International Studies, 1989).

47. Hillel Ticktin, "The Barriers to the Market and the Necessary Rise to Nationalism," paper presented at the 23d National Convention of the American Association for the Advancement of Slavic Studies, Miami, Florida, November 23, 1991.

Chapter 2

The "Third Worldization" of Russia and Eastern Europe

Andre Gunder Frank

What went wrong in the Socialist East? The usual answers range from "everything" from its opponents, to only "Stalinism" or even "nothing," according to its erstwhile supporters. The answers encompass policies, ideologies, and periods dating from the first Soviet government and revolution in 1917 (or one could start even earlier, with the birth of Marxism in 1848) to those of the last government and reforms of Mikhail Gorbachev beginning in 1985. About this last Soviet period, opinions range from the "if it ain't broke, don't fix it" position of those who thought nothing much was wrong, to arguments that the whole "system" was unworkable. Many critics in the middle, including Gorbachev himself,[1] acknowledged some failures and the need for the kind of change proposed by perestroika but stopped short of embracing a complete transformation. Others, however, regard Gorbachev's efforts at reform as misguided and literally counterproductive. Some argue that were it not for Gorbachev's own policy errors, the Soviet Union and its economy could have survived for some time, if not indefinitely. Among these critics are Michael Ellman and Vladimir Kantorovich[2] and Stanislav Menshikov,[3] to whom we shall return.

All these answers and others like them to be reviewed here are at best half-truths; the old adage has it that they are worse than no answer at all. However, they all focus primarily, if not exclusively, on ideological reasons attributed to socialism, or they are concerned primarily with organizational and policy failures inside the Soviet Union and Eastern Europe. They also leave real-world economic reasons out of consideration.[4] But the answer to the question of "what went wrong" should be sought much more in the material reality of our one-world economy than in any ideological discussion of "socialism" or even in the policies of the former Soviet Union and Eastern Europe.

To begin with, these regions entered the competitive development race in the world economy with an enormous historical handicap. From a realistic, nonideological perspective, their efforts, albeit under the socialist flag, were much less to build socialism than to catch up. For a while, they seemed to succeed—before they failed. However, the reason for continued backwardness in the East is not so much ideological socialism or political planning, now universally faulted and rejected, but much more the historical economic differences and continuing contemporary relations between the two parts of Europe in the world economy.

Historical Background in the World Economy

The division of Europe into a more developed "West" and a less developed "East," with a "Central Europe" geographically and economically in between, stems at least from the sixteenth century—or the ninth.[5] Jeno Szucs observed that "a very sharp line was in fact to cut Europe into two parts from the point of view of economic and social structure after 1500."[6] The dividing line has run remarkably close to the Elbe River and the "Iron Curtain" of the forty years following World War II. "It is as if Stalin, Churchill and Roosevelt had studied carefully the *status quo* of the age of Charlemagne on the 1130th anniversary of his death."[7] Moreover, "the old Roman *limes* would show up on Europe's morphological map, thus presaging right from the start the birth of a 'Central Europe' within the notion of the 'West.' "[8]

Western Europe already exported manufactures and Eastern European agricultural and mineral raw materials by the time of the sixteenth-century expansion. In addition, Western Europe used its access to the gold and silver of the Americas to pay for its imports from, and economically to colonize, the East—in Europe and beyond. Later, and until World War I,

> the whole history of the Hapsburg state was an attempt to balance
> the unbalanceable while being squeezed somewhere between the two

extremes of East-Central Europe. The only consequent structural element in that formula . . . [was] the setting up by the Hapsburgs of a diminished—East-Central European—copy on an "imperial scale" of the division of labor drawn up by the nascent "world economy" on a larger scale. . . . The Hapsburgs had no chances in the Western sector of the world economy either. So the House of Hapsburg settled down to a division of labor between West (industrial) and East (agricultural) through the economic structure within its own, East-Central European, political framework. . . . In the "Hapsburg division of labor," Hungary was cast in the East's role [with its hinterland, and Austria governing Bohemia in the West's].[9]

Thus, historically, Eastern Europe, albeit culturally European, was never economically developed like Western Europe. Therefore, their people have little historical claim to become West European now. Only part of the eastern part of Germany, the Bohemian and Moravian parts of the Czech Republic, and in some sense part of Hungary, Slovenia, and maybe part of Croatia, plus perhaps the Baltic republics, were historically similar to Western Europe.

It is little wonder, then, that these countries sought a way out of their bind through "socialist" development.[10] For a while and against all odds, including postwar Marshall Plan aid that was restricted to Western Europe and continued Western Cocom and other embargoes against the East, the East seemed to succeed.[11] They had massive increases in electric, coal, steel, and oil production to show for their efforts. In 1957, the Soviet Union was the first to launch a human-made satellite, Sputnik, and it so outpaced the United States in the production of engineers as to put a real scare into the Americans. Few people regarded Khrushchev as a hollow boaster when a few years later he vowed, "We will bury you"—in the competitive development race in the world economy. East Germany advanced to the world's ninth industrial power. By various economic and social indices—industrial production, the development of human capital (health and education)—several countries in Eastern Europe narrowed the gap and in some cases even overtook countries in Western, not to mention Southern, Europe in the 1950s and 1960s.[12] In the 1970s, the Soviet Union and Eastern Europe still held their own and maintained the recently narrowed gap in this world economic competition. Eastern Europe did so, however, at the cost of running up debts to the West, when recessionary lower growth rates in the West encouraged loans to the East. The Soviet Union achieved some kind of parity in the arms race and significant successes in space. In the 1980s, however, the Soviet Union and Eastern Europe all missed the technological train—and lost the race.

Seventy years of the politics and ideology of "socialist development" in the Soviet Union and forty years of the same in Eastern Europe— not to mention the development of socialism itself—seem not to have substantially and definitely changed the economic positions of these regions, either relative to each other or to Western Europe. Over the entire postwar period, the East-West gap and the relative positions of the states within the East changed very little.

Indeed, there is some question whether these forty years even changed their internal class structure much. If there was any change, it was mostly the decline of Bohemia, Moravia, Hungary, Slovenia, and perhaps the Baltics in Central and "socialist" Europe relative to the rise of parts of Spain, Italy, and Greece in "capitalist" Southern Europe. Industrialization, of course, modified the class structure every-where in Europe, but apparently not more and perhaps less in the East than in the West and South. Therefore, only the above-mentioned regions in Central Europe now have a fighting chance to recuperate their historical positions in Europe, and that in competition with South-ern Europe. Public opinion in Southern Europe already shows itself very aware of this threat, while in Central and Eastern Europe it still appears even unaware of the problem.[13]

To summarize in other words:

1. There is only *one* world system, and the claim expressed by Stalin in *The Economic Problems of Socialism* shortly before his death in 1953, and by still others since then, that there are "two world systems," one capitalist and the other socialist, is an illusion. This illusion was derived from the notion of "politics [and ideology] in command," which was proposed by Mao and Lenin but is equally shared by Reaganites and end-of-history theorist Francis Fukuyama. In the real world, economics is in command.

2. In particular, the worldwide competitive process of capital accu-mulation is the motor force of history. In this regard, Marx was right to stand the idealist Hegel on his head. In this competitive race for capital accumulation, the "socialist" economies of Eastern Europe

started out with an enormous handicap, which—except temporarily—they were not able to make up, let alone overcome. So they lost the race. As is the rule in other kinds of races, most of the competitors also lose; only a few win—and they only temporarily so.

3. The center-periphery structure in the world system is alive and well. Indeed, polarization is growing apace in the "really existing world capitalist system." Even World Bank calculations demonstrate it. The principal center-periphery division between the rich North and West and the poor South and East is of long standing, and it is steadily growing deeper. Within Europe, this same division has existed for over a thousand years. The fact of center-periphery division has characterized the world system for millennia, and this division between two "worlds" has existed for some half a millennium.

This long-standing economic and structural (and consequently political and cultural) division of Europe has been perpetuated to this day and promises to continue for some time to come. Ironically, many of the "Second World" East Europeans who sought to join the "First World" West will find themselves in the "Third World" South instead.

As the foregoing quotation about the history of Eastern Europe and the Hapsburgs suggests, as does experience since 1989, it was an ideological illusion to group Eastern Europe and the Soviet Union into a "second" world of their own, relegating the South to a "third" world. Both the East and the South were and remain in the "second" world.

The First World has placed obstacles in the way of, if not combated, states seeking to rise from second- to first-world status. For decades, Western embargoes and other obstacles directed against the East were covered with the fig leaves of Cold War ideology. Yet, today many of these same Western policies, and even some Cocom trade restrictions, continue for reasons of naked economic competition, as we will observe below. Should we not regard the Cold War as principally an ideologically disguised yet crude attempt by the West to keep the East, and of course the South, in second place? Of course, this strategy, which included an arms race to spend the East into bankruptcy, CIA machinations, and myriad other tactics,[14] was successful. A "minor" cost was the politically motivated support to South Korea and Taiwan, which permitted them to compete effectively if not yet to achieve first-world status. Permitting the already-developed Germany and Japan to grow poses greater costs and threats. With the demise of "socialism," these costs are exacerbated, and the center-periphery structure and conflict is only further reinforced, or, rather, more exposed.

4. The alternation between hegemony and rivalry continues. The "American century" lasted twenty years, from the mid-1940s to the mid-1960s. Since then, the renewed rivalry of Western Europe and Japan—but not of the Soviet Union, as I have emphasized again and again—has challenged American hegemony. Now the Cold War is over and Germany and Japan have won, as I have repeated since at least 1988. When President Bush launched his "New World Order" with the Gulf War against Iraq, he proclaimed the twenty-first century American as well. But even to pay for that war, Bush had to send his secretary of state, James Baker, hat in hand to Germany and Japan. Then he had to go to Japan himself as a traveling salesman for the Big Three automobile companies, who have all experienced economic troubles in the face of competition from Japan. After World War I, as Charles Kindleberger aptly put it, Britain could not, and America still would not, take in hand the reins of the world economic system and prevent world depression. Now the United States can no longer do so, and Japan will not or cannot, as depression threatens again.[15]

5. The economic cycle also remains on its roller-coaster ups and downs. Since the mid-1960s, the "Kondratieff" long wave has been in a down phase, and we have seen shorter cyclical recessions and recoveries. Since 1989, we are in the fifth cyclical recession of this long economic crisis, and it threatens to become *the* crisis in the crisis— so much so that President Bush had to downplay his new world order or delete it altogether from his speeches. Even so, he lost the 1992 election because of the economy.

Transition: From Second to First or Third World?

The political and ideological changes in Eastern Europe through which its people aspire to join the First World in Western Europe threaten instead to place Eastern Europe economically in the Third World— again, for that is where it was before. Poland has already been Latin-americanized. The former dependent agricultural (and temporarily, oil) export economy par excellence of Romania will be lucky if it can recover that position, now in competition with Bulgaria, which developed agribusiness for export during the "socialist" regime.

The same problem obtains a fortiori in the former Soviet Union. Some parts of Russia and Ukraine were Westernized by Peter the Great and industrialized by him, Witte, and Stalin. But most of the former Soviet Union still has at best a Third World economy, like Brazil, India, and China, which also have industrial capacities, especially in military hardware. The Transcaucasian and Central Asian regions are economically not so likely to be Latinamericanized as Africanized or—God forbid—politically Lebanonized, like the former Yugoslavia. From there, war and "ethnic cleansing" may soon spread elsewhere through the Balkans; we have already seen a bitter glimpse of the foreseeable future for many of the region's peoples.

Many of these regions now face the serious prospect, like Africa, of being marginalized out of the international division of labor. Their natural resources have been squeezed dry for the benefit of industrial development farther north, and now the regions and their peoples can be discarded. In Russia, President Boris Yeltsin took this position regarding Central Asia. On the other hand, it is understandable that the peoples of the southern regions, exploited in the past, now demand a different relationship. Similarly understandable is the appeal to—or discovery of—"traditional" ethnic and national identities and the rise in interethnic strife as a response to aggravated economic deprivation, which included 30 percent unemployment in parts of Central Asia even during Soviet times. However, political "independence" and interethnic strife offer the people of Central Asia or Central Africa little economic hope for the future. On the contrary, the erection of politically motivated ethnic and other barriers to economic interchange, and even exploitation, threatens to return them to the backwaters of history.

The revolutions of 1989 in Eastern Europe and the breakup of the Soviet Union were not at bottom responses to supposed differences in economic and political policies between the "socialist" East and the "capitalist" West. Instead, these revolutions were more the consequence of the individual states' participation in a single world economic system and its present world economic crisis. This crisis evoked important similarities between the economic policy responses of the East and the West, and especially those of the South in Latin America, Africa, and parts of Asia.

The world economic crisis spelled the doom of the "socialist" economies much more than did "socialist planning" or the "command economies" that are now almost universally blamed for the failure. Not unlike the Third World economies of Latin America and Africa, the Second World economies of the Soviet Union and Eastern Europe were unable to bear the pace of accelerated competition in the world economy during the period of crisis. Like every previous one, this economic crisis forced widespread economic restructuring and political realignments. It is true that the "command" organization of a planned economy and political bureaucracy were instrumental in depriving the economies of Eastern Europe and the Soviet Union of the flexibility they needed to adapt to the world economic crisis and to meet the technological revolution which that same crisis engendered elsewhere. However, many Third World market economies also failed, as did important sectors in the industrial world, most notably in the United States. In the meantime, Japan Inc. and the newly industrialized countries (NICs) of East Asia relied on important state political and economic actions to promote their technological advance and adjustment.

World Economic Crisis and Policy in Eastern Europe and the Soviet Union

We may return to the question of "what went wrong." Far from looking for the answer only, or even primarily, in the internal structure, policies, or ideology of the Soviet Union and Eastern Europe, we must seek it in the structure and development of the world economy in general and in the recent world economic crisis, and particularly in its present fifth recession.

The world economic crisis has been expanding and deepening in Eastern Europe, the Soviet Union, and its successor states. This crisis and related economic factors have contributed materially to the success of various social, ethnic, and nationalist movements in mobilizing so many people for such far-reaching political ends. The decade of the 1980s, indeed beginning in the mid-1970s, came to be called "the period of stagnation" in the Soviet Union, and it generated an accelerating economic crisis and a real deterioration of living standards in most of Eastern Europe.[16] Significantly, especially in Eastern Europe, this period also brought an important deterioration in its *relative* competitive standing and standard of living compared to Western Europe and even to the NICs in East Asia.

Regarding the states of Eastern Europe, the 1970s and 1980s—and indeed the 1990s—make amply clear that "socialism" was largely irrelevant to their failure. For East European policies—and their consequences—were hardly any different from those of the "capitalist" Latin American debtor countries, which failed equally.

In the 1970s, the countries of Eastern Europe (and "socialist" countries everywhere) switched from import substitution industrialization (ISI) to import-led growth. They sought to fuel their growth by importing technology and capital from the West, which they intended to pay for by exporting the derivative manufactures back to the West and the world market. Actually, their strategy was only the supply constraint–scarcity economy version of the selfsame "export-led growth" strategy. That was to import technology in order to export manufactures, and it was pursued by the demand-constrained surplus economies of the East Asian and South American NICs. Moreover, the East Europeans continued with their export promotion to the Soviet Union and each other.

Unfortunately for them, and for the peddlers of ideological models for success, the East European NICs failed no less than the South American ones did and a few Southeast Asian ones as well. No doubt, there were domestic reasons for all these failures as well as world economic factors. The latter were caused by the world economy in crisis, which permitted only a few successes to penetrate the protected and recessionary import markets in the West and the world generally.

The "solution" everywhere was to run up debts. In the 1970s, moreover, crisis-reduced domestic investment opportunities in the West made credit-financed exports to the South and the East all the more necessary and welcome. So the banks, awash with investable money, loaned and loaned. Debts piled up in the South American and East European NICs alike, and in some Southeast Asian ones, like the Philippines and Indonesia, as well. This debt economy prospered until the renewed recession in 1979–82 turned the "solution" into yet another problem. The recession obliged closure or restricted access to this South/East casino and its replacement during the 1980s by Reaganomic roulette in the U.S. casino instead.[17]

Those who now find ideological discomfort in the failure of "really existing socialism" and the "success" of world-market, export-led growth would do well to make the following comparisons with "really existing capitalism":

In the 1970s, the same export- or import-led growth strategies were adopted by Communist party–led governments in the East (Poland, Romania, Hungary) and military dictatorships in the South (Argentina, Brazil, Chile). Neither their differences in political ideology nor in economic "system" were sufficient to bring about significant differences in their political and economic responses to the world economic crisis. These same economic strategies, with heavy reliance on foreign debt, then generated the same (debt) crisis within the crisis. Significantly, the new crisis began in Poland in 1981, before the more usual dating in Argentina and Mexico in 1982.

Then in the 1980s, the same debt-service strategies, modeled on International Monetary Fund (IMF) policies, were adopted and implemented by Communist party–led governments in the East (Poland, Hungary, Romania, Yugoslavia) and by military dictatorships, other authoritarian governments, and—it is important to emphasize—their successor democratic governments in the South (Argentina, Brazil, Mexico, the Philippines). There were variations on the theme of debt service, but it is difficult to correlate, let alone explain, them by reference to the political color or ideologies of regimes or governments. The most stellar pupil of the IMF was Nicolae Ceausescu in Romania, who actually reduced the debt until the lights went out, first for his people and then for himself. In Peru, on the other hand, the newly elected president, Alán García, defied the IMF and announced he would limit debt service to no more than 10 percent of export earnings. Actually, Peru's payments were less than that before he assumed office, and they rose to more than 10 percent under his presidency. Real income fell by about half. The novelist Mario Vargas Llosa sought to succeed García, after moving politically from the center-left to the extreme right. But what does that mean, if anything? Alberto Fujimori won the presidential election through his opposition to Vargas Llosa's economic program and then turned around and applied the very same policies in what became popularly known as "Fujishock."

Communist General Jaruzelski in Poland and the populist Sandinistas in Nicaragua also imposed IMF-style "adjustment" and "conditionality" on their people. Both did so *without* the benefit of pressure from the IMF, since Poland was not a member and Nicaragua had no access to it. In Nicaragua, there was "condicionalidad sin fondo," that is, conditionality without the Fund (*fondo*) and without any bottom (*fondo*) or end to the Sisyphean policy. Hungary had the most reformed economy and the most liberal political policy still led by a Communist party in the Warsaw Pact. Yet Hungary paid off the early 1980s principal of its debt three times over—and meanwhile doubled the amount it still owed! That is more than Poland or Brazil or Mexico, which on the average paid off the amount of debt owed only once or twice, while at the same time increasing its total only two times. No matter, the Solidarity government that replaced General Jaruzelski and the Communist party in Poland then benefited from IMF membership and imposed even more severe economic sacrifices on its population than its predecessors had. In Hungary's first free election, all parties promised to follow the IMF prescriptions.

Moreover, the Western IMF and its policies were the "secret weapon" and de facto ally of the erstwhile opposition groups in these countries. They are now in power, or making their bid for it, thanks primarily to the economic crisis, and secondarily to the political one, engendered by the implementation of IMF-supported austerity policies. So now there is neither an economic nor a political alternative to further such policies, which are tied to IMF and other Western advice and conditions.

In the 1980s, the East European NICs, like the South American and African ones, also lost their capacity to compete in export markets. As for all the dependent "developing" economies, by far their most important supply constraint was and remains that of hard-currency foreign exchange based on the U.S. dollar. For that reason also, the East Europeans maintained and tried to increase their intra-COMECON (Soviet Bloc) trade with each other and the Soviet Union, which was not paid for in dollars. Therefore, as we will note below, the dollarization of former COMECON trade in the 1990s will all but dry up this intraregional trade while simultaneously blocking any extraregional replacement, because dollarization can only exacerbate the most critical supply constraint, which is foreign-exchange shortage.

This foreign-exchange problem was intensified by the debt crisis, and it became both a cause and then a consequence for missing the high-tech train, which left the East European economies standing on side tracks in the 1980s. If the East European NICs had become, indeed had even remained, more competitive in the world market than the East Asian NICs, there would have been no 1989 revolution, Fukuyama's and our own celebration of democracy notwithstanding.[18] Now their failure is universally attributed to socialism's shortcomings, and Eastern Europeans have come to share the Reaganomic and Thatcherite belief in the "magic of the market" as the sure-fire alternative. Freeing the market and market freedom came to be seen as the solution to all problems on the way to paradise, when in fact in the short run they can only deprive Eastern Europeans of the partial protection they had before. Greater inequalities of income and mushrooming unemployment are dismissed as "small" costs. Moreover, few are willing to consider the real costs of privatizing or converting East European economies, and particularly their military sectors, which once accounted for perhaps 25 to 50 percent of goods production but have since lost many of their export markets.[19]

The political irony is that "really existing socialism" failed not least because of the unsuccessful implementation of import- or export-led growth models and IMF-style austerity policies in the East. Yet "really existing capitalism" pursued the same models and policies in the South and also failed. However, nobody in the West or East says so, and nobody in the South any longer has a plausible "socialist" alternative to offer. Why was there a change of system in part of the East in the face of failure, but none in the South as a consequence of the same failure? The argument made by Jeane Kirkpatrick, Ronald Reagan's ambassador to the United Nations, that totalitarian countries in the East do not change, while authoritarian ones in the West do, is debatable. So is the question of whether there was a change of system or "an end to history."[20]

The "Special Case" of the Soviet Union

The Soviet economy, it has been claimed, was more isolated and independent than the East European economies. However, the Soviet economy was also integrated into the world economy through the East European economies on which it depended for industrial goods, as well as being directly linked into the world economy. Even in the Soviet Union, therefore, domestic economic organization and policy were not the only or even the main reasons for its economic failure.

In line with this reasoning, Fred Halliday offers an answer to "what went wrong"—he suggests not "socialism" or even "capitalism," but rather "a singular collapse." He argues that no one factor is solely responsible, although the internal weakness of the Soviet system played a major role. He denies substantial significance to international factors,[21] among which he includes competition in technology and in

Afghanistan. Yet it was the failure to compete in the world economy, compounded with its internal crisis, that led to the post-1985 changes in the USSR.[22] However, Halliday also claims that "this interstate competition, comprehensive as it was, is not sufficient to explain how, why, and when the communist system collapsed."[23]

Halliday concludes that "it was not the 'market,' in any direct sense, of intervention within these societies and economies, that contributed to their demise."[24] Rather, he attributes the collapse to dynamics which began with the rise in the price of oil, giving the USSR a windfall profit. However, he discounts arguments that the same rise in oil prices imposed unanticipated hardships for the oil-importing countries of Eastern Europe, and that the decline in oil (and gold) prices after 1981 deprived the Soviet Union of much-needed foreign exchange. Over 90 percent of its hard-currency earners were in this market. It thus seems questionable that this did not have a major impact on Soviet economy or society.

Moreover, as already noted, the Soviet Union, like the East European NICs, pursued export-promotion strategies no less than other nations, only with less success. The deepening crisis in the economies of Eastern Europe also affected the Soviet Union. It depended on them for imports of essential manufactures which they produced with technology that they in turn were required to, but increasingly could not, import from Western Europe. Thus, both the external and thereby the internal economy of the Soviet Union was affected by the economic crisis in Eastern Europe at the same time that it was already hard hit by the decline since 1981 in prices for gold, oil, and gas. This denied the Soviet Union the foreign exchange it needed to bypass Eastern Europe and buy directly from the West.

Halliday does not attribute much significance to the arms race in general and "Star Wars" in particular: "Important as it is, there are reasons to qualify the import of the arms race explanation as the major factor behind the Soviet collapse."[25] He goes on to explain, "The very high rate of [Soviet] military expenditure as a percentage of GNP is but another way of saying that GNP itself was rather low. . . . In absolute terms the U.S. was outspending the USSR. The focus must, therefore, be as much on the efficiency and allocative mechanisms of the civilian sector as on the claim of the military on GNP."[26] On the face of Halliday's argument alone, it could equally well be the other way around. GNP was already low, and growth rates declined and then stagnated in the 1980s.[27] Therefore, it could also be argued that the increased military expenditures, coming on top of declining foreign-exchange earnings, affected efficiency and allocative mechanisms negatively or at least impeded their improvement. If that is so, then contrary to Halliday, both the "market" and the "arms race" did indeed intervene in Soviet economy and society.

However, it should be noticed that the "Second Cold War" arms race itself was also market driven. To begin with, the Second Cold War was started by President Carter in mid-1979, several months *before* the Soviet Union invaded Afghanistan. It involved the NATO agreement to increase military expenditures by 3 percent a year after inflation, the "double track" decision to place American Pershing II and Cruise missiles in Western Europe, and to play the "China card" against the Soviet Union. The Soviet invasion of Afghanistan followed in December 1979, when perhaps the Soviets miscalculated that détente was already a lost cause. The American political and military response, and subsequent escalation, was much stronger than expected, even in America.[28] Why? Not by happenstance did all this begin in 1979, precisely at the beginning of an economic recession that lasted until 1982, the longest-lasting and most severe downturn since World War II—until the present one beginning in 1989. In every recession since World War II, each administration has escalated military engagement and/or expenditures, as President Bush did again against Panama and Iraq.[29]

The 1979 economic recession and inflation, probably more than the Iran hostage crisis, cost Jimmy Carter the election and ushered Ronald Reagan into the presidency. He called the Soviet Union an "evil empire" and started "Star Wars" with the express purpose, documented by Sean Gervasi, of outspending the Soviet Union to its knees. So there is the half-truth in his spokesperson's claim to have won the Cold War. But Reagan did not invoke this policy before putting into place the remainder of "Reaganomics." Reaganomics was no more than the continuation or escalation of the "monetarist" and "supply-side" policy already inaugurated by Jimmy Carter, when *he* (and not Reagan) abandoned Keynesianism in 1977 and appointed Paul Volker to head the Federal Reserve in the 1979 recession, where he continued to carry out Reaganomic monetarist policy all through the 1980s.

The costs of the crisis, and especially of the 1979–82 recession, were shifted onto the backs of those throughout the world economy who could least afford their burden and least defend themselves. Monetary and fiscal policies and debt service were the instruments, as Desai pointed out.[30] However, the debt crisis—which emerged during the 1979–82 recession—removed the South and East from availability as borrowers of last resort to prop up demand in the economies of the West. A replacement was needed, and it was found in the United States, which by 1986 had become the world's largest debtor.

The instrument was still the same monetary and fiscal policy, except that now it was called "Reaganomics" and functioned through "military Keynesianism" or "Star Wars." Reagan's renewed increase of military expenditures, coming on top of Carter's, generated the famed American "twin deficits" in the federal budget and the foreign currency account. U.S. deficit spending was necessary, not only to support the American economy, but to keep the entire Western economy afloat during the 1980s. This world economic imperative and the inevitably uneven distribution of its costs benefited parts of the West, including Western Europe, Japan, and the East Asian NICs who were dependent on the American market. However, it was this same world monetary and fiscal policy that pushed Latin America, Africa, Eastern Europe, and the Soviet Union into an economic depression that is already more severe than that of the 1930s. A major, but always unmentioned, difference between the Soviet Union and United States in the 1980s was that the former had no one to bail it out of bankruptcy. The latter, however, received massive capital contributions from Western Europe and Japan, as well as involuntary support through debt service from Latin America, to plug up the American foreign trade and domestic budget deficits that were generated by military spending.[31]

Taking this into consideration, Halliday's claim that the world market did not intervene in the Soviet economy or society is highly questionable. Instead, he and many others asserted that "the central feature of the collapse" was "the ideological dimension . . . [that] was in some ways decisive."[32] "The central feature of the collapse . . . [was] the collapse [of] underlying self-confidence . . . first among the leadership and, then within the population as a whole."[33] This led to Gorbachev's change of heart. Yet, Gorbachev himself asserted time and again that there was no alternative to perestroika, in view of the serious problems faced by the Soviet economy. These were vastly aggravated by the pressures emanating from the world economy of which it was a part. Indeed, in the opening pages of chapter 1 of his book *Perestroika*, Gorbachev explained its "origins":

> Perestroika is no whim. . . . Perestroika is an urgent necessity. . . . The country began to lose momentum. . . . Analyzing the situation, we first discovered a slowing economic growth . . . to a level close to economic stagnation. . . . A country that was once quickly closing on the world's advanced nations began to lose one position after another . . . [in] scientific and technological development, the production of advanced technology.[34]

Soviet perestroika and Russian economic reform, as well as East European privatization, have destroyed old forms of economic organization before new ones were put in place. In particular, the Soviet Union made the serious mistake of starting perestroika where it is most difficult: in industry and trade instead of agriculture. Adopting the Chinese model and beginning privatization on the land, even if the Soviet Union has relatively less agriculture and peasant enterprise, could have increased food supplies to the cities and built up political capital for Gorbachev. Instead, both the Soviet Union and especially Eastern Europe began by making the industrial and commercial state monopolies subject to market forces and permitting them large measures of private monopoly power. The result was, of course, that they raised prices to consumers and intermediaries, which brought inflation. At the same time, inflation was (and mostly still is) fed by burgeoning state deficits, which have been managed by printing money faster and faster. Significant causes of these deficits were increased arms expenditures during the "Star Wars" era and higher subsidies to or prices from the state and privatized enterprises. The result was inevitably a breakdown of the supply system coupled with runaway inflation. Instead of serving the consumer (not to mention the worker) better, liberalization, both before and since the "revolution," has brought the economy to a halt. Since 1989, and especially 1991, the breakup of COMECON and the shift to the dollar as the currency of trade within and between Eastern Europe and the former Soviet Union also disrupted demand and supply and therefore drastically reduced production and employment.

Therefore, the medium-term economic irony has been that domestic economic and political liberalization and the abolition of COMECON and intra-Soviet trade relations broke up the only available avenue for international East-East trade. Eastern and Central Europe and most of the former Soviet republics are dependent in various ways on fuel and other raw materials from Russia. This dependence is partly physical, based on the existing network of oil and gas pipelines and railways, but it is also economic, since these countries cannot import and pay for fuel originating elsewhere. This in turn is a factor of their dependence on manufactured exports to Russia and to each other, which they cannot sell in the West because they are not competitive there. The East also has difficulty selling its manufactured goods in the South, where the West and East Asia have been increasingly compelled to increase market share to compensate for domestic and export markets lost to the new recession. Moreover, especially under French pressure, the European Economic Community (EEC) is reluctant to reduce its tariff barriers to imports from the East, whose low prices threaten Western agricultural, steel, chemical, textile, and other markets, particularly in the recessionary times of the early 1990s.

The conversion of East European and former Soviet trade from rubles to dollars only exacerbated the problem of their mutual economic dependence. The result can only be that the short-term economic depression and unemployment in each country is exacerbated by the decline of its export markets elsewhere in the region and the impossibility of replacing them with markets in the West and South. East German industry, of course, lost all of its export markets in the East as soon as it adopted and required payment in the strong deutsche mark. It was particularly dependent on those markets after its capacity to export to the West was all but eliminated by heightened competition and lagging technology during the 1980s. It is no wonder the export-dependent economy of East Germany is in depression.

Dollarization and regionalization among the republics of the former Soviet Union and Yugoslavia and elsewhere extend the same problem to those countries, where again the new ideology and politics are replacing the old international economic organization before a new one can takes its place. Therefore, another economic irony is that, after the cancellation of its foreign debt, the next best thing Eastern Europe and the former Soviet Union could get from the West would be a fund of convertible currencies to maintain their regional trade network until it could be replaced by more multilateral East-West trade.

The talk of new Western economic aid to the East is no more than a smokescreen for continuing exploitation in the form of the debt-service funds that flow from the increasingly impoverished East into Western bank coffers. Former Romanian ambassador Silviu Brucan estimates that the total debt of over $150 billion generates an annual flow of $10–15 billion, which is more than the entire capital of Jacques Attali's European Bank of Reconstruction and Development. Indeed, the *International Herald Tribune* reported an annual obligation—not all of it paid—of $11 billion on a debt of $70 billion from the Soviet Union alone.[35] The reduction of the Polish debt by half after the 1989 revolution was the quid pro quo in exchange for Poland's starting to pay interest on the remaining half; until then it had paid no interest at all.

Ellman and Kantorovich and Menshikov argue that first Gorbachev's economic advisers and then Yeltsin and Gaidar made serious policy mistakes.[36] These include several of the "domestic" ones mentioned above. To them Ellman and Kantorovich add "weakening, or removing altogether three crucial load-bearing 'bricks' . . . the central bureaucratic apparatus, the official ideology, and the active role of the party in the economy."[37] Menshikov also stresses mistaken or inadequate measures in respect to the informal "shadow" economy, which importantly complements the formal one. But these observers, like most others, largely neglect the international political and economic forces that played equal or greater roles and influenced what internal policies could be implemented.[38]

In fact, these policies and measures were also "mistaken" responses to economic exigencies over which the political leadership in the Soviet Union—and a fortiori in Eastern Europe—had scarce control before their revolutions and virtually none afterward. Now they are completely beholden to world-market forces, to Western institutions like the World Bank and the IMF, and to advisory "missions" such as those of Jeffrey Sachs of Harvard. That is, politics was *not* in command all that much; especially and ironically, politics in the East was and is not in command. If any politics has been in control in the East, it is that of the West! Neither has ideology governed, despite claims to that effect by Chirot, Desai, and even Hobsbawm.[39]

The results of these policies of the East and West are doubtful at best. In the short run, the accelerated incorporation of the East into the world market has had two ironically contradictory results. First, the East is still unable to compete effectively—the less so for having lost the partial protection that "socialism" afforded it and its people. But even so, some of its products—agricultural, raw material, and industrial—are perceived as a threat in the West, particularly now in recession-plagued Western Europe.

In the longer run, the incorporation of Eastern Europe and parts of the former Soviet Union into a European economic bloc may help Western Europe weather the storm of the world economic crisis, by strengthening its ability to compete against the Japanese-led East Asian and U.S.-led American blocs. The very regionalization of the world economy is a consequence of the same world economic crisis.[40] While multilateralism may be touted at General Agreement on Tariffs and Trade (GATT) talks and elsewhere, the heightened competition brought by this (as well as the previous) world economic crisis has had the effect of promoting the regionalization of the world economy. The EEC and its plans for a regional market after 1992 are only its most institutionalized expression. Western Europe may lose some of the American market on which it is so dependent. Europe will also face increasing competition in the world market from Japan and, with its devalued dollar, from the U.S. itself. Therefore, Western Europe will increasingly need to expand its traditional markets in Eastern Europe and the former Soviet Union, and perhaps in the Middle East and Africa as well. With any remnant ideological obstacles removed, the EEC could and should be extended to include Eastern Europe, even if the latter continues to be dependent on Western Europe.[41] That process is now in full swing, in fact, and the elimination of ideological obstacles is therefore more its effect than its cause.

In this regard, it is useful to note again that the economic colonization of Eastern Europe by its Western neighbors has a centuries-long history. In the world economic crisis of the 1930s and early 1940s, Germany's economic and political colonization of Eastern Europe was in full swing. Moreover, German ambitions were not confined to the East or to political domination in the West. In 1944, German big businesses, some of which still survive under the same name, published advertisements about the postwar European economic union they then foresaw under German management.[42] The same year, an Austrian by the name of Kurt Waldheim submitted his Ph.D. dissertation about the German ideologist Konstatin Franz (1817–91). In its conclusion he wrote approvingly of the

> marvelous cooperation of all European peoples under the leadership of the Reich. . . . To accomplish this, is the national calling of Germany. . . . Germany alone has the inner spirit and world position to put this idea into practice and to make it universal. . . . Through the regeneration of the East, Western Europe will regenerate itself; and through the domination of these countries, it will regain its erstwhile position in the world. Otherwise, it will lose its previous importance ever more to North America . . . and on the other side to Russia.[43]

Conclusions and Perspectives

Perhaps the biggest irony is that the present "transition from socialism to capitalism" is taking place just when another severe recession in the world economy is helping to pull Eastern Europe and the former Soviet Union deeper into depression. For this reason, celebrations of the events of 1989 as liberation in the East and victory in the West may have been premature. The peoples of the former Soviet Union and Eastern Europe were supposed to be offered some of the benefits (as well as some of the costs and discipline) of free-market Western democracy through various vehicles of reform: first by making the Soviet economy responsive to market forces under glasnost and perestroika; then through the "shock-therapy" reforms of Gaidar in Yeltsin's government in Russia; and through privatization and expanded democracy in Eastern Europe. East Europeans sought to become like West Europeans; the Soviet people sought at last to join Western civilization. It was understood the transition would be unsettling— smoother or rougher, depending on the skill of those making domestic policy. Many people hoped, and some still do, that the more the old ideological ways are rejected, and replaced with Reaganomic and Thatcherite ideology and practice, the better the policy and the faster and smoother the transition will be.

However, the short-term economic irony is that the transition has accelerated the economic decline of the East, at least in part because it has occurred at the worst possible time. The severe recession in the West has exacerbated the difficulties of transition in the East. By 1990, production in Eastern Europe had declined an average of 20 percent, spelling severe depression and galloping inflation there. More of the same followed in 1991 and 1992. However, this inflation is measured in terms of national currencies which have become worthless. Accordingly, these economies are now "dollarized" or "D-markized." The result is that the real-market value of their properties and goods is suffering a classical and severe deflation against these world currencies; property, land, and skilled labor in the East can be had by Westerners for very little. The value-price differential between the East and the West that has resulted from these unrealistic exchange rates has also generated widespread "free"-market corruption in, and especially a massive smuggling of valuable raw materials out of, the East. These black-market dealings deny needed foreign exchange to the states and their enterprises and, in a vicious downward spiral, generate still greater devaluations of the Eastern national currencies, perhaps to the point that they and their economies collapse altogether. (Ironically, the dollar is increasingly valued only in the socialist or former-socialist East and the underdeveloped South, while it is declining in value elsewhere on the world market.)

Unemployment has ravaged the population in the East, which has little provision for unemployment insurance. In the old days, ideology and full employment made it unnecessary; now the new ideology and bankruptcy make it impossible. In Germany, accelerated unification deepened the depression and aggravated unemployment, which in the East rose rapidly to several million. Ironically, unification was accelerated to avoid mass migration out of the bankrupt East. Yet unification so accelerated the East's bankruptcy and unemployment as to promote even more westward migration, a subject to which we return below.

Thus, policies designed to accelerate economic integration and make producers responsive to market forces are again more effect than cause; and insofar as they cause anything, their effects are again rather the opposite of those supposedly intended. Perhaps more significantly still, the industrial economies of the West, in Europe and elsewhere, are increasingly able to transfer a major part of the costs of adjustment to the world economic crisis to the "Second World" East, as they already have to the "Third World" South. In the process, the Second World is also being "third worldized." *This* is where deliberate policy does come in, however. It is most dramatically visible in the West German "colonization" of the former German Democratic Republic, which is reminiscent of the carpetbaggers who went from North to South after the latter's defeat in the American Civil War. The West is systematically eliminating real and potential competition from the East by forcing even economically sound enterprises into financial bankruptcy and/or buying them up at artificially low prices.[44] The steady procession of "expert advisers" and the IMF policies that already depressed the economies of the South and East in the 1980s are now even more prevalent in the East and only compound its bankruptcy. They counsel "getting the prices right" by increasing the domestic prices of all commodities, including basic consumer goods, to Western levels—but excluding the price of wage labor and not counting their prices in dollars or marks!

Unfortunately also, ideologically promoted privatization is no remedy for the ills of Central and Eastern Europe, any more than stabilization and privatization policy have been in Latin America and elsewhere. Indeed, during the present world recession, these privatization policies can only socialize and aggravate poverty further. The current privatization craze is just as economically irrational and ideologically driven as was the earlier nationalization craze. It makes very little difference whether an enterprise is owned privately or publicly; all have to compete on equal terms in the world market. The only exceptions to this rule are enterprises, public and private, that are subsidized from the state budget or are otherwise supported "in the public interest." Moreover, in the market, both are equal in their ability to make good and bad investments and other kinds of management decisions. In Eastern Europe as elsewhere, whether investment decisions are sound is not determined by whether they are made by public or private agencies. Indeed, Germany's public Treuhandanstalt, which is in charge of privatizing public firms, has been making disastrously bad (dis)investment decisions in the East to serve private big business interests in the West.[45] Privatizing public enterprises one week at bargain-basement share prices that double the next week on the national stock exchange is just as fraudulent a practice as nationalizing loss-making enterprises and paying for them above market value or nationalizing profitable enterprises with little or no indemnification. This practice is all the more egregious in the case of enterprises in the East and the South that are privatized and bought up with devalued domestic currency purchased (or swapped for debt) by foreign companies or joint ventures using foreign exchange from abroad. In sum, the privatization debate is a sham; it is far less about productive efficiency than about distributive (in)justice.

Thus, the legacy of global Reaganomics has been intensified by a worldwide recession and perhaps depression. Political events in the East after 1989 were the direct result of the world economic crisis. We observed above how economic depression is now hitting them too. The hardest hit are the weakest and poorest population segments and regions, such as those in declining industrial regions and in the former Soviet Central Asia, where unemployment rose to over 20 percent before their independence, to which it contributed. The terrible civil war in the former Yugoslavia is a direct consequence of the economic and debt crisis of the 1980s. A different Western policy could have lessened the debt's sociopolitical ravages and avoided dismemberment and civil war in Yugoslavia and perhaps in the Soviet Union as well.

Thus, the short- and medium-term prospects are beclouded by the accelerated impoverishment of Central and Eastern Europe and the former Soviet Union—victims first of the world economic crisis, and then of political and economic policies that have aggravated its regional effects. At least four dangerous and mutually related consequences threaten Europe and the West, especially with another recession battering the world economy and Europe in the early 1990s: (1) accelerated migration from East and South to West; (2) political gains by the radical right; (3) spreading ethnic and nationalist conflict; and (4) the breakdown of existing territorial states and outright war among their successors. These phenomena are often interpreted as unrelated and motivated by cultural, ideological, or political causes. Yet all of them are not only intimately related to each other, they are also ultimately derived from the world economic crisis and the unintended consequences of ill-considered policies to confront that crisis.[46]

The new conventional wisdom claims to account for the ethnic conflict in the former Yugoslavia, and the prospect of similar conflict elsewhere in Eastern Europe and the Soviet Union, by appealing to history. But the appeal is limited to a half-truth about age-old ethnic divisions that were contained for decades under "socialist" rule. Almost nobody discusses the other half of the truth—the historical and current position of these regions in the world economy, factors that are at least as important, and perhaps more so, in accounting for their present political and ethnic debacles.

Thus, it is simply not correct to suppose that Eastern Europe or even the Soviet Union belonged to a separate "system" whose deviant ideology caused their downfall. On the contrary, what caused their misery was their participation in the same world economic system as everybody else. Nor did they have any other choice![47]

Notes

Author's note: I am grateful to Michael Ellman, Hannes Hofbauer and Andrea Komlosy for comments on an earlier draft of this essay. I drew on the minor ones for some factual corrections and stylistic revisions, but I disregarded the major ones that arise out of our disagreements—perhaps to my and the reader's peril.

1. Mikhail Gorbachev, *Perestroika* (London: Collins, 1987).

2. Michael Ellman and Vladimir Kontorovich, *The Disintegration of the Soviet Economic System* (London: Routledge, 1992).

3. Stanislav Menshikov, *Catastrophe or Catharsis: The Soviet Economy Today* (London: Inter-Verso, 1990); and "Russia: Catastrophe or Catharsis?" (paper presented at the Faculty of Economics of the University of Amsterdam, 26 November 1992).

4. Eric Hobsbawm answers the question of what went wrong by pointing to the inability of Russia and Eastern Europe to deal with the world economic crisis of the 1970s and 1980s. See "What Went Wrong?" *Contention,* no. 1 (Fall 1991). Ernest Gellner, in an interview with *Contention,* claims that nothing was wrong. See "A Year in the Soviet Union," *Contention,* no. 2 (Winter 1992). Daniel Chirot recognizes the continuing tensions between capitalist countries and acknowledges that utopia had not arrived. Yet his answer to what went wrong points to the failure of a utopian ideology. See "After Socialism, What?" *Contention,* no. 1 (Fall 1991). These conclusions are shared by Meghad Desai, who sees that "capitalism in its successful restructuring passed on the costs of restructuring . . . to the East Europeans." Socialism was caught by its inability to produce sufficient surplus to be able to service its debts. The failure was in socialism as an ideology. See "Is Socialism Dead?" *Contention,* no. 2 (Winter 1992).

5. Andre Gunder Frank, "Nothing New in the East: No New World Order," *Social Justice* (San Francisco) 19, no. 1 (Spring 1992): 34–61; and "Economic Ironies in Europe: A World Economic Interpretation of Politics in East-West Europe," *International Social Science Journal,* UNESCO, Paris, no. 131 (February 1992): 41–56; *Revue Internationale des Sciences Sociales,* UNESCO, Paris, no. 132 (May 1992): 279–97; and *Revista Internacional de Ciencias Sociales,* UNESCO, Paris, no. 132 (May 1992): 267–84.

6. Jeno Szucs, "The Three Historical Regions of Europe," *Acta Historica Academiae Scientiarum Hungaricae* 29, nos. 2–4 (1983): 133.

7. Ibid.

8. Ibid.

9. Ibid., 172–73.

10. Lenin himself defined the essence of "socialism" as "electricity plus soviets," but he immediately abolished the latter.

11. In 1944, U.S. president Roosevelt dumped his vice president, Henry Wallace, and named Harry Truman as his new running mate. In April 1945, upon Roosevelt's death, Truman became president. Four months later, he dropped the atomic bomb on Hiroshima, thereby deliberately starting the Cold War. In 1947, he announced the Truman Doctrine of containment and launched the Marshall Plan. Henry Wallace, fearing another depression, testified before Congress that the Marshall Plan would lead to a third world war. He proposed an alternative plan to be administered by the United Nations, which would "preclude that American capitalists misuse Marshall's proposals as a pretext to dominate world markets." How different would world history have been if Roosevelt had retained Wallace as vice president? Perhaps this is an instance of domestic politics changing the course of history in the world.

12. Hannes Hofbauer and Andrea Komlosy, "Eastern Europe: From 'Second World' to First or Third World?" (paper presented at the Faculty of Economics of the University of Amsterdam, 1992).

13. Ibid.

14. *Time* (24 February 1992) reports an un-"Holy Alliance" between President Reagan and Pope John Paul II to "save" Poland.

15. Andre Gunder Frank, "World Economic Crisis Once Again," *Economic and Political Weekly* (Bombay) (29 February 1992): 437–38; *Economic Review* (Colombo) 18, nos. 1–2 (April–May 1992): 2–4.

16. See Andre Gunder Frank, *El Desafío de la Crisis* (Madrid: Editorial IEPALA; Caracas: Editorial Nueva Sociedad, 1988).

17. Andre Gunder Frank, "American Roulette in the Globonomic Casino: Retrospect and Prospect on the World Economic Crisis Today," in Paul Zarembka, ed., *Research in Political Economy* (Greenwich, Conn.: JAI Press, 1988), 3–43.

18. Andre Gunder Frank, "East European Revolution of 1989: Lessons for Democratic Social Movements (and Socialists?)," *Economic and Political Weekly* (Bombay) 25, no. 4 (3 February 1990): 251–58; also published as "Revolution in Eastern Europe: Lessons for Democratic Social Movements (and Socialists?)," *Third World Quarterly* (London) 12, no. 2 (April 1990): 36–52, and in William K. Tabb, ed., *The Future of Socialism: Perspectives from the Left* (New York: Monthly Review Press, 1990), 87–105; reprinted

in Charles K. Wilber and Kenneth P. Jameson, eds., *The Political Economy of Development and Underdevelopment,* 5th ed. (New York: McGraw-Hill, 1992), 209–25. See also "No End of History! History to No End?" *Economic and Political Weekly* (Bombay) (1990); also published in *Social Justice* (San Francisco) 17, no. 4 (December 1990), and in H. I. Schiller and K. Nordenstreng, eds., *National Sovereignty and International Communication,* 2d ed. (New Jersey: Ablex Publishers, 1993); "Economic Ironies in World Politics," *Economic and Political Weekly* (Bombay), 26, no. 30 (27 July 1991): 93–102; *Economic Review* (Colombo), (September-October 1991): 1–3, 41–49; "Nothing New in the East: No New World Order," 34–61; and "Economic Ironies in Europe: A World Economic Interpretation of Politics in East-West Europe."

19. The author's personal communication with Andras Brody in Budapest, based on his input-output calculations.

20. See note 18.

21. Fred Halliday, "A Singular Collapse: The Soviet Union, Market Pressures and Inter-State Competition," *Contention,* no. 2 (Winter 1992): 121.

22. Ibid., 133.

23. Ibid., 137.

24. Ibid., 126.

25. Ibid., 127.

26. Ibid., 128.

27. Ellman and Kontorovich, *The Disintegration of the Soviet Economic System.*

28. Only recently new revelations have been published of massive CIA intervention, including in the form of monetary aid.

29. Andre Gunder Frank, "Third World War in the Gulf: A New World Order Political Economy," *Notebooks for Study and Research* (Amsterdam and Paris), no. 14 (June 1991): 5–34; *Endpapers* 22 (Nottingham) (Summer 1991): 62–110; *Economic Review* (Colombo) 17, nos. 4–5 (July-August 1991): 17–31, 54–60, and 68–73; "Third World War: A Political Economy of the Gulf War and the New World Order," *Third World Quarterly* 13, no. 2 (Spring 1992): 267–82; also in H. Mowlana, G. Gerbner, and H. Schiller, eds., *Triumph of the Image: The Media's War in the Persian Gulf: A Global Perspective* (Boulder: Westview Press, 1992), 3–21.

30. Desai, "Is Socialism Dead?"

31. The American economy is threatened with a similar bankruptcy as this inflow of capital disappears in the recession or depression of the 1990s. In Japan, the recession has obliged its financial institutions to repatriate more capital to Japan than the country exports. In Germany, the recession was postponed by reunification because of the conquest of the East German market. However, this boost was dissipated through a German version of "Reagan-

omic" deficit financing in the East. This policy obliged the rate of interest to rise to permit the German state to attract private capital. High German interest rates have also pulled up European interest rates, exerting a further recessionary influence. Thus, the new recession has generated Japanese and German competition for capital, drawing it away from the United States. Yet, this capital has become a habit forming fix; withdrawal symptoms may spell political disaster for the United States and the world.

32. Halliday, "A Singular Collapse," 137–38.

33. Ibid., 135.

34. Gorbachev, *Perestroika*, 17–19.

35. *International Herald Tribune*, 15 October 1991.

36. Ellman and Kantorovich, *The Disintegration of the Soviet Economic System;* and Menshikov, *Catastrophe or Catharsis: The Soviet Economy Today.*

37. Ellman and Kontorovich, *The Disintegration of the Soviet System*, 31.

38. One of Gorbachev's domestic mistakes was his anti-vodka campaign. Through his control measures he lost public political goodwill needed for his reforms, and the state lost precious revenue from the sale and tax on alcohol. Further, black-market prices went up, contributing to inflation, and moonshine alcohol replaced the legal version, generating corruption. Its basic ingredient, sugar, disappeared from store shelves, creating a sugar shortage. More sugar had to be imported from Cuba. The road to hell is paved with good intentions.

39. Politics and ideology were not in command in Washington either. Instead, world economic pressures mediated by political "policy" made the government's share of GNP rise, as in Britain, leading to third worldization. Increased defense spending not only bankrupted the Soviet Union, it nearly bankrupted the United States as well. So far the U.S. economy has been bailed out by Western European and Japanese "voluntary" capital contributions, as well as by Third World and Eastern European debt service. None of these remedies was available to the Soviet Union.

40. See Andre Gunder Frank, *Reflections on the Economic Crisis* (New York: Monthly Review Press; London: Hutchinson, 1981); "Is the Reagan Recovery Real or the Calm Before the Storm?" *Economic and Political Weekly* (Bombay) 21, nos. 21–22 (24–31 May 1986); *El Desafío de la Crisis;* and "American Roulette in the Globonomic Casino," 3–43.

41. I have argued this in Andre Gunder Frank, *The European Challenge* (Nottingham, England: Spokesman Press, 1983; Westbury, Conn.: Lawrence Hill Publishers, 1984).

42. Illustrierte Zeitung Kultur Sonderausgabe 1944. *Der Europaische Mensch.* Leipzig. Reproduced in part with an editorial introduction by Peter Lock in "Rüstungswerbung," *Militarpolitik und Dokumentation* Heft 41–42, Frankfurt am Main: Haag und Herchen.

43. Kurt Waldheim, *Die Reichsidee bei Konstatin Frantz*. Inaugural Dissertation zur Erlangung des Doktorgrades der Rechts-und Staatswissenschaftlichen Fakultät der Universität Wien, 1944. Translated by Andre Gunder Frank.

44. Michael Schneider, *Die abgetriebene Revolution. Von der Staatsfirma in die DM-Kolonie* (Berlin: Elefanten Press, 1990).

45. Ibid.

46. See note 19.

47. Socialist economies were being and would increasingly be integrated into the world capitalist economy. East-South relations were not more favorable to the South than West-South relations. Circumstances offered the economic basis and the desirability for the unification and "Europeanization" of Europe, perhaps including the Soviet Union notwithstanding any ideological differences. "Really existing socialism" in the East was unable to offer a viable alternative. See Andre Gunder Frank, "Long Live Transideological Enterprise! The Socialist Economies in the Capitalist International Division of Labor," *Review* 1, no. 1 (Summer 1977); *Crisis: In the World Economy* (New York: Holmes and Meier; London: Heinemann, 1980); and *Reflections on the Economic Crisis*. See also *The European Challenge: From Transatlantic Alliance to Pan-European Entente for Peace and Jobs* (Nottingham: Spokesman Press, 1983); and "The Socialist Countries in the World Economy: The East-South Dimension," in Lelio Basso Foundation, ed., *Theory and Practice of Liberation at the End of the 20th Century* (Brussels: Bruylant, 1988).

Chapter 3 ━━━━━━━━━━━━━━━━━━━━━━━━

The "End of History" and the Third World

The Relevance of Ideology

Georgy I. Mirsky

Both Francis Fukuyama, with his brilliant and controversial article "The End of History,"[1] and former president George Bush, with his idea of a "new world order,"[2] profess the possibility of a new system of international relations based on common sense, rationality, and the universal recognition of a model that is a final achievement of history: the liberal democratic society exemplified by the United States. Fukuyama does not conceal his belief that Western capitalism is a crowning achievement of human genius, and Bush wished the whole world to recognize it as such and be guided by this simple and seemingly uncontroversial concept.

The question, however, remains: has the Western model been universally accepted? If it were, there would be no need for ideology—only the recognition of a blissful crowning success in historical development, making superfluous any struggle for the hearts and minds of the world's citizens.[3]

One of the great failures of Marxism has been its inability to grasp the importance of nationalism and religion. Focused exclusively on class struggle, Marxists have overlooked the most powerful driving forces and motivational factors of human behavior, both individually and collectively. Now it is precisely these forces, directing and channeling the natural human search for group identity, that are vigorously asserting themselves.[4] What they inspire is an ideology more powerful than Marxism-Leninism. We are just as far from the end of history as from a new world order.

Fukuyama is right when he claims that economic and political liberalism has finally triumphed, and that this means victory for the Western idea. There are no more viable alternatives to liberalism after the collapse of the two major challenges to it: fascism and communism. It is precisely in the countries pursuing the Western model that the class problem—the old, devilish issue of exploitation, the cornerstone Marxist concept—is closer to solution than anywhere else. Of course, there are and always will be the rich and the poor in these countries, and this disparity will always provoke indignation and protest, but experience has shown, at a horrible cost, the inevitable outcome of all attempts to create a "just" society without both rich and poor.

Critics of capitalism who claim that the social ills inherent in this system can be eliminated, given a more just and egalitarian form of social organization, have yet to prove their case. Those who would point to the socialist states where there allegedly was no unemployment have only to look at the results of communist rule and the numbers of jobless that are likely to appear as the whole inhuman structure unravels, leaving behind it an absolutely distorted, hopeless economy as well as a demoralized and helpless people.

Still, attempts to create a just society are bound to continue, and very likely in violent, revolutionary forms. A quarter of a century ago, in the midst of the Chinese "cultural revolution," a respectable Western journal expressed the belief that after that horrible experience, probably nobody in the world would resort to revolution again. The age of revolutions had to be over, if people had any sanity left. Apparently, quite a few people in the world failed to read that article.

The age of revolution is not over and it is hard to see when it will be, if at all. Again and again, in more countries, embittered and impatient young people will mobilize masses against injustice, humiliation, despotism, corruption, and ethnic discrimination. It is inevitable, since the majority of the world's population does not inhabit the countries of the Western model. For these people history is not ending, having accomplished its role and achieved its goals; it is just beginning. What they experience is poverty, misery, and frustration. They know nothing about economic liberalism or political pluralism. They feel anger, and their anger is not going to evaporate. On the contrary, with the old world order based on the U.S.-Soviet confrontation collapsing, and the contours of a new one still quite vague, and with weapons in abundance virtually worldwide, more violence has to be expected.

Jim Hoagland described in the *Washington Post* on 13 February 1992 how he felt while watching on television scenes of young boys in Mogadishu riding in jeeps and shooting at the buildings: "They were smashing offices and apartments into shards and rubble, laughing gleefully as they did. They were systematically destroying the Western-style city." Hoagland considers these scenes as "emblematic of a physical rejection of the West and its artifacts that is taking place in many places in Africa and the Third World. . . . The youths left behind in a decaying former colonial capital . . . were striking out at a Western world that they cannot see, or reach, for leaving them to their fate."

The Third World against the West? Or, to express the same thing in different geographic terms, a North-South confrontation?

The old order was based on the global confrontation of the two systems and the Cold War. Bad as it was, we have to admit that it was an order of sorts. Now, with the total and surprisingly rapid collapse of communism, any semblance of order in the world has all but disappeared. To quote the British weekly the *Economist:*

> The end of the cold war does not mean a world at peace. On the contrary, it may for a time mean an even more violent world, as the sort of local tough who used to shelter under a superpower's protection now finds that he can survive only by the power of his own fist. These people will be the main danger to international order in the next few years. . . . None of them will wield anything like the power the Soviet Union once wielded, but some of them will be militarily strong enough to ignore mere diplomatic disapproval or an economic slap on the wrist.[5]

It is clear that this kind of danger to world stability will have its source primarily in the vast areas of the Third World, especially the Middle East and North Africa. Primarily, but not exclusively, for we must now add to these territories huge areas of the former Soviet Union, especially those inhabited by the peoples of Central Asia and the Caucasus. Moreover, even the eastern and southeastern parts of Europe can be regarded as regions of potentially dangerous conflict. Suffice it to look at Yugoslavia, or rather, what remains of this seemingly civilized and relatively developed European state, which is suddenly displaying the kind of terrible political conflict usually associated with the new nations of the Third World.

Central Asia and Emerging Nationalism

One of the most interesting examples of the continuous relevance of ethno-nationalism and religious revival in the contemporary world is the southern tier of the former Soviet Union.[6] In the prerevolutionary Russian empire, administrative division was not based on ethnic criteria, and boundaries between provinces were not drawn according to the natural historic frontiers that divided national and religious communities. Most of those communities identified themselves in terms of religion rather than ethnicity. From the point of view of the Russian imperial authorities, "religion formed the basis for distinguishing natives from infidels . . . the term 'nationality' in its modern meaning did not exist in this period."[7]

Then, the Soviet regime, having discarded and virtually abolished religion as an identity factor, made the national-linguistic issue a cornerstone of its neoimperial policy. Completely new administrative and territorial units were created based on nationality. The highest form of unit was the union republic, and this status was given only to those republics which had common borders with foreign states and thus were capable, at least theoretically, of seceding from the union. Then came autonomous republics (mostly inside the Russian federation), autonomous oblasts, okrugs, and so on. Thus, at the very beginning, two fateful steps were taken that have led inexorably to the present turmoil. First, the concept of nationality was rigidly linked to the issue of territory, and ethnonational identification became possible largely in terms of territorial units. Second, the principle of de facto inequality became part of the foundation of the new state structure.

The long-term implications of this new organization have been enormous. Since ethnic communities in most cases did not have clearly defined borders, one inevitable result of the rigid administrative delineation has been the creation of ethnonational minorities inside practically all of the republics and other territorial units. Moreover, in some cases, areas inhabited largely by distinct ethnic groups were arbitrarily incorporated into republics with totally different populations. The best-known cases of this kind are Nagorno-Karabakh, which with its Armenian majority was transferred to Azerbaijan, and the two famous and splendid Tadjik cities, Samarkand and Bukhara, which were included in Uzbekistan. But there are many other points of conflict as well. For instance, some districts inhabited mostly by Tartars became part of the neighboring Bashkir autonomous republic; conversely, thousands of Bashkirs live in the Tartar autonomous republic. This situation was probably inevitable anyway, and it is to be found in many other parts of the world: dozens of ethnic communities in Africa live on both sides of state frontiers. But in the Soviet Union, where all but purely economic ties between neighboring nations and ethnic groups were eliminated (including religion), excessive emphasis on the only remaining basis of group identification, the ethnolinguistic factor, could not but breed nationalistic conflicts. And when the iron grip of the omnipotent center weakened, territorial and border issues inevitably became paramount. This process has led to numerous conflicts which, given the lack of political culture and of traditions of civilized behavior, have taken peculiarly ugly forms, such as the mutual massacre of Kirgiz and Uzbeks at Osh in 1990. Unfortunately, more bloodshed in the future is by no means impossible. These patterns of conflict are strikingly reminiscent of some of the worst disputes in Asia and Africa, which is one reason for calling some of the less-developed parts of the former Soviet Union the "new third world."

Another implication of the new Soviet organization was the pattern of assertion, in some cases quite artificially, of a new nationhood closely linked to statehood. The official basis of the blossoming Soviet culture was national in form and socialist in content. It was necessary to ensure the existence of the whole package of vestiges of the modern state in each ethnoterritorial unit. These included an academy of sciences, an opera, a ballet, laureates of Lenin and Stalin prizes to a complete outfit of state institutions and party nomenklatura's jobs and offices. The "root" nationality had to be paramount and leading in every way. In some cases nationhood simply had to be built up, even on rather dubious historical grounds. One striking example is Uzbekistan.

There was never such a thing as an Uzbek nation. The territory of today's Uzbekistan was inhabited by an ethnic community largely descended from Mongol conquerors who had come to these lands in the Middle Ages and had mixed with the sedentary population of the valleys. "Uzbek" was the name of one of those newcomer Mongolian steppe tribes. The community in question had a distinct religious identity—Sunni Islam—but spoke several related languages and was mostly known in the region by the name of "Sart."

Under Soviet power, an unprecedented process of nation building got under way. One of the most widespread local idioms was chosen as the official national language. The term *Sart* was banned altogether. The concept of an Uzbek nation, speaking the Uzbek language and possessing a distinct and ancient culture, had to be asserted to justify the existence of a large union republic. Needless to say, once this process acquired a momentum of its own, national self-assertion and self-identification in terms of the Uzbek nation became inevitable, and the seeds of a potentially powerful Uzbek nationalism were sown.

In all the new republics, strong vested interests were emerging in the existing order: a new party and state nomenklatura, an ever-growing bureaucracy, entrepreneurs prospering within the framework of an unnatural and ugly economic system (dealers in the so-called shadow economy), and so on. What they all wanted was preservation of the status quo, although with a greater degree of autonomy. Socialism and Soviet rule (*Sovetskaya vlast*) for those people were the rules of the game, the factors guaranteeing their existence, but they were not issues of deep conviction and loyalty or ideological and political devotion. And now all of them, practically without exception, have become totally shameless turncoats and adopted nationalist colors. They welcome independence as long as it ensures continuation of their privileges. National sovereignty for them is by no means tantamount to social transformation. A very important phenomenon has been the emergence of the new local intelligentsia. Growing very fast as economic and social development got under way, it became the standard-bearer of this new nationalism.

This writer once had an opportunity to visit some of Baku's oil refineries and observe its truly multinational workforce—Azeris, Russians, Armenians, and so on. Relations between workers of diverse ethnic groups seemed quite satisfactory, problems emerging only at the end of a year when results of the "socialist competition" had to be announced. Inevitably, those awarded first place and premiums were Azeris, as representatives of the "root nationality." Otherwise, no causes for discontent on ethnic grounds appeared to exist. But it was quite different in the party and state apparatuses, as well as among the so-called creative intelligentsia. It is precisely there that the new nationalism blossomed.

The fact is that in most of the republics (with the notable exception of the Ukraine, Georgia, Armenia, and the Baltic states), native professional and entrepreneurial classes were negligible or practically nonexistent prior to the revolution. For instance, in what became Azerbaijan, both business and liberal professions were virtually monopolized by Armenians, Jews, and Russians. The indigenous educated strata consisted mainly of *ulama,* or men of religion, exactly as it was in many Arab countries where professionals and businessmen were largely of alien origin. With the consolidation of the Soviet republics, which brought undisputed educational advances, thousands of people of the "root nationality" emerged with new skills and modern training, as did an inevitable competition for social and economic advantage. In this struggle, the mere fact of belonging to the "root nationality" meant an important initial advantage. The nationality issue became a major vehicle of career building which, of course, was bound to intensify and strengthen nationalist feelings. Later, in the era of perestroika and the collapse of the old order, these feelings, which had been cultivated by the Soviet leadership for decades, were expressed and demonstrated in new and sinister ways.

Roughly speaking, two kinds of local native nationalism were developing in the republics and the rest of the ethnic and territorial units. The first might be called "career nationalism," since it had very little to do with genuine concern for national culture and language, or with a real desire for independence. The clearest manifestation of this kind of nationalism was in the Ukraine. One could spend hours in any government or party office in Kiev and never hear a word spoken in Ukrainian. Even on the streets, one could be certain that if Ukrainian was heard, it would in all probability be an old peasant speaking. And yet it was precisely in Kiev that a bitter covert struggle was in progress for years. It can be described as nothing more than simple infighting over jobs and privileges between the local apparatchiks and the "Moskali," or newcomers from Moscow. As a matter of fact, the local nomenklatura in the republics basically never differed from the "Big Brother" in Moscow, except for ethnic background and knowledge (often quite poor) of the local language. But in order to assert themselves, they had to play the ethnic card, albeit cautiously so as not to be accused of "bourgeois nationalism."

The second brand of nationalism was represented primarily by intellectuals, schoolteachers, university professors, and students. Here, genuine ethnic ideals were being cultivated, national identities openly professed, original languages lovingly restored, and traditional cultural values reborn. It is this second variety of nationalism that was to gain acceptance by the broad masses and acquire an irresistible force, once the grip of the center had weakened and independence suddenly appeared to be within reach.

The strength of this popular feeling, so strikingly manifested in the course of national referenda on the independence issue, especially in the Ukraine, surprised many foreign observers. To understand it, one has to bear in mind that one of the most powerful processes set in motion by perestroika and the subsequent collapse of Soviet power can be characterized as a search for identity.

The point is that every human being needs to be associated with some group, the ethnonational community being only one of many possible collectivities. But in the rapidly disintegrating Soviet Union, positive self-identification was possible primarily in terms of this kind of community. Nationalism could not be but local, limited to a narrow ethnic group, since a broader and all-embracing national entity (like the American nation, for instance) did not exist.

In fact, there has never been such a thing as a Soviet nation. One could ask a Soviet person who he or she was, and the answer would be: "I am a Soviet citizen" or "I am Russian" (or Armenian, Tartar, Jewish, Tadjik, and so on). This means that self-identification was possible either in a purely formal or in a strictly ethnic sense. Of course, there was another category—*sovetskiye ludi* (Soviet people). Millions of people belonging to the species aptly called "homo soveticus" were conscious of the invisible border which separated them from the rest of humanity, but this was no substitute for nationhood. The new politico-ideological community the Soviet leadership was so proud of can be said to have been related to citizenship and enforced loyalty to the paramount state but not to ethnicity.

Now, with the grandiose building collapsing, there is virtually nothing a former Soviet person can identify with except for the ethnic community. State, party, class, profession, and standard of living have deteriorated to such a degree, and everything looks so ugly and worthless, that the only firm ground, the only basis for self-assertion and perhaps even pride, can be found in the sense of belonging to a stable, long-established community, traditionally respected and even sacred. Race and religion, rather than unstable, fragile, and ever-changing values (as many now perceive the political and economic dimensions of life) still provide stability and command respect.

Identity groups usually consolidate precisely on the basis of ethnic or religious-community sentiments, or both. For example, people of

Turkish origin (or at least bearing Turkish names) in Bulgaria represent a distinct identity group, as do Adjarians in Georgia (pure Georgians by blood but Muslim by religion).

The exact ethnic origins of these and similar groups may be subject to debate and controversy, but it really does not matter much. What matters is the sense of belonging to a well-defined community with its own history and traditions and, very importantly, with a record of grievances and suffering or a sense of being an underprivileged minority. To some extent, every such community is a kind of permanently besieged fortress surrounded by enemies. Naturally, this sort of feeling breeds communal solidarity as well as hatred for enemies (who, quite understandably, are most likely to be neighbors). And nationalism, of course, thrives on hatred. The relative weakness of Russian nationalism (as yet), compared to nationalism in the other republics, can be largely explained by the simple fact that, whereas other nations see the Russians as the root cause of their misfortunes, the Russians themselves cannot find anybody to blame for their predicament but themselves.

But this is not the case with the other ethnic communities. Russian domination is for them the source of all evil, and they are vigorously asserting their independence. The horrible vacuum created in the souls of Soviet people during seven decades of communist rule can only be filled, if at all, by nationalism and in some areas, mainly the Muslim regions, by religion. It is against this background that the upsurge of what is called Islamic nationalism in the southern tier of the former Soviet Union should be analyzed.

Adding this new area of potential turmoil to the "traditional" tumultuous countries of the Third World, we can envisage the existence of vast zones of potential unrest representing danger to global security. And the louder the talk about America remaining the only superpower, the stronger the resistance to the growth of U.S. power will be. The world will not recognize the United States as a global policeman.

The Relevance of Ideology

Forces of nationalism, or ethno-communalism, unlike those of Marxism-Leninism, have by no means been spent. There are grounds to think that they will dominate the twenty-first century. It may so happen that history, nearing its "happy end" in the realm of social relations, at least in the countries of the Western model, will bump against upheavals in ethnic and national relationships. Both anti-Western, anti-imperialist xenophobia, as a consequence of Western-led interventions in regional conflicts, and the settling of domestic scores within the Third World are genuine threats to global security.

Now, where does ideology come into all this? Can nationalism be called ideology?

It depends on the definition of the term. We can argue ad infinitum about what exactly ideology is. To the question "Is nationalism ideology?" both positive and negative answers can be argued and sustained. Even if we refute nationalism's claim to be an ideology, what will change? It will certainly not weaken the powerful appeal of nationalism, its tremendous capacity to mobilize and inspire immense masses of people.

Fukuyama maintains that only systemic nationalisms (as, for instance, highly organized national socialism) can be formally considered ideologies on the same level as liberalism or communism. He is probably right, and he draws from this assertion the logical conclusion that nonsystemic nationalisms, lacking elaborate projects of socioeconomic organization, can therefore be compatible with other doctrines and ideologies possessing such projects, including (and this is the quintessence of his thesis) liberalism.[8]

Certainly there is nothing in nationalism that makes it incapable, as a matter of principle, of adapting to liberal and democratic ideas, at least in theory. But the practice looks quite different. It is not accidental that most of the Asian and African societies are far from the Western liberal model. This has nothing to do with xenophobia or hatred of all things Western. The fact is that the very structure of these traditional societies is not well suited to adopt Western liberal values and make them their own.

This does not mean at all that those societies are incompatible with democracy. We see many democratic regimes in the Third World, beginning, of course, with India. All talk about Easterners being organically averse to democracy is pure nonsense. Moreover, the winds of democracy have lately started to blow with astonishing strength in Asia and Africa, to say nothing of Latin America. We have seen the downfall of many a dictatorial regime in the last few years, and the trend is obvious, especially since one of the main sources of antidemocratic, totalitarian tendencies—Marxism-Leninism—has been totally and probably irrevocably discredited.

The problem is different. The democratic organization of government and political pluralism are not tantamount to liberalism, to this "Western idea" which has triumphed in the industrially advanced societies. Usually these terms and concepts are more or less fused together. For example, freedom is often regarded as almost the same thing as democracy. Yet, there is practically absolute freedom of expression and political activity in post-communist Russia, but it can hardly be called a democratic country. Just the same, a democratic organization of a state structure is not equivalent to economic and political liberalism. For the latter to prevail, to penetrate into each cell of the society, to become a natural way of life and mode of thinking, a different set of social traditions and values is needed from that which is dominant now in Asia and Africa. Society there is based on group and clan solidarity, on ethnic and religious communities, on traditionally powerful networks of client-patron relationships. It is not better or worse than the Western society, it is just different. It is another type of civilization.

The political culture based on this civilization is by no means inherently antidemocratic or predisposed toward despotism. However, it is less individualistic than the Western one, more collectivist, with strong paternalistic and authoritarian traits. Any society based on solidarity and collectivism needs ideology much more than one focused on individual achievement. One may call it nonsystemic ideology or even deny its right to be called an ideology at all, but this does not matter.

What matters is that in order to keep solidarity alive, to mobilize masses, especially at times when the nation struggles for political emancipation or against economic backwardness, it is necessary to inspire the population with a set of strong politico-ideological beliefs. Since the socialist ideas of the class struggle of workers and peasants against capitalists and landlords have proven to be irrelevant, and regimes founded on such ideas have collapsed, the nationalistic and religious dimension of political life has emerged paramount. Frustration and anger are channeled not against "domestic exploiters" but against "the others," who may happen to be neighbors or imperialist Westerners. The result may not be ideology in the strictest sense, certainly not a systemic ideology, but it is a powerful psychological motivation on a mass level nevertheless.

Here we can observe a vast difference between this model and the Western one. Highly developed capitalism, that is, a society based on economic liberalism and political democracy, does not, strictly speaking, need ideology as such, at least not at the grassroots level. This system was certainly founded on the ideology of liberalism and continues to be guided by its spirit. The society is organized and ruled on liberal principles. Ideas of freedom and democracy can even now mobilize millions to defend them in the hour of crisis. But, generally speaking, on the level of mass consciousness, ideology does not have a role to play—simply for the reason that the society is organized on quite rational and natural principles. For the majority of the population, basic frameworks for ensuring well-being and political freedom appear to be quite adequate. Demands and grievances, some extremely grave and acute, can be channeled through movements of group protest and mobilization, but there is no need for a mass mobilization on a national scale, except to repulse danger from the outside in wartime. Thus, there exists a state ideology, liberalism, but mass ideology is quite superfluous.

All the movements and leaders who tried to change human nature felt the need for a strong ideology to assist them in creating an unnatural, inhuman society. National socialism, with its ideas of racism, the total negation of freedom, and the subordination of the individual to the state and the führer, was unnatural and inhuman. So was socialist society. Che Guevara once said that the fundamental aim of Marxism was to eliminate individual interest as a psychological motivation. Maybe this was a noble aim, but it was also a monstrous social project; the results of this disastrous experiment are there for the whole world to see.

Now, we may hope that the days of misguided "systemic ideologies" are past. In the Western model we have liberal democracy as the ultimate form of societal organization. (It is far from perfect, but then, can human nature as such be perfect?) Only a minority of the globe's population embraces this model, and so it is far from universal. As to the majority, nationalism (both of a narrow or local and *tiers mondiste* type) seems to be the name of the game.

So much for the relevance of ideology. Whether or not nationalism can be called ideology from the scientific point of view, it increasingly continues to be highly relevant in the Third World, and not only there.

Nationalism per se is not an evil; nor was the idea of social equality and the ending of exploitation. But we know where it has led. Nationalism is a natural phenomenon, and as such it is neither good nor bad;

but it is potentially very dangerous. Perhaps in the coming century it will be the main danger for humanity.

What about religion in this context? Of course, nobody would call religion an ideology, but in terms of inspiring and mobilizing masses, who can argue that there is anything like religious fervor to arouse people? Probably even nationalist appeal is not as powerful. It was argued above that the failure to understand religion and its role in the life of people and society as a whole was a central shortcoming of Marxism. Now religious feeling is vigorously reasserting itself. Marxists, in the company of others who once believed that religion is inherently antimodern, antiprogressive, and thus certain to be superseded by "modern," "scientific" social ideas, now grimly regard the revival of religious sentiment in many parts of the world, especially in the Muslim East. Some are even afraid that the war between communism and the West will be replaced by a war between Islam and the West.

The revival of Islam, or the emergence of what is sometimes incorrectly called "political Islam,"[9] has indeed been powerful. An American expert on the subject, Judith Miller, has put it this way: "More than a decade after the first modern Islamic revolution in Iran, militant Islam is once again on the move, transforming everyday life in the Middle East and challenging the legitimacy of almost every state."[10] This phenomenon can best be explained by the dismal failure of practically all the alternative, secular models of government. To quote a leading expert on Islam, John Esposito, "Modern secular nationalism was found wanting. Neither liberal nationalism, nor Arab nationalism/socialism had fulfilled its promises."[11] Resurgent Islam is replacing moribund secular ideologies, such as Nasserism and Baathism,[12] but also, and most importantly, secular Arab nationalism and Western-style democracy. This virtually leaves Islam as a "true and only path." Frustration over the patent inability of secular (left- or right-wing) regimes to end poverty, injustice, and corruption; deep-seated, decades-long feelings related to the Palestinian issue and to the failure of Arab leaders to overcome their squabbles and intrigues and unite against Israel and America—all have helped channel Arab frustration into what has come to be called Islamism. The leader of the Islamicists in the Sudan, Hasan Turabi, maintains that nationalism used to be an alternative to Islam, but "today if you want to assert indigenous values, originality and independence against the West, Islam has become the national doctrine."[13]

Thus, secular nationalism in a major part of the world appears to be giving way to what might be called religious-inspired or Islamic nationalism. There is little doubt that what we see there is not so much a sudden upsurge of religious feeling, as such, or a rediscovery of Islamic values—these were never eclipsed—but a deepening conviction that it is only by embracing "Islamic ways" that both national and social goals can be achieved. This widespread conviction can rightly be called a kind of ideology and, contrary to Fukuyama's thesis, it is quite relevant and gaining ground in a large part of the globe.

As to the threat of Islam, while there can be no doubt that Islamic fundamentalism in its extremist, militant form can become a real menace to world security (including that of the Western world), Islam as such, as Shimon Shamir rightly put it, "is not the enemy. Muslims are not barbarian hordes, baying at the gates. A Western *Kulturkampf* against Islam would be misguided and self-defeating."[14]

Notes

1. Francis Fukuyama, "The End of History," *National Interest* (Summer 1989).

2. For George Bush's statements formulating his concept of a "new world order," see "Toward a New World Order," *U.S. Department of State Dispatch* 1, no. 3 (17 September 1990); and "Address to the 46th Session of the United Nations General Assembly in New York City," *Weekly Compilations of Presidential Documents* 27, no. 39 (30 September 1991): 1324–27.

3. For a critique of "the end of history" argument, see Samuel Huntington, "No Exit: The Errors of Endism," *National Interest* (Fall 1989).

4. For an excellent work on the dynamics of ethnicity and nationalism, see Nathan Glazer and Daniel Moynihan, eds., *Ethnicity: Theory and Practice* (Cambridge, Mass.: Harvard University Press, 1975).

5. *Economist,* 8–14 February 1992, 13.

6. On the subject of Soviet nationalities, see Alexander J. Motyl, *Thinking Theoretically about Soviet Nationalities: History and Comparison in the Study of the USSR* (New York: Columbia University Press, 1992).

7. Michael Mandelbaum, ed., *The Rise of Nations in the Soviet Union: American Foreign Policy and the Disintegration of the USSR* (New York: Council on Foreign Relations Press, 1991), 19.

8. Francis Fukuyama, *The End of History and the Last Man* (New York: Free Press, 1992).

9. Islam, unlike Christianity and other religions, never was, and could not

be, "apolitical" or "depoliticized," because it never recognized the concept of separation between church and state, between spiritual and worldly power. It is a comprehensive set of guidelines for a way of life, including the organization of society and form of rule.

10. Judith Miller, "The Islamic Wave," *New York Times Magazine,* 31 May 1992, 23.

11. John L. Esposito, *The Islamic Threat* (New York and Oxford: Oxford University Press, 1992), 15.

12. The Baath party, powerful as ever, remains the ruling force in both Syria and Iraq, but it has become nothing more than a vehicle of state, clan, and personal power, and has lost its former mystique and appeal in the wider Arab world.

13. Miller, "The Islamic Wave," 25.

14. Shimon Shamir, "Islam and Democracy" (paper presented at the SOREF Symposium, "Islam and the U.S.: Challenges for the Nineties," the Washington Institute for Near East Policy, 27 April 1992), 41.

Chapter 4 ━━━━━━━━━━━━━━━━━━━━━━━━━━━━━━━━━

The Collapse of the USSR and the Future of the Socialist Model

Elizabeth Kridl Valkenier

The double demise of the USSR, first as a superpower and then as a unified socialist state, has resulted in fundamental changes in the country's domestic and foreign policies. As far as the successor Commonwealth of Independent States' economic relations with the Third World are concerned, however, the break with communism does not signify a comparable break with the past or the arrival of a qualitatively new era. The momentous changes of December 1991 will not bring a complete reversal of economic policies toward the Third World. They will merely make it possible to pursue with greater consequence, and more rigorously, market-oriented policies which had been recognized as necessary during Brezhnev's last years and were beginning to be implemented during Gorbachev's tenure.

Similarly, the vast majority of Third World leaders will not feel orphaned, as did Castro, who stated at the Congress of the Cuban Communist Party in October 1991: "To speak of the collapse of the Soviet Union is to speak of the sun not rising." Very few of them will denounce the new state for having abandoned its international socialist mission. The plain truth is that the Soviet Union ceased to exist on the cognitive map of the Third World as an alternative model and as a source of effective support quite a few years earlier, before it broke up as a state and as a system.

Had the changes of late 1991 taken place in late 1964 with the dismissal of Khrushchev, the opposite would have been the case. During the first decade of active Soviet entry into the Third World, the USSR did indeed pursue socialist economic policies and offered what

88

seemed like a successful development model. Moreover, during those years Soviet words and actions were consistent and presented a solid antithesis to Western modes of operation. Hence they were recognized by the Third World for what they were intended to be.

However, in the intervening twenty-seven years the socialist aspects of Soviet policies had been jettisoned for the sake of cold economic efficiency—more visibly in practice, much less so in rhetoric. Indeed by the time Gorbachev's perestroika arrived on the scene, very little of the original Soviet revolutionary and humanitarian premise was left. Likewise, the once-high regard the Third World had for Soviet views and actions had evaporated. Instead of respect, there was contempt and even recrimination. Instead of being praised or regarded as a welcome alternative to the West, as it was in the 1960s, the USSR had come to be seen by the South in the 1980s as part of the Northern cabal. Soviet-American cooperation during the 1991 Gulf War was not an eye-opener; rather, it was generally recognized as yet another demonstration of the existing situation.

Soviet economic relations with the developing countries comprised three elements: (1) ideological explanations of the workings of the world economy, justified by reference to Marxism-Leninism; (2) a theoretical development model based largely on Soviet experience; and (3) practical economic policies dictated by the Soviet Union's international posture and domestic needs.

Each of the three components underwent substantial modification (but at different rates and not always concurrently), as Soviet policies passed through three stages which roughly coincided with the chairmanships of Nikita Khrushchev, Leonid Brezhnev, and Mikhail Gorbachev. From beginning to end, Soviet theories and behavior were called socialist, yet the first phase was aggressively ideological; the second increasingly pragmatic; and the third, frankly revisionist.

The current, post-1991 phase openly rejects socialism. But coming as it does after the revisions initiated by the Gorbachev regime, it does not, to repeat, constitute as radical a break with the past as does the open renunciation of communism as a state system.

Phase 1, Khrushchev: Aggressive Challenge

During Khrushchev's ascendancy, Soviet economic thinking and behavior in the Third World were an integral part of the systemic challenge to the West. In the decade 1953–64, Moscow looked at the world through the prism of combative Marxist-Leninist categories that explained the workings of international economics in terms of imperialism and saw the world economy divided into two competing markets operating on diametrically opposed principles. As a socialist power, the USSR advocated and supported the economic liberation of the postcolonial states via a noncapitalist path of development. It also launched a socialist aid and trade program meant to expose the inequities of Western practice and to detach the developing countries from Western markets.[1]

This was a decade when there obtained a harmonious complementarity between Soviet theory and Soviet practice, as well as coincidence between Soviet goals and aspirations and those of the developing states. It could plausibly be argued that Soviet security and strategic needs were the basic driving force for Soviet entry into the Third World and not any profound feelings of solidarity or common destiny. Yet the fact remains that Soviet economic theories and behavior did much to facilitate that entry. Soviet anti-imperialist rhetoric did play a role in helping the Third World formulate a collective consciousness. Moreover, the USSR's own development did inspire confidence in the command-economy development model, based on state planning, nationalization, and import-substitution industrialization. Similarly, Soviet aid-trade policies—such as the construction of steel mills, renunciation of ownership equity, extension of low interest rates—not only promoted confidence in the viability of that model but also challenged the West to alter some of its policies.[2]

Phase 2, Brezhnev: Pragmatic Readjustment

Though highly effective abroad, Khrushchev's socialist policies proved to be much too expensive for the USSR to sustain. Hence, during the next twenty years Moscow tried to devise more pragmatic ways of operating in the developing countries, ways that would bring it tangible economic benefits, not just diplomatic or political gains vis-à-vis the West.

Show projects, characteristic of the first period—such as the Aswan dam in Egypt or the Bhilai steel mill in India—were replaced by less ambitious schemes that assured the USSR of repayment. The exploitation of natural resources—bauxite in Guinea or oil in Iraq—on a payback basis were the hallmarks of the new turn. And long-term trade agreements provided a planned underpinning to the whole scheme.

The development model also changed. Instead of promoting its own autarkic industrialization drive of the 1930s as the best method to assure both economic liberation and rapid growth, Moscow now offered another experience. This was the New Economic Policy (NEP) of the early 1920s, when the USSR had had a mixed economy, with a private sector in agriculture and the services, and it had welcomed foreign investment in industrial development.[3]

But it should be noted that despite the notable transmutation in Soviet practice, the ideological goals of the USSR (or its socialist posture) remained unchanged. The rhetoric about the nature of imperialism and capitalism, about the unique, exemplary nature of Soviet aid and trade policies, persisted. The theory of the two competing world economies still held, as did the ultimate goal of detaching the developing countries from Western markets. The USSR strove for an exclusive relationship, claiming to be forming a socialist international division of labor.

During the first decade of Brezhnev's rule, the pragmatic policies did bring the desired results. Soviet trade with the developing countries increased and aid-trade policies became to some extent coordinated with Soviet plans and needs. Moreover, the Soviet model seemed to take firmer hold as the earlier fashion among Third World radicals to opt for Arab or African socialism gave way to the adoption of a "socialist orientation." Similarly, Soviet promotion of a radical East-West confrontation seemed to bear fruit with the formation of OPEC and the oil price hike of 1973.

The upward curve of success came to a halt in the mid-1970s, and the second decade was marked by a series of reversals in the economic sphere. The new wave of decolonization in Africa following the collapse of the Portuguese empire produced destitute radical states which expected generous support from the USSR in the name of international solidarity, just at that juncture when the Soviet Union began to experience falling rates of growth. At the same time, those radical allies, like Iraq, that became rich on petrodollars preferred to spend their new wealth in the West rather than integrate further with the Socialist bloc. Finally, the revitalized Third World began to press demands not only on the West but on the East as well. At the fourth United Nations Conference on Trade and Development (UNCTAD) in 1976, the Third

World countries known as the Group of 77 for the first time refused to acknowledge a special East-South relationship and demanded equal assistance (in terms of the percentage of donor GNP) from East and West alike.

These reversals led to reassessments behind the scenes and readjustment in policies, plus some modifications in official ideology regarding international economics. In the latter 1970s Moscow abandoned the doctrine of two competing world markets, accepting instead the existence of a single world economy over and above its socialist and capitalist components.[4] Similarly, the Soviets gave up the fiction of creating a socialist international division of labor and came to terms with the obvious fact that most of the developing countries were being increasingly integrated with the capitalist markets.[5]

These novel views legitimated the expansion of East-West trade and heralded changes in East-South relations. Among the more telling post-1975 alterations in aid-trade policies was Moscow's abandonment of strict bilateralism and its growing interest in concluding trilateral agreements with the West for economic cooperation in the South.[6] At the same time as it sought more renumerative ventures in the South, Moscow became less generous with its assistance, especially to clients with a socialist orientation. In 1982, feeling the "burdens of empire," the USSR refused Mozambique and Laos full membership in the Council of Mutual Economic Assistance (COMECON).

Not surprisingly, by the early 1980s, Soviet experts began to write with appreciation and some understanding about the contribution that capitalist methods could make to development. At first, only petty traders and small-scale operations were tolerated as consistent with the socialist orientation. But eventually even large-scale enterprises were acceptable. Capitalist institutions and management and work habits, it was acknowledged, were necessary prerequisites for development and growth. Likewise, the former endorsement or advocacy of the nationalization of private foreign and domestic assets disappeared.[7]

Phase 3, Gorbachev: Revisionism

Steps to bring theory and practice together, to bridge the gaps and inconsistencies, were taken only by Gorbachev. True, his efforts to remove ideology as a factor in Soviet international behavior were made in order to update, modernize, and improve the socialist image and performance. Nevertheless, the net result was to render Soviet thinking and behavior hardly distinguishable from that of the Western mainstream. During the years 1985–91, a separate Soviet stand on economic issues concerning the Third World effectively ended.

Gorbachev's open and unqualified recognition of world-wide interdependence was the cornerstone of the new economic thinking. In his address to the twenty-seventh congress of the Communist Party of the Soviet Union in February 1986, the First Secretary spelled out what he called an "integral world." This vision represented a substantial refinement and advance over the concept of a single world market that had entered official parlance in the late 1970s and was narrowly applied in order to legitimate East-West trade. The integral-world theory covered the South as well, for it recognized that objective economic forces were compelling all countries, through ever greater interaction and interpenetration, to be part of the global marketplace.

Reformulating the doctrine on how imperialism operates was a logical corollary of the integral-world theory. Gorbachev did not coin any pungent phrases to encapsulate this revision. All that he did was to stop telling the developing countries to actively oppose imperialist exploitation. For example, at the 1986 Party Congress he did not urge the Third World to resort to unilateral steps to deal with the debt issue. Instead, he urged "cooperation on an equitable basis," arguing that a "fair" negotiated solution was possible. This more moderate, official stance on North-South relations allowed specialists in the USSR to fill in the interstices and to argue outright that the traditional image of neocolonialism, with its "primitive" account of center-periphery interactions, had failed to materialize. Given the fact of interdependence, an equitable partnership between the West and the developing countries was possible.[8]

The acknowledgment of an interdependent world also permitted a nonideological discussion of what caused backwardness and what contributed to development. The onus for backwardness was no longer placed on the operations of imperialism, and Soviet specialized studies shifted attention to such topics as overpopulation, persistence of traditional methods in agriculture, and even to the resistance of Eastern cultures to modernization.

Under Gorbachev, the NEP model of development was relegated to the background. Increasingly and without any reservations, the experience of the newly industrialized countries (NICs) began to be studied and extolled as worthy of emulation. Blind faith in the efficacy of various noncapitalist measures had been jettisoned to such an extent that numerous authors wrote openly of how socialist-oriented countries had experienced stagnation, political conflict, and bureaucratic strangulation, while those which had opted for capitalism had attained high economic growth.[9]

Changes in the rationale for and implementation of aid-trade policies reflected the liberation of economic theory from ideology. Glasnost took hold in the field, and the burdens of empire began to be openly aired in the media as well as in the new representative institutions. (In the later Brezhnev period, when criticism of Soviet aid-trade policies first surfaced in open writings, it was buried in specialized journals or monographs. Even there, a certain decorum was observed: for example, references to the exemplary, "selfless" Soviet policies abounded.) Scholars, journalists, and deputies objected to the size of Soviet foreign-aid appropriations (calculated, it was said, to amount to about a hundred rubles per person—slightly less than an average monthly wage in those days), the extent of unpaid debt (revealed to be 35 billion rubles), the unbalanced nature of Soviet trade, and the wasteful, inefficient use of Soviet assistance by its recipients.[10]

Concurrently a new external strategy began to be implemented. Several institutional and administrative reforms were passed to make this possible. Notably, the Ministry of Foreign Trade and the State Committee on Foreign Economic Relations (GKES, the aid agency) were merged into a single Ministry for Foreign Economic Relations, bringing the various scattered operations under one roof for the purpose of creating an integrated efficient and profitable system. New legislation liquidated the state monopoly on foreign trade that had previously hampered contacts with abroad. It permitted individual economic entities—state-sponsored, cooperative, and private—to deal directly with foreign partners.

As for Soviet economic assistance, here clear notice was served to the Third World that the former preferential arrangements would be curtailed. In July 1990, President Gorbachev promulgated a decree specifying that the USSR "shall build projects abroad on the principle of mutual benefit and mutual interest, being guided in this by international norms and practices . . . and proceed from the fact that economic assistance shall be rendered taking account of our country's real possibilities."[11]

Aid appropriations were cut across the board by 30 percent and 40 percent in the budget appropriations for 1990 and 1991 respectively, as well as reduced in unspecified amounts for individual partners. At the same time, the USSR began to lecture recipients on the efficient use of aid and to prod its political allies—Vietnam, Cuba, Nicaragua—on how to introduce elements of Soviet perestroika to improve their economic performance. These strictures produced more resentment than results—as was the case in Castro's Cuba, which banned a Soviet magazine altogether for printing an article critical of the way the Cuban economy was managed.[12]

In foreign trade an unabashed pursuit of profit became evident. There was a purposeful outreach to the NICs—some of them underestimated in the past (Brazil), others ostracized (South Korea, South Africa). Moscow actively set out to court these countries with trade fairs, information seminars for businessmen, and official visits. When Prime Minister Ryzhkov visited the ASEAN states in early 1990, he worked as hard on linking the potential promised by Soviet economic reforms with the rapid development of Southeast Asia as on warming up diplomatic relations. A retinue of economic advisers, officials, and representatives of the revived Soviet Chamber of Commerce accompanied Eduard Shevardnadze on his diplomatic trips to Latin America (1988) and Africa (1990). As for the traditional trade partners, here Moscow made strenuous efforts to replace preferential (that is, client) relationships with genuine partnerships that benefited both sides. The Soviets began to insist forcefully that the unbalanced trade accounts be settled either through increased purchases of Soviet goods or by outright repayment of debt.

There was heightened interest in dealing with the private sector, in seeking investment that entailed Soviet equity, in setting up consulting firms, and in selling (not giving away) Soviet know-how. In all respects the former "socialist" scruples or political aversions to capitalist profit-making had been scrapped in favor of economic expediency. The agreement in 1990 with the South Africa–based De Beers company to market Soviet diamonds is as good an example as any of the concerns and principles that guided the Soviets during the Gorbachev era.

For the purposes of this essay, it matters little whether the new strategy bore any tangible economic results. What is important is the Third World's response to the new Soviet theory of an integrated world, which effectively renounced the former socialist vision of international economics and legitimated various Soviet policy initiatives that were hardly distinguishable from those of the West.

Responses varied from acceptance to denunciations, depending on how advantageous the pre- and post-1985 arrangements happened to have been to the persons, institutions, and states that were affected. Socialist-oriented states and radical groups openly charged that the USSR had "betrayed" its international mission and sold out to the capitalist powers. Among the Group of 77 and other organizations representing the collective economic interests of the Third World, there was virtual consensus that in accepting and preaching global interdependence the Soviets had found a convenient cover for abandoning their independent stance in order to secure inclusion. The switch also legitimated withdrawing support for various international measures to equalize or improve the distribution of gains, as well as pressing for the USSR's admission into the existing international economic institutions and legal arrangements.[13]

The overall effect of the post-1985 switch was to exacerbate the deterioration of the Soviet image. True, Soviet popularity had been declining since the late 1970s. However, given the persistence of the Cold War, the myth of Soviet identification with and support for various Third World grievances retained some operational validity for both sides. It was only during Gorbachev's tenure that persistent criticism and recriminations came out into the open, so much so that the USSR felt obliged to face the criticisms and answer such allegations as those made by Akbar Zaidi, a professor at the University of Karachi: "The present Soviet thinking about the development towards socialism especially in the Third World, is a complete about turn from what was being said in the past concerning Imperialism and revolution. . . . Thus, the economic considerations of the Soviet economy outweigh by far, the ideological dimension of the theory and practice of developed socialism."[14]

Possible Future Scenarios: The CIS and/or the Russian Federated Republic

What about the guiding principles and future policies of the CIS? Since the collapse of the USSR, the new noncommunist policies in this and other areas have not been shaped into clearcut new programs. Moreover, it is not certain in what form the CIS will survive, nor is the political future of Yeltsin and his Russian Federated Republic assured. Nevertheless, on the basis of the glasnost-era debates concerning Soviet foreign and domestic economic policies that took place before December 1991, it is possible to identify three basic interest groupings among the Russian public and officials in the central bureaucracy: the neoliberals, the moderates, and the conservatives. Each group advocated its own set of policies toward the developing countries before the USSR was dissolved. Their alternative proposals are still likely to be pursued in the foreseeable future.

The neoliberals represent the radical wing of the spectrum. They could just as well be called Westernizers. Their campaign to improve Soviet economic operations in the Third World was closely associated with their goals to introduce a market economy and representative democracy at home, to enter world trade and financial institutions, and to bring about a close rapprochement with the West in foreign policy. Their membership included some prominent political and economic figures: people like Anatoli Sobchak, the mayor of St. Petersburg; Nikolai Shmelov, the outspoken economist and deputy to the Congress of People's Deputies; and Ivan D. Ivanov and Ernst Obminsky (respectively Deputy Chairman of the Commission for Foreign Economic Relations and Deputy Foreign Minister in charge of foreign economic relations during the Gorbachev years), who as early as the late 1970s began advocating opening up the Soviet economy and participating in multilateral trade. In the late 1980s they were seconded by younger economists and political scientists from various research institutes of the Academy of Sciences, especially the Institute of World Economy and International Relations (IMEMO) and the Institute of the USA and Canada, who were in the process of establishing their reputations and gave frequent interviews to the media.

These pro-Western reformers proposed practical measures to place the largest possible number of Soviet economic deals with the Third World on a "commercial basis." They advocated cutting off the ungrateful and costly radical clients and courting instead the NICs, ending barter deals and debt-swapping to redeem the sizable sums that were due to Moscow, and initiating tripartite East-West-South ventures to revitalize trade.[15] They favored steps that would help integrate the USSR into international financial and other institutions.

The radical reformers have occupied a prominent place among President Yeltsin's advisers. Their ideas have informed and driven many of Yeltsin's actions. For example, in the fall of 1991 he said several times that Soviet aid to the Third World should be discontinued. And for the immediate future it seems likely that this orientation will predominate in the policies of the Russian Republic and the Commonwealth because of the ready solutions it offers at a time of severe economic crisis.

In the Russian Federated Republic the market approach already is a matter not only of economic expediency but also of the new national political and cultural identity. It is the aspiration of the republic's Foreign Minister, Andrei Kozyrev, that Russia "take up a fitting place . . . among the most developed and civilized countries of the Northern Hemisphere."[16] As a "civilized" country, Russia, in late December 1991, served notice on Fidel Castro that all subsidies would be terminated and all Soviet troops withdrawn from Cuba. (Here it should be noted that Gorbachev was in the process of reducing Soviet subsidies gradually and by way of negotiation, not by unilateral pronouncement.) But at the same time Moscow also received a mission from the Cuban émigrés in Miami, the Cuban-American National Foundation headed by Jorge Mas Canosa, with which it discussed credit lines to be extended to Russia and alternate sources of goods traditionally imported from Cuba—sugar, nickel, and citrus fruits.[17] Although no final agreement was signed, this particular move on the part of the impatient radicals is the clearest expression of their aspirations: to get rid of costly allies of the socialist period; to take up profitable deals with new partners; and to gain U.S. approval.

The second group, the moderates, is much less enamored of the West and its reform models. It seems that their outlook and program will have a good chance of prevailing in the near future, once emotions calm down and realities begin to be faced. Unlike the radical liberals, the moderates are mainly concerned with workable reforms in aid and trade, tending on the whole not to address, directly or indirectly, either foreign or domestic politics. Their mode of operation is also different. Their views were seen more often in the specialized journals than on the pages of the daily press. And they tried to persuade the elected deputies and the bureaucracy more through interoffice memoranda than through public pressure.

Economists associated with various academic institutions are prominent in this group, and their views seem to be shared by quite a few economists working in the ministries. As a group, they tend to belong to the older generation, to have had considerable experience as scholars and administrators before 1985, and to have served in World War II.

The group's caution is due to several reasons. They are not as optimistic as the radicals about the returns from speedy and unguarded entry into a world market dominated by the capitalist industrial powers, from joining various international institutions and undertaking the incumbent obligations, and from cutting the traditional ties to the Third World. Their lack of enthusiasm for the West is due in part to economic calculations, in part to a certain mistrust of unfamiliar Western ways, which they consider alien.

In my talks with several economists of this persuasion in Moscow, I heard it repeated in passing that the radicals were copying Western methods too uncritically and without any regard to post-Soviet realities. To the moderates, Soviet economic relations with the Third World had a logic created by the centralized state controls, the nonconvertible ruble, and the noncompetitive nature of Soviet exports. Of course, they want to do away with the wasteful and misdirected policies of the past, but they also want to avoid too precipitous a change in patterns and methods. They are fully aware of the persisting weaknesses in the economy, the long tortuous course that reforms will take, and that in the meantime the country could not simply, through sheer force of will, get rid of the traditional partners in the Third World and replace them with the NICs and the West.[18]

In this light even Soviet-Cuban trade is not seen as a drain, but a reasonable enough arrangement. After all, the USSR obtained one-third of its sugar needs from the island, 40 percent of its citrus fruit consumption, one-sixth of its requirements in nickel and cobalt—all of it in rubles. Buying these goods elsewhere would cost $2 billion annually.[19]

The cautious pragmatists argued that widening trade with the developing countries could and should be a priority.[20] Their recommendations centered more on sprucing up bilateral relations than on venturing into the unfamiliar territory of multilateralization. They do not reject multilateralization, but think it wiser to improve existing networks so as to be able to enter the wider field of activity from a stronger position. Good chances for progress are seen in Africa, for example, through concentration on joint agricultural production or mining that will be run according to the efficiency and profit-minded directives of the presidential decree of July 1990. They believe that given the new, practical principles for guiding economic activities in the Third World, the fact that 30 percent of Soviet projects in Africa turned out to be unprofitable is no deterrent.[21]

Finally, there are the conservatives, who on strategic grounds did not discount the Third World as an unwelcome burden. They saw it as a safeguard or as a bargaining chip against the United States. This outlook could easily come to guide Russia's policies in the event of a military or authoritarian takeover. Such a turn could occur in a more distant future should persisting crises lead to unmanageable chaos. At the start of Yeltsin's tenure, the conservative view had a powerful spokesman in Aleksandr Rutskoi, Russia's vice-president. He enjoyed the support of army officers and managers of the military industries, who were also upset by Russia's loss of superpower status and opposed to the rampant infatuation with the West (dubbed "Atlanticism").

Unlike the reformers and the moderates, the conservatives were concerned not with the cost or effectiveness of economic relations with the developing countries, but with the Soviet Union's power position. Within the grouping there were tough hardliners and moderate conservatives.

Until his deposition, Egor Ligachev was the forceful spokesman for the tough line, for those who did not intend to abandon the radical allies under any circumstances. Ligachev justified that position by arguments drawn from the traditional political lexicon that identified Soviet national interests with class interests and international solidarity. After Ligachev's demotion, that vocabulary became discredited. But during the Persian Gulf crisis the old line resurfaced in a somewhat different guise. This time, the tough conservatives spoke up more candidly: in the name of national interests instead of class interests or international obligations. In the words of Dimitri Yazov, defense minister at the time: "We do not have the right to be weakened, despite the positive process of . . . strengthening confidence between different states. In the world there not only remain but also appear now 'hot spots,' which under certain conditions can grow into global conflict. Such a 'spot' appears now in the Near East. And Grenada and Panama are not yet forgotten."[22]

Moderate conservatives are prominent among the older diplomatic corps and academic specialists. Unlike the tough-minded hardliners, they concede that both the economic and military components of Soviet cooperation with the Third World are in need of restructuring—the former because it had not been subjected to rigorous cost scrutiny, the latter because it had grown to "unjustifiable" proportions. However, these more pragmatic conservatives do not condone the harsh criticism voiced by the radical reformers or countenance the policy changes they advocate. They consider the radical criticism as much too one-sided, and their policies as risky unilateral concessions that would leave their country unnecessarily exposed to American pressures.

The moderate conservatives want to ensure that overhauling Soviet policies will be part of a reciprocal process—a process from which the developing states are not excluded and in which the United States also participates, so that a new mode of conduct obligatory on all would emerge. In all this, they are concerned about the loss of credibility by "betraying" the former Soviet partners and the damaging effects of making unilateral concessions.[23]

Possible Future Scenarios: The Muslim Republics

The three paradigms sketched above pertain only to a CIS in which the Russian Republic maintains a leading role, or to some future formation in which the Russian Republic will either stand alone or again have a leading position. Should the CIS break up, then the Muslim republics will face the need and opportunity to deal even more extensively with their immediate neighbors (Turkey, Iran, and China) and with more distant, interested lands (Egypt, Saudi Arabia, and South Korea). Here two models of domestic development and foreign economic relations are possible—the secular and the non-secular, the former being more receptive and the latter less open to interaction with the wider world and its market economy.

At present, the secular scenario is being implemented in varying degrees by leaders of the Central Asian republics, and it is likely to prevail in the near future. The reasons are fairly obvious. The leaders of these republics respect Islam, but their policies are secular and their motivations are purely pragmatic. They will accept money, expertise, and assistance from any source to alleviate immediate needs and to help promote development, and the most attractive deals come from the West. In differing measures, the elites take keen interest in the experience of modernization in Turkey as coinciding with and being applicable to their plans and interests. Furthermore, Turkey offers a gateway to the West with its advanced technology and powerful financial institutions.

At present and in the near future, the non-secular model—an Iranian-type radicalization of domestic economic and foreign policies—is not a likely alternative in the Muslim republics of the CIS. However, one cannot claim with absolute certainty that this scenario is wholly out of the question for a more distant future, given the weak transitional regimes that preside over the introduction of market-oriented institutions. Should economic and political crises deepen, radical fundamentalist sentiments could readily stir some politicians and take hold of the minds of the population. Islamic identity could then become a powerful force in shaping the economic and political life of these states.

For the present and as far as the future of the CIS is concerned, it is significant to note that any type of close economic or other association of the Central Asian republics with their neighbors to the south is generally viewed with apprehension in Moscow. Andrei Kozyrev (in his February 10, 1992, interview with the Portuguese newspaper *Publiku*) has stated that something should be done to counteract that rapprochement: "Today it is necessary to talk about how to include these governments in a civilized, democratic space." The Russian neoliberals take note of the split between the Christian and the Muslim republics of the former Soviet Union and propose to deal with it, in part, by emphasizing the Euro-Asiatic character of the CIS. The conservatives talk tough about preserving Russian hegemony in what used to be Soviet economic space.

The steps taken to attract the Central Asian republics' economies to the Organization of Economic Cooperation, composed of Turkey, Iran, and Pakistan and known as the "Islamic Common Market," are viewed with suspicion in Moscow. It is argued that such plans are aimed at prying these republics away from the CIS (or from their former Slavic partners) and forming political and economic groups that would substantially change the geopolitical situation in the region.[24]

The apprehension expressed in Moscow points up the mutually exclusive paradigms that could come to prevail in different parts of the former Soviet Union. The Russian neoliberal and the Central Asian nonsecular models present radical departures from the Soviet past, and each is based on extensive copying of foreign economic and cultural experiences that are perceived as successful. These foreign models have nothing in common. Conversely, the moderate Russian and secular

Central Asian scenarios present middle-of-the-road visions that do not spell conflict. They permit modernizing many of the old mechanisms, relations, and ties in a manner that does not further undermine stability in the areas that were formerly the USSR.

Future Scenarios: The Third World

This paper has described at some length the evolution of Soviet theory and practice in order to show the extent to which the active, socialist policies that the USSR pursued in Khrushchev's time, and the image of an alternative world economic order it tried to project have eroded or been changed in subsequent decades. Hence, the fact that the USSR has ceased to exist as a socialist state does not, so far as East-South economic relations and mutual perceptions are concerned, constitute a radical break with the past.

Although Gorbachev's perestroika in this and other fields was carried out in the name of modernizing socialism, this is not the way it was perceived in the South. For the South, the theory of an "integral world" and the policies it entailed did not offer an alternative to or an improvement on the existing international system, but betokened the Soviet Union's drive for inclusion in the operations of a world economy shaped and dominated by the capitalist states. In short, the socialist paradigm, as exemplified by the USSR, ceased to be credible in the eyes of the Third World well before the actual collapse of the Soviet Union as a state and as a system.

Yet, the complete demise of the USSR does not spell an end to Marxism or socialism, or to their attraction or applicability to the Third World with its economic problems, domestic and international. In that sense, history has not come to an end, as some people would argue in the West. Neither can they rest assured that the experience in workable economic development in East and Southeast Asia will provide the only guidance for solutions, and that North-South tensions are moving onto a downward curve.

Marxism with its explanations of the inequitable distribution of wealth on both the international and the domestic scales will continue to provide analytical tools that have logical validity and offer emotional solace. As such, it will guide and inspire both marginal geographic regions (Africa) and radical groupings (in Latin America) in the developing world which feel ill-served by the prevailing order. However, it is highly unlikely that a single country (China or Cuba) will in the near future have the opportunity and the power that the USSR had over the past thirty-five years to utilize that discontent in order to create a sphere of influence beyond its borders.

Although Marxism will not present a geostrategic threat on the global scale, its principles will continue to affect international economic negotiations. In one form or another, a definite collective Third World consciousness concerning grievances against the North has been a constant in various United Nations negotiations. The sense of exclusion, of being dictated to or taken advantage of by the West, has been in evidence all along. The immediate issues differ, whether they be the price of raw materials, the settlement of debts, or the salvation of tropical rain forests. But each time the suspicion or conviction that the North is imposing its will and interests on the South complicates the negotiations. Given these persisting perceptions, the fact that the USSR no longer provides an alternative model, supports the developing countries' grievances, or follows less exploitative policies makes no contribution to lessening the North-South tensions. On the contrary, Russian policies and needs will tend to exacerbate these tensions and difficulties by adding a new element—that of the East's competition for the resources of the North. As already indicated, it became clear to the developing countries by 1980 that the Soviet Union sided with the North on such issues as the Law of the Sea and the New International Economic Order (NIEO). The collusion between the West and the East was evident to the South, despite the USSR's continued resort to anti-imperialist rhetoric in various international forums.

From the Third World's viewpoint, then, the collapse of the USSR has added another, even more negative element to the international economic situation. The CIS has become an insistent competitor for large-scale assistance from the rich industrial states and international financial institutions. Moscow's needs and demands for billions in Western assistance and loans inevitably reduce the amounts that will be available to the South. The readiness of the West to oblige does not pass unnoticed in the South; nor, for that matter, does the penchant of the current CIS leadership to identify civilization, progress, and reform with the West.

Altogether, then, the break-up of the USSR and its collapse as a socialist power, and the graphic demonstration that command economics produces disaster, do not necessarily spell "better" economic behavior by the South or fewer "unreasonable" demands on the North. In the immediate future, the USSR's collapse and the choice of the CIS to hitch its fortunes to the Western market economies do not remove or alleviate old irritants in North-South economic relations. Not only are traditional tensions reinforced, but new ones are also created.[25]

Notes

1. The 1961 CPSU Program is the succinct theoretical document of that era. It reads like a communist manifesto for the developing countries, outlining their position in the world market and their expected progress by means of noncapitalist methods.

2. For a detailed discussion of Soviet theories and policies during this and the subsequent periods (up to the early 1980s) see Elizabeth Kridl Valkenier, *The Soviet Union and the Third World: An Economic Bind* (New York: Praeger, 1985).

3. For an excellent review of Soviet aid-trade policies, see Marie Lavigne, ed., *East-South Relations in the World Economy* (Boulder and London: Westview Press, 1989). For the changing development model, see Elizabeth Kridl Valkenier, "Development Issues in Recent Soviet Scholarship," *World Politics* 32, no. 4 (July 1980): 485–508.

4. For this moderate definition, see V. V. Rymalov's entry "World Market," in the *Great Soviet Encyclopedia*, vol. 16 (New York: Macmillan, 1977), 676.

5. See the Soviet Bloc statement to the UNCTAD in 1979, "Evaluation of the World Trade and Economic Situation . . . ," UNCTAD, TD/249 (April 19, 1979).

6. See Christopher T. Saunders, ed., *East-West-South: Economic Interaction between Three Worlds* (New York: St. Martin's Press, 1981).

7. Evgenii Primakov, "Strany sotsialistocheskoi orientatsii" (Countries of socialist orientation), *Mirovaya Ekonomika i Mezhdunarodnye Otnosheniya,* no. 7 (July 1981): 16, and the round-table discussion of the future of capitalism in the developing countries, *Mirovaya ekonomika i mezhdunarodnye otnosheniya,* no. 1 (January 1985): 81–94 (henceforth cited as *MEMO*).

8. N. Volkov and V. Popov, "Has an Era of Neo-Colonialism Materialized?" *International Affairs* (Moscow), no. 11 (November 1988): 107–17. See also P. Khvoinik, "Imperialism: termin i soderzhanie" (Imperialism: the term and its content), *MEMO*, no. 1 (January 1990): 5–19.

9. Aleksei Kiva, *Natsional'no-osvoboditel'noe dvizhenie: teoriya i praktika* (The national liberation movement: theory and practice) (Moscow: Nauka, 1989), gives the fullest treatment of this subject.

10. A. Kortunov, "Soviet Aid: Is it Always Put to Wise Use?" *Moscow News,* December 10, 1989, 6.

11. Text of the decree in *Vneshniaya Torgovlia,* no. 8 (August 1990), Supplement.

12. N. Volkov, "Being True to Principles," *Moscow News,* March 9, 1990, 12.

13. Ellen Brun and Jacques Hersh, *Soviet–Third World Relations in a Capitalist World* (New York: St. Martin's Press, 1990), provides a fine analysis of how Soviet–Third World interests regarding international economics had evolved from solidarity to recrimination.

14. Akbar Zaidi, "The Pause in the Revolution . . . ," *International Affairs* (Moscow), no. 1 (January 1990): 16–17.

15. E. Obminsky, *Global'nye interesy i natsional'nyi egoizm* (Global interests and national egoism) (Moscow: Mezdunarodnye Otnosheniya, 1990), 19.

16. "Russian Diplomacy Reborn," *International Affairs* (Moscow), no. 3 (March 1991): 129.

17. *Foreign Broadcast Information Service,* Soviet Union, December 26, 1991, 7 (hereafter cited as *FBIS*).

18. L. Zevin, "Vneshne-ekonomicheskaya strategiya SSSR vo vzaimosviazanom mire" (The foreign economic strategy of the USSR in the interdependent world), *MEMO,* no. 9 (September 1991): 33–43.

19. Sergei Tarasenko, head of the Assessment and Planning Department, Ministry of Foreign Affairs, in *Moscow News,* no. 52 (January 7–14, 1990): 6.

20. See interview with V. N. Burmistrov, Deputy Minister of Foreign Economic Relations, *Vneshniaya Torgovlia,* no. 9 (September 1990): 11–13.

21. Ibid., and Yuri Popov, "Africa and Soviet Perestroika," *International Affairs* (Moscow), no. 3 (March 1991): 47–50.

22. "Vysokaya otvetstvennost' ofitsera" (The lofty responsibility of an officer), *Krasnaya Zvezda,* August 19, 1990, 2.

23. Andrei Urnov, "The Third World and the USSR," *International Affairs* (Moscow), no. 8 (August 1990): 69–73; Sergo Mikoyan, "Whom Do We Help and How?" *Moscow News,* no. 7 (February 1990): 6.

24. A. Shumilin, "Islamic Realignment," *Komsomolskaya Pravda,* January 14, 1992, 2 (translated in *FBIS,* January 24, 1992, 13).

25. See V. Titov, "Africa in the Post-Confrontational World in the Making," *International Affairs* (Moscow), no. 8 (August 1991): 3–7, for the expression of Soviet apprehensions that the African states, which form an influential bloc at the UN and in the nonaligned movement, cling to "doctrinaire" views on North-South relations.

Part 2

The Soviet Experience in the Third World

Chapter 5 ━━━━━━━━━━━━━━━━━━━━━━━━━━━━━━━━━━━

The USSR and the Third World

A Historical Perspective

Yuri Krasin

The October Revolution of 1917 in Russia and the emergence of the USSR in 1922 inspired great hope for the settlement of long-standing conflicts that had assumed especially acute forms early in the twentieth century. Over a hundred nations and nationalities inhabited the territory of the Russian empire. Many of these had ancient historical roots and unique sociocultural identities. A week after the October coup, the Declaration of the Rights of the Peoples of Russia was adopted. It promulgated new principles in relations between nations and nationalities: equality and sovereignty of the peoples; the right of self-determination, even to the point of separation and establishment of independent states; the abolition of national and national-religious privileges and restrictions; and the free development of national minorities and ethnic groups.

The Declaration on the Establishment of the Union of Soviet Socialist Republics, adopted by the Congress of the Soviets of the USSR in December 1922, put relations between nations, based on those democratic principles, in direct opposition to the capitalist world. "There, in the capitalist camp," the Declaration pointed out, "there are national hostilities and inequality, colonial slavery and chauvinism, national oppression and pogroms, imperialist atrocities and wars. Here, in the socialist camp, there are mutual confidence and peace, national freedom and equality, peaceful coexistence and fraternal cooperation of peoples."[1]

Proceeding from those principles, the Soviet federation of republics offered the peoples in colonies and dependent countries a new type of relationship based on equality and support of their aspirations for liberation. It was a gleam of hope in a world of acute international conflicts and colonial oppression. However, seven decades later that hope had turned to disappointment. The Soviet federation model had disintegrated, and relations with Third World countries had acquired a degree of distrust and even alienation. It is still unclear how Russia and other members of the Commonwealth of Independent States (CIS) will approach their relations with developing countries. A profound reappraisal of values is needed to understand current events and dispel ideological myths. Consequently, it is necessary to consider the USSR's historical experience in its relations with the Third World.

The purpose of this chapter is not to describe past events consistently, to map out and substantiate their cyclical characteristics, but to give a philosophical and historical appraisal of what has transpired in the context of a general view of twentieth-century history, especially its wars and revolutions, which have been exceptionally dramatic and, for the peoples of Russia, extremely tragic.

The October Revolution and the Messianic Impulse

Underlying the USSR's theoretical and practical attitude toward the Third World was the notion of revolutionary messianism. This in turn stemmed from the Marxist concept of the historic mission of the proletariat as the liberator of human society from all forms of exploitation. The October Revolution was regarded by V. I. Lenin and other Bolsheviks as the beginning of the worldwide socialist revolution that would begin the transition from a capitalist socioeconomic formation to a communist one. Liberation movements in the colonial world were interpreted as part of the world revolution and seen as natural allies of the socialist state. Complex processes in underdeveloped regions were artificially reduced to a simplistic "class analysis" and interpreted in the light of the universal antagonism between socialism and capitalism.

Some critics ascribe to Lenin the pronouncement that "the route of the world revolution to Berlin and Paris goes through Peking and Calcutta." There is no conclusive evidence he ever said this, but the essence of this thesis was spelled out in one of Lenin's last articles: "In the last analysis, the outcome of the struggle will be determined by the fact that Russia, India, China, etc., account for the overwhelming majority of the population of the globe. And during the past few years it is this majority that has been drawn into the struggle for emancipation with extraordinary rapidity, so that in this respect there cannot be the slightest doubt what the final outcome of the world struggle will be. In this sense, the complete victory of socialism is fully and absolutely assured."[2]

As for domestic processes in the underdeveloped countries, Lenin believed that in the epoch of transition to socialism "with the aid of the proletariat of the advanced countries, backward countries could go over to the Soviet system and, through certain stages of development, to communism, without having to pass through the capitalist stage."[3] Such were the conceptual positions determining the USSR's policy toward colonial and dependent countries.

In the first few years after the October Revolution, it seemed that world revolution would come about very soon. It was at that time that prominent Bolshevik leaders even spoke out in favor of direct intervention in the East to implement the liberation of the oppressed peoples. In August 1919, Leon Trotsky, for instance, proposed to send the Red Army to India through Afghanistan. At the fourth congress of the Comintern, Nikolai Bukharin advocated the right of a proletarian state to "Red intervention": "The Communist Manifesto points out that the proletariat must win the whole world, but it is impossible to do this by moving a finger; bayonets and rifles are needed here. Yes, the proliferation of the Red Army is the proliferation of socialism, proletarian power, and revolution."[4]

Of course, extremist statements by some Bolshevik leaders were counterbalanced by the more sober-minded positions of other authorities, namely, Lenin, who unambiguously spoke against the "export of revolution." He clearly underscored the impossibility of manufacturing revolution from outside and linked the prospect for the advance of backward countries toward socialism with the quest of domestic social forces for transitional stages and forms of development corresponding to those countries' real conditions. Lenin was not alone in acknowledging the importance of the characteristics and national identity of backward countries. G. Chicherin, the Soviet government's first People's Commissar of Foreign Affairs, wrote in his instruction for F. Raskolnikov, the Soviet ambassador in Afghanistan: "We cannot and must not approach Afghanistan, proceeding from the standards of economically developed nations. Naturally, we should not forget for a moment and disregard the tremendous difference between the communist program and the program that is being implemented by the Afghan government."[5] Later, when it was clear that the capitalist system was getting out of its deep crisis and gradually stabilizing, the USSR's messianic concept of the Third World was modified and adjusted to the new circumstances. The changes formed part of the doctrine of peaceful coexistence between the two social systems. The Soviet Union's messianic role was primarily represented by the new society in the revival of Russia's national provinces and by the political and economic support granted to the anti-imperialist struggle of the peoples in backward countries. On these grounds a mass of propaganda material was produced that included books, booklets, photo albums, and films. It displayed the achievements of the Soviet national republics in economics and culture, and in resolving contradictions between nationalities and furthering peoples' friendship. The so-called complete solution of the nationality problem had culminated in the creation of a new historical community, the united Soviet people.

The essence of the messianic approach to the Third World, with all its modifications, remained consistent throughout seventy years: an orientation toward solving the problems of backward countries within the framework of the world confrontation between socialism and capitalism, a belief in the liberating effect of socialism on the Third World, and priority assistance to socialist-oriented countries and movements. This essence was formulated clearly in the thesis of the sixth congress of the Comintern in 1928: "All basic questions of the revolutionary movement in colonies and semi-colonies are directly connected with the great struggle constituting our epoch, between the capitalist and the socialist systems." This view revealed the prospects "for backward colonies' noncapitalist road of development and the possibilities for a bourgeois-democratic revolution to turn into a proletarian socialist revolution in advanced colonies, with the aid of victorious proletarian dictatorships in other countries."[6] Thus, the problems of colonies and dependent nations were viewed in the context of confrontation, and those countries themselves were regarded as a kind of battlefield between the two social systems.

Such views were not groundless. They were based on revolutionary romanticism during the period of the most acute crisis of early monopoly capitalism. Drastic changes in the system of capitalist relations at the beginning of the twentieth century had generated sharp contradictions and conflicts. Both the October Revolution and the consequent upsurge in worldwide revolutionary movements grew out of these changes. It seemed that capitalism would collapse very soon under this pressure. The whole situation was characterized by the ferocity of the struggle, which naturally brought about a confrontational mentality and a confrontational policy. A class-conflict perspective dominated both in ideology and politics.

Later, the capitalist system survived its crisis, demonstrating its ability to make essential modifications. An opportunity to overcome the confrontational stereotypes of political thinking and action had been created. Yet, Soviet policy stuck to the logic of the crisis period of early monopoly capitalism, continuing to embrace obsolete views of the capitalist system's inevitable collapse and the more favorable prospects for Third World development under socialism. This inertia of confrontational thinking and behavior was encouraged by acute conflicts and independence struggles in the Third World, but to a much larger extent, it was determined by dogmatic, class-confrontational thinking under the Stalin regime. Proposed schemes were increasingly divorced from reality. Consequently, it seemed more and more as though a futile attempt was underway to outwit history and force the long and complex course of Third World progress to conform to artificial concepts of noncapitalist development and socialist orientation. Soviet policy did not correspond to real economic and sociopolitical conditions in those countries and reflected only one (by no means major) trend of their development.

The priority of ideology also favored a selective receptivity to information regarding actual developments in Third World countries. Information coming from those countries through various channels was sifted out and adjusted to fit standard ideological clichés. Everything that contradicted dogmatic schemes was disregarded. Researchers specializing in developing countries did not have any objective information and were themselves captives of the class-confrontational way of thinking and Stalinist dogma.

Reality avenges itself on the policy that inadequately perceives it. This is what happened to the USSR's policy toward Third World countries. The results were opposite to the goals set. How was this manifested?

First of all, the excessively ideological policy led to a selective approach to Third World nations. Backing was given to countries whose leaders declared their adherence to socialist goals and employed Marxist-Leninist rhetoric. But the verbal façade often concealed authoritarian regimes whose leaders pursued egoistic goals, corporate or personal.

Second, a militaristic tone prevailed in relations with Third World countries. In assistance and support, emphasis often shifted from the economy and culture to military aid. Suffice it to say that the military component of the total amount of aid to developing countries reached nearly 80 percent. Today it is the portion of aid exerting the hardest pressure on Russia's budget, and it has resulted in chronic indebtedness. The share of the twenty developing countries that have received 97 percent of Soviet arms supplies in the Third World amounts to 96 percent of Third World debt to the Soviet Union.[7]

Third, and most important, the USSR's economic and military aid to Third World countries proved to be extremely counterproductive. A kind of historical irony is reflected here: the goals set yielded the opposite results. Socialist-oriented countries in fact found themselves in an economic stalemate, characterized by inadequate and "immature" material and social prerequisites of further development and transformation. Their economic development was largely retarded and deformed. There were constant vacillations in their policies, recurrent attempts to use capitalist methods, and a tendency to become excessively dependent on the Soviet Union. In the last analysis, the breakup of the totalitarian, state socialist system in Eastern Europe and in the USSR was followed by the collapse of socialist-oriented regimes in the Third World. In general, we can certainly say that historical experience castigated the concept of the Third World's development in the mainstream of the world revolution and revealed its incongruity with the major historical trends in the evolution of backward countries in the twentieth century.

But good history cannot overlook the positive effects of the Soviet Union's involvement with the Third World. One has only to remember what the map of the world looked like in 1917, right after World War I. It pictured a motley assortment of colonial possessions. The peoples of Asia and Africa were directly dependent on the great powers, while in Latin America semicolonial dependence was more typical. Today the picture is completely different. Former colonial provinces have become politically independent states, subjects and not objects of world history, as Lenin predicted. Awareness of humanity's moral and political responsibility for the Third World's development and progress has taken root in international public opinion.

This outcome undoubtedly reflects the influence of the October 1917 revolution: it gave an impetus to the liberation struggle of colonial peoples. It is no wonder that the victory of the October Revolution was followed by a tide of liberation movements that swept over a whole group of colonial and semicolonial countries. China, Korea, India, Turkey, Iran, Indonesia, and Afghanistan were all influenced by the liberation ideas of the October Revolution. They evoked a positive response even in remote Latin American countries. The words of Emiliano Zapata, a general of the Mexican revolution, are quite revealing in this respect: "The cause revolutionary Mexico and newly liberated Russia are fighting for, is the common cause of all mankind, one which all oppressed peoples are deeply interested in."

Its influence on colonial nations continued when the Soviet Union entered the stage of intensive modernization. Very few gave a thought to the tremendous costs of that process. Third World liberation-movement leaders primarily regarded the Soviet experiment as a model for modernization that produced quick results and formed an industrial basis for national liberation and independence. Jawaharlal Nehru, India's prominent political leader, wrote in this regard:

> But, most of all we had the example of the Soviet Union which in two brief decades, full of war and civil strife and in the face of what appeared to be insurmountable difficulties, had made tremendous progress. Some were attracted to communism, others were not, but all were fascinated by the advance of the Soviet Union, in education and culture and medical care and physical fitness and in the solution of the problem of nationalities—by the amazing and prodigious effort to create a new world out of the dregs of the old.[8]

Neither should one forget the influence of Soviet foreign policy on liberation movements in colonial and dependent countries in the 1930s, when the danger of fascism was increasing. It would be proper to remember the support given to China in the struggle against Japanese aggression and to Ethiopia in resisting the Italian invasion, and of course, the massive response in Afro-Asian colonial zones following the defeat of Nazism and Japanese militarism. This triggered off a new wave of national liberation movements, which led to the collapse of colonial empires and to the emergence of new independent states. The Soviet Union's prestige grew as a result of its great contribution to the destruction of world reactionary forces and to the creation of favorable conditions for the victory of national liberation revolutions. Thus, relations between the USSR and the Third World cannot be assessed in a partisan manner.

Its revolutionary messianic ideology unquestionably deformed Soviet policy toward those countries. However, this ideology was organically linked with the revolutionary sentiments of local radical nationalist forces, inspiring them in their struggle for liberation. The Soviet Union's support of this struggle in many ways contributed to the success of national liberation movements and helped colonial peoples win independence.

Yet, an objective assessment of Soviet policy toward the Third World conclusively reveals the utopian revolutionary messianism that predicted the liberation of the world's oppressed peoples and the overthrow of capitalism as a social system. This vision, explicable as an exaggerated reaction to the crisis of early monopoly capitalism, increasingly lost its connection with real life. The theory of noncapitalist development and socialist orientation was incompatible with the socioeconomic realities of the newly free countries. It hampered understanding of their actual problems, to the detriment of the countries themselves as well as Soviet interests.

What were the actual results of their socialist orientation? The first wave of countries opted for this course in the 1960s. Their ruling regimes increasingly showed their populist natures, along with tendencies to borrow Bonapartist traditions and copy despotic oriental stereotypes of political behavior. In the last analysis, they in fact turned into autocratic regimes headed by populist leaders.

The second wave took place in the 1970s. There was an attempt to create Leninist-type vanguard parties, committed to Marxism, that would be the main force of advance toward socialism. But those parties gradually began to merge with the state, dragging their countries into stagnation and leading them into economic and social deadlock. Socialist-oriented nations found themselves in a deep crisis whose resolution required rejecting ideological utopias and leftist-extremist experiments in favor of a search for opportunities for capitalist relations and foreign capital.

In the last few decades, the Soviet Union steadily lost its attraction as an example for the Third World. The initial achievements of the Soviet national republics in economics and culture were replaced by hardships rooted deeply in specific Asian social structures that are difficult to modernize. In totalitarian societies, those structures were not so much changed as reproduced in other forms and then preserved. In the guise of "socialist nations" constituting, according to official ideology, a single historical community (that is, the Soviet people) were sociocultural realities with distinctive features of relations inherent in Eastern societies.

Soviet Central Asia: The Failed Experiment

With the breakup of the Soviet Union, the realities of traditional Central Asian societies manifested themselves with all their contradictions. Everyone could see the features of Eastern civilization that had not changed. The "communal" rather than the "civic" relationship was at the center of social being. The family-kinship group (*avlod, qaum, toifa, heish, gru,* etc.) still remained the microcosm that determined society's economic, legal, cultural, and ideological workings. Individual and personal principles of consciousness had never crystallized out of the communal system.

It is clear that economic modernization could not be organic in such conditions. Rather, it was in some way superimposed on traditional structures, leaving them intact in their essence. This gave rise to a deformed, dualist economy—on the one hand, developed industry, implanted from the outside and subordinated to the center, and on the other hand, mainly monocultural agriculture using predominantly manual labor. Over 50 percent of the factories in the Central Asian republics were under Soviet control, 40 percent were under Union-republican control, and only 7–10 percent were wholly under republican control. The gap between industry and agriculture can be illustrated as follows: Uzbekistan produced 70 percent of the Union's total cotton yield, but the republic's share of the textile industry made up only 4 percent.[9] This dualism also permeated relations between the nationalities. The Russian-speaking population was typically employed in industry and the local population in agriculture. The share of the Russians in industry was three times higher than that of the local nationalities, whereas in agriculture it was extremely small—around 3 percent in Uzbekistan, Tajikistan, and Turkmenistan. The mechanical imposition of new industries on the Central Asian economies did not create a demand for industrial labor among the local population and could not raise the people's standards of industrial culture. For this reason, the shortage of labor in industry coincided with surplus labor resources among the indigenous population.

In addition, there were unresolved ethnic contradictions. The history of the former Soviet Central Asian republics is marked by active ethnic migrations. It is hard to find a more diverse settlement pattern among various nationalities. Over forty ethnic groups live in the Ferghana Valley alone. Ethnic separation hardly decreased throughout the period of the USSR's existence; market-economy mechanisms were unable to dissolve ethnic groups into a single nation. This is one of the reasons for acute conflicts between nationalities and ethnic groups.

The Soviet Collapse, the Third World, and Westernization

The experience of the peoples in backward regions of the USSR—indeed, the whole experience of the Third World—challenges the universality of the Marxist conception of history as a sequence of socioeconomic formations. This approach, on the whole, reflects the development of the European technogenic civilization, but it is clearly inadequate for an analysis of the historical process in the countries of the East. Attempts to squeeze the Third World's complex and contradictory evolution into the scheme of transition from capitalism to socialism are doomed to failure. Other approaches are necessary.

This has become especially clear today, when a radical shift of axes in the world's development is under way. The East-West contradiction, as a contradiction between two social systems, has sunk into oblivion. The North-South contradiction of world development is coming to the fore. Its resolution will determine not only the Third World's destiny, but also the future of humanity.

The technological revolution in no way alleviates this contradiction. The gap between the two regions in production, in per capita consumption, and in living standards is not narrowing but expanding. In 1965 the difference between industrial and low-income countries in GNP per capita averaged $8,500, whereas in 1987 it exceeded $14,000.[10]

It is possible to foresee that the North-South contradiction will predominate in the coming century. The most acute problems of humanity will be centered around it. Under conditions of overall interdependence, destructive tensions in the Third World will not remain localized. They are already reflected in the industrial countries:

1. The population explosion in the Third World is increasing the flow of immigrants into the developed world. This migration cannot be stopped by legal, economic, or military methods. Further, the North-South contradiction is reproduced in more acute forms within the industrial countries, in relations between the local population and immigrants. In the process new forms of alienation and inequality are generated, and chauvinism and right-extremist political tendencies are nurtured.

2. Ecological problems in the Third World, such as the destruction of forests, erosion of soil, and drought, are causing irreversible changes in the Earth's climate and in the global ecological system as a whole, affecting the vital interests of all countries and peoples.

3. Increasing domestic tensions in the developing countries create favorable conditions for terrorism, which—particularly with the threat of nuclear technology escaping strict governmental controls—could lead to much more serious consequences in the future.

4. Normal, stable functioning in our economically interdependent world community is simply unthinkable as long as there are areas of mass discontent concentrated in the Third World.

To date, there has been no convincing program to resolve the North-South global contradiction. This task needs much research, hard questions, and careful reflection. But one thing is clear: the solution of this problem is possible only within the framework of a new thinking that regards the world as a contradictory whole in which all elements of the system depend on one another. This calls for a concerted effort from the entire world community in developing the mechanisms of a nonviolent and consciously conducted world.

Cessation of confrontation between social systems ensures much success along this line. The process of disarmament, which has already begun, will positively influence the developing countries. In the two decades between 1970 and 1989, arms purchases in Third World countries amounted to over $375 billion. If the heavy burden of militarization is relieved, this would help solve their external debt problem. According to UN experts, the developing countries' renunciation of arms imports would reduce their indebtedness by 20 to 30 percent and lead to higher rates of economic growth.[11] The documents of the Stockholm Initiative Conference (April 1991) emphasize that a worldwide reduction of the arms race in the 1990s alone could release some $1.5 to $2 trillion.[12] The disarmament and the development of the Third World are two sides of the same coin.

It is important to realize that cooperation in the world community in response to the challenge of global problems is not a unilateral process of the world's becoming "Westernized." There is an urgent need for new thinking to overcome the one-sided Western view of its principles, as well as for means to implement such new thinking. Despite the wholeness of the world and commonness of humanity's major achievements, the Eastern nations have their own sociocultural realities, values, traditions, and specific ways of thinking. Therefore, the way to our diverse world's unity does not go through the borrowing of "the Western model" by all peoples, nor through the arithmetical addition of the experiences of various countries, but through a complex synthesis of unique cultures and civilizations.

Social thought and practical politics are just beginning to grope for ways and forms of resolving the global contradiction between the North and the South. One thing is clear: a fundamental reorganization of the world order, both economic and political, is unthinkable without the constructive interaction of all countries and peoples. It requires a synthetic generalization of the sum total of the world's historical experience and the whole diversity of cultural and life values.

Russia, the CIS, and the Third World

The role of the Commonwealth of Independent States that emerged in the territory of the former USSR and its relations with the Third World should be assessed in the light of this worldwide perspective. Ideological myths of revolutionary messianism no longer intoxicate the social consciousness of the citizens of the former USSR. Sobriety is accompanied by the increasing aspiration to understand one's place in world development. Perhaps in this difficult quest for transition from the past to the future, the peoples of the former Soviet Union will be able to make their own indispensable contribution to the great synthesis of cultures and civilizations that is becoming an urgent need for humanity's survival and progress. There are solid historical grounds for such a contribution.

The Russian identity as a country and a state is not national. Russia developed from a community of multiple nationalities and ethnic groups inhabiting its territory since time immemorial. The Russian element was a kind of natural historical melting pot of two civilizational cultures—the East and the West. Rudyard Kipling wrote, "East is East, and West is West, and never the twain shall meet." But Russia, situated between the two civilizations, demonstrated in its historical dynamics their unique contradictory interaction. This fact often attracted attention in Russian social thought. Russian philosopher Nikolay Berdyayev explained that the complexity and tragic character of Russia's historical destiny resulted from the collision and struggle between its Eastern and Western elements. "Russia cannot define itself as the East and put itself in opposition to the West, Russia must also become aware of itself as the West and East-West, uniting, not separating both worlds."[13]

Isn't it the East-West contradiction which conceals the mystery of those shocks that Russia has been experiencing in the twentieth century?

It is hardly possible to appraise the prospects for the development of the Commonwealth of Independent States, formed on the USSR's territory, while ignoring the two historical streams—Eastern and Western—which are organically interlaced in the vast space of Russia.

The Commonwealth has emerged from powerful forces created by economic breakdown and disintegration. The unitary state, only formally called federation, has collapsed. Centrifugal tendencies still prevail, for there are factors behind them that promote disintegration. This turmoil is primarily a powerful response (not only of the elite, but also of the masses) to the former totalitarian regime's imperial policy, and to relapses into imperial thinking in the statements and behavior of some Russian political leaders and intellectuals. This response has merged with the increasing national self-consciousness in the republics. Moreover, there are factors connected with the general situation of the breakup and the inertia of disintegration. On this basis, mass consciousness develops the idea that it is easier to get out of the crisis alone, rejecting any possibility of a return to totalitarian centralism. The reassertion of the national identity of peoples with an ancient history and specific culture, which have been long denied freedom of expression, also works in this direction. The behavior of national political elites is an essential disintegrative force. Their private interest consists of securing those "patrimonies" that have formed after the empire's breakup. Egoism and ambition are expressed on different grounds, but their common denominator is the aspiration to preserve those positions which help the elites determine the policy of national states.

The currently dominant centrifugal trends must not prevent us from seeing the opposite, centripetal tendencies. On a broad historical scale, integrative factors are preserved at the level of extremely deep processes. These are not only organic economic ties that have taken decades to form, but also cultural and demographic relations. But the main thing is that the age-old common historical experience has been well pressed into the layers of common psychological and sociocultural stereotypes and world views. These factors are already manifesting themselves, thereby giving impetus to centripetal processes.

We can hardly expect that integrating factors will work in full force in the near future. It would be particularly hasty to overestimate the vitality and possibilities of the current framework of the CIS, a framework that lacks a solid structure, capable of installing the prerequisites for even a loose confederation. But in the long run, the integrative factors will manifest themselves, for Russia's centuries-old history is not only that of an empire. Rather, it embodies, as mentioned above, a complex process of the merger of various national cultures and traditions of peoples throughout the vast space of Russia. Naturally, the revival of union statehood is in no way predetermined, even in the distant future. Integrationist trends will not necessarily prevail over centrifugal forces. The former states of the USSR are experiencing a period of major changes in the whole system of relations between nationalities and socioeconomic ties. During such periods of rapid change, traditional connections—economic, social, and political—are disrupted. There is a wide range of opportunities to develop new relations. The subjective factor plays a decisive part in the choice of opportunities in such times. If the new states fail to produce the forces able to alleviate and later to neutralize the disintegrative factors, an entirely new system of geopolitical ties may arise in the former Union's territory—not without the influence of external regional and global actors (that is, outside the CIS). Those new ties can in the course of time prove to be stronger than Russia's magnetism in relation to the other states of the former Soviet Union and even to its own national-state structures.

Furthermore, if integrationist trends prevail in the long run, there will be a lengthy period of collision of interests and their reconciliation, various disturbances and conflicts, before a sufficiently solid foundation for a new union of states is created.

Russia is at a crossroads with its excruciating task of overcoming the heritage of a totalitarian system. It is faced with the question of whether the disintegration of the Soviet Union will lead to the loss of its unique synthetic identity and its global and regional influence, or if it will retain the role of integrator of the diverse sociocultural experience of the peoples in the European and Asian parts of the former USSR.

The answer to this question will determine whether Russia will regain its greatness as a world force, or if its future will bring decline and degradation. It is not only the destiny of Russia and its neighbors that is at stake, but also the question of whether another barrier dividing the East and the West will be created, or if a bridge, which will help humanity solve the global problem of the Third World, can be built to unite them.

Notes

1. *The First Congress of the Soviets of the USSR* (Moscow, 1923), appendix 1, p. 8.

2. V. I. Lenin, *Collected Works,* vol. 33 (Moscow: Progress Publishers, 1966), 500.

3. Ibid., 244.

4. *IV vesmirny kongress Kommunisticheskogo Internatsionala. Izbrannye doklady, rechi i rezolutsii* (The Fourth World Congress of the Communist International: selected reports, speeches, and resolutions) (Moscow, 1923), 196.

5. *Arkhivy raskryvayut sekrety* (Archives disclose secrets) (Moscow, 1990), 195.

6. *Kommunisticheski Internatsional v dokumentah* (The Communist International in documents) (Moscow, 1933), 837.

7. *Mirovaya Ekonomika i Mezhdunarodniye Otnoshenia,* no. 9 (1991): 40.

8. Jawaharlal Nehru, *The Discovery of India* (Oxford: Oxford University Press, 1988), 372.

9. *Vostok,* no. 5 (1991): 122, 124.

10. *Mirovaya Ekonomika i Mezhdunarodniye Otnoshenia,* no. 9 (1991): 34.

Data from the *Report of Independent Group for Finance Flows in Developing Countries,* chaired by H. Schmidt (Hamburg, 1989), 3.

11. See *Mirovaya Ekonomika i Mezhdunarodniye Otnoshenia,* no. 3 (1991): 139.

12. See *Mirovaya Ekonomika i Mezhdunarodniye Otnoshenia,* no. 9 (1991): 114.

13. N. Berdyayev, *Sub'da Rossii* (The destiny of Russia) (Moscow, 1990), 28.

Chapter 6 ━━━━━━━━━━━━━━━━━━━━━━━━━━━━━

Russia's "New Thinking" and the Third World

Viktor A. Kremenyuk

The introduction of the principles of "new thinking" into Soviet decision making in the years 1985–90 brought visible benefits both to the Soviet Union and to the world at large. While this much is widely recognized and does not demand proof, what is sometimes overlooked is that the new thinking raised several important issues for Soviet foreign policy. Among these were (1) how to avoid major destabilization in the Third World while the Soviet Union was actively seeking accommodation with the West in the area of strategic relations; (2) what new directions should have been introduced into Soviet–Third World relations to coincide with the changes in Soviet relations with the West; and (3) whether changes in both Soviet-Western relations and Soviet–Third World relations would inevitably lead to the growth of nationalism in the international system, thus creating new areas of instability.

These and other related questions have not been resolved, while the situation has become much more complicated with the collapse of the Soviet Union and the emergence of independent states. It is difficult, if not impossible, to speak of a coordinated foreign policy of the Commonwealth of Independent States (CIS) because, to a large extent, Soviet policy has been fragmented into the individual politics of fifteen nations. And while significant shifts are not yet evident in the relations of the former Soviet republics with the West, changes have become significant and far-reaching in their dealings with the Third World. To what extent these can be traced to "new thinking" remains to be seen. However, it is evident that the foreign policies of all the former

Soviet republics have inherited the ideas of "new thinking" while trying at the same time to differentiate their specific interests from those of the Soviet Union.

In order to understand better what impact the "new thinking" had on Soviet and post-Soviet relations with the Third World, it would be appropriate to consider what new aspects it introduced. Compared with traditional Soviet policy, what impact did these innovations have in the Third World, and what aspects of Third World politics have influenced relations within the CIS? It is important to remember that the CIS itself constitutes a whole new "world" of North-South relations; thus, it is understandable that the factor of the Third World plays a crucial role in post-Soviet development.[1]

New Thinking versus Class Struggle: Crisis in Soviet–Third World Relations

For many years the essence of Soviet policy in the Third World consisted of the principle of class struggle against what was depicted as "imperialism," that is, the domination and influence of the developed Western nations over the former colonies.[2] This policy consisted of two main parts: first, the building of alliances with a number of nations considered "socialist" or of "socialist orientation";[3] and, secondly, the courting of a number of nonaligned nations judged to be politically and economically useful to Soviet interests, as long as they kept at some distance from the West.[4] The first group consisted of countries such as Cuba, Vietnam, North Korea, Angola, Afghanistan, Ethiopia, the Congo, and Nicaragua, while the second included India, Indonesia (until the anticommunist coup in 1965), Egypt, Syria, Nigeria, Iraq, and Libya.

Different as they seem, both courses served the same goal: to prevent Western domination in the Third World and to increase Soviet clientele among the newly liberated nations. These were regarded as a "historical reserve" for the expansion of communist ideas and as allies in the worldwide confrontation with the West.[5] This ideological motive was mixed with a significant degree of traditional Russian imperialistic thinking, based on the realities of the geopolitical setting of the southern and eastern periphery of the Russian borders. For many years, official communist propaganda categorically rejected even the hint of some parallel between the Soviet and Russian policies in that area.

However, the objective truth remains that in both policies there were many similarities which may be explained by geographical as well as historical factors.

While acquiring features of a modern European state, the Russian empire was moving south and eastward, filling the vacuum of power which for centuries existed in Central Asia after the collapse of the Timur empire, and which had turned the local states, as well as the states in Transcaucasia, into objects of Turkish-Persian rivalry. The need for stable and manageable borders pushed the Russian empire to interfere vigorously in these areas. Its aim to install order in the vast spaces of Eurasia resulted in the expansion of its territory, until its borders came close to such entities as China and Japan in the Far East, and British India in the South. Basically, the same power considerations pushed Soviet Russia to retain firm control over these spaces, though, of course, its imperial expansion had a significant ideological element.

The Russian expansion produced two important consequences for Soviet policy in the Orient and in the Third World. The first concerned mainly the approach to local authorities and local traditions. The second related to the big-power game in distant areas which intermixed with rivalry and alliances in Europe.

The Russian imperial attitude toward local traditions and local authorities was largely liberal. Russian governors and military commanders lived in separate settlements or military garrisons without building luxurious residences in the living quarters of the ancient cities. Thus, cities such as Tashkent, Alma-Ata (Vernyi), and Bishkek came into existence. Troops were stationed predominantly in the border areas, where they were instrumental in safeguarding the borders of the empire against traditional forays by nomads. Religious and civil matters, where they existed prior to Russian intervention, continued to be administered by local authorities and were not subject to Russian rule. The local elite was welcome to join Russian service through proper education. This approach created more or less stable entities since, without undue interference into local traditions, the empire provided military security, nonviolent resolution of local feuds, and the development of industry and trade.

Soviet rule, while inheriting some of these features, in other respects went too far in reshaping local societies. Religion was banned and the religious were persecuted. Traditions such as polygamy, ritual clothing for women, and religious education were prohibited. Local authorities were dismissed, and the Soviet system was installed instead. Nomads were forcibly settled, hunters were made to become cattle breeders, free trade was banned, and the "noble" trade of the caravans was prohibited. Land reform was imposed, in disregard of Islamic traditions and attitudes toward property. Collective farms were enforced, as were the "liberation" of women, the secularization of life, and industrialization under the central-planning system, and local communist parties were created as subsidiaries of the All-Union Communist party.

This policy unarguably contributed to the modernization of the former Russian colonies. They were turned into industrially developed parts of the general economic system, with a large portion of the younger generation becoming European-educated, ideologically loyal professionals. Special emphasis was placed on local industrial development during and after World War II. During the war, a significant part of the Russian industrial complex was moved to the Asian regions of the country. The production of arms, even of sophisticated aircraft, was started in Tashkent, Alma-Ata, Frunze (Bishkek), and Ashkhabad. Thousands of professionals moved in from Central Russia and the Ukraine. After the war, but in anticipation of a new one, the policy of developing these areas continued and increased in traditional industries such as cotton growing and the production of raw materials. The "virgin lands" campaign in the mid-1950s brought hundreds of thousands of new settlers from Russia and the Ukraine to Kazakhstan and other republics.

Such rapid modernization—carried out without due consideration for human needs and traditions, and without adequate development of other sectors of the economy and society—produced serious pockets of unrest, resistance, and disloyalty. The local elites, while paying tribute to the central authorities, would violate both the committment to ideological purity and economic contribution to the central plan. Fake "millions of tons" of cotton were accompanied by bribes and corruption from Uzbekistan and other republics.

The local elites also supported nationalistic feelings among some parts of the intelligentsia and cultivated the religious leaders. Interest in the Asian republics significantly increased during the years of the Afghanistan war, which was not only unpopular among the local population, but stirred feelings of solidarity among Muslims in neighboring countries. Dozens of young Uzbeks and Tadjiks deserted the Soviet troops in Afghanistan.[6]

With respect to big-power relations, the Russian empire and the Soviet Union followed approximately the same line of conduct, with minor alterations. Thus, both were equally uninterested in interfering in remote areas at the initial stage of their expansion. Russia was too concerned with its positions in Europe (the Baltic states, Poland, and the struggle with Turkey over control of the Black Sea), and the Soviet Union was preoccupied with Germany and Japan, in addition to facing the threat of an anti-Soviet *cordon sanitaire* in Europe. However, as soon as these fears were more or less settled, both joined the other great powers in active politics in the colonial periphery, though their immediate and long-term interests were different.

The Russian empire viewed the colonies mainly from a geostrategic and security perspective. This may explain why the Russians were reluctant to become engaged in areas far from their own territory.[7] Hence, the Russian emperor refused to take the Kingdom of Hawaii under his protection in the early nineteenth century, although such a request was sent to him through the commander of the Russian naval expedition. The main colonial interest of the Russian empire, as it may be assessed now, a century later, was concentrated on its borders with China and Japan, control over what Lord Curzon called the "pivot of the hinterland" (Central Asia), and permanent pressure on the Turkish territories of Asia Minor where the Armenian population lived (Kars and Erzurum).

The Soviet version of colonial expansion—that is, its policy in the Third World—developed in a different manner, though it began in the post–World War II era as a typical Russian endeavor (claims to Turkey, Soviet troops in northern Iran), as well as through Comintern-type activities (assistance to Communist parties in China and North Korea). Soviet premier Nikita Khrushchev began a worldwide policy of support for newly liberated states. He established close relations with Egypt, India, and Indonesia, and lengthy alliances with Vietnam and Cuba; and he sponsored Soviet forays to the Congo (Zaire), Ghana, Mali, and other African states. The initial purpose of that thrust is evident. From the early days of the Eisenhower administration, U.S. Secretary of State John Foster Dulles pursued a policy of "encirclement" as part of a general strategy of Soviet containment. Dulles envisioned the creation of U.S.-sponsored alliances in the Middle East (the Baghdad Pact, 1954),[8] Southeast Asia (SEATO, 1955), and the Far East (U.S.-Japanese, U.S.-South Korean, and U.S.-Filipino security arrangements followed the American engagement in Vietnam during the battle of Dien Bien Phu in 1954).[9] Soviet colonial expansion served to counter this policy.

Although that policy helped to forge the Soviet-Chinese alliance, it also encouraged the Soviet government to reevaluate its negative attitude of the late 1940s and early 1950s toward nonalignment (which paralleled the American approach). The result of this reevaluation included assistance to Egypt with Soviet weapons in 1954–55 and the establishment of relations with India, Burma, and Indonesia, which were followed by generous Soviet economic and military aid.[10] Thus, the main nonaligned nations received political and economic support which helped them to convene the Bandung Conference in 1955 and the first Conference of the Heads of States and Governments in Belgrade in 1961. Through these policies, the Soviets managed to subvert the U.S. policy of encirclement and to prevent the formation of a chain of pro-American military alliances along the perimeter of the USSR. They also gave the Americans to understand that through some "painful points" in the Western position, such as Suez or the Congo, the Soviets could strengthen their position in relations with the West.

Soviet policy in the Third World underwent further development following the U.S. defeat in Vietnam. Essentially, it was an American idea that the Third World was a battleground by proxy in the superpower rivalry.[11] And in this respect, the military failure of U.S. forces in Vietnam was regarded by Soviet leaders as evidence of U.S. military weakness and its inability to install a Pax Americana in the Third World. Hence, the idea of building a Soviet system of alliances and of increasing Soviet power-projection capabilities became quite popular in the 1970s, leading to decisions to intervene in Angola (1975), Ethiopia (1977), Nicaragua, and Afghanistan (1979). These political strategies were paralleled by developments in Soviet military thinking, especially in naval doctrine.[12]

In following the principle of class struggle, the Soviet Union went too far in its Third World ventures and produced a crisis in its foreign policy. On the one hand, the policy of increased involvement in the Third World drained Soviet resources and weakened the Soviet economy. It permanently complicated Soviet-American relations, as well

as its relations with the whole Western alliance. It also prompted the
first fragile voices of protest and dissent within Soviet society, following
growing losses in Afghanistan and frustration among the population.[13]

On the other hand, there was increasing disillusionment about Soviet
capabilities among its closest allies, some of whom could not accept
actions such as the war in Afghanistan. And finally, there were feelings
of concern and alienation among those nations of the Third World
that had managed to develop strong economic ties and friendly relations with both East and West. It was evident that Soviet policy had
not won the sympathies of the Third World (with some few exceptions),
while it had required too much of a sacrifice for Soviet society. It can
be stated with full evidence that the Soviet policy in the Third World
not only heavily contributed to the general crisis of Soviet society, but
itself reached a critical stage of development in which the interests of
further expansion contradicted the interests of the survival of the
communist system.

New Thinking: Concession or Soviet Self-Interest?

There are two distinct points of view among those who are interested
in the "new thinking." Was it a concession to the West, a retreat of
the Soviet empire forced by its losing the Cold War to the West, as
Francis Fukuyama suggests?[14] Or was it a sober decision to reconcile
the extent of Soviet involvement in the Third World with the availability of Soviet resources?[15] By the early 1980s, inadequate resources
had created a serious crisis in Soviet efforts both to continue active
involvement in the Third World and to match U.S. President Reagan's
new buildup of strategic and conventional weapons. Accordingly, these
alternative views not only have some basis in fact, but may also explain
the origins of "new thinking" in general and as it pertains to the Third
World in particular.

The Soviet literature—for example, by Gorbachev, Shevardnadze,
and Yakovlev—is somewhat ambiguous about the origins of the new
thinking. These writers tend to stress its positive aspects, its respon-
siveness to the concerns of all nations, and its applicability to international rapprochement and reconciliation. All that is true and has been
confirmed by both Western and Third World observers. However, one
question remains. Why did all this not happen ten years ago, in the
early 1970s, during the U.S.-Soviet détente? To what extent was it

a unilateral, unprovoked Soviet decision, and how much was it a recognition of the futility of the traditional goals and of the useless waste of Soviet resources? This is one of the most crucial questions for understanding both the general origins of "new thinking" and its consequences for the Third World.

Failure to answer these questions gives way to speculation on the real nature of the new thinking. That is why Fukuyama's article has gained such notoriety; the author had reason to regard the introduction of new thinking as a retreat of the Soviet empire and Marxist-Leninist ideology under the burden of confrontation with the West. It seemed to be the result of the failure of Soviet doctrine in confronting Western liberalism. Since a serious analysis may yield other explanations for the new thinking, it is important to examine its origins and its policy objectives in the Third World.

As it seems, new thinking was a blend of virtue and necessity. As a virtue, it emerged from a group of liberal-thinking top functionaries in the Soviet leadership. Their backgrounds, education, and outlook (which developed as a critical response to developments in the Soviet economy and society by the end of the 1970s and the early 1980s) led them to an alternative view of the future of the Soviet system. They understood that practically all the reserves and assets of the Soviet system (central planning, political unity, social integrity, ideological control, etc.) had been exhausted by the late 1970s, and some new model of development had to be introduced.[16]

The first approach in this direction was to mobilize the remaining resources in order to perfect the established system. However, the more the leadership under Gorbachev proceeded with that task, the more evident it became that the whole system had to be restructured. Thus, after years of trial and error, the concept of perestroika was worked out, meaning not only perfection of the social order in the USSR, but the establishment of a new order based on democratic principles, a market economy, respect for human rights, and ecological security.

In his polemics with hard-liners, Gorbachev very often used the following argument: it would be naive, he used to say, to imagine that the Soviet leadership had the choice in 1985 to try to make a new start or to continue the previous policy. There was no choice. The decision to undertake a new mode of development was the only way out of imminent crisis. Thus, perestroika was not the result of abstract thinking influenced by Western achievements, but a bitter necessity in order to avoid the complete collapse of the nation and subsequent chaos. Perhaps in terms of tactical solutions to minor difficulties, there could have been choices and alternative decisions, but regarding the most serious and urgent matters, there was no chance that the old Soviet model could survive.

In arguing for the necessity of perestroika, Soviet leaders quite often used the case of foreign policy to strengthen their position. It was clear that one of the heaviest burdens for the ailing Soviet economy was its security forces and foreign policy commitments, including the cost of strategic and conventional forces, the navy, the security apparatus (KGB), the war in Afghanistan, and assistance to friends and allies in Eastern Europe and in the Third World. Under the conditions of Mutually Assured Destruction, all these efforts could provide only a marginal advantage to the Soviet Union, if any. However, they consumed enormous amounts of resources and effort. Besides, in order to catch up with the U.S. administration's proclaimed goal of increased military spending (begun by President Jimmy Carter in 1980 and multiplied by Reagan in 1981–82), the USSR had to continue to spend enormous resources on the modernization of its strategic arsenals, which not only drained the national economy, but also created the danger of mismanagement, not to mention the risk of inadvertent nuclear war.

In the midst of such tremendous waste of Soviet resources and the insignificance of its results, an environment was created for the implementation of the principles of new thinking in the Soviet foreign policy arena. The nomination of Eduard Shevardnadze as Soviet foreign minister in 1985 initiated a rapid process of de-ideologization of Soviet foreign policy. Within the next several years agreements were signed on the withdrawal of Soviet troops from Afghanistan, the destruction of intermediate nuclear forces, the reduction of strategic arms, and the reduction of conventional forces in Europe. The whole context of Soviet-Western relations has changed, putting an end to the Cold War relationship. New thinking could claim credit for completely changing the nature of the international system which emerged after World War II.[17]

But new sources of trouble appeared in the world. One of these was Eastern and Central Europe. Demolition of the Berlin Wall in November 1989 led to the reunification of Germany. The economic might of Germany was now complemented by territorial gains. The other source of trouble in Europe became Yugoslavia, where the process of disintegration of the federation was accompanied by fierce civil war. Ethnic and border troubles appeared throughout Eastern Europe.

The primary significance of these sources of trouble lay in the fact that such postulates of new thinking as the creation of a democratic and just "new world order" once the Cold War was finished proved to be false. It was expected that with the winding down of conflict between the superpowers, it would be possible to create an atmosphere in which all nations would enjoy security and pursue economic development. In reality, however, it appeared that the Cold War confrontation had kept frozen dozens of conflicts on ethnic, territorial, and other issues. Once the Cold War had disappeared from the international system, the system itself began to disintegrate, loosing the ties which had kept it together. The hardest blow came from the quick disintegration of the Soviet Union following the unsuccessful coup of August 1991.

Even before the end of the Cold War brought such unexpected results to the situation in Europe and in the former Soviet Union, the international system had experienced a severe shock from the Gulf crisis, which followed the Iraqi aggression against Kuwait in August 1990. Though the Iraqi troops were eventually forced out of Kuwait in early 1991 through military action by the U.S.-led coalition, both the crisis in that area and the general confusion in the Third World continued. The unstable and unpredictable situation in Iraq, the growth of fundamentalist forces in Iran and Lebanon, and the waves of instability projected from both the Armenian-Azerbaijani conflict over Nagorno-Karabakh and from political upheaval in former Soviet Central Asia, have contributed substantially to the continuation of tensions in the area. It has become evident that with the winding down of the superpower rivalry, hidden pockets of instability, which were dormant for years, have become activated and have burst out as new sources of war.

These facts have emphasized the other side of the situation in the Third World. While the superpower rivalry had kept some of the potential conflicts under a certain control, the transformation of relations between the Soviet Union and the United States was not followed by parallel changes in the peripheral areas, as happened in the early 1970s.[18] On the contrary, it was assumed that the end of the rivalry would lead to the superpowers' withdrawal from the Third World and a decrease in their support to traditional friends. That has produced two different responses. First was anxious anticipation of the decrease in foreign assistance. This was especially so for countries such as Cuba, Ethiopia, and Angola, as well as for those which were suffering from a food crisis, such as Somalia, Sudan, and Bangladesh, and from other forms of underdevelopment found in Burma, Nepal, and Algeria. The second type of response was one of relief on the part of those who regarded a possible withdrawal of the superpowers from the Third World as an opportunity to fill the vacuum on the regional level.

These developments in the Third World have redounded upon the policies of the superpowers. In the United States they have provoked a serious debate within the foreign policy community about the U.S. role in the Third World, especially its most strategically important areas: the Middle East and Persian Gulf, Southeast Asia, the Caribbean, and Central America. Sometimes, American "activism," though having popular support, as in the case of the Gulf War, was regarded, especially by both isolationists and radical critics, with skepticism. It was assumed that given the continuation of the United States' superpower status, a "unipolar world" might become counterproductive for American interests. Soviet policy (until December 1991, when the Soviet Union officially ceased to exist) regarded the evolution of the Third World with growing concern, since it posed potential threats for Soviet domestic affairs and for some border areas in Transcaucasia and Central Asia.

Soviet foreign policy, in turn, has passed through several critical stages which tested and in the long run undermined the importance of new thinking. The first crisis for Soviet foreign policy in this period was the anticommunist revolutions in Eastern Europe. Watching the communist regimes in Hungary, Poland, Czechoslovakia, East Germany, Romania, and Bulgaria come down, under the impact of perestroika, the Soviet leadership had to resist any temptation to interfere in these events. It had to disregard pressure from the conservatives and thus "bless" the end of its sphere of control in Europe. The second crisis was caused by the unification of Germany. This was a special case both for the Soviet elite and the Soviet population, because of bitter memories of the German invasion of 1941–44 and the necessity to give up the first socialist state on German soil. This crisis was also successfully addressed by Gorbachev's government in the spirit of new thinking, against which open attacks were expressed in the Soviet press and by the public.[19]

The third crisis was caused by the Iraqi invasion of Kuwait. The Soviet government was quick in protesting the invasion, together with the United States and most of the international community.[20] However, it was evident that the Soviet government was in a difficult position, because Iraq had been a Soviet ally since 1973. The Iraqi armed forces had been trained by the Soviet military and were equipped with Soviet weaponry. Iraq had almost always enjoyed Soviet diplomatic support, even when the rest of the world protested its use of chemical weapons against the Kurds in 1988. Thus, the Soviets bore part of the responsibility for Iraq's aggression against Kuwait. Even while protesting the Iraqi action, the Soviet government avoided mentioning the Soviet-Iraqi Treaty of 1973 and saw no reason for abrogating it. Finally, the Soviets were reluctant to join forces with the twenty-six other nations that sent troops (some only symbolic forces) to the Gulf area. Instead, they tried to play a self-appointed role as intermediary during the crisis.

By the time of the Persian Gulf crisis, the position of the liberals in Gorbachev's administration had weakened significantly. (Shevardnadze's resignation was open evidence of that.) Gorbachev no longer had carte blanche for foreign policy decisions but had to clear his actions with the hard-liners, who insisted that the Soviet Union distance itself from the United States and take measures to help Iraq diplomatically (as evidenced by Yevgeni Primakov's trips to Baghdad and to Washington). They hoped that Iraq would militarily withstand allied forces' attack and that this would give Soviet policy more weight. This, in turn, would open a way to discredit the new thinking and to declare it an "antinational" policy.[21]

Although the military victory of the allied forces put an end to those hopes, the continuing crisis in Soviet foreign policy increased the importance of several of its elements for the Third World. First, the Soviet Union was quickly turning from a donor of foreign assistance to a consumer of it, thus becoming a rival to the Third World. Second, the inability—and sometimes even the open refusal—of the Soviet Union to continue to assist its closest allies in the Third World either turned them into open critics of Soviet policy (Cuba, North Korea) or helped to overthrow Marxist regimes in Ethiopia, Angola, and Nicaragua. Even such staunch supporters of the Soviet Union as the Vietnamese preferred to distance themselves and begin seeking accommodation with their former enemies. Third, the Soviet crisis in the

Third World immediately found its way into the domestic realm, creating a gap between the "North" (Russia and the other Slavic republics) and "South" (Transcaucasia and Central Asia).

It might be suggested that the deepest scars of Soviet misbehavior in the Persian Gulf crisis pertained to Soviet-Islamic relations. These were never very successful, even before the crisis, because of the war in Afghanistan and the Islamic nations' disapproval of the position of Islam in the Soviet Union. But usually this tension was counterbalanced by the Soviet role in the Middle East, where Moscow consistently supported the Arab radicals. This time, since a Soviet quasi-ally had attacked an Arab country and the Soviet Union was reluctant to take decisive measures, anti-Soviet feelings among the Islamic nations significantly increased. Thus, when the Soviet Union collapsed and disintegrated into the CIS, the Islamic factor had become crucial. It determined the relationship between Russia and the Islamic republics and between Russians and Muslims within the Russian republic itself. Indeed, two Islamic republics, Chechen and Tatar, have since seceded and opted for full independence.

The Post-Soviet Period

In December 1991 the Soviet Union ceased to exist as a nation. In its place was created the Commonwealth, a loose arrangement of states having some elements of coordination but basically wherein each state pursues its own foreign policy goals with little regard for the others. Soviet policy as such has been split into fifteen different policies, each prompted by an individual republic's desire to assert its independence and sovereignty, to find its own focus, and to extend relations primarily to its neighbors or to states regarded as friendly based on religion (the Islamic republics), language (Azerbaijan and Turkey, Moldova and Romania, Tadjikistan and Iran), history, and geographical proximity. A totally new picture has emerged where there once was a single Soviet foreign policy.

This could not help but affect traditional Soviet relations with the Third World. Previous alignments were based roughly on Cold War principles, with the Soviet Union supporting political groups and governments in the Third World because of their anti-Americanism. With the dissolution of the Cold War along its central front, in U.S.-Soviet relations, an easing of tensions in the peripheral areas did not follow automatically. Confrontations in the Middle East, Cambodia, the Korean peninsula, and in Cuban-American relations continued. And that, as already mentioned, placed the Soviet Union in an awkward, confused position, leading to a crisis with the Persian Gulf War. The disintegration of the Soviet Union has changed the picture completely. No sovereign state among the former Soviet republics was inclined to continue support to the former Soviet clients, for both political and economic reasons.

This change has created a completely new atmosphere in regional conflicts. There was a danger that the Bush administration, for domestic political reasons (the presidential elections of 1992), might try to "flex American muscle" overseas. That possibility never materialized, because the American public was becoming less inclined to encourage the President's forays abroad. Another aspect of the new atmosphere in regional conflicts was the prospect of peace for some of them: the Middle East, following the Madrid Conference of 1991; Cambodia, following a UN-sponsored truce and subsequent national elections; and Korea, following the bilateral agreement on North-South dialogue on national reconciliation. The same should be said about South Africa, Afghanistan, Somalia, and Ethiopia. But not all the hopes in these areas have been realized. The Arab-Israeli conflict unexpectedly reversed direction. In February 1992, there was another "small war" across the Lebanese border between Israeli military forces and Hezbollah militants. Later, with Israel's deportation of four hundred suspected Palestinian Islamic activists to southern Lebanon, the peace talks were brought to a halt.

It was clear that the regional conflicts were changing in different directions, and it was difficult to find a single response to them. On the one hand, discussions of "multilateralism" became frequent, with the emphasis on the necessity for all the large powers—the permanent members of the UN Security Council—to find a consensus on peace keeping and conflict resolution. This was regarded as one of the main avenues toward the creation of the "new world order." In this context it is important to remember the UN Security Council summit in late January 1992, as well as discussions of multilateral efforts in Europe in response to the Yugoslavian crisis. On the other hand, it was evident that the big powers continued their policies of supplying arms to critical areas, disregarding the possible consequences for regional peace and security. In this respect, the situation in the Persian Gulf, where a new round of the arms race began in 1992, has acquired special importance.[22]

The other side of the disintegration of the Soviet Union and its effect on Third World affairs concerns the new policies of the states of the former Soviet Union. Some of the "Northern" Soviet republics have continued to be involved in the Third World. The Russian Federation had acquired, as part of its Soviet heritage, permanent participation in peace efforts in regional conflicts. Consequently, it had a special role in discussions with other weapons suppliers concerning the possibilities of arms control in the Third World, while nevertheless assisting the most deprived nations of the region. The other Slavic republics also continued to operate in the Third World, though on a more sporadic basis. Ukraine has continued some arms supplies to Third World areas, and Belarus was developing trade relations with Iran and some Arab states of the Middle East and Persian Gulf area.

As to the Soviet "South," the situation there has completely changed. The republics with predominantly Muslim populations, including Azerbaijan, Uzbekistan, Tadjikistan, Turkmenistan, Kyrgyzstan, and most of all Kazakhstan, have emerged as new and important actors in the Islamic world. Special importance is attributed to Kazakhstan, the largest among the Muslim republics and the only possessor of strategic nuclear arms. Though from the very beginning the Kazakh leader insisted that his republic would prefer non-nuclear status, he was reluctant to destroy the nuclear arsenal as part of the U.S.-Soviet START Treaty of 1991 and is pursuing the development of an independent Kazakh space program. Kazakhstan occupies a pivotal position between the old Soviet "North" and "South"—that is, between the Slavic republics and the non-Russian Islamic states. (Almost half of its population is Slavic, and there are significant German and Korean elements.) These factors, added to its natural wealth and developed industry, have given it a leading role among the former Soviet Union's least developed republics. It has exercised a visible restraining role in the foreign policy of the other Islamic republics, though it could not, of course, inhibit them from taking a more active role in international Third World politics.

In 1991, Azerbaijan applied for and was granted membership in the Organization of Islamic States. This was a major diplomatic opening for the former Soviet republics. Azerbaijan actively began to establish working relationships with its immediate neighbors, especially Iran and Turkey. It chose to emphasize its special relationship with Turkey, based on historical ties and language kinship and a certain similarity in their anti-Armenian postures. At the same time, Azerbaijan could also count on a special relationship with Iran, given that northern Iran is populated by native Azeris. The Iranian government could not ignore the role that this fact could play in establishing close relations between the two states, although it may also be viewed with concern by Tehran.

The four republics of the Central Asian region were more active in establishing relations with the Arab world and Pakistan. They were evidently anticipating assistance from rich Arab countries as well as markets for their industries. Sometimes this was cause for concern—when, for example, the Tadjik government promised to start exporting enriched uranium without due international inspection.

In trying to generalize about these developments, it is clear that the former Soviet "South" was actively seeking a new identity. These republics' traditional reliance on the Russian security umbrella (which was renewed following the host of agreements on the status of the CIS Joint Forces and on the Joint Border Command) and on Russian economic input, together with the continuation of traditional ties between Asian producers of raw materials and Russian industrial consumers, was in growing measure accompanied by a desire to establish closer economic and cultural relations with their southern neighbors.

This much had been long expected. The other side of that same process, the stirring of some underdeveloped and non-Christian parts of Russia proper, was unanticipated and concerned Russia's leaders. Some Islamic republics in the Russian Federation, such as Tatarstan and Bashkorstan, as well as the Islamic population of the Northern Caucasus, demonstrated interest in having independent ties with the Islamic world. The Buddhist Kalmyks and Buryats wanted to have relations with the Buddhist countries. Although the Russian leadership regards itself as the representative of both its Christian and non-Christian populations in its foreign relations, this trend could potentially threaten the integrity of the nation.

In assessing the importance of these events for the Third World, it is obvious that the reemergence as independent actors of a significant number of Islamic (or pro-Islamic) "Southern" republics in the former Soviet Union can change some of the important balances in world politics. First, the sheer number of Islamic states has increased, making them much more influential in the UN (where the former Soviet republics have already been accepted). Second, they have immediately increased the significance of fundamentalism, which can be observed both in Algeria and Iran (the latter convened the group of the Islamic "common market" with the full participation of Azerbaijan, Uzbekistan, Turkmenistan, Kyrgyzstan, and Tadjikistan, with Kazakhstan as an observer). Third, it will inevitably give much more emphasis to the problems of development, which until recently were widely ignored by the international community.

All this may significantly change the traditional patterns of world politics and add to the existing confusion, as some of the former colonies and dependent territories gain the status of highly developed states, while the newcomers to the world community will increase the competition for international financial and other resources. What is especially important is that these changes will be accompanied by the further expansion of the Islamic factor in world politics, which may change political dynamics in the Middle East, the Indian subcontinent, Southeast Asia, Turkey, and the Balkans. It would be wise to consider all these and similar novelties and to prepare for their consequences in advance.

Conclusion

Events in the Third World following the upheaval in the former Soviet Union suggest some important conclusions. First is that the international role of the Russian Federation may need to be increased. On the one hand, Russia will continue to play an important but difficult role in the global strategic balance and in European development. It will continue to support global strategic stability through the controlled reduction and destruction of the excessive nuclear potential, both in U.S.-Russian relations and in the whole nuclear club, including France, the United Kingdom, and China. As a part of Europe, it will have to carry out its obligations to reduce its conventional armaments, as well as managing its complex military (both nuclear and conventional) relations with the other republics—Ukraine, Belarus, the Baltic republics, Moldova, and Kazakhstan.

However, of special importance will be the Russian role in shaping the future of the former Soviet Islamic republics. It is evident that Russia possesses enormous possibilities for becoming the main sponsor and promoter of further changes in these states. Both the historical traditions mentioned above and current realities (existing economic interdependence, the Russian minorities in all these states, the Russian-educated professionals and democratic-oriented political figures, mixed marriages) give Russia a unique chance to play a conciliatory and constructive role in assisting the new states to acquire their own international stature without overplaying the Islamic factor and without the danger that their advent on the international scene will sharpen the North-South confrontation and the differences between the Islamic and Western worlds. But to play such a role, Russia itself will have to go through a significant process of change and development.

Notes

1. This has been analyzed in some recent publications on Russian foreign policy. See A. Bogaturov, M. Kozhokin, and K. Pleshakov, "Mezhdu Vostokom i Zapadom" (Between East and West), *Nezavisimaya Gazeta,* 25 September 1991.

2. This may be traced in the writings of one of the most important writers on the Third World in the Communist party. See K. N. Brutents, *Sovremennye nationalno-osvoboditelnye revolutsii* (Contemporary national-liberation revolutions) (Moscow: Politizdat, 1974).

3. G. B. Starushenko, *Sotsialisticheskaya orientatsia v rasvivayushikhsia stranakh* (Socialist orientation in developing countries) (Moscow: Politizdat, 1977).

4. I. I. Kovalenko, ed., *Dvizhenie neprisovediniya* (The non-aligned movement) (Moscow: Nauka, 1985).

5. The official position of the Communist Party of the Soviet Union on this issue is articulated in several documents of the twenty-fifth, twenty-sixth, and twenty-seventh congresses. In 1976, at the twenty-fifth congress, Secretary General Brezhnev spoke of the "definite support" of the newly liberated states: *Materialy XXV svezda KPSS* (Materials of the twenty-fifth congress of the CPSU) (Moscow: Politizdat, 1976), 11–16. In 1981, at the twenty-sixth congress, Brezhnev spoke of the "fragmented picture" in the Third World and of the different directions of Soviet policy with regard to states of "socialist orientation" and the rest of the Third World: *Materialy XXVI svezda KPSS* (Materials of the twenty-sixth congress of the CPSU) (Moscow: Politizdat, 1981), 11–15. In 1986, at the twenty-seventh congress, the new party secretary general, Mikhail Gorbachev, spoke of "contradictions" between the West and the Third World and emphasized the need for their "peaceful solution": *Materialy XXVII svezda Kommunisticheskoy Partii Sovetskogo Soyuza* (Mate-

rials of the twenty-seventh congress of the CPSU) (Moscow: Politizdat, 1986), 17–18.

6. Some of these aspects of the Soviet war in Afghanistan were discussed in "Lessons of Afghanistan," *SSHA: ekonomika, politika, ideologya,* nos. 6–7 (1989).

7. P. A. Chikhachev, *Velikiye derzhavy i vostochny vopros* (Great powers and the Orient) (Moscow: Nauka, 1970).

8. The Baghdad Pact was officially established on 24 February 1955. This reference to 1954 is to the treaty between Turkey and Iraq that was the basis for the Baghdad Pact.

9. Townsend Hoopes, *The Devil and John Foster Dulles* (Boston: Little, Brown, 1973).

10. Nikita Khrushchev, *Khrushchev Remembers,* translated and edited by Strobe Talbot (Boston: Little, Brown, 1970), 430–35.

11. Formulated as an academic concept in the late 1950s by T. Schelling, Henry Kissinger, M. Taylor, Morton Halperin, and others, this idea became part of John F. Kennedy's official policy of "flexible response." Yu. M. Melnikov, *Vneshnepoliticheskiye doktriny SSHA* (U.S. foreign policy doctrines) (Moscow: Nauka, 1970).

12. S. G. Gorshkov, *Morskaya moshch gosudarstva* (States naval power) (Moscow: Voyenizdat, 1976).

13. One of the first criticisms of Soviet Third World endeavors to appear in the Soviet media was D. Volsky, "My i tretiy mir" (We and the Third World), *Izvestiya,* 21 December 1988.

14. Francis Fukuyama, "The End of History," *National Interest* (Summer 1989): 3–18.

15. This line is perfectly reflected in Mikhail S. Gorbachev, *New Thinking for Our Country and the World* (Moscow: APN Publishers, 1988).

16. As one of the main statements of this necessity, the report by Mikhail Gorbachev to the twenty-seventh congress of the CPSU may be consulted (*Materialy XXVII svezda KPSS,* 22–24).

17. Eduard Shevardnadze, *Moy vybor* (My choice) (Moscow: Novosti, 1991).

18. In Soviet literature it was analyzed in V. Avakov and V. Kremenyuk, "Sistema vzaimodeystvia mezdunarodnykh knofliktov" (System of interrelation of international conflicts), in V. Gantman, ed., *Mezhdunarodnye konflikty sovremennosti* (Contemporary international conflicts) (Moscow: Nauka, 1983).

19. The decisions on Eastern Europe and Germany were openly attacked by such party hard-liners as Egor Ligachev and by conservative military com-

144 The Soviet Experience in the Third World

manders such as General Makashov. Their remarks about these "self-defeating decisions" appeared in early 1990 in *Pravda* and *Krasnaya Zvezda*.

20. The joint Soviet-U.S. communiqué was announced on 3 August 1990. See *Izvestiya*, 4 September 1990, 1–2.

21. There was a special publication in the conservative *Sovetskaya Rossiya*, which vehemently attacked the supporters of new thinking and declared them to be "war-mongers" (*Sovetskaya Rossiya*, 22 February 1991).

22. "Sneaking in the Scuds," *Newsweek* (22 June 1992): 20–24.

Part 3

Moscow, the United States, and the Third World

The Dynamics of U.S.-Russian Interaction in the Third World during the Gorbachev Era and Beyond

Alvin Z. Rubinstein

For forty-five years—from 1945 to 1990—the United States and the Soviet Union engaged in an intense rivalry in the Third World. For the most part, their rivalry was competitive rather than confrontational. Its scope was global yet remained relatively low-risk, because it was waged in regions that were peripheral to each other's core security community—Moscow's October 1962 attempt to implant nuclear missiles in Cuba is the only exception to this proposition—and because the rivalry occurred in an essentially bipolar world, which meant that neither depended on the alignments of secondary states for its security. The Third World was seen as a vast strategic preserve in which transient alignments and endemic instability provided each adversary with attractive options that could be adapted to changing ambitions, perceptions, and opportunities.

Explanations for the origins, dynamics, and transformation of the U.S.-Soviet rivalry in the Third World exceed the actual causes. Although theoretical formulations can suggest numerous possibilities, a regard for reality requires careful attention to context and thus makes efforts to compare different eras and different rivalries most difficult. Mindful that alternative assessments are possible, what follows is one attempt at explanation.

Three features distinguished the U.S.-Soviet rivalry from previous great-power rivalries of the nineteenth and twentieth centuries. First, there was the nuclear dimension. As nuclear powers, both the United States and the Soviet Union were careful not to exceed the bounds of what they could do in the "gray areas" of the Third World in which

147

they competed. Moreover, each realized that setbacks there could be borne without fear that a significant shift in the central strategic balance of power might result. Second, their rivalry unfolded in a weak, politically multipolar environment in which their clients were independent nation-states. Decolonization had legitimated the state system. This had the effect of constraining the actions and ambitions of each superpower. It also imposed a kind of deemphasis on ideology in their dealings with the clients they selected. In the absence of a readiness to use military power to establish unquestioned control, as Moscow did in Afghanistan in December 1979, neither superpower could impose its will on a dependent client state. Each played according to the rules of the international system, in which nation-states are universally recognized as the principal political actors in the diplomatic realm. They did so for domestic reasons and for flexibility in pursuing national interests abroad. Finally, the third distinctive feature of the U.S.-Soviet rivalry was its preoccupation not with the quest for additional real estate, but rather with a combination of strategic denial and strategic advantage.

Any analysis of their rivalry needs to make clear the distinction between an imperial policy and an imperialist policy, though characteristics of both were present to some extent, as we shall see. In the nineteenth century, Russian policy was imperialistic, as Moscow expanded its dominion and absorbed huge areas of Central Asia.[1] But the policy followed by the Soviet Union and the United States in the Third World may be termed an imperial policy and differentiated from an imperialist policy in a number of ways.[2] First, an imperial policy, in contrast to an imperialist one, is impelled primarily by considerations that are political and strategic, not territorial or economic. Its impetus derives from a desire to weaken an adversary through far-ranging and adroit maneuvers and manipulation. It embraces the concepts associated with an indirect strategy. It aims at intrusiveness and influence-building in friendly client states, not their domination or incorporation. Second, an imperial policy accepts the disparity in power between patron and client, recognizes the formal equality between them as sovereign states, and assumes that cooperation is a matter of mutual self-interest. Although asymmetrical, the relationship brings advantages to each party. A patron may be unable to impose its preference on the domestic or foreign policy behavior of a dependent state, but it may nonetheless be satisfied with the regional and global advantages that it sees as stemming from facilitating the client's general policy orientation. Thus, by helping a client do what it wants to do, the superpower finds a result that is beneficial, one that helps improve the strategic context within which it conducts its diplomacy and carries on its rivalry with its key adversary. Only in Afghanistan did Moscow discard such a relationship in favor of a blatant imperialistic grab to control real estate and install a compliant puppet regime. Everywhere else in the Third World from 1953 to 1990, it came by invitation, its assistance a response to requests from diverse clients.

Third, an imperial policy is ideally patient, consistent, and cost-effective. Having a prime adversary clearly in mind, it operates on the assumption that incremental gains in contested areas can, over time, bring a qualitative improvement in the strategic position. Finally, it views Third World actors as pawns, useful to have but for the most part readily disposable. It downplays, but does not completely ignore, ideology as a motive for foreign policy. The ideological residual may well be the result of a need to exaggerate an external threat in order to strengthen the leadership's domestic legitimacy. For example, notwithstanding glasnost and accounts by a number of former Soviet officials and academicians, no conclusive material has appeared explaining the decision to intervene militarily in Afghanistan in December 1979; nor do we even know which or how many Politburo members actually were involved.[3]

As with other putative models, the imperial model has its limitations, because political choices are often the result of idiosyncratic considerations that defy analysis by distant observers. The role of a few key personalities looms large, but no archival evidence has been provided to permit a searching analysis of how decisions were made in the Brezhnev Kremlin, or, indeed, how key decisions were made under Gorbachev. Whatever approach is used—one that emphasizes balance-of-power considerations, a psychologically derived one that stresses the critical role of misperceptions on both sides, a Marxist-based or an imperial one—the Cold War that attended the end of the Second World War was, as with all previous historical instances of "cold war," a product of specific, concrete circumstances.

Stalin's Role

The U.S.-Soviet rivalry in the Third World was an outgrowth of Stalin's attempt to extend to the Middle East the expansion of Soviet power in Europe at the end of the war.[4] Even before the war ended, Stalin's imperialist ambitions surfaced. On 19 March 1945 the Soviet government informed the Turkish government, which had maintained an uneasy neutrality during the war, that it would not renew the 1925 friendship treaty unless Ankara returned the districts of Kars and Ardahan in eastern Anatolia and provided bases on the Straits. At the Potsdam conference of July 1945, Stalin demanded the return of the districts, which had been given to Russia in 1878 following the Russo-Ottoman War of 1877–78, but then returned to Turkey in 1918 by the Treaty of Brest-Litovsk and formally accepted by Moscow in the Russo-Turkish treaty of 1921.

The issue simmered while the problems of Germany and Eastern Europe dominated and soured Western relations with the Soviet Union. Stalin overplayed a strong hand. Instead of requesting reasonable concessions that might have brought some accommodation, especially in regard to security in the Black Sea region, he made a determined bid for domination. Over the course of the next year, Moscow pressed for revision of the 1936 Montreux Convention, arguing that Turkey's refusal to agree to joint Soviet-Turkish regulation of the Straits jeopardized the USSR's security. Its case received short shrift in Washington, which was convinced that the Soviet Union was responsible for the civil war in Greece.

Iran was also a target for Stalin's expansionist ambitions. It had been occupied by the Soviet Union and Britain on 25 August 1941 to forestall a possible pro-German orientation, assure Western control of the oil fields, and maintain a secure transit route for shipments of war matériel to the war-torn Soviet front. The country was divided into two zones of occupation: the Soviets occupied the provinces of Azerbaijan, Gilan, Mazanderan, Gorgan, and Khorasan; the British held the southern part of the country. Tehran was treated as a neutral enclave. British forces withdrew after the war, in accordance with the provisions of the tripartite treaty of 29 January 1942. The Soviets, however, consolidated their position, frustrated the Iranian government's efforts to reassert its authority in the occupied provinces, and encouraged separatist revolts. Under Soviet tutelage, autonomous Azerbaijani and Kurdish republics were proclaimed in December 1945 and January 1946, respectively, prompting Iran to complain to the UN Security Council. Over the next eighteen months, Iran and the Soviet Union engaged in intensive negotiations, the result of which was a Soviet military withdrawal, a reassertion of Iranian control, and a Moscow that was checkmated by the astute diplomatic moves of Iran's prime minister. For the first time since the end of the war, a targeted victim had escaped the Soviet net.

By early 1947, U.S.-Soviet relations had frozen. The Truman Doctrine and the Marshall Plan set U.S. policy; the establishment of the Cominform in September 1947 accelerated the Sovietization and communization of Eastern Europe.

Stalin's probes in the Middle East ended, and his attention focused on domestic recovery from the war, and on Europe and the Far East. But his policy polarized relations with Turkey and Iran, though neither country had threatened his security. His heavy-handed diplomatic pressure and unmistakable territorial designs on his two neighbors pushed them into closer ties with the United States, and prompted the United States to begin its active military-strategic involvement in the Middle East. Thus, unwittingly, Stalin bequeathed to his successors the formidable task of unhinging the U.S.-inspired military alliances that, for the first time in Soviet history, posed a genuine threat to the Soviet homeland from the Middle East. His policies, to which Washington overreacted, made the containment of Soviet expansion and influence in the Middle East a major concern of U.S. foreign policy.

Moscow's Forward Policy: The Era of Optimism and Commitments (1953–80)

Moscow's policy in the Third World came of age under Khrushchev, and in the process generated a strategic-political tension with the United States that took on global dimensions. After Stalin's death in March 1953, Soviet leaders undertook a series of major changes in policy toward the Third World, nowhere more dramatically than along their southern tier. They moved to normalize relations with Turkey, Iran, and Afghanistan. For example, in a diplomatic note to Ankara on 30 May 1953, the Soviet government acknowledged that its previous policy had been a mistake, and it said that "the Soviet Union has not any kind of territorial claims on Turkey."[5] Comparable concessions were made to Iran and Afghanistan; the result was a relaxation of tensions and a normalization of relations.

The success of Soviet policy inhered in its gradualist and accommodating character. With diplomatic normalization, Moscow extended economic and (in the case of Afghanistan) military assistance on favorable terms. It concentrated on strengthening bilateral ties and did not set conditions, such as the legalization of communist parties or changes in a courted country's military alliances. It deferred to the domestic and regional priorities established by the Turkish, Iranian, and Afghan leaderships. By way of contrast, the U.S. extension of the policy of containment was conceptually flawed, because it ignored the diverse and often divergent interests of the countries it sought as allies. In its preoccupation with building alliances, Washington stressed the Soviet threat long after the regional actors had discounted its immediacy or probability and had directed their primary security efforts elsewhere. As a result, policy divergences became evident in U.S. relations with Turkey, Iran, and Afghanistan by the late 1950s and early 1960s; and they transformed regional politics in the Arab East and South Asia and inadvertently prepared the way for Khrushchev's forward policy.

Not content with securing the USSR's southern tier, Khrushchev shifted Soviet foreign policy from a continental-based strategy in world affairs to a global one, which enjoyed general support among the major contestants for political power during the succession crises between 1953 and 1957. (Molotov was probably the lone dissenter to Khrushchev's decision to become heavily engaged in the Arab world.) Ironically, it was the deterrent policy of the United States during the pre-missile era, when U.S. nuclear superiority was paramount, that facilitated the USSR's entry into and courtship of key Third World countries such as India, Egypt, Iraq (after 1958), and Ghana. The U.S. policy of ringing the Soviet Union with military and refueling bases in nearby states to enhance the nuclear-strike effectiveness of the U.S. Strategic Air Command's long-range bomber force was perceived by the Soviet leadership as a threat to their national security. Even more important, the polarization that this encouraged ran counter to the thrust of the forces of nationalism in the Third World, which aimed at shedding all traces of former Western domination and at steering an independent course in world affairs. By applying its containment policy uncritically to the Third World, the United States facilitated Khrushchev's determination to set the Soviet Union on an activist and greatly expanded course there. With checkbook and olive branch, Khrushchev courted key countries, exploited regional conflicts, and provided arms to countries opposed to Western (mainly U.S.) policy, irrespective of their ideological orientation or political system. Over the years, the policy was extended, refined, and strengthened; indeed, Brezhnev was to carry it much further. Not until Gorbachev's time was it reversed.

The approach Khrushchev developed and the forms of involvement he pioneered brought the Soviet Union into the mainstream of Third World politics. Economic assistance was expanded; increasingly, military assistance overshadowed economic aid; friendship treaties and cultural accords were promoted to reassure clients, deepen the Soviet presence, and discourage accommodation with the United States. With flexibility and a verve that had theretofore been absent from Soviet policy, Khrushchev gave client regimes the wherewithal that made it possible for them to pursue policies that were, as he shrewdly discerned, essentially congruent with his own aims. Optimistic and convinced that the situation in the Third World was ripe for "socialism," he was doubtless spurred on by the dramatic improvement the USSR had achieved in less than two years in its relations with Afghanistan, India, Egypt, and Indonesia. He sensed in the Third World, a region he called a "zone of peace" at the Twentieth Congress of the Communist Party of the Soviet Union (CPSU) in February 1956, a free-hunting ground where the Soviet Union might be able to improve its overall political and strategic position relative to the United States.

For the Soviet Union, strategic denial meant, concretely, thwarting U.S. policies, undercutting its alliances and alignments, complicating its diplomacy, diverting its resources away from Europe to areas and issues that were peripheral to Moscow's concerns and ambitions, and seeking ways that would prevent the United States from utilizing regional advantages or that would exact a stiff price for them. To this end, Khrushchev pioneered a differentiated approach that downgraded ideological considerations: support for regimes that opposed U.S.-sponsored military pacts and arrangements; encouragement of those who opted for nonalignment politically and the noncapitalist path of development economically; friendship with any regime at odds with the United States; and perhaps most important of all, exploitation of regional conflicts. In the 1950s this meant support for Afghanistan against Pakistan, and for Egypt and Syria against Iraq (until July 1958, when a military coup overthrew the pro-Western Hashemite monarchy). In the 1960s and early 1970s the USSR supported Cuba against the United States, Egypt and Syria against Israel, India against Pakistan, Iraq against Iran, and the People's Democratic Republic of

Yemen (PDRY) against Oman, and so on. Whether exploiting intraregional polarization (which was not, it should be noted, created by the Soviet Union, but inhered in the region's historic and political animosities), normalizing relations with countries prepared to enter into closer ties with the USSR, or encouraging positions antithetical to U.S. policy and interests, Moscow proceeded pragmatically, tailoring its assistance and commitments on a case-by-case basis.

It remained for Brezhnev to move the USSR's policy from one primarily geared to strategic denial to one forcefully striving for attainment of strategic advantage. The pivotal development that heralded the coming of age of Moscow's power projection capability in the Third World was the Kremlin's quick decision to rearm and protect Egypt and Syria after their defeat in the 1967 June War. Moscow's readiness to intervene militarily on behalf of prime clients was presumably the result of deliberations that weighed certain considerations: (1) the opportunity factor, which derived from regional instability and the alacrity with which beleaguered local actors turned to the Soviet Union; (2) the inability or unwillingness of the United States to use its power to affect regional outcomes; (3) the role that clients could play in providing compensatory advantages that would strengthen the Soviet position; and (4) the coming on line of a military capability that permitted greater strategic assertiveness.[6]

Military assistance strengthened the political links between Moscow and prized clients, deepened the Soviet presence in the Arab world, and raised the ante in the U.S.-Soviet rivalry in the Third World. Washington, then mired in the Vietnam morass, perceived Moscow's increased projection of military power as a challenge to its position and interests. The acquisition of military privileges had long been an objective of Soviet military planners. From 1955 on, when a treaty of friendship was signed with North Yemen and Moscow helped modernize Hodeida's port facilities, they had sought a foothold on the southwestern part of the Arabian peninsula, so as to be positioned to affect developments in the Red Sea, Gulf of Aden, and Arabian Sea region. This accounted, at least in part, for Moscow's willingness to underwrite Egyptian President Gamal Abdel Nasser's 1962–67 intervention in the North Yemeni civil war (Egypt's "Vietnam"). Thus, long before 1970 when the United States acquired Diego Garcia as a base in the Indian Ocean, Soviet planners evidently were thinking of ways of acquiring privileged access in the Mediterranean Sea, the Arabian Sea, and the

Indian Ocean. Neo-Mahanism was very much a conceptual consideration underlying the USSR's construction of a "blue-water" fleet from the late 1950s on, a result of Admiral of the Fleet Sergei G. Gorshkov's success in persuading political leaders of the need for limited command of the seas in areas important to Soviet foreign policy interests.[7] In a major work justifying the naval buildup, Gorshkov cited Peter the Great to cement his case for both a strong army and navy: "Any potentate with a land army has one hand but he who also has a fleet has two hands."[8]

After Egypt's defeat in June 1967, Moscow's reward for its massive infusion of arms and advisers was extensive military privileges, including naval access and depots at Alexandria and Sollum. (However, these were terminated in 1976 by Anwar Sadat, who had decided on a pro-U.S. orientation in order to regain Israeli-occupied Egyptian territory.) In the 1970s and early 1980s, the Soviet navy acquired varying degrees of military privilege in Syria, the PDRY, Somalia, Cuba, Vietnam, and Ethiopia (though these were acquired only at the cost of having to relinquish the bases in Somalia). Moscow was increasingly confident in its military instrument and had reason to see developments in the Third World as essentially favorable to Soviet interests, and it was reinforced in this view by the hard-currency windfall that it reaped in the early 1970s, as a consequence of the sharp rise in the international price of oil. The upshot of all of this was such that at the CPSU's Twenty-sixth Congress in February 1981, Brezhnev could proclaim, "No one should have any doubts, comrades, that the CPSU will consistently continue the policy of promoting cooperation between the USSR and the newly free countries, and consolidating the alliance of world socialism and the national liberation movement."

A combination of commitments, opportunities, and misperceptions of the importance of linkage in U.S. diplomacy drove Brezhnev's policy in the Third World, essentially in ways that were antithetical to his interest in a U.S.-Soviet détente. The incongruity of assuming that he could use Soviet power to undermine the United States in the Third World at the same time that he sought détente to obtain Western credits, isolate China, stabilize the nuclear arms race, and improve relations with Western Europe seems to have escaped the Kremlin leadership. Or perhaps they were captives of their own distorted ideological formulations and thought both could be reconciled.

In any event, the imprint that Brezhnev made on the Third World tableau destroyed détente. Starting with the aid to North Vietnam that proved so cost-effective in military terms, and continuing with the protection and patronage provided Egypt and Syria after the June War, the commitment of Soviet combat forces to safeguard Nasser from defeat in the 1969–70 war of attrition along the Suez Canal, and the rejection of American overtures for joint efforts to halt the 1973 October War in its early stages, Brezhnev conveyed the impression that Moscow would not forego opportunities or jeopardize its ties to clients in the interest of a broad accommodation with the United States. His behavior in Angola in 1974–75, in Ethiopia in 1977–78, and Cambodia in 1978–79, coming as it did with the deployments of the SS-20s in Europe, demonstrated an assertiveness designed to make the most of military power for the attainment of political objectives. The invasion of Afghanistan in December 1979 was the final straw in the collapse of détente. In retrospect, one can argue that Khrushchev's attempt to implant nuclear missiles in Cuba in the fall of 1962 was a gamble that might have brought a far-reaching change in the strategic balance of power between the United States and the Soviet Union. By contrast, none of Brezhnev's military moves could have had such an effect; indeed, their net effect was to bring on the enormous U.S. military buildup of the Reagan years, and with it the realization by a new Soviet leadership that Brezhnev had produced a stagnation so widespread that it would require major shifts in Soviet policy at home and abroad.

Gorbachev and the Crisis of Stagnation

Glasnost and perestroika had their roots in Gorbachev's determination to tackle the profound economic crisis that faced the country when he came to power in March 1985. As he later wrote, he realized that in the late 1970s the economy had begun to lose momentum and was performing badly: "Economic failures became more frequent. Difficulties began to accumulate and deteriorate, and unresolved problems to multiply. Elements of what we call stagnation and other phenomena alien to socialism began to appear in the life of society. . . . A country that was once quickly closing on the world's advanced nations began to lose one position after another. Moreover, the gap in the efficiency of production, quality of products, scientific and technological development, the production of advanced technology and the use of advanced techniques began to widen, and not to our advantage."[9]

According to one Western analyst, "Soviet GNP per capita, measured in purchasing power parity, amounted to less than a third the U.S. level in 1985 and 1986. This boosts the defense share of GNP to possibly a quarter of GNP or more."[10] Military and foreign policy expenditures were draining Soviet resources into unproductive channels, at a time when labor productivity was falling, the return on investment declining, and corruption and inefficiency growing.

Gorbachev set out to reform the system, but in the end destroyed it, without creating stable or functioning institutions in its stead. He started with political reforms, which acquired a momentum of their own, but he failed to introduce real economic reform.

Our focus here is on the evolution and dynamics of the U.S.-Soviet rivalry in the Third World. Attention to the contributory domestic and foreign developments will be kept to a minimum. Although we do not know all the influences and considerations that shaped the specifics of Gorbachev's policy toward the Third World and the rivalry there with the United States, the record is sufficiently substantial for some tentative generalizations and preliminary assessments.

Gorbachev's Third World policy went through three phases: concern over inherited problem areas, but essential continuity (March 1985 to mid-1986); new thinking and the demilitarization of regional conflicts (late 1986 to 1989); and accommodation and cooperation (1990 and 1991). Each phase had discernible characteristics and implications for U.S.-Soviet rivalry; and each was the consequence of the upheaval occurring in Soviet domestic politics and of the changes in the overall Soviet-American relationship.

Concern but Continuity: March 1985 to Mid-1986

During his first year in power, Gorbachev faced dilemmas in the Third World for which there were no obvious solutions. According to Harry Gelman, Soviet leaders saw themselves "engaged in efforts to consolidate precarious advances of the past, and they cannot disengage from these efforts without accepting setbacks that however disguised, will be generally recognized as humiliating Soviet defeats. The Gorbachev leadership perceives itself as involved in a worldwide struggle to repel U.S. efforts to eliminate a whole series of as-yet-unconsolidated Soviet geopolitical positions in the Third World staked out in the 1970s."[11]

The continuing Soviet war in Afghanistan, where more than 120,000 troops were bogged down in an endless struggle against the Mujahideen resistance, was particularly frustrating. But Soviet arms and advisers were also heavily engaged in military campaigns on behalf of beleaguered regimes in Angola, Ethiopia, and Kampuchea. Syria, Iraq, and Libya were major recipients of advanced Soviet weapons. Cuba and Vietnam commanded extensive subsidies. Involvement in Nicaragua was a continuing source of tension in U.S.-Soviet relations.

Gorbachev received Third World leaders from India, Ethiopia, Syria, Vietnam, Madagascar, Laos, Nicaragua, Mozambique, and Zimbabwe. His message was the same: the Soviet Union supports the struggle of "freedom-loving" peoples and will continue to provide assistance to these countries. His aim was to reassure prime clients of the continuity in Moscow's foreign policy. The Soviet media condemned "U.S. neoglobalism," epitomized by direct military interference in the internal affairs of Afghanistan, Angola, and Nicaragua.[12] In its year-end editorial, *Pravda* blamed the United States for "the emergence and expansion" of tensions in the Third World.[13]

In his report to the Twenty-seventh Congress of the CPSU on 26 February 1986, Gorbachev devoted less attention to the Third World than to any other part of the world or any other major foreign-policy problem facing the Soviet leadership. Of the approximately five thousand words that he devoted to the "Basic Objectives and Directions of the Party's Foreign Policy Strategy," a mere 150 touched on Third World issues, and two-thirds of these spoke of Afghanistan. He did reaffirm the CPSU's "invariable" solidarity with "the forces of national and social liberation" and close cooperation "with socialist-oriented countries, with revolutionary-democratic parties, and with the Nonaligned Movement."[14] However, since Stalin's death and Moscow's surge of involvement in the Third World, no Soviet leader had, on such an occasion, spent so little time on the "zone of peace," the national liberation movement, the various regional conflicts, and the prime targets of Soviet commitment and concern. Judging by the speech, Gorbachev's priorities were domestic problems, nuclear issues, and improvement in U.S.-Soviet relations. He gave no hint of his thinking about regional conflicts, the issues that were worsening U.S.-Soviet relations.

Gorbachev's approach suggested flexibility, but Soviet behavior in various regional conflicts demonstrated a sameness. Despite hints of disillusionment among some Soviet scholars with the benefits from subsidizing clients (even in Brezhnev's time, there had been official sanction for friendly Third World countries to expand their economic ties with Western sources, in order to ease the financial burden and pressure on Moscow), the actions of the Soviet government did not signify impending retrenchment or curtailment of commitments.

In the economic sphere, Gorbachev pushed expanded relations with India, Kuwait, Zimbabwe, Iran, and Egypt. Nothing much materialized in 1985 and 1986, but the visits of delegations and the signing of protocols reflected Moscow's desire for closer ties. Gorbachev hoped that commerce would consolidate the diplomatic ties that were established in the fall of 1985 with Oman and the United Arab Emirates, and that improved economic relationships could be established on a businesslike basis with countries that had hitherto been peripheral to Soviet diplomacy, such as Mexico, Brazil, and Singapore.

Overall, Gorbachev's activism attested to the Third World's continued importance in Soviet foreign policy. Arms transfers were still the principal currency for securing political investments. Soviet assistance was stepped up to embattled clients—Afghanistan, Ethiopia, Angola, Cambodia, and Nicaragua, who sought to stave off challenges from U.S.-backed anticommunist insurgencies.[15]

New Thinking and the Demilitarization of Regional Conflicts (1986–89)

There is merit in the argument that for the first year or so in power, Gorbachev groped for an approach to regional conflicts that was protective of Soviet stakes, yet less confrontational and more receptive to some melioration of the rivalry with the United States. More and more, the men around him, especially Foreign Minister Eduard Shevardnadze (who carried out sweeping personnel changes in the Ministry of Foreign Affairs), Anatoly Dobrynin (who had been ambassador to the United States from 1962 to 1986), and Aleksandr Yakovlev (one of the intellectual forces behind glasnost), appreciated the complexities underlying Third World conflicts and argued that it be "treated not as an arena for the advance of socialism, but rather as a problem area in East-West relations."[16] In this way, issues could be approached in other than a zero-sum fashion. There had, of course, been such voices in the late 1970s and early 1980s, but they were far removed from those in power; moreover, their writings tended to be couched in stereotypical ideological classifications and Aesopian suggestiveness.[17]

By mid-1986, three developments nudged Gorbachev toward implementing "new thinking" in the Third World arena. First, the Chernobyl nuclear disaster in April 1986 brought home to him how mismanaged and inefficient the economic and industrial infrastructure really was. The need for reform, for attracting foreign investment, for embarking on broad-based modernization was even more urgent than Gorbachev had at first thought. Second, Gorbachev's initial efforts supporting military solutions to lingering regional conflicts had proved futile: Soviet-generated military offensives in 1985 and 1986 failed to achieve their objectives. Finally, Gorbachev came to appreciate that the U.S.-Soviet rivalry in the Third World was interfering with his efforts to promote better relations with the United States and complicating his aim of a broad reconciliation with the West.

In a major speech in Vladivostok on 28 July 1986, Gorbachev accepted Beijing's preconditions for an improvement in Sino-Soviet relations: a reduction of Soviet forces in Mongolia and solutions to the festering regional conflicts in Afghanistan and Cambodia. With his announcement that by the end of the year, six regiments would "be returned to the motherland," he opened the way for UN-sponsored talks to find a political settlement acceptable to the United States and the Soviet Union.[18] To underscore the seriousness of his desire for a diplomatic solution to the festering regional conflicts that had adversely affected U.S.-Soviet relations in the past, Gorbachev stressed certain points in an interview on 23 July 1987 with the Indonesian newspaper *Merdeka*.[19] He acknowledged that each regional conflict had its own roots and its own specific cure. In regard to Afghanistan, he maintained that "in principle, the question of the withdrawal of the Soviet troops" from the country has already been decided, and "we favor a speeding up of the withdrawal." In addition, he singled out the Cambodian problem and the Iran-Iraq War as regional conflicts that needed solutions. By the time he spoke at Krasnoyarsk in September 1988, the Geneva agreements had spelled out the timetable for the withdrawal of Soviet forces from Afghanistan, regional talks under UN auspices were making progress toward settlements in Angola, Namibia, Nicaragua, and Cambodia, and the eight-year-long Iran-Iraq War had been stopped. Gorbachev's sweeping proposals included an offer to withdraw Soviet forces from Cam Ranh Bay in Vietnam in return for a U.S. withdrawal from Subic Bay and Clark Airfield in the Philippines; and a call to make the Indian Ocean a zone of peace.

When former foreign minister Eduard Shevardnadze spoke to the USSR Supreme Soviet on 24 October 1989, the U.S.-Soviet relationship in the Third World no longer had a conflictual edge to it. The fundamental pattern of hostility and rivalry had been dramatically altered. According to Shevardnadze, "It is important to stress that both the Soviet and U.S. leaderships are directing their attention to long-term prospects for increasing positive and constructive cooperation in bilateral relations and on the whole series of world problems.[20] He started by noting that free elections were scheduled for Nicaragua and that the United States would accept the results. (Perhaps surprisingly to many in Moscow and Managua, and Washington as well, the Sandinistas were defeated and relinquished power in April 1990.) Regarding Afghanistan, he noted that the Soviet withdrawal had led Soviet leaders to "adopt a new scale of evaluations and criteria of our own behavior," and these would be in accord with United Nations principles:

When more than 100 UN members kept condemning our action for a number of years, did we need anything else to make us realize: We had placed ourselves in opposition to the world community, had violated norms of behavior, and gone against common human interests.

I am of course talking about the introduction of troops into Afghanistan. There is a lesson to be learned from the fact that in this case too there were also gross violations of our own legislation and of our own intraparty and civic norms and ethics.

I am saying this as someone who was a candidate member of the CPSU Central Committee Politburo at that time. M. S. Gorbachev and I happened to be together at the time, and we learned about it from radio and newspaper reports. A decision which had grave consequences for our country was made behind the party's and the people's back.

Shevardnadze lauded the UN's role in helping to end various regional conflicts and noted that "for the first time in many years not one Soviet soldier is participating . . . in military operations anywhere in the world." And, he added, the Soviet Union was actively involved in settling regional conflicts in every part of the world.

Under Gorbachev, the Soviet leadership realized that continuation of the U.S.-Soviet rivalry in the Third World was detrimental to the aims of détente, reconciliation, and disarmament. Between 1986 and 1989, the transformation in Moscow's imperial policy in the Third World became apparent. It was manifested in four major changes in Soviet policy, which may be categorized as follows: (1) deemphasis on the military as a foreign-policy instrument; (2) acceptance of linkage in U.S.-Soviet relations; (3) encouragement of political settlements of regional conflicts; and (4) movement to reduce the costs and nature of Soviet imperial policy.[21]

Deemphasis on the military as a foreign policy instrument. The shift away from heavy reliance on the military as a means of achieving political goals is the most significant difference between Gorbachev's Third World policy and that of his predecessors. Afghanistan was the watershed. As Gorbachev said on 8 February 1988, "any armed conflict, including an internal one, can poison the atmosphere in an entire region and create a situation of anxiety and alarm for a country's neighbors. . . . That is why we are against any armed conflicts." Downgrading the military as an instrument of political influence-building in Third World regions was a prerequisite for U.S.-Soviet détente.

For their part, Soviet analysts were encouraged by glasnost and the official call for "an influx of fresh ideas" and "a scientific analysis of past experience and a study of 'blank' and 'obscure' areas" of foreign policy to write more openly and critically.[22] None, during the 1986–89 period, was as direct and unequivocal as Professor Vyacheslav Dashichev, head of the Foreign Policy Department of the USSR Academy of Sciences Institute of Economics of the World Socialist System. He was the first Soviet analyst to blame Brezhnev publicly for the collapse of détente in the 1970s and early 1980s, arguing that "the United States, paralyzed by the Vietnam debacle, reacted strongly to the expansion of Soviet influence in Africa, the Near East, and other regions":

> The expansion of the Soviet sphere of influence reached critical limits in the West's eyes with the introduction of Soviet troops in Afghanistan. . . . Could such a severe exacerbation of tension in Soviet-Western relations . . . have been avoided?
>
> Unquestionably so . . . the crisis was caused chiefly by the miscalculations and incompetent approach of the Brezhnev leadership.[23]

What was new and pathbreaking about Dashichev's critique was his reliance on a classical balance-of-power analysis to show the shortcomings of Moscow's imperial strategy. There was no obeisance to any class-based considerations:

> People, V. I. Lenin pointed out, live within a state, and every state exists within a system of states which are in a condition of a certain political equilibrium relative to one another. Any desire on the part of a major state (or bloc of states) to sharply expand its sphere of influence produced a disruption of this equilibrium. To restore it, other states united within an 'anticoalition' against the potentially or actually strongest state (in a given region or in the world). . . .
>
> The hegemonist, great-power ambitions of Stalinism repeatedly jeopardized political equilibrium between states, especially those of East and West. . . .
>
> By the early seventies the Soviet Union had reached a level of nuclear missile forces that made global nuclear conflict unacceptable to the United States. A period of East-West détente started. . . .
>
> Détente gave the Soviet Union a chance to reduce confrontation with the West and thereby prevent the buildup of the 'anti-coalition' forces. . . . It soon transpired that détente was acceptable to the United States and its allies only if the international political and military status quo was preserved.

But, argued Dashichev, Soviet policy proceeded headlong, without any clear sense of the country's true national interests.

More typical of "new thinking" were critical assessments written in the old style—that is, they were theoretical, overly generalized, heavily larded with Marxist terminology, and focused on what was happening in the Third World as a result of indigenous and Western actions, with no or little attention to the responsibility that Soviet policy bore for the existing situation. Georgy Mirsky, a senior researcher and distinguished analyst of Third World developments at the USSR Academy of Sciences Institute of World Economics and International Relations (IMEMO), asked, "Where is the Third World heading?" He acknowledged that the social sciences in the Soviet Union had depended on inadequate tools and data in the past.[24] The political leadership in the Third World (its superstructure in Marxist-Leninist terminology) and not socioeconomic relationships or the level of development had determined the "choice of paths." Mirsky discussed the weakness of the leftist forces, the failure of "socialism," and the conflicts arising out of the struggle for development, implying that Soviet policy was led astray by virtue of its incorrect assessments of these forces. Academician Yevgeny Primakov, former head of IMEMO, and an alternate member of the CPSU Central Committee and adviser to Gorbachev on Middle East affairs, asserted that "war and the use of force in general should be ruled out from interstate relations," and that "it would be wrong to reduce everything to colonialism," that regional conflicts had arisen because of other reasons as well.[25] However, very much a cautious, establishment Academician, he added that this should not be interpreted to forbid "the possibilities of national and social liberation forces from making use of every means at their disposal to ensure their legitimate rights." He was never one to get out ahead of the official line. A. Kolosovskii, a deputy foreign minister, acknowledged that regional conflicts in the Third World were a destabilizing force and that they had prevented the establishment of stable and normal relations between the United States and the Soviet Union.[26] He contended that the West's extensive economic interests explained its "many relapses into unconcealed colonialism and military approaches," but, unlike Vyacheslav Dashichev, he said nothing about the USSR's responsibility for what had occurred. From reading Aleksandr Kislov, a Middle East specialist and IMEMO's deputy director, one might conclude that the USSR was enticed into Third World conflicts by the "imperialist powers" that had sought to weaken the USSR and scatter its resources.[27] He denied that the USSR's interference was primarily prompted by "its geopolitical offensive," as Western analysis have alleged.

However, "new thinking" in Soviet academic writing lagged behind the movement in the diplomatic arena. Regional settlements outpaced the emergence of a new openness in Soviet analyses. In Afghanistan, the UN-crafted agreement ended the direct Soviet military involvement in February 1989. In Africa, Moscow's support was crucial for the success of the U.S.- and UN-brokered agreement that ended the civil war and Soviet-Cuban combat involvement in Angola in December 1988 and that brought independence to Namibia, and with it a transformation of politics in Southern Africa. Indirectly, by fostering regional settlements, Gorbachev's policy served to force the government of South Africa to free Nelson Mandela, dismantle the system of apartheid, and open talks with black leaders for democratic power-sharing reforms. The waning of Soviet support doomed the previously Soviet-subsidized dictatorial regime of Mengistu Haile Mariam in Ethiopia: Mengistu ended the war with Somalia in 1988 and, failing in his efforts to stamp out secessionist movements, fell from power in 1991. Regional settlements, certainly to the extent that foreign interference was formally ended, were also concluded in Nicaragua and Cambodia. In Syria, long a prized client, President Hafez Assad was put on notice by Gorbachev that the absence of diplomatic relations between the Soviet Union and Israel "cannot be considered normal" and that though the USSR would continue to provide arms, the Syrians had to realize that they would not be strengthened to the level of strategic parity with Israel.[28] The downgrading of military means in the Third World was in keeping with Gorbachev's call for the "demilitarization of international relations," a theme he sounded in his speech before the U.N. General Assembly in December 1988.

Acceptance of linkage in U.S.-Soviet relations. Unlike previous Soviet leaders, Gorbachev accepted that there was a contradiction between the USSR's projection of power in the Third World and its attempts to improve relations with the United States. As noted earlier, the most direct ascription of culpability to Moscow for the failure of détente was Dashichev's in May 1988. Dashichev's explicit linking of Soviet behavior to the West's hostility is still the exception in Russian writings on the Third World. During the 1986–89 period, focused attention to this subject was more apt to be found in Soviet journals and on Moscow radio and television programs than in serious academic writings. Scholars such as Viktor Kremenyuk of the USSR Academy of Sciences Institute of the USA and Canada and Aleksei Vasil'ev of its African Institute were among the few who forthrightly admitted that problems were created by the USSR's imperial rivalry with the United States, that Moscow often failed to take into consideration a "balance of interests," and that Moscow was to blame for an excessive funneling of arms to clients in the belief "that the more arms you pour into a country the greater the influence, including political influence, you win there."[29]

Growing recognition of the importance of linkage was also evident in Moscow's repeated calls for U.S.-Soviet cooperation to solve regional conflicts and problems, and in the wide-ranging and continuous discussions that took place between American and Soviet officials. The relationship between Secretary of State James Baker and Foreign Minister Eduard Shevardnadze became quite close, based on trust and respect. The implication of this changed attitude was that if the superpowers were to cooperate in the Third World, not only would they be able to end or sharply limit the cycle of ever-more-costly and dangerous regional conflicts, but their own relationship would not suffer as it had in the past.

Encouragement of political settlements of regional conflicts. In addition to promoting the resolution of those regional conflicts noted earlier (Afghanistan, Angola, Nicaragua, Cambodia, the Horn of Africa), the USSR made a concerted diplomatic effort to establish contacts with all sides in other regional disputes in the interest of fostering negotiated settlements. Gorbachev inched toward the restoration of diplomatic relations with Israel, exchanging de facto consular missions. He helped persuade PLO chairman Yasser Arafat to state publicly, as he did in Geneva in December 1988, his acknowledgment of Israel's right to exist, acceptance of UN Security Council resolutions 242 and 338, and renunciation of terrorism.

In the Persian Gulf, Moscow joined with the UN Security Council in passing resolution 598, which served as the basis for the cease-fire that was eventually arranged in August 1988 and ended the fighting between Iraq and Iran. In this instance, however, its policy was not as disinterested as in Angola, possessing a competitive as well as a cooperative aspect: "Playing a complicated double game of trying to improve relations with both sides of the conflict, the Soviets sought to weaken American efforts to build a consensus against Iran, while positioning themselves to pose as mediators to end the war."[30]

At a conference on foreign policy and diplomacy held for his staff on 25 July 1988 and devoted to an examination of key shortcomings and requirements of Soviet diplomacy in the era of perestroika, Shevardnadze stated that, given "the overriding task of diplomacy—to seek friends for the country or at least not acquire enemies," one priority was "to conduct energetic dialogue and talks with all countries without exception on the main areas of world politics."[31] Moscow's adherence to this principle, as in talks with Israelis and South Africans, counseling moderation to the PLO, courting countries with which it had strained relations in the past (Iran, Egypt, Sudan, Chile, and Indonesia), and reiterating the inappropriateness of military means for the realization of diplomatic ends, was integral to Gorbachev's policy of conveying to client and competitor alike his serious interest in finding peaceful solutions to regional conflicts. By the end of 1989, he had profoundly altered the policy he had inherited.

Movement toward reducing the costs and nature of Soviet imperial policy. Underlying Gorbachev's policy of perestroika was the conviction that resources had to be redirected from unproductive military and political purposes to the economic and social development of Soviet society. Significant cuts were essential not only at home in the military sector but also abroad in subsidies to prime clients like Cuba and Vietnam. As Melvin Goodman has noted, "Escalating costs of aid to Third World economies as well as large foreign debts have caused the Soviets to become increasingly impatient with poor economic performance":

> In addition to Soviet criticism of economic management of some of Moscow's closest Third World clients, Soviet commentators have acknowledged shortcomings in assistance programs to the Third World. Few Soviet clients have the infrastructure to absorb Moscow's large mineral and metals processing plants or massive hydropower installations, and Soviet agricultural and industrial technology is not easily transferred to tropical countries with small-scale industry. . . . The USSR's credit terms are no longer as favorable as Western terms (Soviet credit terms are based on 17 years to repay; Western countries allow an average of 30) and only a small percentage of Soviet programs are established as grant aid. (More than half of Soviet aid programs are in ten countries; Western countries extend aid to more than 150.)[32]

After returning from a trip to Africa in March 1990, Shevardnadze deplored the quality of Soviet assistance and goods and the past reliance on "pseudo support" in the form of "weapons and arms, mainly."[33] Partially in response to complaints voiced in the Soviet parliament, President Mikhail Gorbachev issued a decree on 24 July 1990 requiring that "economic assistance shall be given with due regard for our country's actual possibilities."[34] This put "socialist" clients on notice that aid and trade would be increasingly determined by principles of "mutual advantage and mutual interests," and not for strategic or political reasons. Moscow's overextension of its resources was forcing a retraction of its imperial outreach.

Cost-reduction efforts, suggestive rather than substantive in the late 1980s, by 1990 and 1991 took on unconcealed urgency, as the Soviet economy declined from stagnation to quasi-anarchy in the wake of a rise of ethnic assertiveness and the disintegration of political stability. According to INTERFAX, the reliable independent news agency that had emerged as a competitor to TASS, the USSR's major debtors in the Third World were Cuba, Vietnam, Mongolia, Iraq, India, Syria, Afghanistan, Yemen, Nicaragua, Ethiopia, and Algeria; and virtually all of them were falling behind with their debt repayments.[35] Moscow could no longer afford the costs of an imperial policy. Economic collapse at home ended the willingness to assume burdens in pursuit of foreign policy goals. What was possible in the 1970s—when the rise in the price of oil brought windfall accumulations of hard currency, and arms sales could be partially paid for by wealthy Third World clients—was no longer possible in the USSR's reduced economic circumstances of the early 1990s.

Accommodation and Cooperation: 1990–91

By 1990 Gorbachev was committed to a historic accommodation with the United States and a comprehensive reconciliation with Western Europe. As a concomitant to his negotiation of major arms control agreements, termination of Moscow's empire in Eastern Europe, and unification of Germany, he moved from rivalry to cooperation in the Third World. The Persian Gulf War proved conclusively that the Soviet Union and the United States were no longer adversaries. Not only did Moscow not oppose the U.S. policy of reversing Saddam Hussein's aggression against Iraq, it actually supported through the UN Security Council a progressively increased pressure against Iraq. Moscow's support of various UN resolutions made possible the U.S.-organized international coalition that defeated Saddam Hussein, though Soviet scholars chose not to mention this fact to avoid angering the Iraqis.[36] Perhaps nothing illustrated more convincingly the end of Moscow's perception of an American threat; no longer could Moscow justify an imperial policy aimed at undermining U.S. positions and interests in the Third World.

Soviet retrenchment was unmistakable: assistance to Cuba and Vietnam was cut back, as much a consequence of domestic instability as strategic design; advisers and arms to Ethiopia, Mozambique, Nicaragua, and other lesser clients were also sharply reduced. Moscow was no longer willing, or able, to bear the costs of an activist policy in the Third World: the combination of the desire for improved relations with the United States, the urgency of domestic concerns, the costs of maintaining a forward policy, and the obvious political disadvantages of doing so placed a premium on cooperation with the United States in the Third World.

Whatever hopes Gorbachev had for hanging on to the essentials of the dearly bought Soviet position in the Third World were rudely shattered by the unanticipated consequences of the abortive coup of 19–21 August 1991 mounted against him by close party associates. When the coup collapsed and Gorbachev was returned to Moscow from detention at his summer residence in the Crimea, history was already dropping the final curtain on the entity known as the Union of Soviet Socialist Republics.

On 13 September 1991 the Soviet Union and the United States agreed to stop all arms transfers to their clients in Afghanistan by 1 January 1992. This climaxed two years of inconclusive bargaining, in the aftermath of the formal Soviet military withdrawal. The agreement was a function of Gorbachev's increased need for U.S. economic assistance, the purging of hard-line, conservative elements on whom he had depended up to the time of the coup, and the desire of both parties to put the Afghan battleground behind them. In September, too, Moscow hinted at further cutbacks in assistance to Cuba, Vietnam, and other clients. On 18 October, Secretary of State Baker and Foreign Minister Boris Pankin announced in Jerusalem that invitations were being sent under their joint sponsorship to Israel and the main Arab parties to the Arab-Israeli conflict to attend an international conference on the Middle East which would open in Madrid on 30 October 1991. Moscow also used the occasion to restore formal diplomatic relations with Israel. Although the impetus for the conference came from Washington, Moscow's involvement was important symbolically. It made the exclusion of the UN and the European Community possible and facilitated the participation of Syria and the PLO.[37]

In his attempt to restore the health of a sick society, Gorbachev shed forty-five years of rivalry, an ideological tradition, and an imperial system. The Third World, instead of being a battleground, became a proving ground where Soviet accommodation would, he hoped, elicit the credits, the diplomatic support, and the entrée into international economic organizations such as the World Bank, IMF, and GATT that the Soviet Union desperately needed. He may even have projected an approach to economically viable or well-off Third World countries (Iran, Iraq, Algeria, Saudi Arabia, the Gulf emirates, Mexico, Indonesia, and the like), in which closer economic relations would contribute to the USSR's rejuvenation. However, the post-coup chain of destabilizing events made moot the strategy that may have guided Gorbachev's policy. The dissolution of the Communist Party of the Soviet Union, the rejection of Marxism-Leninism and the ideological underpinnings of the Soviet sociopolitical and economic system, the unstoppable separatist surge in Ukraine, Armenia, Georgia, and elsewhere, the growing ethnic violence, the worsening economic plight, and the final scene in the power struggle between Mikhail Gorbachev and Boris Yeltsin—these diffused power, threw the legitimacy of existing institutions into doubt, and mortally weakened Gorbachev.

Epilogue

The end came with breathtaking suddenness. On 9 December 1991 the presidents of Belarus, Russia, and Ukraine met in Minsk, declared "that the USSR has ceased to exist as a subject of international law and as a geopolitical reality," and formed a commonwealth.[38] The president of the USSR, Mikhail Gorbachev, disputed the authority of the three presidents to act without having the matter resolved according to constitutional methods and "with due regard for the will of their people."[39] But driven by the overwhelming mandate for independence shown in the referendum held on 1 December in Ukraine and by Yeltsin's determination to sweep Gorbachev off the political stage, eleven republics (only Georgia and the Baltic states refused to join) agreed at Alma-Ata on 21 December 1991, to the creation of the Commonwealth of Independent States (CIS). On 25 December Gorbachev resigned as president of the Soviet Union, insisting that although he favored "the independence of nations and sovereignty for the republics" he at the same time supported "the preservation of the union state and the integrity of this country." Six years and nine months after becoming absolute ruler of the Soviet Union, he presided over the end of communism and of the communist system that Lenin had founded.

The demise of the Soviet Union ushers in a period of enormous uncertainty. Unlike other empires of this century, the Soviet empire collapsed because of actions by a leadership dedicated to its reform, and not as a result of defeat in war. The historian Walter McDougall asks, will the post–Cold War era see a renewal of "economic competition among the capitalist states reminiscent of the rival imperialisms of 1871–1914?":

> So long as the ex-superpowers refrain from isolationism, the potential for conflict will always remain. The United States, being a naval and commercial power and the world's largest economy, will continue to have far-flung, if not global, interests. The Russian state will continue to be absorbed in the politics of Eastern Europe, the Middle East, the Gulf, the Indo-Persian Corridor, and the northwest Pacific. But one can hope, at least, that while regional conflicts in the world may increase, Russian-American tensions and proxy battles may not.[40]

If the Commonwealth of Independent States takes hold and transforms the relationships of the former union republics of the USSR into a dozen independent and loosely connected states with internationally recognized and legally delineated borders, the geopolitics of central Asia and the Middle East will have been profoundly changed. In that event, Russia would no longer be a Middle East power, because the exercise of true independence (the end of Moscow's control, the creation of national armies, and the conduct of independent foreign policies) by Georgia, Armenia, and Azerbaijan in the Caucasus, and by Kazakhstan, Turkmenistan, Uzbekistan, Kyrgyzstan, and Tajikistan in Central Asia would separate the republic of Russia from the Middle East. Turkey, Iran, and Afghanistan, which have lain in the shadow of Russian/Soviet military power throughout the nineteenth and twentieth centuries, would no longer face a perennial imperialist threat from the north. Success of the CIS would mark the end of Russia's 450-year-old multiethnic empire.

However, if the CIS proves ephemeral and, after a period of reorganization, if the potential of Russia is harnessed to a new surge of expansion in search of security against foreign attack and for the Russian ethnic groups that dot the Central Asian landscape, a return to familiar great-power politics and rivalry is likely. In any event, whether the CIS succeeds or fails, the phenomenon of Islamic self-assertiveness in Central Asia and the Caucasus is inevitable, though the character of these emerging Islamic states is far from discernible at this preliminary and transitory stage. Probably all that can be said with some sense of optimism is that for the foreseeable future, at least, the politics and ambitions of small and medium states will overshadow those of the great powers on the Central Asian–Middle Eastern heartland region, which has attracted so much strategic speculation in this century.[41]

The leaderships of small countries have it in their grasp to develop internal cohesiveness and friendly ties with great powers, and thereby to secure their newly found independence. This will require wisdom and an absorption with building for the future rather than dwelling on the past.

Notes

1. For example, see Dietrich Geyer, *Russian Imperialism: The Interaction of Domestic and Foreign Policy 1860–1914* (New Haven, Conn.: Yale University Press, 1987). Geyer's analysis examines czarist expansionism, but also decision-making influences, economic influences, and domestic unrest. A more traditional focus on expansionism in quest of territory is David Gillard, *The Struggle for Asia 1828–1914: A Study in British and Russian Imperialism* (London: Methuen, 1977). Gillard's narrative traces the expansion of Russia and England across the Eurasian land mass.

2. For studies that do not make this distinction, see for example, Michael W. Doyle, *Empires* (Ithaca, N.Y.: Cornell University Press, 1986), chapter 1; and Benjamin J. Cohen, *The Question of Imperialism* (New York: Basic Books, 1973), chapters 1 and 2.

3. In a recent memoir, Academician Georgii A. Arbatov writes that the decision was made by Leonid Brezhnev, Dmitrii F. Ustinov, Andrei Gromyko, and Yuri Andropov; he also attributes particular importance to Ustinov's insistence on a military intervention, even to the point of overriding the advice of top Soviet military leaders. G. A. Arbatov, *Zatyanuvshcheesya vzydorovleniye (1953–1985): svidetel'stvo sovremennika* (Overly long recovery, 1953–1985: testimony of a contemporary) (Moscow: Mezhdunarodnye Otnosheniya, 1991), 229–30. In 1989, Red Army general Valentin I. Varrenikov stated that Defense Minister Ustinov overruled his military advisers, but he did not try to explain Ustinov's motivations (*New York Times*, 19 March 1989). Other accounts include Mikhail Suslov, the party ideologist, as a pivotal decision maker. See also Cynthia Roberts, "Glasnost in Soviet Foreign Policy: Setting the Record Straight?" *Report on the USSR* (15 December 1989): 4–8.

4. For example, see Bruce R. Kuniholm, *The Origins of the Cold War in*

the Near East: Great Power Conflict and Diplomacy in Iran, Turkey, and Greece (Princeton: Princeton University Press, 1980).

5. Royal Institute of International Affairs, *Documents on International Affairs 1953* (London: Oxford University Press, 1956), 277–78.

6. Alvin Z. Rubinstein, *Moscow's Third World Strategy* (Princeton: Princeton University Press, 1990), 127–28.

7. See Bradford Dismukes and James M. McConnell, eds., *Soviet Naval Diplomacy* (New York: Pergamon Press, 1979); Bryan Ranft and Geoffrey Till, *The Sea in Soviet Strategy* (Annapolis, Md.: Naval Institute Press, 1983); and Robert Waring Herrick, *Soviet Naval Theory and Policy: Gorshkov's Inheritance* (Annapolis, Md.: Naval Institute Press, 1988), esp. chapters 7 and 8.

8. S. G. Gorshkov, *The Sea Power of the State* (Annapolis, Md.: Naval Institute Press, 1979), xi.

9. Mikhail Gorbachev, *Perestroika: New Thinking for Our Country and the World* (New York: Harper and Row, 1987), 5.

10. Anders Aslund, "How Small is Soviet National Income?" in Henry S. Rowen and Charles Wolf, Jr., eds., *The Impoverished Superpower: Perestroika and the Soviet Military Burden* (San Francisco: ICS Press, 1990), 49. The other essays show the Soviet military's inordinate consumption of the country's resources, to the detriment of all other sectors of society. Soviet and Western economists have confirmed the basic findings, in many cases presenting even more doleful assessments of the Soviet economy's plight.

11. Harry Gelman, "Gorbachev's Dilemmas and His Conflicting Foreign Policy Goals," *Orbis* 30, no. 2 (Summer 1986): 241.

12. *Pravda*, 26 December 1985, 5.

13. *Pravda*, 31 December 1985.

14. The text of Gorbachev's speech in the translation of the Foreign Broadcast Information Service: FBIS/Party Congress, 26 February 1986, O-33.

15. David B. Ottaway, *Washington Post*, 11 June 1986.

16. Francis Fukuyama, *Gorbachev and the New Soviet Agenda in the Third World* (Santa Monica, Calif.: RAND Corporation, June 1989), 13. See also Viktor Yasmann, "The New Soviet Thinking in Regional Conflicts: Ideology and Politics," *Radio Liberty Research*, 3 December 1987, 3.

17. The nuances of these esoteric debates among leading Soviet scholars have been carefully examined by Western scholars such as David Albright, Galia Golan, Jerry Hough, Roger Kanet, Robert Legvold, and Elizabeth Valkenier. One of the best, and generally overlooked, Soviet books is V. P. Lukin, *Tsentry sily: kontsepsii i real'nost'* (Center of power: conceptions and reality) (Moscow: Mezhdunarodnye otnosheniia, 1983). Lukin, who is now active in the Russian Foreign Ministry, offered an analysis of an emerging politically

multipolar system that contrasted starkly with the essentially bipolar, dichotomous Marxist-Leninist formulations of Soviet establishmentarian orthodoxy. He disagreed with, for example, Yevgeny Primakov, who saw emerging Third World power centers for the most part as U.S. proxies. He also downgraded the use of force as an instrument of foreign policy long before this was embraced by Gorbachev.

18. *FBIS/USSR National Affairs*, 29 July 1986, R-18–R-19.

19. *FBIS/SOV*, 23 July 1987, CC7–CC8.

20. *FBIS/SOV*, 24 October 1989, 42–51.

21. This section is drawn from Rubinstein, *Moscow's Third World Strategy*, epilogue.

22. See, for example, Eduard Shevardnadze's speech in July 1988. "The Nineteenth All-Union CPSU Conference: Foreign Policy and Diplomacy," *International Affairs*, no. 10 (October 1988).

23. Vyacheslav Dashichev, "Vostok-Zapad: poisk novykh otnoshenii" (East-West: the search for new relations), *Literaturnaya Gazeta* (18 May 1988), 14. See also Andrei Kozyrev, "Confidence and the Balance of Interests," *International Affairs*, no. 11 (November 1988): 3–12.

24. G. Mirsky, "K voprosy o vybore puti i orientatsii razvivayushchikhsia stran" (On the problem of the path and orientation of developing countries), *Mirovaya ekonomika i mezhdunarodnye otnosheniye* (hereafter cited as *MEMO*), no. 5 (May 1987): 77–81; see also "Avtoritarizm i vlast' voennykh 'tret'em mire'," (Authoritarianism and military power in 'the third world'), *MEMO*, no. 7 (July 1989): 44–54.

25. Yevgeni Primakov, "USSR Policy on Regional Conflicts," *International Affairs*, no. 6 (June 1988): 3–9.

26. A. Kolosovskii, "Regionalnye konflikty i globalnaya bezopasnosti" (Regional conflicts and global security), *MEMO*, no. 6 (June 1988): 32–41.

27. A. Kislov, "Novoe politicheskoe myshlenie i regionalyne konflikty" (New political thinking and regional conflicts), *MEMO*, no. 8 (August 1988): 39–40.

28. *FBIS/USSR International Affairs*, 28 April 1987, H7.

29. See "The USSR and the Third World," *International Affairs*, no. 12 (December 1988): 137–41.

30. Fukuyama, *Gorbachev and the New Soviet Agenda*, 42–43.

31. "The Nineteenth All-Union CPSU Conference," 21.

32. Melvin A. Goodman, *Gorbachev's Retreat: The Third World* (New York: Praeger, 1991), 156.

33. *FBIS/SOV*, 26 April 1990, 9.

34. *Izvestiya*, 24 July 1990.

35. *FBIS-SOV: National Affairs*, 6 December 1991, 36.

36. For example, see Victor Kuvaldin, "Long Echo of the Short War," *International Affairs,* no. 7 (July 1991): 20–29. On the other hand, it should be noted that among Soviet critics of Gorbachev, perestroika, and "new thinking," there were those who deplored the alacrity with which he deferred to U.S. wishes and accelerated the USSR's imperial decline: for example, V. Lukashevich, *Krasnaya zvezda,* 25 May 1991, and A. Golts, *Krasnaya zvezda,* 13 June 1991, as translated in *FBIS/SOV,* 4 June 1991, 13–15, and 17 June 1991, 6–8, respectively.

37. Thomas L. Friedman, *New York Times,* 30 October 1991.

38. *FBIS/SOV,* 10 December 1991, 56.

39. Ibid., 15.

40. Walter A. McDougall, "Speculations on the Geopolitics of the Gorbachev Era," in A. J. Rieber and A. Z. Rubinstein, eds., *Perestroika at the Crossroads* (Armonk, N.Y.: M. E. Sharpe, 1991), 353.

41. Milan Hauner, *What is Asia to Us?: Russia's Asian Heartland Yesterday and Today* (Boston: Unwin Hyman, 1990).

Chapter 8 ━━━━━━━━━━━━━━━━━━━━━━━━━━

America's Post–Cold War Military Policy in the Third World

Mark N. Katz

The Third World was an extremely important arena in the Cold War competition between the United States and the Soviet Union. Both sides frequently employed military means in their contest for influence in Asia, Africa, and Latin America. These included arms transfers, the dispatch of military advisers, the acquisition of bases or "facilities," support for allied military intervention, and, on occasion, direct super-power military intervention. While nuclear weapons and Europe were arguably more important arenas of superpower competition, the Third World was the most active. Those who feared a wider conflict between the United States and the USSR often foresaw it resulting from a Third World clash that escalated uncontrollably. Although Soviet-American rivalry in the Third World never did escalate into a direct conflict between the superpowers, it appeared that such might occur on some occasions—most notably, during the 1962 Cuban missile crisis.

A key feature of the Cold War in the Third World was the fierce competition between the superpowers for allies. Each one actively sought to maintain its existing allies and to convert the other side's allies into its own. All Third World countries became "vital" to the two superpowers. Even if a particular Third World country was not especially important itself, it was often located near countries that interested Washington and Moscow more. Neither superpower was willing to accept that a Third World state could remain truly non-aligned. Each tried to ensure that a Third World nation's nonalignment leaned toward it and not its rival.

At the beginning of the Cold War in 1945, virtually the entire Third

World was in the American sphere of influence; almost none of it was in the Soviet sphere. As the Cold War progressed, however, America tended to lose allies as the Soviet Union tended to gain them. This trend culminated in the 1970s, when pro-Soviet Marxist regimes came to power in several countries in Asia, Africa, and Latin America. The Soviets, of course, lost allies on several occasions. Moscow also struggled mightily, and in the end ineffectually, to retain many of its Marxist allies during the 1980s.

Despite Moscow's problems in the Third World throughout the Cold War, and its ultimate withdrawal from it at the end, policy makers in Washington regarded the United States as on the defensive against aggressive Soviet diplomacy and support for insurgency in Asia, Africa, and Latin America. There was great fear in Washington that the emergence of a Marxist regime in even the poorest Third World country would enable Moscow to spread revolution or otherwise gain influence in more important neighboring countries. Thus, each and every Third World country was militarily important to the United States, if only because of Washington's fear of what would happen if that country became a Soviet ally.

The Cold War is now over. Soviet influence in the Third World has essentially vanished. Indeed, the Soviet Union itself disappeared in 1991, and Moscow has essentially abandoned the few remaining communist governments in the Third World that were traditional allies—Cuba, Vietnam, and North Korea. Soviet-American competition in the Third World has completely ended. Indeed, Moscow and Washington have collaborated on a number of efforts at regional conflict resolution, some more successful than others. While there were differences in how Washington and Moscow responded to the Iraqi invasion of Kuwait, Moscow voted in favor of the UN Security Council resolution authorizing the American-led military intervention against Iraq, an action which would have been virtually inconceivable during the Cold War.

Russia and the other former Soviet republics are now experiencing an acute economic crisis. Moscow could not compete now with Washington for influence in the Third World even if it wanted to. It is highly doubtful, however, that the Cold War will reemerge at any time in the foreseeable future. If Russia evolves into an established democracy, Moscow is likely to see its interests served through close political and economic cooperation with the West. Under these circumstances, Russia would have no interest in competing with the West for influence in the Third World in a way that would damage Moscow's relations with the West. A democratic Russia is unlikely to see any net advantage resulting from influence in the Third World that would compensate it for poor relations with the West. This does not mean that a democratic Russia would have no interests in the Third World. It is likely, though, to pursue those interests in coordination with the West rather than in competition with it. If anything, a democratic Russia is likely to see the Third World as a competitor for aid, trade, and investment from the West.

At present, it seems much more likely that Russia will continue along the path toward democracy, if only because the attempt to reimpose a dictatorship appears highly difficult to initiate and sustain, as the coup plotters of August 1991 learned. If some form of dictatorial regime does reemerge in Russia, however, the Cold War will not necessarily be revived. The August 1991 plotters were plainly signaling the West that they would not alter Gorbachev's foreign policy course.[1] A dictatorial regime in Russia would also want Western economic assistance during the current economic crisis, which it probably could not resolve by itself. Even if hostile East-West relations did recur, there would not necessarily be a revived Cold War in the Third World. A dictatorial regime in Moscow would probably be too preoccupied with suppressing domestic opposition, especially if it tried to bring the non-Russian republics back under its rule. Under these circumstances, Moscow would probably be unable to divert military resources to the Third World away from its own internal security needs.

If indeed Russia is likely to be unwilling or unable to compete vigorously with the United States for influence in Asia, Africa, and Latin America, what does this mean for American military policy toward the Third World?

During the Cold War, Soviet commentators often described American foreign policy as "imperialist." This, however, is not the predominant view in the former USSR now. There are many in the Third World, though, who still think of the United States as an imperialist power. Third World Marxists saw the USSR as a bulwark against American expansionism during the Cold War. Many non-Marxists in the Third World viewed the Cold War as a process by which the two superpowers acted to limit each other's expansionism. Many in the Third World believe the collapse of the Soviet Union means that there is no longer another superpower available to check American expansionism. Further, there is considerable fear that the U.S.-led defeat of Saddam Hussein's armed forces signals the ends of America's "Vietnam syndrome," and that America's post–Cold War interventions in Panama and the Gulf mark the beginning of an expansionist phase in U.S. foreign policy.

There are, however, important factors that militate against increased American interventionism in the post–Cold War era. A close study of the period reveals that American policy makers undertook military intervention in the Third World in order to halt what they considered to be Soviet expansionism. Sometimes what America intervened against was not in fact Soviet expansionism. Those American policy makers responsible for intervention, though, always believed that they were acting to "halt the spread of communism."

The collapse of the Soviet Union, of course, means that there is no longer a global Soviet threat to American interests. Since Soviet expansionism has come to an end, intervention to halt it is no longer necessary.

Of course, those who argue that the United States is an imperialist power see the collapse of the Soviet Union not as a disincentive to American intervention, but as providing an opportunity for it to expand. This view, however, does not adequately account for the role that public opinion plays in American foreign policy making. Even during the Cold War, the American public often demonstrated its opposition to intervention. This was shown not only by its demand that the United States withdraw from the Vietnam conflict, but also by congressional unwillingness to sanction U.S. military involvement in the Third World thereafter. Congress, for example, ended military assistance to the anti-Soviet forces in Angola (1975–76) and limited American military assistance to the Nicaraguan contras during the 1980s. Members of the Reagan administration found ways to aid the Nicaraguan rebels covertly and illegally during the mid-1980s, but this assistance was halted when the Iran-contra operation became public knowledge.

The American public and Congress became less willing to sanction military intervention or assistance, sometimes even when the White House claimed that it was necessary to counter the threat of Soviet expansion. Either the American public did not always believe that Soviet expansionism was actually occurring, or they doubted that it challenged American interests sufficiently to justify the human and material cost required to halt it. Indeed, it was these costs that contributed to serious domestic economic and political problems in the United States and led American politicians to fear the consequences of involvement in a protracted conflict.

At present, and probably into the future, the American public is only likely to sanction military intervention under two conditions: (1) when the public is persuaded that there is a direct, imminent threat to American vital interests for which it considers a significant human and material cost worthwhile; or (2) when intervention advances a less important aim, but succeeds in such a short period of time that effective opposition does not have time to develop.

The risk that any American administration contemplating intervention abroad faces is that if it becomes prolonged, the public will not support it, leading to negative consequences at the polls. Thus, a sensible administration is likely to avoid any intervention in pursuit of a less-than-vital interest when it is likely to be at all prolonged and to involve anything more than a minimal loss of American lives. Yet even when the public is persuaded that a vital interest is at stake and it is willing to support a large-scale intervention, the administration will not necessarily rush to intervene. For no matter how popular intervention may be at first, domestic support may decline dramatically if it becomes prolonged and costly.

There have been cases where American intervention has succeeded in a very short period and at a relatively low cost—Grenada and Panama are the most recent examples. It is doubtful, however, that there are many places where intervening forces could achieve their objective so quickly and easily. Under what conditions would the American public support large-scale intervention in the post–Cold War era? There is no longer a Soviet Union to pose a global threat to American interests. Indeed, presidents Bush and Yeltsin all but declared that Russia and America had become allies—an attitude that President Clinton also shares.[2] If another state attempted to achieve global dominance as the Soviet Union did in the past, a new Cold War would emerge and the Third World would probably be an important arena of competition in it. At present, however, no other state appears either desirous or capable of attempting to achieve global dominance.

If the American public was often unwilling to support intervention when there was a threat to global hegemony, it is doubtful that it would support large-scale intervention at a time when there is no such threat. What American interests, then, are so vital that an American administration would risk and the American public would tolerate large-scale and perhaps prolonged conflict to defend them?

Different Americans will answer this questions differently. A debate is now occurring not only about what America's vital interests are in the Third World, but even whether there are any. Although it may wound the *amour propre* of many in the Third World to realize it, the reason this debate is occurring is that the Third World was primarily important to the United States in the context of the Cold War. With its end, some Americans have argued that the Third World, or at least most of it, possesses no intrinsic value to the United States. Others see it as a potential source of threat through the possible proliferation of nuclear weapons and other means of mass destruction. There are many other points of view as well.

What follows is my own view of what Washington and the American public are likely to view as U.S. vital interests in the Third World. In my view, these are four: (1) deterrence of conflict involving weapons of mass destruction; (2) prevention of efforts to achieve regional hegemony; (3) maintenance of Western access to the world's sea lines of communication (SLOCs); and (4) maintenance of Western access to oil.

Weapons of Mass Destruction

All countries, including the United States, seek to avoid being attacked by weapons of mass destruction. During the Cold War, the United States devoted considerable effort to deterring such an attack against America or its allies by the Soviet Union, which possessed nuclear and chemical weapons arsenals, and which had a biological weapons capability too. With the end of the Cold War, the American fear of a Russian attack has all but disappeared, as has the Russian fear of an American attack.

Even during the Cold War, however, the USSR, the United States, and their closest allies held a common fear of nuclear weapons proliferation beyond the existing nuclear weapons states. In 1968, the superpowers jointly sponsored the Non-Proliferation Treaty (NPT), through which all non-nuclear states adhering to it agreed to renounce the acquisition of nuclear weapons forever.

With the Cold War now over, and with the spread of weapons

technology to many countries, America, Russia, and other Western nations have become increasingly concerned about the acquisition of weapons of mass destruction by Third World states. Whether such a concern is just or legitimate can be debated; that this concern exists in the West, however, cannot be denied.

The United States has sought to prevent the spread of nuclear weapons to the Third World through diplomatic efforts aimed at encouraging those states which have not yet ratified the NPT to do so. At the same time, the United States has coordinated with its allies an effort to deny technology and resources that could be used in a nuclear weapons program to those states that have refused to sign the NPT.

In my view, this effort is unlikely to succeed. Relatively rich nations determined to acquire nuclear weapons may well be able to do so. And although the production of nuclear weapons is a long, complex process, chemical and biological weapons can be made relatively easily. Several Third World states already possess weapons of mass destruction, and many more can and probably will acquire them in the near future.

It has been observed that up to now, states possessing nuclear weapons have sought to avoid war with each other. Some believe this trend can continue into the future. Others, however, doubt whether it will continue if more states acquire nuclear capability.

Except under the most exceptional circumstances, the only rational response for America and any other power fearing a nuclear threat in the Third World will be the same one that America and its allies adopted toward a nuclear Soviet Union: deterrence and containment. If the Soviet Union, which was the most powerfully armed nuclear state in the world, did not launch a nuclear attack against the West because it feared an overwhelming American second strike, it is highly doubtful that a much less well armed Third World state would think it could launch a nuclear attack against an established nuclear power and avoid massive retaliation.

Notwithstanding the rhetoric about North-South conflict, Third World nations appear to have fewer disputes with the advanced developed countries than with one another. The main danger of nuclear proliferation in the Third World is not from North-South nuclear confrontation, but from conflict between Third World nations involving nuclear weapons. The temptation to use, or threaten to use, these weapons may be especially great in conflicts where one side possesses them while the other does not.

Nations which acquire nuclear weapons and behave in a manner their neighbors consider aggressive are likely to find those neighbors rushing to initiate or strengthen alliances with the great powers of the West. Indeed, those nations feeling threatened by nuclear-armed neighbors may well request protection from the established great powers. Simple possession of nuclear weapons, then, may not necessarily give states a significant military advantage over their neighbors. Indeed, the proliferation of nuclear and other weapons of mass destruction may result in America and its allies' gaining and retaining a greater degree of military access to Third World countries than would have occurred otherwise in the post–Cold War world.

The proliferation of weapons of mass destruction in the Third World, then, is not likely to lead to direct American military intervention to halt or reverse this trend. Instead, it will lead to an American-led effort to deter attacks on the North and the North's allies in the South through maintaining the ability to launch an overwhelming retaliatory attack.

The Threat of Regional Hegemony

With the end of the Cold War, no power now threatens to achieve global hegemony. However, several Third World powers could seek control of their particular region. Saddam Hussein's Iraq is an obvious example of a state that has attempted this recently and may well try again.

The United States and its allies can be expected to oppose the efforts of any state to achieve regional hegemony, not just because this might threaten Western interests in that region, but also for fear that any state that did achieve regional dominance could all the more easily act to harm Western interests beyond that region. For the most part, however, the American public is unlikely to tolerate direct U.S. military involvement to counter a potential regional power in most areas of the Third World which it did not think was linked to a global effort to achieve hegemony.

Attempts to achieve regional hegemony, however, will probably not require direct Western military intervention in most instances. Such attempts are likely to be resisted most actively by the countries neighboring the aspiring hegemon that are its targets; they are likely to turn to America and its allies for military assistance to counter their expansionist neighbor. In most instances, this Western military assistance should be able to help such states thwart the ambitions of an aspiring regional hegemon.

But as American intervention to drive Iraqi forces out of Kuwait shows, there are occasions when the American public will support direct intervention to halt regional expansionism. This case, however, is probably an exception. To begin with, the Persian Gulf region is considered particularly vital to American interests. It is difficult to think of other regions that Americans would regard as being similarly vital. In addition, the Iraqi threat to the relatively weak Gulf Cooperation Council (GCC) states was so great that they could not possibly have defended themselves successfully without external assistance. Although there may be other instances in which a very large state quickly overwhelms a small one, this is probably not the typical situation that will arise. In a more even contest, the defenders could probably hold off the attacking forces either with their own resources or with military assistance (but not direct intervention) from abroad.

Access to Sea Lines of Communication

The United States has a long tradition as a maritime nation, dependent on trade with other nations to maintain its military and economic strength. Historically, the United States has not tolerated any attempt to restrict its access to any international waterway, a principle that is likely to remain part of American policy indefinitely.

American policy seeks to maintain the "freedom of the seas" not just for trade purposes, but also to maintain naval access to the rest of the world. In the post–Cold War era, the United States may come to value this naval access even more highly than before. Now that there is no longer a threat of Soviet expansionism, countries which hosted American military facilities in the past may no longer be willing to do so; the Philippines is one example. Furthermore, strong domestic pressure is growing in the United States to reduce the costs of maintaining bases abroad by bringing American troops home.

If there is to be an American military presence abroad in the future, it may well be primarily a naval one. With only a handful of foreign military facilities, the navy can be present in most regions of the world. This arrangement is also more desirable for Third World allies that prefer not to have American military forces stationed on their soil but do want some American presence nearby.

One of America's two post–Cold War interventions was directly related to maintaining American access to the SLOCs. Its intervention in Panama did serve to oust an unpopular dictator and restore democracy to that country. This American intervention, however, occurred just before the Panamanian government was to appoint a Panamanian administrator for the canal under the terms of the U.S.-Panamanian treaty of 1977, which called for a gradual American turnover of the Canal Zone to Panama.[3]

It must be emphasized that American intervention in Panama was acceptable to both American and Panamanian public opinion, because the U.S. action ousted an unpopular dictatorship and restored democracy. It is unlikely, however, that the United States would have gone to such lengths unless a vital American interest—such as access to an extremely important waterway—was also at stake.

Intervention in Panama was also acceptable to the American public because it was very brief and involved relatively little loss of American life. Intervention to maintain access to other waterways is also likely to require relatively little effort, and thus to be acceptable to American public opinion. Further, any Third World state seeking to block access to international waterways will not only find itself opposed by the United States and its Western allies, but also by neighboring Third World states. Wherever the threat of lost access to an international waterway arises, America is likely to undertake intervention to remove that threat, and this intervention is likely to receive broad international support.

Western Access to Oil

The Iraqi conquest of Kuwait in August 1990 was reversed within a few months by an enormous UN-sanctioned and U.S.-led military effort to expel Iraqi forces from that country. Why was the Bush administration able to rally the support of the American public and many governments for this operation? The atrocity of Saddam Hussein's actions contributed to their determination to expel Iraq from Kuwait. But this was probably not the most important factor. The decisive factor was that the Iraqi conquest of Kuwait and the potential for expansion into Saudi Arabia threatened a vital Western interest— access to oil.

There should be no doubt that access to Persian Gulf oil is of vital interest to the West. Western countries depend on the Persian Gulf to supply them with a significant percentage of their current oil consumption, and this dependence is expected to increase in time. Only four countries in the world have proven oil reserves which will last over a century at current rates of production. All are Persian Gulf states: Iran, Iraq, Saudi Arabia, and the United Arab Emirates. Most other countries' reserves will be exhausted within ten to twenty years, at current rates of production.[4] Of course, more oil is being and will be found in other countries. But unless new discoveries outside the Persian Gulf region rapidly outpace the West's oil consumption, the West will become increasingly dependent on the Persian Gulf.

During the Cold War, American foreign policy makers were animated by the fear that the Soviet Union would gain control of the Persian Gulf region and then either deny the West access to the region's oil or drive the price of oil up dramatically. In either case, policy makers feared that the West would suffer extraordinary economic damage that would also drastically affect its defense capabilities.[5]

The threat of Moscow's gaining control over the Persian Gulf has ended. America and the West, though, continue to fear the possibility that any one power might gain control of the entire region and its oil resources, thereby putting it in a position to threaten the strength of Western economies.

Because of its unique economic importance, no other part of the Third World is as vital to the West as the Persian Gulf region. Although America would undoubtedly act to thwart an attempt to achieve hegemony in other areas of the Third World, it is difficult to envision in this post–Cold War era where the American public would feel so threatened that it would sanction a U.S. intervention on the scale of the one undertaken against Iraq.

Would the United States undertake direct intervention in the Persian Gulf region again? If any state outside the GCC invaded or threatened to invade any of the GCC states, the question can be answered in the affirmative with a high degree of confidence. External attack, however, might not be the only threat to the GCC countries. Graham Fuller, the well known former U.S. government analyst and expert on the Middle East, has predicted that internal threats to the monarchical regimes of the GCC are virtually certain to arise.[6] What will the United States do if (or when) they occur, especially in Saudi Arabia?

This would be a difficult case for the American polity to decide. Saudi Arabia is seen as vitally important to America. Intervention to repel an attack by another state against it would probably seem justified to the American public. But intervention to suppress an internal insurgency may not be acceptable, not least because of the memory of Vietnam.

There are currently two schools of thought about how America should react to such a situation. One can be called the "Washington" school, while the other can be called the "Tokyo" school.

Just as it was for the Bush administration, Saudi Arabia is of paramount importance to the Clinton administration. Its importance for this group stems from the fact that the West is heavily dependent now and will become increasingly dependent over time on oil from the Persian Gulf. The Kingdom, though, is seen as being primarily important because the two most populous states of the Persian Gulf—Iran and Iraq—have poor relations with America and the West generally.

For the Washington school, these two factors magnify the importance of Saudi Arabia and the other GCC states. Indeed, the Washington school sees the continued rule of the monarchical regimes in the GCC states as being of fundamental importance for American interests. The leaders of the GCC states also see cooperation with America as being in their interests. The Washington school fears that the downfall of the GCC monarchies would lead to the rise of anti-American governments in these countries. If the entire Persian Gulf region were ruled by governments hostile to the West, they might cooperate to cut off or limit the West's access to the Gulf's oil.

What makes Saudi Arabia more important than the other GCC states, of course, is that it is the most powerful of them. Internal uprisings in any of the other GCC states could probably be crushed with Saudi forces. The other GCC monarchies, however, could probably do nothing effective to quell an insurgency in the Kingdom. Indeed, the overthrow of the Saudi monarchy would probably be quickly followed by the overthrow of all the other GCC monarchies.

While the Washington school sees the preservation of the existing (or remaining) pro-American regimes in the Persian Gulf as being vital to American interests, the Tokyo school does not. This school of thought takes its name from Japan's policy thrust toward the Persian Gulf, which also has adherents in the United States. According to this school of thought, it really does not matter what regimes are in power in any of the Persian Gulf states. Whether the regimes are pro-Western or anti-Western, they all have an interest in selling their oil. If they do not sell their oil, or if they cannot do so because they charge too high a price for it, then the economies of the Persian Gulf states will suffer. Whatever their political orientation, then, all the Persian Gulf states can be expected to pursue their economic interests not only by seeking to sell their oil to the West, but to do so in competition with other states that export oil. This school of thought points out that despite the coming to power of a generally anti-Western government in Iran in 1979, Iran has continued to sell oil to Japan and other countries.

The merits and demerits of these two schools of thought are being debated. For the purposes of this study, a determination about which one is right is less important than suggesting which is likely to prevail in the United States and thus shape American military policy toward the Persian Gulf.

The Washington school is likely to prevail at least in the near future. This is because Washington policy makers are unlikely to change their minds about the importance to American interests of preserving the monarchical GCC governments.

But will this viewpoint prevail in the long run? So long as the West remains heavily dependent on oil from the Persian Gulf, the Washington school is likely to prevail. America and its allies are likely to work hard to ensure that an anti-Western regime does not come to power in Saudi Arabia.

It is possible, however, that the enormous political transformation that has occurred in the USSR will result in the West becoming less dependent on Persian Gulf oil. The former USSR currently has proven oil reserves of 57 billion barrels—5.6 percent of the world's total—which are expected to last only 13.6 years at current rates of production. By contrast, Saudi Arabia possesses 257.5 billion barrels of proven reserves—25.5 percent of the world's total—which will last well over a century at current rates of production.[7]

The former Soviet Union, however, was not only the largest country in the world (Russia alone still is), but is the largest area of the world in which modern Western oil exploration and extraction methods have not yet been applied. The quality of the USSR's oil technology was widely acknowledged to be significantly inferior to that of the West. Indeed, it appears that the decline in oil production in the former Soviet Union might not necessarily be due to the depletion of its oil reserves, but instead to the exhaustion or even disintegration of its oil-extraction capability.

The USSR has traditionally produced significantly more oil than it has consumed, but in the past it had to supply oil to its petroleum-poor allies in Eastern Europe and elsewhere, which could not pay for it in hard currency. Relieved of this obligation, the former USSR now has more oil available to sell for hard currency. Indeed, oil-rich Russia may decide that its economic interests will be better served not by bartering its oil for goods from the other republics of the former USSR, but by exporting as much oil as it possibly can to buyers with hard currency.

It is, of course, impossible to foretell whether in fact massive new oil reserves will be found in the former USSR and to what extent Russia and any other oil-rich republics will increasingly export their oil for hard currency. But to the extent that more oil is found in and exported from the former USSR, the West will become less dependent on Persian Gulf oil. And to the extent that its dependency declines, the preservation of the Saudi monarchy may become less compelling to the American public. While it may still be willing to defend the Kingdom against external attack, probably it would not sanction U.S. intervention to defend the Saudi monarchy against any internal threat, especially if access to Saudi oil was no longer seen as particularly vital.

If substantial new oil reserves are discovered in the former USSR, the Tokyo school may replace the Washington school in the United States. This is not likely to happen, though, unless substantial new oil reserves are indeed found in the former USSR.

Conclusion

The post–Cold War era is likely to bring decreased American intervention in the Third World. With the end of the Soviet attempt to achieve worldwide hegemony, and in the absence of any similar threat, American concern about the Third World is likely to be much less than it was previously.

America does, of course, have interests in the Third World separate from the Cold War. As the interventions in Panama and the Persian Gulf demonstrated, Washington still regards some of its interests there as important enough to justify military intervention. These actions, however, do not signify an American willingness to undertake intervention anywhere in the Third World, now that the former USSR poses no obstacle to Washington. Panama and the Persian Gulf happened to be directly related to interests (access to the Panama Canal and to Persian Gulf oil) which the American public and Congress do indeed regard as vital to the United States, without reference to the Cold War. However, relatively few vital American interests remain in the Third World, in the absence of a need to contain an attempt to achieve global hegemony. Most American security interests in the Third World can be effectively pursued by the United States through means other than direct intervention.

Indeed, they will have to be pursued by other such means. The American public is highly unlikely to support any form of prolonged foreign intervention, unless it is firmly convinced that America's vital interests are at stake. In the post-Vietnam era, no American administration has sought to risk involvement in a prolonged conflict for fear of the political consequences that will ensue. It is highly significant that armed intervention against Iraq was sanctioned by the UN Security Council—an action that this body had never before approved, except in the anomalous case of Korea—before it was sanctioned by the U.S. Congress. This shows that Congress is not likely to rush to approve American intervention in the Third World in the post–Cold War era. With the downfall of the Soviet Union, the American public is not likely to regard most of the Third World as having sufficiently vital significance for the United States to justify costly intervention.

Notes

1. See "State of Emergency Committee's Statement: 'A Mortal Danger Has Come,'" *New York Times*, 20 August 1991.

2. Ann Devroy and R. Jeffrey Smith, "U.S., Russia Pledge New Partnership," *Washington Post*, 2 February 1992.

3. Linda Robinson, "Dwindling Options in Panama," *Foreign Affairs* (Winter 1989–90): 187–205.

4. *BP Statistical Review of World Energy* (June 1991): 2.

5. Mark N. Katz, *Russia and Arabia: Soviet Foreign Policy toward the Arabian Peninsula* (Baltimore: Johns Hopkins University Press, 1986), 3–12.

6. Graham E. Fuller, *The "Center of the Universe": The Geopolitics of Iran* (Boulder, Colo.: Westview Press, 1991), chapter 6.

7. *BP Statistical Review of World Energy* (June 1991): 2.

Chapter 9

The End of the Cold War and the "New World Order"

Implications for the Developing World

Roger E. Kanet and James T. Alexander

The dramatic developments in the international system during the past several years have had a major impact on relationships between the former Soviet Union and the United States on the one hand and between the so-called superpowers and the developing countries of Asia, Africa, and Latin America on the other.[1] This paper will examine developments in Soviet and U.S. foreign policy since 1985, explain the factors that contributed to change in their foreign policies and to the winding down of the Cold War, and finally discuss the implications of these developments for relations between the United States and the Soviet successor states and for the developing countries themselves. The emphasis throughout the discussion will be on the policies of the two countries toward the Third World.

Two concepts, new thinking in foreign policy and new world order, are essential to an understanding of these policy shifts. For the reform leadership in Moscow, new thinking in foreign policy became both the analytic tool explaining the need for dramatic changes away from confrontation with the West in Soviet foreign policy and the justification for changes in policy.[2] Briefly stated, new thinking called for the reduction in, even elimination of, confrontation with the West, a lessening of the Soviet commitment to military capabilities, and a focus on rationalizing and making more cost-effective Soviet foreign policy. Included in all of this was a greater emphasis upon the normalization of relationships with the United States and other industrialized capitalist states and a reduction in Soviet commitments throughout Eastern Europe and much of the Third World—commitments viewed increas-

ingly by Soviet leaders and analysts as too costly and counterproductive. By 1989 new thinking had already resulted in significant shifts
in Soviet foreign policy behavior, including behavior throughout the
developing world. This included the withdrawal of Soviet troops from
Afghanistan; an active role in attempting to resolve conflicts in Angola,
Cambodia, Ethiopia, and Nicaragua; and the shifting of Soviet relations with Third World clients to principles of mutual benefit. The
term *new world order* was really a euphemism for reducing Soviet
military and economic commitments throughout the developing world.

It is important to recognize that by the mid-1980s, neither of the
superpowers was able to use its overwhelming military and economic
resources for purposes of effectively projecting power or controlling
conflict situations in the Third World. Neither country was able to
dictate terms to its allies or clients, as is demonstrated by U.S. relations
with Israel and El Salvador and Soviet relations with Afghanistan and
Ethiopia. Although both superpowers could provide assistance in ways
that exacerbated local or regional tensions, neither was really able to
resolve those tensions in ways favorable to its own objectives. To a
substantial degree, this situation was recognized by President Mikhail
Gorbachev and his advisers and lay, in part at least, at the base of the
shift in Soviet policy.

While new thinking in Soviet foreign policy was resulting in significant changes in behavior throughout the Third World, the United
States began to reassess its own positions. Prior to the end of the
superpower confrontation and the Cold War, U.S. policy throughout
the Third World had been influenced to a substantial degree by a
concern for the expansion of Soviet influence in regions viewed as
important to overall U.S. interests. This "zero-sum" approach to relationships in the Third World had characterized large aspects of both
U.S. and Soviet policy until the late 1980s.

With the reduction of confrontation between the United States and
the Soviet Union, one important factor motivating earlier U.S. policy
was eliminated. However, the challenge to Western—including American—economic interests in the Persian Gulf region represented by
Iraq's invasion of Kuwait in August 1990 and the longer-term potential
for Saddam Hussein to influence both regional and global politics
resulted in a dramatic reassessment of the foundations of U.S. policy.
This reassessment resulted in President Bush's call for a new world
order. Though many have viewed this term as a mere political slogan

meant to facilitate the creation of the coalition that defeated Iraq, the concept does have concrete meaning. It is a reformulation of the basic historical principles that underlay U.S. policy throughout the twentieth century.

In effect, the United States has made favorable relations with countries—including developing countries—and the continued supply of development assistance to them contingent upon their acceptance of certain key principles: political pluralism, liberal democracy, and free enterprise economic systems. Examples of this policy are especially visible in relations between the United States and several states in Latin American and in Africa, most notably Kenya, where the United States and its European allies have attempted to use economic aid as a means of influencing domestic political and economic structures.

In sum, the paper will argue that the end of the Cold War and the collapse of the Soviet state have dramatically reduced factors that influenced both Soviet and U.S. policy in the past. Russia and the other successor states of the USSR are likely to focus much more narrowly on domestic and regional concerns and on relations with the major industrial states, thus devoting far less attention to the Third World than the USSR had done in the past. At least for the foreseeable future, the member states of the Commonwealth of Independent States (CIS) will not be in a position to provide economic assistance to developing countries, though some may become important suppliers of sophisticated military hardware as a means of earning hard currency. A major exception is likely to occur in the emerging states of Central Asia, which are already gravitating toward expanded relationships with Muslim countries throughout the Middle East.

The United States, as indicated in the call for a new world order, is likely to be far more selective in its relationships in the Third World. In part, this will result from the elimination of concern about the Soviet threat. It will also, however, be influenced by the weakened economic situation of the United States and its likely inability to commit the amount of resources to international political activities that was committed in the past.

For a large number of the poorer states of Asia, Africa, and even Latin America, the post-Cold War period will probably be one of reduced access to resources from the industrialized world. Countries viewed as strategically significant—because of either their importance for U.S. and Western economic vitality or the emergence of strong military capabilities in a region that might threaten stability—are likely still to be the objects of significant U.S. interest.

Now that we have outlined the major thrust of the argument of the paper, we will turn to a more detailed examination of its key components. We will first trace the development of Soviet policy toward the developing countries under Gorbachev. This will be followed by an examination of the meaning of new world order in recent U.S. policy. Finally, we shall discuss the implications of the changes in Soviet policy (and of the demise of the Soviet Union) and the shifts in U.S. views and policies for the countries of the developing world.

From New Thinking to the Fragmentation of Consensus: Soviet Policy toward the Developing World under Gorbachev

In spring 1985, when Mikhail S. Gorbachev assumed the leadership of the Communist Party of the Soviet Union (CPSU), relations with the developing countries were still at the center of Soviet foreign policy. When the Supreme Soviet dissolved the Soviet Union less than seven years later, active Soviet involvement had virtually disappeared in most regions of the Third World. Central to an understanding of the process of Soviet decline is an understanding of the commitment of the Gorbachev leadership to fundamental reform, the general failure of that reform, and the implications of those developments for Soviet foreign policy.

As we have noted, despite growing evidence that Soviet analysts were already questioning the focus of Soviet policy throughout the developing world, the Soviet Union in 1985 remained deeply involved in regional conflicts in the entire Third World—from Cambodia and Afghanistan in Asia to Angola in Africa and Nicaragua in Central America. After 1985 the USSR underwent revolutionary changes in both its domestic and foreign policy aimed at revitalizing the economic, social, and political foundations of the system.

Soviet optimism concerning the direction and pace of international developments and prospects for the expanded role of the USSR had peaked in the mid-1970s. Major developments in Soviet nuclear capabilities, the rise of Marxist-Leninist regimes in the Third World, and the general withdrawal of the United States from international politics contributed significantly to that optimism.[3] Nevertheless, less than a decade later the Soviets found themselves increasingly on the defensive internationally. Relations with the West had deteriorated into a new arms race. In the Third World the USSR had been virtually frozen out of participation in key developments in the Middle East, and a number of its new allies or clients (Afghanistan, Angola, Cambodia, Ethiopia, and Nicaragua) had failed to create stable political-economic systems and were increasingly challenged by domestic insurgencies supported ·by the United States and other countries.[4] The result was a growing demand for Soviet military and economic support, including the direct takeover by Soviet troops of responsibility for the security of the Marxist-Leninist regime in Afghanistan, which led to widespread criticism by many developing countries. In yet another area the Soviets found that the attractiveness of their socioeconomic-political model had weakened. The unity of the Soviet-led world Communist movement had shattered long ago. In Western Europe Communist parties had lost domestic support, declared their independence from Moscow, or both. In the Third World a growing number of Marxist regimes were modifying their commitment to socialism and reestablishing or strengthening economic and political ties with the West.

These problems arose at the very time when the weaknesses of the Soviet economy were becoming more apparent. By the beginning of the 1980s, economic growth rates had, in the words of General Secretary Gorbachev, "fallen to a level close to economic stagnation." The technological gap between the Soviet economy and the economies of its major competitors, including a number of newly industrialized countries (NICs), was expanding.[5] After decades devoted to catching up with the West in a broad range of fields and of establishing themselves as a global power, the Soviets now faced the prospect of stagnation and decline. The weaknesses of the Soviet economy raised questions about the possible overextension of international commitments and limited the relevance of the USSR for many of the most pressing of international problems—economic development, international trade, and hard-currency debts.[6]

After he assumed the leadership of the CPSU, Gorbachev spoke repeatedly of the domestic and foreign policy problems facing the USSR. He committed himself to a major reform, or perestroika, of the entire Soviet system as a means of resolving these problems. The basic argument that he presented to support this reform can be summarized as follows. First, the economic problems of the USSR and the technology gap between the Soviet Union and the West were undermining the ability of the USSR to support the legitimate needs of the Soviet population or to ensure its military security and its global standing in the twenty-first century. Second, economic reform, or perestroika, within the framework of socialism was essential in order to overcome the economic problems and technological weaknesses of the USSR that threatened too to undermine its international status; also required as a precondition for economic reform was a reform of the political process that would make officials more responsive to the needs of economic rationality.[7] Third, to overcome entrenched bureaucratic forces resistant to change, a more open but still controlled political system that encouraged criticism and rationality in support of reform was required—thus the need for openness and democratization. Finally, policies were needed to enable the Soviets to benefit more fully from advances in the international economy and to accomplish, by means other than primarily military, major Soviet foreign policy objectives. Perestroika became Gorbachev's call for major reform with the goal of revitalizing the economy, closing the technology gap, and turning the USSR into a fully competitive global superpower.[8] As was clear from the vantage point of early 1992, the expectations of General Secretary Gorbachev and his advisers concerning their ability to turn around the Soviet economy were not fulfilled. The economy continued to decline. Openness and democratization contributed to the opening up of Soviet domestic politics, to growing opposition from conservative elements in the USSR, and to the disintegration of the unified Soviet state.

Between Gorbachev's rise to power in 1985 and the dissolution of the Soviet state in late 1991, Soviet policy toward the developing world went through three basic stages. In the first period, which can be labeled the period of great expectations, lasting from 1985 until approximately 1988, the promotion of new political thinking did not really coincide with a comparable change in policy or behavior. The dominant Western response during this period was that new thinking was largely tactical and did not represent a break with the grand design that had undergirded Soviet policy in the past.

The second period, which was characterized by a flurry of new foreign policy initiatives from Cambodia in Southeast Asia to Nicaragua in Central America, lasted from 1988 until mid-1990. It was during this period that the reality of the structural changes in Soviet policy in the Third World was increasingly recognized in the West—

as well as the reality of changes in other aspects of Soviet foreign and domestic politics.

The third period of Soviet Third World policy under Gorbachev began in 1990 and lasted until the demise of the Soviet state. In effect, this was a period in which any consensus on Soviet foreign policy fragmented, individual republics eventually succeeded in asserting their autonomy, and the Soviet leadership was forced to focus almost exclusively on domestic concerns. Although new thinking continued to dominate official foreign policy statements, growing evidence emerged of opposition to official policy, including that in the developing world. The resignation of Foreign Minister Eduard Shevardnadze in December 1990, the hard-line anti-Western attacks on Western banks by the new prime minister, Valentin S. Pavlov, and the shifting Soviet position on the confrontation in the Persian Gulf were all evidence of this move away from the roots of new thinking.[9] The failure of the coup of August 1991, however, led to a radical reinterpretation of Soviet commitments throughout the developing world.

The Period of Great Expectations

Before we begin our assessment of the implications of recent developments on the future policies of the Soviet successor states in the Third World, it is essential to trace in more detail the evolution of Soviet policy through the three periods after Gorbachev's selection as head of the CPSU in March 1985. Although Gorbachev dramatized the problems facing the Soviet Union in both the domestic and international arenas, he was neither the first nor the only important Soviet personality to outline the need to turn the USSR around.[10] In his report to the Twenty-seventh Party Congress in February 1986, Gorbachev outlined the contents of new political thinking when he raised issues seldom if ever discussed publicly by Soviet political leaders in the past. The major points that he mentioned included recognition of the existence of "global problems, affecting all humanity" that required "cooperation on a world-wide scale," explicit stress on the interdependence of states, the argument that "it is no longer possible to win an arms race, or nuclear war for that matter," and strong criticism of the "infallibility complex" that had characterized previous foreign policy.[11]

Gorbachev's views drew heavily on those of academic analysts who had already discussed in the 1970s most of the issues that were to be placed on the agenda of the top political leaders after 1985. New thinking, as these views were termed by Gorbachev, became an integral element of Soviet assessments of developments in and policy toward the Third World. The three major concerns raised about Soviet involvement in the Third World related to the escalating costs involved in supporting client states, the failure of Soviet allies after independence to create stable political systems and functioning economies, and the negative impact that involvement in the Third World had on other Soviet policy concerns—in particular, relations with the United States.

Thus by early 1986 the official Soviet intention to reduce direct Soviet commitments to Third World clients was evident. Besides raising the issue of the cost of supporting Third World allies, the Soviets now questioned the long-term viability of some of their client states and increasingly criticized the policies of some of them. This new concern about Soviet policy in the Third World had an important impact on a reconceptualization of regional conflicts and the most appropriate Soviet response to those conflicts. In the past, Soviet analysts and politicians had charged that Western imperialism was the primary source of regional conflict and recognized that the USSR had an obligation to support progressive groups throughout the Third World. Early in the Gorbachev years a new interpretation began to dominate official Soviet statements. Gorbachev himself argued that "regional conflicts in Asia, Africa, and Latin America are spawned by the colonial past, new social processes, and recurrences of predating policy, or by all three." The objective, according to Gorbachev, is to find a political, not a military, solution to these conflicts. He went on to argue that every country has a right to determine its own political orientation and that neither of the superpowers should intervene in domestic conflicts.[12]

By 1987 the intellectual foundations for a shift in Soviet policy had been established; however, the question that then arose concerned the degree to which that new assessment influenced actual Soviet behavior. In fact, throughout 1988 and 1989 the Soviet leadership initiated a number of important modifications in Third World policy aimed at reducing the areas of conflict with the West, limiting the drain on Soviet resources, and extricating the USSR from involvement in regional conflicts in which the prospects for success seemed virtually nonexistent.[13] The Soviets moved forcefully on a variety of fronts to modify important aspects of their past policy throughout the Third

World. Chief among these changes were the reassessment of security and economic commitments to radical Marxist-Leninist regimes—like those in Afghanistan, Angola, and Ethiopia—that were challenged by internal opposition. Finally, questions were raised about the long-term benefits either to the USSR or to recipients of the major arms transfer programs of the Soviet state.

New Foreign Policy Behavior

We turn now to a brief examination of the actual changes in Soviet–Third World behavior during 1988–89. By far the most dramatic and significant of the changes was the decision made in early 1988 and implemented over the next year to withdraw Soviet combat troops from Afghanistan. After initial efforts to pacify the country by conquest and to exert greater pressure on Pakistan to accept the new status quo in the region, it soon became clear that the Communist government of Afghanistan, despite massive Soviet economic and military support and the direct involvement of well over 100,000 Soviet troops, was not capable of defeating the anticommunist rebels. The military and political costs involved, as the USSR attempted to normalize relations with both the United States and China, and the growing unrest at home in the face of escalating Soviet casualties contributed to the decision to withdraw. The Soviets did not abandon the government of Najibullah, however, which it correctly considered capable of stabilizing its control. The Communist government of Afghanistan continued to receive large amounts of economic and military aid until the end of 1991, when a U.S.-Soviet agreement no longer to support allies in the civil war went into effect.

In Southeast Asia the Soviets influenced the Vietnamese decision to withdraw combat troops from Cambodia by late 1989. In southern Africa they contributed to the resolution of the conflicts in both Namibia and Angola by playing an important behind-the-scenes role in the negotiations that resulted in the Cuban decision to withdraw their forces from Angola.[14] Initially, as in Afghanistan, the Gorbachev leadership apparently hoped for a military solution to the civil war. But when it became clear that the Popular Movement for the Liberation of Angola was unable to assert full control over Angola, the Soviets pushed strongly for negotiations that resulted in a cease-fire and the reduction of Cuban troops in the country.

In Central America a parallel development occurred as the Soviets first encouraged the Sandinistas in Nicaragua to permit an open and competitive election and, later, accepted what for them were the very negative results of that election.[15] Overall, during 1988 and 1989 the Soviet Union either encouraged or accepted a series of developments in relationships with Marxist-Leninist client states throughout the Third World that resulted in their military withdrawal, the beginnings of a negotiated solution to a long-standing conflict, or the reduction of their overall military and economic commitment to a client regime.[16]

Closely associated with the shift away from strong support for clients in regional conflicts was the questioning of the cost and long-term value to the USSR of both the military and economic relationships that had been established since the mid-1950s. For example, an editorial in *Izvestiya* in early 1990 provided specific information on the size and nature of the debt to the USSR. Of the 85.8 billion rubles owed to the Soviet Union through 1 November 1989, 37.2 billion were owed by socialist developing countries and an additional 42 billion rubles by other developing countries.[17] The editorial made clear that the amounts owed to the USSR were not likely to be repaid quickly enough to help the Soviet economy. Another Soviet author noted that the debt owed to the USSR was the result of "economic, ideological, and military-political miscalculations."[18]

There were those who virtually called for the USSR to abandon all commitments throughout the Third World and to focus exclusively on the solution of domestic problems.[19] In sum, from 1988 until some time in early 1990 the Soviet Union pursued a number of policy changes that resulted in a reorientation of its policies in key conflict regions throughout the Third World. It began to reduce commitments to some of its established allies. New thinking had indeed evolved into new behavior patterns.

Fragmentation of Foreign Policy Consensus and the End of the Soviet State

It is ironic that at the very time when the USSR could expect to begin profiting from the changes it had initiated in its foreign policy, the domestic consensus on that policy had already begun to fragment. Soviet policy in Asia, Africa, and Latin America during the late 1980s resulted in a rapid reassessment in the West of the nature of Soviet foreign policy and the prospect of the USSR's entering the international community as an equal and beneficial contributor to the emergence of a new international order. While political leaders and analysts in the West praised the Gorbachev leadership for its pragmatic approach to regional conflicts and other foreign policy concerns—witness especially the early stages of the Persian Gulf conflict—voices emerged in the Soviet Union that condemned Gorbachev, Foreign Minister Shevardnadze, and other reformers for a foreign policy of capitulation. Thus began the third stage of Gorbachev's policy toward the Third World, a period of growing internal confrontation within the Soviet Union itself, of division concerning the very roots of foreign policy, and of a gradual weakening of the position of the reformers that, prior to the end of 1990, resulted in Shevardnadze's resignation.

Throughout 1990 the debate on Soviet foreign policy became extremely vocal. Shevardnadze, the architect of much of this new policy, was the target of extremely critical comments by those who charged him and Gorbachev with having abandoned the security interests of the USSR in Central Europe by permitting, even encouraging, the demise of Marxist-Leninist regimes and unilaterally committing the USSR to withdrawal of its troops from the region. Elsewhere Shevardnadze and Gorbachev were accused of abandoning the interests of their allies throughout the Third World.

In response to the charge that the USSR was abandoning the Third World, Shevardnadze noted in an interview in spring 1990 that it was true that the Soviet Union was in the process of reducing the intensity of some of its Third World contacts. He argued, however, that without solving its domestic economic problems, the Soviet Union would be in no position to help developing countries in the future. He noted as well that in most of the regional conflicts to which the USSR had been a party, military solutions simply did not exist.[20]

With the resignation of Shevardnadze in December 1990, Soviet foreign policy began to shift away from virtually complete cooperation with the United States in both bilateral relations and regional conflicts. In the Persian Gulf crisis, for example, Soviet policy became more complex and included verbal support for U.S. policy, efforts to protect the government of President Saddam Hussein while also strengthening ties with moderate Arab states, and also activities meant to normalize relations with Iran.[21] Not until summer 1991, after the attempted constitutional coup in which Prime Minister Pavlov and others tried through parliamentary means to strip executive powers from the office of President Gorbachev and give them to the prime minister, did Soviet policy once again shift back to the policies that had characterized the Shevardnadze period. It was the coup of 19 August, however, that had the major impact on Soviet policy, both in general terms and in relationship to the Third World.

The Coup and Its Aftermath

The failed coup accelerated the multifaceted process of disintegration of the Soviet Union and culminated in its formal dissolution four months later. The three Baltic states had already regained their national independence in the first half of September and, much like their neighbors in East-Central Europe, now faced the uncertainties of establishing independent economic and political systems. Eleven of the remaining twelve former union republics established an as yet amorphous Commonwealth of Independent States through which they agreed to cooperate in areas of mutual concern—military security, transportation, and the like.

The coup represented a desperate attempt by a handful of hardliners to stem the tide of the changes that had been unleashed by Gorbachev's reform program and were now sweeping the Soviet Union and threatening its collapse. Chief among these changes were those associated with the nationality question and with the relationships between the central authorities in Moscow and the union republics. Though Gorbachev had fought assiduously to suppress secessionist demands and to retain central authority over the entire country, his personal authority and that of the central state and party apparatus were in serious decline. The new union treaty that had been negotiated in spring 1991 and was to be signed on 20 August recognized the changed political relationships between the center and the republics. The draft agreement illustrated the growing power of republic-level officials, such as Boris Yeltsin in Russia and Nursultan Nazarbaev in Khazakhstan, and the fact that political initiative had shifted from the center to the republics. The timing of the coup was meant to forestall the signing of the new Treaty of the Union, which would have legalized further decentralization of state power.

Rather than salvaging centralized authority, the coup speeded up the process of disintegration. The three Baltic republics left the Union, while eleven of the remaining twelve declared their independence but continued discussions about future cooperation. In the ensuing months the signing of the treaty was put on hold while the republics jockeyed to strengthen their demands for greater authority. A treaty of economic community between eleven of the remaining republics and the center was signed in October, with Ukraine acceding to the treaty on 4 November. All the while, President Gorbachev fought to maintain the authority of the central government.[22] In a televised speech on 3 December 1991 he repeated his plea to the republics not to leave the Union and warned of dire consequences, even civil war, should his arguments not be heeded.[23]

The impasse between President Gorbachev and the presidents of the union republics was broken on 8 December with the announcement that the presidents of the three Slavic republics—Belarus, Russia, and Ukraine—had agreed to form the Commonwealth of Independent States, thereby undercutting Gorbachev's efforts to retain a confederative state with a strong central presidency. Within a week all the remaining republics except Georgia joined the Commonwealth. On 25 December Gorbachev resigned as president of the Soviet Union, and a rump session of the Supreme Soviet dissolved the USSR, bringing to an end the seven-decade experiment in "centralized federalism."[24]

Between the abortive coup of August and the dissolution of the Soviet state, President Gorbachev continued the dramatic shifts in Soviet policy as they related to the developing world. Most important were the agreement with the United States to stop the supply of all military equipment to the warring parties in Afghanistan and the announcement in September 1991 that the USSR would withdraw its military forces from Cuba, virtually eliminate its other military support to the Cubans, and put economic relations between the two countries on a pay-as-you-go basis.[25]

During all of these developments the USSR was acting as a great power in decline committed to reducing the costs of its foreign involvements as much as possible. Initially efforts were made to retain as much Soviet involvement and influence as possible while simultaneously making that involvement more efficient and cost-effective. By 1990, and especially after August 1991, Soviet policy was characterized by an almost complete withdrawal from areas of previous commitment. We turn now to a discussion of U.S. policy toward the developing world during the recent past, as the confrontation between the United States and the Soviet Union waned.

The "New World Order" and U.S. Policy in the Third World

Writing in 1955, the noted American political philosopher Louis Hartz argued that U.S. foreign policy was a captive of its own unique past. This resulted in a form of messianism and the formation of a "liberal absolutism" according to which the United States tried to mold the outside world to its expectations. Hartz argued that to succeed in the global competition with the USSR, the United States had to adapt its ideals to the realities of the world and reach "a new level of consciousness, a transcending of irrational Lockeianism, in which an understanding of self and an understanding of others go hand in hand."[26]

From the perspective of today, four decades after Hartz wrote, we find that U.S. foreign policy makers only partly followed his advice. Throughout the Cold War the intense competition with the Soviet Union in the Third World translated into intense competition for influence that often required compromising ideals. With the decline of the Cold War and the accompanying disappearance of the Soviet threat, U.S. foreign policy makers have had a great deal more flexibility in pursuing their policy in the Third World. The Bush administration took advantage of that flexibility.

Above all else, President Bush showed a commitment to constructing and following international legal norms. This commitment was first expressed in the strict adherence of the United States to UN resolutions during the Persian Gulf War. Closely tied to international legal norms was Bush's search for uniformity in international relations. This was a rather vague approach to achieving agreement among nations, a sort of businessman's attempt to begin negotiations with a clean slate. This process was most apparent in October 1991 in the preparatory period for the Middle East Peace Conference held in Madrid.

Yet, while aspects of Bush's foreign policy might have achieved the "new level of consciousness" that Hartz recommended, the framework in which that policy was expressed might have been but a new example of extending the concept of America's "manifest destiny" to the outside world. While Bush denied a vision of a *Pax Americana,* the overall foreign policy strategy that he had outlined in the Third World indicated otherwise. While Hartz was correct to note that at the height of the Cold War in the 1950s the export of Americanism was doomed to failure, the recent collapse of the USSR as an international actor makes such a policy objective less improbable. For example, a Soviet military officer has noted of U.S. goals, "The United States is the only superpower, and it is predestined by fate itself to rule the world. And it at once becomes obvious that the new concept [new world order] is not actually that new. It is a question of the same old *Pax Americana*."[27]

It is important to understand the actual meaning of the U.S. policy committed to creating a new world order and to determine the degree to which it has actually resulted in new behavior patterns. A careful assessment of the evolving meaning of the concept and of the policies associated with it shows that U.S. policy in the Bush years can be divided into roughly three periods. In the initial period, up until the time of Iraq's invasion of Kuwait, the United States pursued different policies in the Middle East, Latin America, and Asia.[28] The concept of a new world order emerged in the rhetoric of the Persian Gulf crisis. Finally, in the postcrisis period, a more general policy associated with the concept was extended throughout much of the Third World.

While the decline of the Soviet bloc was the most significant set of events leading to a change in U.S. policy toward the Third World, the initial implications of that decline were unclear. Although some evidence of the changing quality of superpower relations appeared as a result of Soviet policy shifts in Afghanistan, Cambodia, and Angola, it was not until the Iraqi invasion of Kuwait that the full nature of that change became evident. Although the Persian Gulf crisis and the shift in the nature of the U.S.-Soviet relationship serve as the dividing line between pre- and postcrisis U.S. policy in the Third World, it is important to note that the division is not a sharp one. The precrisis period exhibits aspects of new world order policy that are also evident in postcrisis policy, while the postcrisis era exhibits aspects of policy that have long been evident in U.S. foreign relations.

The Prewar Period: Begging Unity

Although U.S. policy gave evidence of some changes during 1990, for the most part precrisis Bush foreign policy did not exhibit uniformity and consistency. The comparison of U.S. policy in the Middle East, Latin America, and Asia shows striking differences. It was largely reactive and differed from region to region according to the level of U.S. influence. This resulted in policies of persuasion in the Middle East, domination in Latin America, mediation and flexibility in Asia, and noninvolvement in Sub-Saharan Africa. As for incongruities within regions, they occurred primarily where the United States had its greatest influence, in Latin America. Across all regions, however, Bush's foreign policy exhibited aspects of postcrisis policy—an appeal to law, the recognition of an expanding role for international organizations, regional uniformities, and the call to democratic and economic reform. What these disconnected elements lacked that appears in the postcrisis period was a unified strategy for their achievement and a vision of the future.

The Middle East. In this region the Bush administration focused primarily on the Arab-Israeli conflict. As had been true since the Persian Gulf War, Secretary of State Baker attempted to lay the groundwork for a peace conference. The preliminary goal was the achievement of a tentative uniformity of perceptions between Palestinians and Israelis before negotiations could start. U.S. policy exhibited the belief that only through compromise could the foundations be laid for an international conference.[29] While compromise had already been an element of U.S. policy in the region, support for Israel was slipping as other actors were included in the peace process. For example, Baker told the American Israel Political Action Committee that peace required a halt to Israeli discussions of a "greater Israel" that would arise through the annexation of the occupied territories. He linked peace negotiations with a halt in the settlement of these territories as a part of recognizing Palestinian political rights.[30]

The changing U.S. perceptions of Arab-Israeli relations included the requirement that the Palestinians (though not the Palestine Liberation Organization) participate in the negotiations. In striving to build a foundation that included the Palestinians, Baker also made it clear that the United States did not support the PLO. Twice in 1989 the United States threatened to cut off funds to any UN agency considering recognizing it as more than an observer organization. Bush suspended the dialogue between the United States and the PLO following the latter's refusal to condemn a May 1990 attack on Israel by one of its splinter organizations.[31]

Latin America. The spread of democracy was the primary focus of the Bush administration's policy in Latin America. The two major areas of attention before the Persian Gulf crisis were Panama and Nicaragua. While policy in the Middle East and Asia largely focused on diplomatically encouraging an environment for future elections, in the cases of Nicaragua and Panama, Bush's policy was one of intervention. In Nicaragua continued economic sanctions were coupled with financial support for the Contras and for the internal opposition. In Panama initial hopes were that General Manuel Noriega would be removed through the electoral process. Following fraudulent elections, the United States condemned the results, instituted economic sanctions, and called for a popular overthrow of Noriega. The failure to achieve Noriega's overthrow led to the U.S. military intervention, which President Bush justified in part by claiming to have had international support.[32] Yet, as he eventually admitted, this support had not been readily forthcoming from Latin American states, which have long been wary of U.S. intervention in the region. Secretary of State Baker further justified the invasion on the basis of articles in both the UN and OAS charters that permit self-defense.[33] For reasons that will be discussed below, these same principles were applied in the Persian Gulf crisis in a manner that was more acceptable internationally.

Bush's policy in Nicaragua was built on a more solid foundation. Early in the process he called for multilateral cooperation among the Latin American countries on the issue of the civil war in Nicaragua. Yet contradictions in policy were evident, since only a month earlier these same countries questioned whether proposed U.S. aid to the contras violated the regional peace agreement that called for their disbanding.[34] Baker raised the classic American paradox in Latin America: the desire for the legitimacy derived from multilateral support for policies that were determined by the United States. The policy that was followed in Nicaragua did not raise strong protest from the countries of the region, nor was it as intrusive as the invasion of Panama. Yet the U.S. provision of special campaign funds for opposition candidates was only a less direct way of setting policy in its sphere of interest.[35] Furthermore, by not rescinding U.S. economic sanctions until after the February 1990 election, Bush offered the Nicaraguan voter a choice between continued economic hardship under the Sandinistas and the possibility of improvement under the opposition candidate, Violetta Chamorro.

The U.S. policy in both Nicaragua and Panama was meant to ensure a democratically elected government. To achieve the goal, the Bush administration initially pursued a minimalist strategy of letting the democratic process flow naturally. Undesirable results and/or unfavorable prospects, however, resulted in increased U.S. involvement in order to achieve the desired objective of democracy. This was then followed by the provision of economic aid meant to help build democracy, spark economic development, and demilitarize the national forces.[36]

Asia. Reflecting its less powerful position in Asia, U.S. policy was more flexible there than in Latin America. Negotiations to end the crisis in Cambodia dominated U.S. involvement in the region. Even before Bush's inauguration, Baker set two goals for this process: Vietnamese withdrawal from Cambodia and barring a return of the Khmer Rouge to power.[37] A shift toward establishing relations with the Vietnamese-backed government was conditioned on the guarantee that any future coalition government would reserve power for Sihanouk. In Afghanistan U.S. policy was also flexible, as it focused on possibilities for a negotiated settlement and popular elections.[38] Finally, fearing Pakistani nuclear development, Bush tried to slow down the Pakistan-India arms race by requesting that Rajiv Ghandi, then prime minister of India, meet with Benazir Bhutto, the Pakistani leader at that time.

Bush's precrisis policy exhibited the major elements of postcrisis policy, but policies were not applied uniformly. In one situation Bush called for compromise in the Middle East, while in another he had U.S. forces invade Panama. Furthermore, while he had received international support for the embargo of Panama, ex post facto appeals for support of the unilateral invasion were not very successful. In essence, as exhibited by these inconsistences, Bush had no single vision on which to found U.S. policy. Yet, sparked by the declining importance of East-West confrontation, he soon saw the opportunity afforded the United States, as the sole remaining superpower, to shape the world in its own image. This meant not only altering defense doctrines but also developing a strategy to ensure the spread of democracy. In his State of the Union Address of 31 January 1990 President Bush noted that it was time for the spread of democratic freedoms and free-market economies. This process would be served through the strength and ability of American leadership to defend its own national interests.[39] Thus the decline of the Cold War would allow Bush to integrate many aspects of traditional American foreign policy into a vision of the future. The initial test of his vision would occur following the Iraqi invasion of Kuwait. Learning from the negative reactions to the invasion of Panama, Bush began to build a foundation of legality before any action had taken place.

The War: The Art of Rhetoric

The actual policy that arose out of the Persian Gulf crisis did not depart from that of the earlier period. What was a departure, however, was the development of the foundations for a coherent strategy to carry out the mission in the Persian Gulf. The strategy differed greatly from that used in Panama because of the consistent application in the latter situation of a combination of openness, international and UN participation, and strict adherence to international law. It is true that U.S. influence in the Middle East is not comparable with that in Latin America. Yet what was significant about the strategy employed in the Persian Gulf was the role that it played in shaping Bush's vision for the future. As will be shown, this was to be a universal, not a particular, application of American foreign policy. But George Bush's conception of universal policy envisioned employing U.S. leadership to spread American ideals to the world. In essence he argued that a Pax Americana (though he denied it) combined with the decline of the Soviet Union permitted the practice of a more integrated and coherent U.S. policy.

Initial statements by President Bush following the Iraqi invasion of Kuwait were based on traditional principles of U.S. foreign policy and rested on four points: (1) an unconditional Iraqi withdrawal from Kuwait; (2) the return of the legitimate Kuwaiti leadership; (3) a long-standing U.S. commitment to security and stability in the Persian Gulf; and (4) the protection of American lives. Realizing that any threat to oil supplies also threatened U.S. economic health, Bush instituted sanctions against Iraq. Compared with past practice, however, there were certain differences. Instead of unilaterally sending troops, as was done in Panama, the United States was "requested" to provide military assistance by the Saudi Arabian government. Furthermore, President Bush exhibited the same strong stand against Iraq that had led to "victory" in the Cold War.[40]

By 15 August Bush recognized the benefits of a world role in the crisis, although old habits of unilateral action were being exhibited. He called for the implementation of the UN resolutions condemning the Iraqi aggression while (as in Panama) justifying the U.S. initiation of a naval blockade of Iraq on an ex post facto appeal to international legality based on Article 51 of the UN charter.[41] While recognizing the importance of the crisis to help reestablish U.S. credibility, Bush explicitly raised the prospects for a new world order to arise out of the cooperative spirit engendered by the common defense of the region.[42] Secretary of State James Baker was even more explicit when he stated that the post–Cold War world order stood at a critical junction and that the Iraqi invasion was a defining moment of a new era. Baker saw an opportunity to solidify the ground rules of the new era on the basis of the UN. Moreover, as Bush had done before him, Baker linked the impediments to the flow of energy resources from the Middle East to the health of the global economy, a threat particularly to the viability of the struggling democracies in the world.[43]

In an example of the new U.S.-Soviet relationship in the post–Cold War era, Bush and Gorbachev issued a joint statement calling for the acceptance by Iraq of all UN resolutions. They also envisioned a postcrisis world in which the erstwhile enemies would work together to set up a regional security structure.[44] Finally, Bush explicitly added a fifth objective to the four that he had noted at the outset of the crisis— the establishment of a new world order. With this announcement, he made a more systematic effort to define the substance of that order. Basing his concept on the immediate principles of halting aggression and allowing the free flow of oil, Bush saw the opportunity for the nations of the world to prosper in harmony under the umbrella of a United Nations free to carry out the roles envisioned for it by its founders. He went on to predict that U.S. leadership would be an integral part of the new "world partnership." Furthermore, he believed that the Persian Gulf operation would restore U.S. credibility by affirming that there is no substitute for American leadership against tyranny. In keeping with this theme, postcrisis U.S. leadership would have a lasting role in the security of the region through mediation, security agreements, and a curb on the proliferation of weapons of mass destruction.[45]

Speaking before the UN, President Bush described his vision of the UN's role in a postcrisis world. He optimistically predicted the continued spread of democracy and greater economic prosperity and peace that would be accompanied by a decline in the proliferation of weaponry. Closer to home, he envisioned the Americas as the first "democratic hemisphere." In addition to its response to the Iraqi invasion, Bush predicted expanded UN participation in solving environmental and drug problems, limiting terrorism, resolving the debt burden, and aiding refugees, as well as its traditional role in peacekeeping. In all, Bush expected the United Nations to be an active force in future world politics.[46]

Throughout this entire period, however, Bush's vision of multilateral participation in a cooperative future of international relations was inconsistent with an evident attempt unilaterally to control the direction of events in the Persian Gulf. While Secretary of State Baker claimed to welcome all diplomatic efforts to solve the crisis peacefully, rhetoric emanating from Washington seemed to preclude this possibility as early as 15 August 1990, as did the quick U.S. rejection of the French and Soviet plans.[47]

The final prescription for the new world order (really a summary of the development of Bush's foreign policy throughout the crisis) was expressed on 29 January 1991 in the State of the Union Address. President Bush described the universal aspirations of mankind as peace and security, freedom and law. These characteristics, he claimed, were being exhibited in the twenty-eight-nation coalition against Iraq. Reverting to patriotism, or what might be interpreted as Pax Americana rhetoric, Bush said,

> For generations America has led the struggle to preserve and extend the blessings of liberty. And, today, in a rapidly changing world, American leadership is indispensable.
>
> But we also know why the hopes of humanity turn to us. We are Americans, we have a unique responsibility to do the hard work for freedom. And when we do, freedom works.
>
> Yes, the United States bears a major share of leadership in this effort [the Persian Gulf War]. Among nations of the world only the United States of America has both the moral standing and the means to back it up. We are the only nation on this earth that could assemble the forces of peace.[48]

Very briefly, George Bush envisioned a world ruled by law and rationality moving toward the freedoms of democracy; this was to occur under the guidance of the United States in areas of political, economic, and military affairs. While in his concept the United States would be heavily involved in this process, the participation of other countries would be encouraged, particularly under the umbrella of international organizations.

As would be expected, foreign policy initiatives in other regions of the world were minimal during the crisis. From a strictly legalistic perspective, the policy that was publicized was largely in keeping with Bush's rhetoric. In promoting international cooperation, Bush's initiatives were clearly exhibited in four instances. First, a Gulf Crisis Financial Coordinating Group was formed to provide aid to those Third

World countries hit hardest by the economic embargo against Iraq.[49] Second, the United States supported a UN Security Council plan to form a governing council of the four competing factions in Cambodia. Subsequently this council and efforts to solve the Cambodian crisis were placed entirely under UN supervision. To employ the UN in this fashion in such a sensitive region could not have occurred during the Cold War. Third, while following long-term U.S. policy, Bush suspended foreign aid to Pakistan because of its advancing nuclear program. Finally, the confirmation of most favored trade status for Mongolia illustrated the impact of Bush's economic rhetoric.[50]

The Postwar Era: Policy Coherence?

At the end of the Persian Gulf War, U.S. foreign policy makers faced a much different situation from that which existed following the Panama invasion. In Panama the focus of the U.S. attack had been the removal of General Noriega; the removal of Saddam Hussein had not been a part of the UN resolutions and, thus, of official U.S. policy. Realizing that the United States was committed to following UN guidelines, Baker repeated the preinvasion policy in Panama by calling on the Iraqis to overthrow Hussein by hinting that his overthrow might result in lighter reparations for Iraq. Baker's comments apparently contributed to the rebellions of Shiites in the south and the Kurds in the north.[51]

Despite some inconsistencies, U.S. foreign policy after the Persian Gulf War was more integrated. In a speech shortly after the termination of the war, Bush codified the U.S. objectives for the Middle East as (1) shared security arrangements with Arab countries; (2) controlling the proliferation of weapons of mass destruction; (3) a peace accord between the Arabs and Israelis; and (4) fostering economic development in the region as a part of the peace process. This last point was to be fulfilled through the redirection of military resources in both the region and the United States. In recognizing a new world based on the "principles of justice and fair play," Bush reiterated the linkages between the decline of the Cold War and the enhanced position of the UN.[52] This approach to foreign policy demonstrated continuity with the process that had originally formed the UN coalition prior to the war. But President Bush's policy had gained greater coherence. If nothing else, this coherence came from clearly stated objectives. In addition, while past rhetoric consisted of words that had little substance, for the most part since summer 1990 Bush consistently attempted to apply the four objectives announced for the Middle East to U.S. policy throughout the world.

In the area of security arrangements, initial attempts to establish a permanent military base in Bahrain or store weapons in Saudi Arabia did not succeed. Yet new security pacts were signed with Kuwait and Qatar, while old security arrangements with Saudi Arabia and Bahrain were enhanced.[53] Attempts to limit weapons proliferation have been closely related to the security arrangements. At first, the U.S. commitment focused on destroying Iraqi capabilities in the areas of nuclear and chemical weapons. This soon became a comprehensive plan for the entire Middle East that involved the members of the Security Council and eventually spread to the issue of arms sales to the Third World as a whole.[54] Major successes in this area occurred soon after the abortive Soviet coup, when the United States and the Soviet Union agreed to halt the sale of military equipment to the warring parties in Afghanistan, and the USSR announced that it would virtually eliminate its military commitments to Cuba.

The Mideast peace process, another central element in Bush's proclaimed policy, was characterized by U.S. efforts to get the Israelis and the Arabs to negotiate a settlement to the issues that divide them. In essence, Secretary of State Baker tried to build a uniform base of compromise upon which to establish the negotiations themselves. As before, this meant excluding direct PLO participation because of Israeli opposition while at the same time pressuring the Israelis by refusing to consider the request for $10 billion in loan guarantees to fund settlement construction.[55]

Though President Bush failed to require postwar democratic reforms from the Kuwaiti emir, the driving forces behind his foreign policy were related to strengthening the growth of market economies and the spread of democracy. He was convinced that the economic progress exemplified by free markets was the "soil in which democracy grows best." While denying any desire to create a Pax Americana, Bush proclaimed the movement toward a "*Pax Universalis* [a process] built upon shared responsibilities and aspirations." While the Pax Universalis appears to define U.S. policy on certain diplomatic levels, it was especially in the area of economics that Bush had tried to mold the internal policies of Third World states.[56]

While "rewarding" Egypt for its role in the Persian Gulf War, the

U.S. forgiveness of part of the Egyptian debt was made contingent on economic reform. Furthermore, the instrumental use of foreign aid and economic incentives was not limited to Egypt. Rather, it became an integral part of policy also in Latin America and Africa.[57] As a clear by-product of the end of the Cold War, U.S. policy makers no longer have to compete primarily with the Soviet Union for influence in the Third World. This means that the United States could be more direct and open in requiring that Third World states desirous of aid comply with the free-market and democratic reforms demanded by the Bush administration. In essence, such a noncompetitive situation places the United States in a strong position to use assistance as an instrument to influence states in need. Reciprocally, Third World states are in a weakened position, for to participate in the international system they must relinquish a certain degree of their sovereignty.

As noted earlier, the Bush administration's foreign policy was no longer a haphazard collection of diverse initiatives; it was based on a vision of expanded U.S. influence tied to international legality and uniformity. Bush's attempts to expand presidential powers in the allocation of foreign aid provide a broad overview of those objectives: (1) the promotion of democratic values; (2) the strengthening of American competitiveness; (3) the promotion of peace; (4) the protection of the United States from transnational threats; and (5) the meeting of humanitarian needs. As has been stated previously, Bush wanted to use foreign aid as an instrument to ensure the achievement of American policy goals.[58]

The Demise of the USSR and the "New World Order": Implications for the Developing World

Even before the disintegration of the Soviet Union and the end of its role in the developing world, voices were heard that warned of the implications of new thinking for the developing countries. For example, the Indian scholar Zafar Imam has concluded that "new thinking has led to more civilized relations among the great powers. Yet, the emerging international system does not promise to produce equivalent gains for the Third World."[59] He points to the fact that the reduction of the role of the USSR as a provider of economic and military support will be of considerable importance to those countries that have depended on the Soviet Union in the past. Moreover, the United States and the international financial agencies in which the United States plays a major role are likely to increase their political demands on potential recipients of development assistance, while a substantial portion of the aid that formerly went to the Third World is being redirected toward Central Europe and the former Soviet Union.[60] As we have noted in discussing the development of U.S. policy in the brief period since the end of the confrontation with the Soviet Union, many of Imam's concerns have already come true.

For the foreseeable future, the successor states of the USSR are not likely to play a significant role in the developing world. First of all, domestic political and economic concerns will draw the majority of the leaders' attention; they will also have to focus on relations with other former republics that, in many respects, will provide the major security challenges for Russia, Ukraine, and others. In relations with countries outside the former Soviet Union, greatest attention will be given to the major industrial states of the West and East Asia for the purpose of obtaining financial assistance, developing markets, and stabilizing the international security system. As we have seen in the policies of Russia and Ukraine, only developing countries capable of meeting the former's economic needs or directly relevant for their security are likely to gain lasting attention. For Russia and Ukraine this includes the East Asian NICs, the oil-producing countries of the Middle East, and countries near the southern borders of Russia. For the emerging countries of Central Asia and Azerbaijan, ties with nearby Muslim countries that can provide assistance of various types are likely to expand in importance. But to a very substantial degree, relations between the Soviet successor states and the developing world will reverse former Soviet–Third World relations. Rather than the USSR's providing political, military, and economic support to developing countries, the successor states will seek such support from a small group of developing states.

This development will likely contribute, at least for the foreseeable future, to the probability that the United States will continue to pursue policies of the sort outlined above. As we have argued, current U.S. policy shows a general uniformity through the greater role that legal norms, compromise, and international organizations play as instruments of policy rather than as its ends. Part of the process includes aspects of idealism and self-interest that are expressed in the term *Pax Americana*. The United States emerged from the Persian Gulf War with restored credibility and world recognition that it was now the only superpower. The changes of the past few years signify greater policy latitude for the United States when it deals with the Third World; this latitude has been most notably exhibited in the instrumental use of foreign aid to accomplish objectives. In addition, the dissolution of the USSR has given U.S. foreign policy a dominant position on the UN Security Council (though the long-term role of China is as yet unclear). Finally, while the commitment to international legality has been strong, the Pax Americana includes the tendency to justify policy on legal technicalities. This has been most obvious in the effort to justify as defensive measures the invasion of Panama and the institution of the blockade of Iraq.

It is too early to determine whether or not the policies of the new world order will play a long-term role in international relations. Among the primary considerations in predicting the future of these policies are current economic problems of the U.S. economy. Many criticized President Bush for devoting too many resources to foreign policy rather than solving domestic problems. Foreign aid is expensive—especially so when foreign debt is forgiven. Not only does increasing the U.S. deficit augur poorly for the future strength of the U.S. economy, but it also signifies an increasing inability to continue to provide economic aid. If one of the key American objectives in the 1980s and beyond has been to restore U.S. credibility as a world leader, the inability to provide continued aid, coupled with growing U.S. indebtedness, will not instill international confidence in the leadership of the United States. The Clinton administration's commitment to deficit reduction and containment of government spending—including foreign aid— underlies the inherent tension in the new world order policies where ambitious political objectives and rhetoric are tamed by the realities of limited economic means. Furthermore, while neither the Soviet Union nor its successors are any longer U.S. competitors in the Third World, the same cannot be said for Germany and Japan. It is likely that they will be less concerned with the types of government and economy that exist in developing countries as long as these countries can provide a stable climate for investment. Thus in the long term it will be to the interest of at least some developing countries to focus their relations on developed countries other than the United States.[61]

If the Pax Americana portion of U.S. foreign policy has a dubious future, what are some long-term positive factors that may arise out of the end of the Cold War? It would appear that for whatever end the Bush administration was committed to legality and uniformity as the basis of policy, the Clinton administration has reiterated the commitment to the same principles. The rising role of international organizations should provide the structure to continue the development of these factors long after the current U.S. strategy is altered. Moreover, the elimination of superpower competition in the developing world should reduce the level of militarization of regional conflicts and contribute to weakening the role of the military in the domestic politics of many former superpower client states. Finally, since the process of political and economic liberalization visible in much of the Third World has domestic roots independent of U.S. pressure, that process should continue to flourish independent of possible U.S. policy changes.

Notes

1. The authors are aware of the fact that terms such as *developing countries* and *Third World* are inadequate for referring to the large number of countries at various levels of socioeconomic or industrial development to which they refer. However, lacking an adequate alternative concept, we will use these terms interchangeably to refer, in a form of shorthand, to the noncommunist countries of Asia (except for Japan), the Middle East, Africa, and Central and South America. We will also periodically use the term *superpowers* to refer to the USSR and the United States. We are well aware of the exaggerated implications of this term, but we find it useful, again as a form of shorthand.

2. For a perceptive overview of these issues, see Paul Marantz, "The Decline of the Ideological Impulse: Marxism-Leninism Withers Away," *Crossroads: An International Socio-Political Journal* (forthcoming).

3. See Alexei Kosygin, "Direktivy XXIV S'ezdu KPSS po piatiletnemu planu razvitiia narodnogo khoziaistva SSSR na 1971–1975 godu," *Pravda*, 7 April 1971, 6.

4. See Mark N. Katz, ed., *The USSR and Marxist Revolutions in the Third World* (Cambridge and New York: Cambridge University Press, 1990).

5. Mikhail Gorbachev, *Perestroika: New Thinking for Our Country and the World* (New York: Harper and Row, 1987), 19. Abel Aganbegyan, Gorbachev's chief economic adviser in 1986–87, maintained that growth actually ceased in this period. See his *The Economic Challenge of Perestroika* (Bloomington and London: Indiana University Press, 1988), 1–3.

6. This argument is developed in full in Edward A. Kolodziej and Roger E. Kanet, eds., *The Limits of Soviet Power in the Developing World: Thermidor in the Revolutionary Struggle* (London: Macmillan, 1989); and Paul Dibb, *The Soviet Union: The Incomplete Superpower* (Urbana: University of Illinois Press, 1986).

7. In an important article, two Soviet analysts developed precisely this argument. See Alexei Izyumov and Andre Kortunov, "The USSR in the Changing World," *International Affairs*, no. 8 (1988): 46–56.

8. Mikhail S. Gorbachev, "Politicheskii doklad Tsentral'nogo Komiteta KPSS XXVII S'ezdu Kommunisticheskoi Partii Sovetskogo Soiuza. Doklad General'nogo Sekretaria Tsk KPSS Tovarishcha Gorbacheva M. S. 25 Fevralia 1986 goda," *Kommunist*, no. 4 (1986): 29. See also Jerry Hough, *Opening Up the Soviet Economy* (Washington, D.C.: Brookings Institution, 1988).

9. See the different periodization of Gorbachev's foreign policy in S. Neil MacFarlane, "The Management of Soviet Decline in the Third World," *Crossroads: An International Socio-Political Journal* (forthcoming).

10. See, for example, Elizabeth K. Valkenier, *The Soviet Union and the Third World: An Economic Bind* (New York: Praeger, 1983), 16; and Tatiana Zaslavskaia, "The Novosibirsk Report," *Survey*, 28 (1984): 88–108.

11. Gorbachev, "Politicheskii doklad," 18–19, 36, 41.

12. Gorbachev, *Perestroika*, 117, 173–74, 187.

13. See the relevant chapters in Kolodziej and Kanet, eds., *The Limits of Soviet Power in the Developing World*, and in Kanet and Kolodziej, eds., *The Cold War as Cooperation: Superpower Cooperation in Regional Conflict Management* (London: Macmillan, 1991).

14. See "Kubintsy ukhodiat iz Angoly," *Izvestiya*, 3 September 1990.

15. See W. Raymond Duncan, "Superpower Cooperation in the Caribbean and Central America," in Kanet and Kolodiziej, *The Cold War*.

16. For a discussion of changing Soviet perceptions on regional conflicts see, among others, Andrei I. Kolosovskii, "Regional'nye konflikty i global'naia bezopasnost'," *Mirovaia ekonomika i mezhdunarodnye otnosheniia*, no. 6 (1988): 321–24; and A. K. Kislov and A. V. Fropov, "Rol' ssr i SShA v uregulirovanii regional'nykh konfliktov (nekoroye itogi krizisa v Persidskov zalive)," *SSha: Ekonomika, politika, ideologiia*, no. 7 (1991): 3–10.

17. "Unikalnyi dokument," *Izvestiya*, 1 March 1990, 3.

18. Elena Aref'eva, "Miloserdie ili vse zhe ideologiia?" *Izvestiya*, 24 July 1990, 1.

19. Andrei Kolosov, "Reappraisal of USSR Third World Policy," *International Affairs*, no. 8 (1990): 69–73; and Andrei Kiva, "The Third World's Illusions and Realities," *International Affairs*, no. 10 (1991): 30–39.

20. "Press-konferentsiia E. A. Shevardnadze," *Pravda,* 27 March 1990, 5.

21. See Robert O. Freedman, "The Soviet Union, the Gulf War, and Its Aftermath: A Case Study in the Decline of a Superpower," *Crossroads: An International Socio-Political Journal* (forthcoming).

22. See Ann Sheehy, "The Union Treaty: A Further Setback," *Report on the USSR* 3, no. 49 (1991), 1–4.

23. Printed in *Report on the USSR* 3, no. 50 (1991): 31–32.

24. Alexandr Rahr, "Is Gorbachev Finished?" and Stephen Foye, "From Union to Commonwealth: Will the Armed Forces Go Along?" *Report on the USSR* 3, no. 51/52 (1991): 1–7.

25. See Suzanne Crow, "Strategic Withdrawal Resumes," *Report on the USSR* 3, no. 39 (1991): 7–9. On the announcement concerning Cuba see INTERFAX in English, 6 September 1991, in *FBIS-SOV* 91–175, 10 September 1991, 13. On the strongly critical Cuban response see "Moscow Announces Withdrawal of Troops, Havana Protests," *Izvestiya,* 13 September 1991, 1, in *FBIS-SOV* 91–179, 16 September 1991, 19.

26. Louis Hartz, *The Liberal Tradition in America* (New York: Harcourt Brace Jovanovich, 1955), 286–87, 308.

27. Col. M. Ponomarev, "Bush's 'New World Order' Seen as 'Old' Idea," *Krasnaya Zvezda,* 17 May 1991, 3, translated in *FBIS-SOV* 91–98, 21 May 1991, 13.

28. Compared with other regions, Sub-Saharan Africa, with few exceptions, had not played an important part in U.S. policy during the presidency of George Bush. Therefore, we will make little reference to the region in this paper.

29. Thomas L. Friedman, "P.L.O. and Israel to Get Bush Ideas on Mid East Peace," *New York Times,* 12 March 1989, 1.

30. James Baker, "Excerpts from Baker's Mideast Talk," *New York Times,* 23 May 1991, 10.

31. Robert Pear, "Baker Would Ask Cutoff of Funds if U.N. Agencies Upgrade P.L.O.," *New York Times,* 2 May 1990, 12.

32. George Bush, "A Transcript of Bush's Address on the Decision to Use Force in Panama," *New York Times,* 21 December 1991, 19. The four points of the justification were (1) the safety of U.S. lives; (2) the defense of Panamanian democracy; (3) combating drug traffic; and (4) the protection of the integrity of the Panama Canal Treaty.

33. James Baker, "Excerpts from Statement by Baker on U.S. Policy," *New York Times,* 21 December 1989, 19.

34. Thomas L. Friedman, "U.S. Asks Venezuela to Put Pressure on the Sandinistas," *New York Times,* 31 March 1989; "Baker Plea for Interim Contra Aid Evokes the Skepticism of Congress," *New York Times,* 4 March 1989, 1.

35. Robert Pear, "U.S. Revises Plan to Aid Opposition in Nicaragua Vote," *New York Times*, 22 September 1989, 1.

36. George Bush, "Excerpts from the President's News Session on Foreign and Domestic Issues," *New York Times*, 14 March 1990, 14.

37. "Excerpts from Baker's Testimony to Senate Foreign Relations Committee," *New York Times*, 19 January 1989, 8.

38. Thomas L. Friedman, "Gorbachev Accepts Deep Cuts in European Forces as Equal; Baker Hints Shift on Germany," *New York Times*, 10 February 1990, 6.

39. "Transcript of Bush's State of the Union Message to the Nation," *New York Times*, 1 February 1990, 22.

40. "Excerpts from Bush's Statement on U.S. Defense of Saudis," *New York Times*, 9 August 1990, 15; and "Excerpts from Statements by Bush on Strategy in Gulf," *New York Times*, 12 August 1990, 12.

41. "Excerpts of News Conference by Bush on Budget and Gulf," *New York Times*, 15 August 1990, 21.

42. "Excerpts from the President's News Conference on the Gulf Crisis," *New York Times*, 31 August 1990, 11.

43. "Excerpts from Baker Testimony on U.S. and Gulf," *New York Times*, 5 September 1990, 14.

44. "Text of Joint Statement: 'Aggression Will Not Pay,' " *New York Times*, 10 September 1990, 7.

45. "Transcript of President's Address to Joint Session of Congress," *New York Times*, 12 September 1990, 20.

46. "Transcript of the President's Address to U.N. General Assembly," *New York Times*, 2 October 1990, 12.

47. "Remarks by Baker at News Conference in Geneva on Standoff in the Gulf," *New York Times*, 10 January 1991, 14.

48. "Transcript of President's State of the Union Message to Nation," *New York Times*, 30 January 1991, 12.

49. Clyde H. Farnsworth, "New Group to Direct Flow of Crisis Aid," *New York Times*, 30 January 1991, 12.

50. On these issues see "US Opens Talks with Cambodian Communists," *New York Times*, 6 September 1990, 7; Michael R. Gordon, "Nuclear Issue Slows U.S. Aid to Pakistan," *New York Times*, 1 October 1990, 4; and "Mongolia Gets U.S. Trade Aid," *New York Times*, 22 January 1991, 7.

51. Clifford Krauss, "New U.S. Hint on Hussein," *New York Times*, 4 March 1991, 8.

52. "Transcript of President Bush's Address on End of the Gulf War," *New York Times*, 7 March 1991, 8.

53. Patrick E. Tyler, "Gulf Security Talks Stall over Plan for Saudi Army,"

New York Times, 13 October 1991, 1; Eric Schmitt, "U.S. Negotiating New Security Pacts in Gulf," *New York Times,* 1 August 1991, 6.

54. On this issue see "Bush Plan for Iraqi Arms," *New York Times,* 16 November 1991, 12; Andrew Rosenthal, "Bush Unveils Plan for Arms Control in the Middle East," *New York Times,* 30 May 1991, 1; and Alan Riding, "Talks Begin on Arms Sales to Third World," *New York Times,* 9 July 1991, 3.

55. "Excerpts from President Bush's News Session on Israeli Loan Guarantees," *New York Times,* 13 September 1991, 10.

56. "Excerpts from Bush's Address to General Assembly: For a 'Pax Universalis,' " *New York Times,* 24 September 1991, 14.

57. Clyde H. Farnsworth, "Egypt's 'Reward': Forgiven Debt," *New York Times,* 10 April 1991, D1; Clifford Krauss, "Chamorro Wins Bush Promise on Debt," *New York Times,* 18 April 1991; and Jane Perlez, "Ethiopian Factions Seek Broad Coalition," *New York Times,* 2 July 1991, 9.

58. Jane Battaile, "Bush Seeks Expanded Powers on Foreign Aid," *New York Times,* 14 April 1991, 14.

59. Zafar Imam, "The Implications of Perestroika for the Third World, Particularly Asia," in Roger E. Kanet, Deborah Nutter Miner, and Tamara J. Resler, eds., *Soviet Foreign Policy in Transition* (Cambridge and New York: Cambridge University Press, 1992), 233.

60. Ibid., 227.

61. It is important to note as well that a U.S. attempt to shape the world will encounter resistance from the varied cultural traditions that exist in the Third World. For the development of this argument in the context of the last years of the superpower competition see Edward A. Kolodziej, "The Diffusion of Power within a Decentralised International System: Limits of Soviet Power," in Kolodziej and Kanet, eds., *The Limits of Soviet Power in the Developing World,* 3–35.

Part 4

Regional Studies

Chapter 10 ▬▬▬▬▬▬▬▬▬▬▬▬▬▬▬▬▬▬▬▬

Russia, Africa, and the End of the Cold War

Stephen Neil MacFarlane

Introduction

There is a tendency in current Western literature on the Soviet Union (or former Soviet Union) to conclude that with the collapse of the USSR—and for that matter, with the gradual retrenchment of the Soviet presence in regions such as Africa prior to that collapse—it is no longer important to dwell on Russia and the Third World. Certainly, given the current problems facing Soviet successor states, it seems unlikely that they will play much of a role in the near term in the international relations of Africa.[1]

The withdrawal or collapse of Soviet influence, however, has important consequences for African politics and security. These deserve examination by Africanists and specialists in the international relations of what we once called the Third World. Moreover, the evolving situation in the former USSR has important potential implications for Africa's place and role in the world economy, independently of the policies adopted by successor states specifically toward Africa. Third, Russia has not dropped off the map altogether. We may assume that eventually the economic and political situation will stabilize, that its evolving relationship with neighboring states will become more predictable, and that consequently it will reemerge in time as a more active player in the Third World and, arguably, in Africa.

In this context it bears mention that Russia's relations with Africa predate the Bolshevik revolution. Although some of the interests it pursued there were historically specific and are not obviously relevant in today's world, others have a more permanent geopolitical character. These may be expected to propel Russia in particular into a more active African diplomacy. In short, it seems a bit premature to write off the successors to the USSR in the consideration of the political and security environment of Africa.

The Cold War and Its Legacy

The Cold War in Africa is now over, in large part as a result of a cumulative Soviet decision to reduce the level of competition and then to abandon it.[2] To understand the implications of this process for the African political environment, one must first address what the impact of the Cold War itself was.

Africa has been remarkably conflict prone for the last two decades.[3] The roots of its conflicts during this period lie in the colonial territorial, social, and economic legacy of (1) contested borders and irredentism (for example, the case of Somalia); (2) exploitative and illegitimate social structures (for example, apartheid); (3) low levels of national integration;[4] (4) the weakness and frequent illegitimacy of postcolonial state structures and the shortage of capable cadres; and (5) poverty, two consequences of which are an intense competition within states for extremely scarce resources and often extreme inequities in income distribution.

The process of modernization and the challenge that it constitutes to traditional institutions and social structures contribute to tension and conflict within and between societies. Ideological factors, and in particular the intensity of nationalism and its spread to substate actors, are a third contributor to the incidence of interstate and civil violence. In short, it is reasonably easy to develop a sufficient explanation for conflict in Africa without specific reference to the agency of the super-powers or to processes in world politics.[5] Nonetheless, it is striking that the two major conflicts of Africa in the 1970s and 1980s—the Angolan war of liberation and subsequent civil war, and the various conflicts on the Horn of Africa—were characterized by considerable Soviet and American involvement, while in many other cases, other actors (for example, France in Chad and Belgium in Shaba) were frequently perceived to be defending the interests of one or the other bloc in the Cold War. It is also striking that both of these major conflicts were settled or ended during the process of superpower détente and disengagement of 1985–91. It appears, therefore, somewhat simplistic and inaccurate to dismiss altogether the causal role of the USSR and the United States and the global competition between them in the explanation of war in Africa.

In the first place, although the roots of conflict have largely been indigenous and/or the result of the colonial legacy, the choice of local actors to use force to deal with conflict is influenced considerably by the availability of the instruments of violence. Local actors, be they liberation movements or states, lacking the capacity to produce military instruments, seek them elsewhere. Providing military instruments to local actors serves as a means of entry into regional politics for external actors seeking influence, ideological affirmation, status, or strategic position. These ends—and the denial of the same to their adversary—were exactly the objectives the superpowers pursued in their Cold War rivalry. The currency of influence—arms—in turn gave local actors the means to use force to deal with civil and regional adversaries. It was, for example, the Soviet arms assistance program that provided Siad Barre's Somali government with the military capacity to challenge Ethiopian control of the Ogaden in 1977.

This effect pertained not merely to the initial choice of force as an instrument of policy but to the duration of conflicts that ensued. As long as the instruments of organized violence were reasonably freely available, there was no compelling reason for local actors involved in conflicts within the region to seek peaceful resolution of them.

In Angola, for example, as long as the Popular Movement for the Liberation of Angola (MPLA) and the Union for the Total Independence of Angola (UNITA) had assurances of the more or less permanent flow of weaponry from their superpower patrons (the USSR and the United States respectively), there was no persuasive reason to settle for less than victory. Likewise, as long as Mengistu Haile Mariam was provided with an apparently inexhaustible military lifeline from the USSR, he had no obvious reason to compromise on his vision of state centralization and personal power in Ethiopia and to approach seriously the Eritrean demands for autonomy or Tigrean demands for the reform of the central state. In this sense, superpower competition both heightened the propensity of local actors to use force to deal with conflict and reduced any incentive for serious effort at conflict resolution through compromise. To judge from the Angolan and Ethiopian conflicts, superpower involvement also increased the lethality and the collateral damage associated with civil conflict.

There is perhaps some reason to probe further here and to ask whether this perpetuation of conflict was merely an ancillary consequence of the superpower competition or whether the proximate objective of the superpowers was in fact to perpetuate conflict. In theory, anyway, since it was the existence of conflict that created the dependence of local actors on external support and that therefore provided an important basis of superpower influence, one can understand why the superpowers might have perceived such an interest. The argument has been made in the literature on Soviet policy in Southern Africa that in the early 1980s the USSR had no interest in a settlement of the conflict between Angola and South Africa because it was that conflict which made the USSR necessary to Angola.[6]

To the extent that the Reagan Doctrine was designed to inflict clear defeats on the USSR and hence to reverse the apparent tide of history in favor of socialism, which many had perceived in the late 1970s, the United States had little interest in serious efforts to wind up conflicts such as that involving UNITA in Angola until the Soviet Union was willing to settle on American terms.[7] The same conclusion is suggested more strongly if one perceives the Reagan Doctrine as part of a broader Reagan administration strategy to weaken the USSR by forcing it to expend scarce resources unproductively. In this sense, there was perhaps symmetry in the causal roles of the superpowers.

One might of course argue that had it not been the Soviets and Americans supplying the parties to these conflicts, it might well have been someone else. There was (and is) no shortage of arms in the international market. The point is that most suppliers in that market have one or two primary motives—profit or political and strategic interest. The principal participants in these two conflicts did not have the means to pay for weapons in the open market. The pursuit by the United States and the Soviet Union of objectives other than economic gain in the region led them to provide weapons on terms that the protagonists in these conflicts could afford. The two conflicts were largely unrelated to the political and strategic interests of other powers beyond the region.[8]

It is also plausible that the Cold War–related competition affected the internal social and political structure of recipient states. The heavy emphasis on military instruments in superpower assistance to local actors increased the domestic political influence of military establishments. This was particularly obvious in Soviet assistance programming (for example, in Somalia and Ethiopia), but the political evolution of Zaire suggests that in certain instances American involvement had similar effects. In a more general sense, Soviet and American assistance favored and sustained those elements of the political spectrum most sympathetic to their objectives while frustrating the aspirations of those opposing them.

At the level of the region as a whole and of subregions within it, since it tended to be weaker states that benefited disproportionately from external assistance (they were the most likely to invite superpower involvement on terms acceptable to the United States and the USSR), the effect of external involvement was to prevent stronger regional actors from attaining regional preponderance or hegemony. Taking the southern African subregion as an example, it is obvious by any measure (population, industrial capability, defense production, military capability) that the Republic of South Africa was a potential regional leader.[9] There was no means whereby other regional actors could independently balance South Africa and thereby restrain it. The foreign and defense policy of South Africa in the late 1970s displayed the country's clear desire to dominate the region in order to safeguard its domestic political order. But Soviet (and Cuban) assistance to frontline states—in particular to Angola—and to the liberation movements constrained South African aspirations and left its quest for hegemony incomplete.

The final point to make here concerns attempts by the global community to have a role in the management and resolution of regional conflicts. The competition between the USSR and the United States extended into the UN itself and—given that both enjoyed a veto on Security Council actions—substantially circumscribed that organization's ability to arbitrate or to resolve regional conflicts in which the United States and the USSR found themselves opposed. This too favored the perpetuation of conflict in both the Horn and Southern Africa.

Before going on to examine the implications of change the end of the Cold War had for the African political and security environment, I should mention two further effects of competitive Soviet involvement. The first is that the Soviet Union—presumably out of a desire to build influence and status in the region—structured its competitive behavior in large part in such a way as to defend and to strengthen widely held regional norms. Most people in the region will underline the fact of American and Western opposition or indifference to the process of national liberation and to the completion of that process in Southern Africa, and the contrasting Soviet support of that process. There seems to be little reason to quarrel with the proposition that Soviet assistance to the liberation movements in Portuguese Africa (in conjunction with that of China and of regional actors such as Guinea and Zambia) accelerated the final collapse of the Portuguese Empire in Africa.

To take another example, there are a number of instances in which Soviet assistance to states threatened by the irredentism of their neighbors (Ethiopia, for example) or by internal secessionism (Nigeria) prevented substantial alteration of the postcolonial territorial status quo in Africa.[10] One may of course question whether the maintenance of this status quo makes sense in terms of long-term African interests, but there is no doubt that this maintenance is a fundamental norm of states in Sub-Saharan Africa.

Second, the interest of the USSR in expanding its presence in Africa and its influence over regional actors gave African states substantially greater room for maneuver in their relations with the West than they might otherwise have enjoyed. The fears of Western powers of "losing Africa" rendered them less insistent in the pursuit of their economic and strategic interests. These fears were also conducive to larger flows of assistance from the West and the United States in particular than would otherwise have obtained. Perhaps less constructively, the regional perception—fostered by the USSR for some time—of the existence of a more equitable alternative to participation in the international capitalist economy, and of an alternative model of development allowing them to escape the travails of capitalist construction and to accelerate the process of economic development, brought efforts in some states to dissociate themselves from or reduce their dependence on the Western economies.

The Soviet decision to restructure its foreign policy in the Third World and in Africa in particular was the principal cause of the termination of Cold War competition in Africa. The consequences for Africa of the end of the Cold War follow quite logically from the above discussion.

The disappearance of superpower competition from Africa has reduced competitive arms transfers and other forms of military assistance to local actors. If the availability of military assistance from the superpowers enhanced the propensity of regional actors to use force in their efforts to resolve conflicts in which they were involved, then the disappearance of this assistance will make the choice of force less likely.

To the extent that continuing flows of such assistance gave local actors a disincentive to seek to resolve military conflicts in which they were involved, the disappearance of such assistance will give them an incentive to seek negotiated solutions. Doubts on the part of both UNITA and the MPLA concerning the long-term availability of superpower military assistance, for example, contributed to their (regrettably short-lived) acceptance of a negotiated solution to Angola's internal war.

Alternatively, in situations of asymmetric dependence on external assistance (as in Ethiopia), the more dependent party is likely simply to lose as flows of such assistance diminish. Either way, it seems reasonable to suggest that the probability of settlement of conflicts fed by the Cold War is enhanced by that competition's disappearance. It is no accident that the ending of the Cold War has brought the resolution of the two conflicts most directly related to it.

This hardly means, of course, that peace will break out, since there is an entire array of conflicts in the region in which the superpowers have not been competitively involved and which are, therefore, not obviously susceptible to resolution in the post–Cold War context. One might cite here the civil wars in Somalia and Sudan or, for that matter, the collapse of the Liberian state.

Likewise, the ending of the Cold War rivalry and the consequent stanching of the flow of resources to military establishments in African states may have some effect in reducing the influence of the military in the domestic politics of African states that had previously had the dubious benefit of such assistance. With the end of the Cold War, for example, the survival of Mobutu Sese Seko is of less significance than it was previously to the United States, and the U.S. government is consequently less indulgent of his manifest abuses of elementary civil and human rights. The events in Zaire in 1991 suggest that the political balance may be shifting away from the president and his military supporters and toward his opposition.

At the level of regional politics, the ending of the Cold War and the consequent diminution in the balancing behavior of external actors open the way for potential regional hegemons to exercise their power in order to control events in their regions. The behavior of Nigeria (via ECOWAS) in Liberia in 1990–91, for example, suggests that in the post–Cold War environment regionally dominant states are likely to play a stronger role in the management of regional security. At the moment, the other logical hegemon—South Africa—is distracted by internal issues. Assuming that these issues are resolved without the collapse of the state, one may expect that South Africa too will come to exercise a regionally dominant role in Southern Africa, a role stemming not merely from its intrinsic power and power potential but also from the clear economic dependence upon it of other states in the subregion.

A further effect of the ending of the Cold War, in Africa as elsewhere, is the substantial enhancement of the capacity of the UN to act constructively to manage and resolve regional conflicts or to assist regional and other actors in such efforts. The clearest example from Africa is the role of the UN in assisting in the withdrawal of South African forces from Angola and in the implementation of Namibia's transition to independence.

The primary impediments to a UN role in crisis management and conflict resolution in the Third World used to be the permanent rivalry in the Security Council between the USSR and the United States and the tendency of the two superpowers to find themselves on opposite sides of the security issues under consideration within the UN. The principal limitations now are the limitations on the UN's organizational and financial capacity to handle the array of security-related tasks thrown its way as a result of the end of the Cold War and the reluctance (which may well be justified) of the organization to move beyond mediation and peacekeeping to more active forms of involvement in regional conflict.

The third problem with the organization is whether it has the will to act with regard to African conflicts. The organization of effective international action to manage crises and resolve conflicts in Africa depends not just on the UN's capacity but also on a perception among major players within it that they have an interest in regulating the conflict in question. In the Angolan-Namibian case, two of the major actors in the organization were involved, sought to disengage, and saw advantages in using the good offices of the UN to facilitate the resolution of this sore spot in their relations. This case is exceptional. There was no particularly strong U.S. or Soviet incentive to engage the UN in the settlement of the Ethiopian conflict. The permanent members have no obvious political or security incentive to engage the organization's efforts in the Sudanese civil war, while there are numerous conflicts elsewhere in which they find their interests far more strongly engaged (Yugoslavia and Cambodia, for instance). It is highly probable that the limited capacities of the organization will be fully stretched in dealing with items higher on the agenda of those who determine its policies.

The obvious exception here is the coalition intervention in Somalia at the end of 1992. This case, however, reflects the foreign policy making freedom of a president in the last days of his administration, and his desire after a humiliating electoral defeat to go out a winner. It was also a product of a television barrage of human misery untypical of Western media coverage of African conflict. For these reasons, the case is idiosyncratic and not a harbinger of greater UN action in the region. The mounting difficulties faced by UN forces in 1993, more-over, will reinforce the organization's reluctance to intervene actively in African conflict.

Even if the UN were so inclined, the prospect of a more effective security management role for the UN is small comfort for those who are concerned about American preeminence in the organization after the collapse of the Soviet Union. It is widely perceived in the South that the UN may become an arm of American foreign policy in the context of evolving American unipolarity. The Persian Gulf War, the UN initiative which was widely perceived to be a cloak for American regional policy, appears to confirm such concern.

It is not my brief to comment on the thesis of unipolarity in general. Suffice it to say here that it is difficult to envisage the United States playing the role of global policeman. The domestic economic situation in the United States demands the reallocation of resources to domestic tasks. The American public is tired of the global mission of American power and views the end of the Cold War as an opportunity to refocus attention on domestic problems. The social frustration of economically marginalized racial minorities evident in the May 1992 riots in Los Angeles adds urgency to this refocusing of the American agenda on internal issues.

In Africa specifically, the associated concern is that the departure of the Soviet Union and the weakness of its successors leave the field open for the imposition of American hegemony. One reason that Nigeria in particular was not enthusiastic about international intervention in the Liberian crisis was a sense that it was dangerous to involve the United States when there was no balancing power active on the continent. In my view, the notion that the United States will take advantage of the end of the Cold War to impose an American hegemony is tenuous, not only for the reasons mentioned above but also because in Africa specifically (as opposed to, say, the Persian Gulf), there is no compelling reason for involvement. Conflicts in Sub-Saharan Africa do not impinge on the concrete interests of the United States. The principal reason, historically, for American engagement—bipolar competition with the USSR—is gone. Nothing has taken its place. The real danger seems to be not so much American domination but a lack of interest and a corresponding diminution in the flow of resources into Africa. It bears mention that some other traditionally active external powers in Africa (France, for instance) are also trimming their investments and commitments.

The net effect of declining political interest is that external involvement in Africa (other than humanitarian) will be largely structured on the basis of narrow perception of economic interest.[11] This may be a good thing, but since the perceived political significance of Africa has diminished and since there is no longer any perception of alternative economic orders in which to participate (for example, the international socialist division of labor), the bargaining power of African states has withered. The terms of such interaction, therefore, are likely to be less advantageous.

Moreover, it was argued in the last section that Soviet policy was effective in strengthening and sustaining regional norms concerning liberation and in protecting the inviolability of frontiers within the region. The disappearance of the first function is perhaps not terribly significant, since the process of political liberation has been completed (for example, in the independence of Namibia, gained in 1990) or is in its final stages (the movement toward constitutional reform in South Africa). The disappearance of the second may well be more significant, since the states of Africa are frequently weak and are often challenged from within by groups seeking secession or from without (the issue of irredentism). The departure of the Soviet Union removes what has been an important prop to this norm of regional behavior. The declining political interest of both superpowers renders it far less likely that external actors will move to forestall any erosion of this norm.

Decolonization brought only partial independence for Africa, since it coincided with the regional activation of the Cold War. Many African states went from colonial status to being objects of Soviet-American competition. In this sense, the end of the Cold War is the completion of the process of political liberation. African politics and international relations are likely to be more autonomous of global processes since the collapse of the USSR than at any time in the history of independent Africa. They will be free of the disadvantages of providing the patch of grass on which the elephants contest. But they will also lose the advantages of such interest.

Russia, Africa, and the World Economy

The mention of economic interchange brings us to the more specific issue of the impact on Africa of change in the USSR. The collapse of the USSR will have impacts on both the trading and the financial position of Africa. In the short term, the dominant feature of post-Soviet participation in the international economy is the economic disaster that the successor states currently face.

One consequence of the economic collapse is the effective cessation of Soviet-bloc economic assistance to African states.[12] Another is the disastrous shortage of foreign exchange faced by the former Soviet Union, coupled with the profound need for imports of basic necessities and capital goods, given the state of domestic production and the collapse of the internal system of economic exchange. There are few ways in which the former Soviet Union can, in the short term, address the foreign exchange problem. Little of Soviet production is marketable in hard-currency markets. The most obvious exception, however, is natural resources. Moreover, the supply available for export is expanding since the economic crisis reduces the capacity of the Soviet economy to consume resource output.[13] The decrease in domestic demand for many of these minerals may be long-term as well since a post-Soviet economy converting its defense industries and, one hopes, making the transition to technology-intensive growth will be less metal consumptive than in the past. The net effect of released supply and a critical need for foreign exchange is the likelihood of rapid release of stocks and new production onto international markets.

The probable consequence is a reduction in price. This is obviously bad news for other producers, particularly since prices in mineral markets are already soft as a result of the weak international economy.[14] In recent interviews with Canadian mineral executives, I was told that this type of behavior has already been detected in areas of the mineral marketplace where there is significant overlap between Soviet and Canadian production.[15] As is evident from table 1 (pp. 238–41), there are numerous minerals in which the USSR and Africa jointly produce the bulk of world output (chromite, cobalt, diamonds, gold, manganese, palladium and platinum, and vanadium, for example). The rapid and/or uncontrolled sale (or alternatively, dumping)[16] of substantial quantities of product by the former Soviet Union will consequently have particularly intense negative effects on already struggling African economies.

In other instances, such as copper, although the former Soviet Union and Africa do not enjoy predominant market share, the sudden dumping of large quantities of output could have substantial negative effects on price, particularly given already weak demand. In the case of copper, this is an industry upon which certain African countries (Zaire and Zambia, for example) depend extremely heavily for foreign exchange. In general, data on foreign exchange earnings of African states underline the critical role of mineral exports for many.[17] In short, one can envisage a strong negative impact on African resource producers stemming from the resource trading patterns of post-Soviet states.

The implications of the collapse of the USSR in international finance are also bleak. In the first place, flows of public assistance from the former USSR and the Eastern European states have dried up as they seek to resolve their own domestic economic crises. Second, the political constituency for public assistance to foreign states is not terribly strong in most democratic polities. Governments consequently have a hard time squeezing resources out for such programs. As was noted earlier, the most frequent approach to building domestic support for foreign aid in the United States was to cite the Soviet threat and the need to counter it. That is now gone. The result is that it is more difficult now than it was before to justify foreign public assistance.[18]

The other side of the coin is that the pool of recipients has expanded substantially with the collapse of the Soviet Union and the political transition in Eastern Europe. The absorptive capacity of these states with regard to foreign assistance is near infinite. On grounds of security interest and concern over European stability and such issues as uncontrolled migration, the needs of these former communist states are clearly a priority matter. Estimates of public credits and grants to the former Soviet Union during 1991 were approximately $20 billion. The United States and its Western allies announced a $24 billion aid package to the former USSR in 1992.

The point is that the pool of such funds is limited while the demand for them has grown markedly. Increases in public assistance to Eastern Europe and the USSR will have to come at least in part out of funds that otherwise would have been sent elsewhere. Although the data are inconclusive as yet, there is good reason to expect that one consequence of the collapse of communist systems in Eastern Europe and the USSR will be a reduction in public assistance to African states from traditional donors.[19]

The picture is not much brighter in the realm of private investment flows. These have been sluggish in Africa over recent years in any case.[20] There are good business reasons for European and North American firms to concentrate their activities in Eastern Europe and the former Soviet Union. The human capital base is highly developed, while labor costs are low. Certainly, in Eastern Europe in any event, infrastructure is more substantial. Most of these countries are potentially quite rich and are therefore potentially attractive markets for light industrial goods and consumer durables. From the North American perspective, the Eastern European countries in particular have the distinct benefit of proximity— and probable preferential access to—the unifying European Community (EC) market.[21] By contrast, the human capital base in Africa is less developed and infrastructure is generally poor, while in most cases, as a result of size, the market potential of African countries is poor. And, finally, Sub-Saharan African countries do not enjoy the advantage of proximity to developed markets.

There remain significant obstacles to substantial Western private investment in the former Soviet Union and Eastern Europe—legal ambiguities, a lack of financial infrastructure, and political instability— but it is not obvious that these disadvantages are any less substantial in Africa. Moreover, substantial progress has been made and is being made in clearing away many of the legal impediments to investment and growth in the former Soviet Union and Eastern Europe. The conclusion here is that the opening of the Eastern European and former Soviet states to foreign investment on often very attractive terms (as

Table 1. Production of Selected Minerals, 1988 (sub-Saharan African countries, USSR, world totals)

Chromite (in metric tons)

South Africa	4,200,000
Zimbabwe	600,000
USSR	3,240,0001
World total	11,665,717
Percent world total	
Africa	41
USSR	28

Cobalt (recoverable cobalt content from mine output, in thousands of pounds)

Botswana	642
South Africa	1,600
Zaire	56,000
Zambia	14,700
Zimbabwe	278
USSR	6,300
World total	96,781
Percent world total	
Africa	76
USSR	7

Copper (in thousands of metric tons)

Botswana	24.4
Congo	1
Mozambique	0.2
Namibia	40
South Africa	170.1
Zaire	530
Zambia	400
Zimbabwe	16.9
USSR	640
World total	8,453.4

Table 1 continued

Percent world total

Africa	14
USSR	8

Diamonds (in thousands of carats; parenthetical figures refer to subtotals for gem and industrial diamonds)

Angola	1,000 (950 + 50)
Botswana	15,229 (10,801 + 4,428)
Central African Republic	343 (284 + 59)
Ghana	352 (49 + 303)
Guinea	146 (136 + 10)
Ivory Coast	20 (15 + 5)
Liberia	167 (67 + 100)
Namibia	938 (901 + 37)
Sierra Leone	175 (100 + 75)
South Africa	8,382 (3,739 + 4,643)
Swaziland	150 (60 + 90)
Tanzania	150 (105 + 45)
Zaire	19,000 (3,800 + 15,200)
USSR	11,000 (4,500 + 6,500)
World total[a]	93,999 (43,606 + 50,393)

Percent world total

Africa	49
USSR	12

Gold (in troy ounces)

Botswana	900
Burkina Faso	90,000
Burundi	1,000
Cameroon	250
Central African Republic	12,268
Congo	500
Ethiopia	20,000
Gabon	2,500
Ghana	372,979

Table 1 continued

Guinea	10,300
Ivory Coast	300
Kenya	5,000
Liberia	21,753
Madagascar	2,894
Mali	85,000
Namibia	5,100
Rwanda	300
Sierra Leone	13,000
South Africa	19,881,126
Sudan	2,500
Tanzania	3,000
Zaire	140,000
Zambia	10,000
Zimbabwe	475,000
USSR	9,000,000
World total	58,453,814
Percent world total	
Africa	36
USSR	15

Manganese (in thousands of short tons)

Gabon	1,145
Ghana	111
South Africa	1,568
USSR	3,000
World total	9,175
Percent world total	
Africa	30
USSR	33

Palladium and Platinum (in troy ounces)

Ethiopia	150
South Africa	4,285,000

Table 1 contined

Zimbabwe	1,600
USSR	3,900,000
World total[a]	8,667,633
Percent world total	
Africa	49
USSR	45

Titanium (concentrate, in short tons)
1. Ilmenite and leucoxene

Sierra Leone	46,427
USSR	507,000

2. Rutile

Sierra Leone	139,286
South Africa	61,000
USSR	11,000

3. Titaniferous Slag

South Africa	772,000
World total[a]	6,726,554
Percent world total	
Africa	15
USSR	8

Vanadium (production from ores, concentrates, and slag, in short tons)

South Africa	18,060
USSR	10,600
World total[a]	33,660
Percent world total	
Africa	54
USSR	31

[a]Does not include U.S. production because this information is withheld by producers. Generally U.S. production of these minerals is sufficiently small that it does not significantly affect percentages.

in the Chevron deal with Kazakhstan) is causing and will cause a substantial redirection of global investment flows at the expense of less developed regions such as Africa.

In short, the collapse of the Soviet state and the end of Soviet hegemony in Eastern Europe have substantial negative implications for Africa. They erode the market position of African mineral exporters. In addition to removing a major rationale for foreign assistance to African states, they have diverted substantial flows of scarce public assistance funds to new recipients. It is likely to redirect foreign investment away from the less developed South to new targets in the East.

There are painful ironies here. Changes in political systems and in law and regulations governing foreign business activity make conditions in Africa today more ripe than they have ever been before for substantial foreign economic activity. Yet experience thus far suggests that there is little if any private sector response. More broadly, the discrediting of Marxist political and economic recipes, coupled with the disappearance of Soviet willingness to underwrite such experiments, has produced what appears to be a wave of democratization in African states (for example, the transition to pluralist political systems in Mozambique, Angola, Zambia, Tanzania, Benin, and Kenya). This is a development occasioned by the ending of the Cold War, which, rhetorically at least, the United States has been seeking for years. Sustaining it, however, requires economic stabilization and significant growth. Yet the end of the Cold War also reduces the probability that these requisites of successful democratization will be achieved.

The only light in this otherwise bleak picture is that in the longer term, these events will open new markets for certain African exports. Notably, assuming that the Eastern European and former Soviet states stabilize their financial and current account positions, and given their climatic characteristics, these developments open potentially substantial new hard currency markets for tropical produce.

Russian Interests and the Future of Russian Policy toward Africa

The third dimension of this analysis concerns the future of Russian policy in Africa.[22] As noted earlier, given the Cold War animus of Soviet policy in Africa in the modern era, there is a tendency to write Russia off altogether since the Cold War is over. This seems premature for at least two reasons.

First, there is the possibility of reversal of the course of the former Soviet Union. The possibility of a reactionary coup d'état in Russia is not out of the question. Although the consequences of such a reversal would be felt most intensely in the domestic context, there might well be foreign policy implications as well. In this context there is apparently some concern about a possible revitalization of competitive policy in the Third World, of a return to the old pattern of cultivation and encouragement of radical socialist-oriented regimes and involvement in regional conflicts. This concern is promoted in part by Russian leaders and academics themselves in the hope, presumably, of frightening the West into being more forthcoming. Although I sympathize with the intent, I do not agree with the prognosis. First, any successor regime in the former USSR will face exactly the same intractable economic, political, and social problems faced by the current one. These will take a long time to work out. It seems probable, therefore, that the attention of policymakers in the former Soviet Union will be directed primarily toward the solution of these internal problems for the foreseeable future.

One could, of course, argue that a future reactionary regime, in its effort to sustain popular support at home, might attempt to compensate for the domestic crisis through an activist foreign policy. But it is hard for me to believe that the Russian populace would be much excited by the prospect of winning back influence over a Cuba or a Vietnam, let alone an Ethiopia or a Benin. The ideological basis for such activity has been irretrievably shattered.

Next, and in a related vein, there is little impression in Africa itself that the USSR has much to offer as an alternative to the West. The alternatives of so-called socialist orientation, noncapitalist development, and the international socialist division of labor have little if any remaining credibility. Last, any rekindling of foreign policy activism directed against the West in the Third World would carry costs to the former Soviet Union hugely exceeding any perceived benefit.

The question of perceived benefit leads me to a final comment. Change in Soviet and post-Soviet policy toward the Third World in general and Africa in particular was a result not merely of economic crisis, domestic political transformation, and the desire for improvement of relations with the West. It resulted also from a process of learning from experience that prior policies did not work and that the conceptual apparatus upon which these policies were based was fundamentally flawed. Intervention tended to produce entanglement. Assistance did not buy durable influence. Activism carried substantial costs in other areas of Soviet foreign policy. Changed Soviet behavior in the Third World was, in other words, partly the result of a cognitive transformation that was produced by a radical disjuncture between orthodox theory and the political realities of the Third World. One cannot change worldviews the way one changes a pair of trousers. The revision of Soviet perspectives on the Third World constitutes a durable constraint on a return to the activism of the past.

Yet the improbability of a return to forceful messianism and Manichaean universalistic competition does not imply an end to Russia's role and impact. Russia had a policy in Africa prior to the Bolshevik revolution. Part of it had to do with an earlier global political rivalry— that with Great Britain. One of the two major episodes in Imperial Russia's African policy was specifically related to this earlier global contest. Russian intervention in the Boer War was seen as a means of placing pressure on Britain and weakening her in the context of the confrontation over Southwest Asia.[23] This seems not terribly relevant to our purpose.

The second, however, is less historically specific and relates to permanent geopolitical interests of the Russian state. Russia, like the United States, is both an Atlantic and a Pacific power. As such, again like the United States, it has a stake in developing and preserving secure access to maritime communications routes between its western (Barents, Baltic, and—via the Mediterranean or the Suez Canal—Black Sea) and Pacific littorals. This interest is particularly strong for Russia since, while it enjoys one of the longest coastlines in the world, the great bulk of it, the Arctic coast, is next to useless.

Such considerations give any successor regime in Russia a permanent concern with the affairs of the Mediterranean, the Red Sea, and the Indian Ocean. In other words, there exists a permanent Russian interest in the eastern and northeastern littoral of Africa. In this context, it is noteworthy that there was, prior to the revolution, a long-standing Russian interest in the affairs of Ethiopia, occasioned in part by Russian Orthodox affinity for their Coptic brethren but also by a growing awareness of the strategic importance of the Red Sea region in the context of the opening of the Suez Canal.[24]

Although issues relating to sea lines of communication and strategic choke points are likely to be less contentious in the post–Cold War international environment than they were in the nineteenth century and for a time in the Cold War, the fundamental interest in the Red Sea and Indian Ocean region remains. One can expect the development of Russian policies that reflect this interest. Moreover, the resurrection of orthodoxy in Russia may well bring efforts to reconstruct meaningful ties between the Orthodox and Coptic churches. Such a happening could play some role in the formulation of Russian policy toward this region as well.

Finally, during the post–World War II period, Soviet policy makers and diplomats developed a substantial track record and presence in Africa, and Russia continues to have a substantial diplomatic infrastructure throughout the region. They developed the habit, moreover, of being there and sought and appreciated the status associated with involvement in regional affairs, here as elsewhere. During the late Gorbachev era, Soviet policy displayed a desire to reduce commitments and costs but also a sensitivity to the desirability of sustaining this status. Although Russia has become weaker and somewhat dependent on outside assistance, there is little indication to my knowledge that they have abandoned their self-image as a great power and their desire for the rights normally associated with such status in international affairs. As they work their way through their internal problems, one may expect such preoccupations to resurface more clearly in Russian foreign policy. In this sense, one may expect a renewal of Soviet involvement in Africa as a whole.

The nature of this involvement, however, is likely to be substantially different. It will reflect limited strategic, economic, and diplomatic interests rather than universal ambitions. It will reflect specific regionally focused objectives rather than a global competitive agenda. It will not revolve around issues of conflict and social transformation but will be more clearly willing to work within the status quo and to strengthen it or to work for peaceful change where such change is deemed necessary or desirable.

Somewhere Yevgenii Primakov said that what the Soviet Union wanted in the Gorbachev era was to be treated as a normal state, by which I believe he meant a state with concrete and legitimate interests that was willing to pursue these in a nonconfrontational way and that expected to be treated as a legitimate and respected member of the international community. It is this normalcy, rather than withdrawal, that I expect in Russian policy in Africa.

Notes

1. I am referring in this paper principally to the Sub-Saharan region of Africa.

2. The reasons for this trend in Soviet politics are amply analyzed in the literature on the evolution of Soviet policy in the Third World under Gorbachev. For a representative treatment of this question with specific reference to Africa, see S. Neil MacFarlane, "The Evolution of Soviet Perspectives on African Politics: 1975–1990," in George Breslauer, ed., *Soviet Policy in Africa* (Berkeley, Calif.: Institute for International Studies, 1992), 5–47.

3. The great bulk of conflict in Africa, however, has occurred at the substate rather than the interstate level. Wars between African states have been very rare. For an illuminating discussion of this point and of its implications for the African state, see Jeffrey Herbst, "War and the State in Africa," *International Security* 14, no. 4 (Spring 1990): 117–39.

4. This is, of course, also the product of preexisting ethnic and religious diversity.

5. This is one of the critical limitations in the application of conventional theories of international politics to conflict in Africa and elsewhere in the Third World. On this point, see K. Holsti, "International Theory and War in the Third World," in Brian Job, ed., *The Insecurity Dilemma: National Security of Third World States* (Boulder, Colo.: Lynne Reiner, 1992), 37–60.

6. See, for example, Seth Singleton, "From Intervention to Consolidation: The Soviet Union and Southern Africa," in R. Craig Nation and Mark V. Kauppi, eds., *The Soviet Impact in Africa* (Toronto: Heath, 1985), 120. This is a variant of the "spoiler" hypothesis with regard to Soviet policy toward Third World conflict.

7. On this point, see Stephen S. Rosenfeld, "The Guns of July," in William Hyland, ed., *The Reagan Foreign Policy* (New York: New American Library, 1987): 203–19.

8. The Israeli support of the Mengistu regime at various stages of its history and the Iraqi and other Arab support of the Eritrean liberation fronts suggest that in the instance of the Horn, there were alternative external suppliers. But none of them had a supply capacity comparable to that of the USSR.

9. Taking 1991 as an example (subsequent to a substantial reduction in the size of the South African Defense Force), South Africa's population was 37,354,200; its gross domestic product for 1990 was $101.57 billion; its defense budget was $4.11 billion; and there were 72,400 personnel in its armed forces, with a trained reserve of 360,000. Military equipment included 250 tanks, 1,600 reconnaissance vehicles, 1,500 armored infantry fighting vehicles, 1,500 armored personnel carriers, 350 towed artillery, and 259 com-

bat aircraft. South Africa has substantial capability to produce artillery, armored vehicles, combat aircraft, and missiles. Comparable figures for Angola, Namibia, Botswana, Zambia, Zimbabwe, and Mozambique are 47,935,800 total population; $25.54 billion total GDP; $3.55 billion total defense budget; 238,600 total personnel in active service and 50,000 organized reserves; 708 tanks; 419 reconnaissance vehicles; 140 armored infantry fighting vehicles; 213 armored personnel carriers; 841 towed artillery pieces; and 383 combat aircraft. The raw data overestimate the military capability of neighboring states since training standards are in general lower and equipment maintenance is less systematic. Moreover, South African forces are under a single command while those of neighboring states are not. And given that the bulk of the military capability of neighboring states came from Soviet assistance programs that are no longer operating, one may expect the military balance to shift further in favor of South Africa in years to come. Data are taken from *The Military Balance, 1991–1992* (London: IISS, 1991), 125–48.

10. The issue of national integration in Soviet policy in Africa is ably treated in Helen Desfosses Cohn, *Soviet Policy Toward Black Africa: The Focus on National Integration* (New York: Praeger, 1974).

11. This affects not only Western but also Russian involvement in the regional economy. Russian specialists commenting on future economic ties with Africa stress concrete mutual interest and profitability as the basis for that country's economic relationship with Africa. It is appropriate in this context to note the effect that Russia may be in a position to provide human capital to developing countries to assist in development. Such transfers of expertise, however, are likely to be concentrated on countries with a capacity to pay for technical services. This rules out much of Sub-Saharan Africa.

12. The OECD noted this trend in *Development Cooperation: 1991 Report* (Paris: OECD, 1991), 155.

13. On the other hand, one may expect that the economic crisis is also affecting the capacity of enterprises in the former Soviet Union to produce them. This is already clear in energy production. Which process has greater velocity is unclear.

14. If one takes 1980 as the base year for a metals and minerals price index, price trends in nonfuel mineral markets from 1985 are as follows: 1985–70; 1986–66; 1987–85; 1988–112; 1989–1290; 1990–108; 1991–100. These figures are approximate averages for the years in question, as prices fluctuate dramatically within each calendar year. Note, however, the overall downward trend from the peak in 1989 to approximate equality with 1980 price levels by 1991. Figures are from the *IMF Annual Report* (Washington, D.C.: International Monetary Fund, 1991), 3. UNCTAD underlined the vulnerability of African economies to the external economic environment and in particular to

fluctuations in commodity prices in *Trade and Development Report* (New York: United Nations, 1990), 43.

15. Interviews in Kingston, Ontario, in November 1991. The minerals affected included aluminum, nickel, and possibly gold.

16. By dumping, I mean the disposal of output on international markets at a price lower than production cost. In the case of the former Soviet Union, this is hard to identify, since there remains little correspondence between real and nominal (currency) cost of inputs (capital and labor).

17. Taking 1989 as an example, mineral share of merchandise export earning for a sample of African countries was: Sierra Leone—41 percent; Nigeria—94 percent (this example is not terribly relevant, given the prominence of oil exports in Nigeria's trading position); Zaire—85 percent; Ghana—29 percent; Togo—53 percent; Zambia—92 percent; Guinea—83 percent; Mauritania—45 percent; Liberia—35 percent; Angola—95 percent (of which, again, a substantial portion is accounted for by oil); Zimbabwe— 17 percent; Congo—76 percent; Cameroon—48 percent; and South Africa— 46 percent. Data are from World Bank, *World Development Report, 1991* (London: Oxford University Press for the World Bank, 1991), 234–35. Combining data in table 1 with the figures here, it appears that Sierra Leone, Zaire, Ghana, Zambia, and South Africa are particularly vulnerable to change in Russian export behavior.

18. There is considerable evidence of a weakening in the American commitment to the provision of official development assistance during the Gorbachev era. In 1982–86, for example, ODA (Official Development Assistance) constituted 0.24 percent of U.S. GNP. By 1989–90 it was at 0.17 percent. The share of ODA in the federal budget, meanwhile, slipped from 1 percent in 1985 to 0.6 percent in 1989. Data are from OECD, *Development Cooperation, 1991*, 125, 129.

19. In this vein, the OECD noted in page 17 of its 1991 report on development cooperation that there was as yet no indication of any major aid diversion from the developing countries to Eastern Europe and noted the reaffirmation in June 1991 of the OECD ministerial council's commitment that cooperation with the developing countries was not to be diminished by support for countries in Central and Eastern Europe. It should be noted, however, that this conclusion was based on 1990 data on assistance to Eastern Europe and therefore precedes the collapse of the Soviet Union itself and its emergence as a major competitor for aid.

20. Net resource transfer data between OECD countries and Africa, for example, show no increase in private flows between 1988 and 1991. In 1980, ODA made up $12 billion out of the $23 billion net transfer, whereas in 1990, ODA was $17 billion out of the $22 billion total, which suggests that the relative importance of private investment in total resources transfer had dimin-

ished markedly. Figures are denominated in 1989 dollars. Data are taken from *Development Cooperation, 1991, 86.*

21. Moreover, there is a substantial incentive for West European enterprises to invest in Eastern Europe for export of output back to the EC as well. This allows them to take advantage of lower labor costs and more permissive regulatory and taxation environments while the likely extension of trade preferences to the Eastern European states limits the tariff costs of cross-border movement of goods.

22. It presumes that the Russian Republic remains more or less intact, which is of course a debatable presumption. The failure to include other post-Soviet polities reflects these states' limited potential for the projection of power and for sustaining broader foreign policies in the Third World.

23. Edward Wilson gives a detailed and well-documented account of this episode in Russian foreign policy in *Russia and Black Africa Before World War II* (New York: Holmes and Meier, 1974), 78–93.

24. On this point, see Wilson, *Russia and Africa*, 15, 24, 73–78. Russian activity during the nineteenth century in Northeast Africa was of course strongly conditioned by the rivalry with Britain.

Chapter 11 ━━━━━━━━━━━━━━━━━━━━━

Russia and the Asia-Pacific Region

Toward a New Doctrine

Gennady Chufrin

Introduction

Russia is a Eurasian power whose geographic location and demographic composition as well as its material and spiritual life and its past and future are tied inseparably to both the West and the East. It follows logically, therefore, that Russian national interests—formed in such a geopolitical, economic, sociological, and cultural environment—can have neither an exclusively Western nor exclusively Eastern focus. Nevertheless, in the not so distant past, Soviet foreign policy had an obvious tilt toward the West because of the priorities it gave to developing relations with the United States and Western Europe.

Soviet neglect of the East came under criticism in the past, but at least at that time it could be justified to a certain extent by the modalities of a global Soviet-U.S. confrontation that called for a concentration of Soviet political, economic, and military efforts in the direction of the West. With the end of the Cold War and the discontinuation of the political and military confrontation with the United States, however, the motives for the previous Soviet foreign policy have become groundless. Meanwhile, as the Asia-Pacific region grows into a new center of world civilization, and as it has become clear that the world community is entering a new, Pacific era, the East is assuming a very important role for Russia.

Because of the dissolution of the Soviet Union and amid a continuing acute political and economic crisis on its territory, a Russian "Eastern" policy must be formulated. Such a policy should take into account both the necessity of replacing military priorities with economic ones and the emergence of new sovereign states (former Soviet republics) in Central Asia and in the Caucasus, as well as the fact that Russia enters the international arena now in a very weakened political and economic condition. Only a few years ago, the Soviet Union was considered to be another superpower, at least militarily. Even that is no longer the case. Even with its military forces sharply reduced in size and firepower, the new Russia remains a formidable military force, but certainly not at the level of the mid-1980s. This is particularly true in the Asia-Pacific region, where Russian ground forces are now smaller in size than those of China, North Korea, South Korea, and even Japan. What remain as the last vestiges of former Soviet military might are the Pacific navy and the nuclear force, but even these are shrinking in size.

And yet in spite of all the current difficulties, Russia remains not only a regional but also a global power, which means that its international interests are not to be reduced to relations with bordering states alone but should involve relations with other nations also. The relative importance of relations with any particular country, however, may depend upon concrete circumstances.

The end of the Cold War does not signify the advent of a nonconflictual era, either in relations between great powers or in intergovernmental relations in general. On the one hand, the end of bipolarity in international relations, irrevocable as it seems, is a welcome development since it means the end of the hegemonic, imperial, and highly confrontationist policies of two superpowers, of an incessant arms race, and of a dangerous balancing on the brink of a global nuclear holocaust. On the other hand, however, the end of bipolarity may result in the growth of international instability caused by the sharpening of territorial, religious, ethnic, caste, ideological, and other contradictions at regional or interstate levels, which had been previously contained by the rigid modalities of the global confrontation. Another potential source of international instability is connected with the remaining asymmetry of great power interests in the contemporary world, although the new competition may take new forms.

Threat perceptions are also bound to be changed. If, for instance, a threat to Russian national security coming from the West has been reduced to a minimum, threats from the East have not only not disappeared but even intensified. Moreover, the disappearance of the Soviet

Union as one of the principal balancing forces in the Asia-Pacific region may activate the efforts of other powers to fill the vacuum. A special danger for Russian national interests may come from Islamic fundamentalism. One may also expect that the power ambitions of some of the regional states, such as Japan or China, may grow to such proportions that they may endanger the security situation in the Asia-Pacific region.

Therefore, the new Russian Pacific doctrine that is currently being formulated at the official level and that is widely discussed by the general public should take all these factors into account.

Russia and the Asia-Pacific States: Bilateral Relations

On the list of Russian foreign policy priorities in the Asia-Pacific region, the East Asian states—that is, China, Japan, Mongolia, and both North and South Korea—are bound to come first because of obvious geographical, political, strategic, and economic reasons.

In analyzing the global strategic situation in which the Soviet Union found itself at the beginning of the 1980s, the Soviet Defense Ministry noted with grave concern that the Asia-Pacific region in the immediate proximity of Soviet borders presented an important source of military threat to the USSR.[1]

It is no wonder that many Soviet analysts and observers expressed at that time fears that the United States, using its politico-military agreements with Japan and South Korea, was in fact trying to form a triangular alliance between Washington, Tokyo, and Seoul aimed at playing an important role in the global confrontation between the United States and the Soviet Union.[2] The growing U.S. military threat was perceived as especially painful given a background of highly strained Soviet-Japanese relations and an almost open confrontation with South Korea.

In addition, Sino-Soviet relations had grown from bad to worse in the course of the last twenty years, while U.S.-Chinese relations had developed into a wide strategic cooperation, challenging the Soviet Union directly and indirectly in regional conflicts in Afghanistan and Cambodia. Thus it is clear that by the middle of the 1980s the Soviet Union found itself in a strategic isolation in the Pacific and East Asian region that was highly detrimental to its national interests. Such a situation developed as a result of two groups of factors, the first of which was determined by the ever intensifying Soviet-American confrontation on the global and regional levels and the second by the serious and sometimes even tragic mistakes of Soviet foreign policy planners who often failed to distinguish real from imaginary Soviet interests in the Pacific and East Asian region.

It was therefore a formidable task indeed that was placed in front of the new Soviet political leadership that came to power in the mid-1980s—either to pursue the previous foreign policy in the Pacific and East Asia, thus risking further international tension, or to try to change it radically without at the same time jeopardizing national security interests. The choice was made in favor of the second option, focusing on constructive approaches to various highly sensitive and difficult problems in the international relations of the Asia-Pacific region. As a result, the Soviet Union succeeded in dramatically improving its relations with practically all of its counterparts in the region during the next five or six years.

China

Without any doubt, normalization of Sino-Soviet relations became a major event in the international life of the region. In May 1989, interstate relations between the Soviet Union and China were formally normalized after three decades of animosity, and two years later an agreement was reached between them, settling their long-standing dispute over the eastern Sino-Soviet border.

That agreement was of special importance, not only for the Soviet Union but now also for Russia, because it resolved one of the thorniest issues in Soviet-Russian relations with China. In spite of that achievement, the extensive Sino-Russian border continues to constitute a constant and very important geopolitical factor in bilateral relations between the two giant neighbors. Completing border talks with Peking on the common border, reaching an agreement with Chinese authorities on the demilitarization of an area on both sides of the border, and transforming that area into a zone of intensive bilateral economic cooperation remain, therefore, among Moscow's main priorities in its relations with China.

Economic ties between the two states, which have recently been developing at a very fast rate, constitute another important factor in Russian-Chinese relations. Russia is unlikely to jeopardize these since they now provide for a substantial part of Russian trade in the Asia-

Pacific region. There is every reason to believe that favorable trends in the Russo-Chinese trade and economic cooperation will continue to develop and diversify. This optimistic forecast is based both on the success of the last few years and on a number of high-level agreements reached between Moscow and Peking between 1989 and 1991.

The main reason for the dramatic growth of bilateral trade (its volume increased almost eightfold during the last decade) was obviously a political one—the complete normalization of Soviet-Chinese relations in 1989. It is worth noting here that the resumption and subsequent expansion of Soviet and Russian-Chinese trade became possible not only because of the resumption of intergovernmental economic and trade exchanges but also to a large extent because of the very quick growth in the border trade between the two countries, the establishment of direct links between enterprises, and the conclusion of numerous barter deals and contracts providing for industrial and scientific cooperation.

Russo-Chinese relations may not, however, develop entirely without difficulties since Moscow and Peking now regard many international as well as domestic events differently. One of the potentially explosive issues is China's human rights problem. If Russia joins other civilized nations in condemning human rights violations by Chinese authorities, this will certainly create a serious strain in Russo-Chinese relations.

Another highly explosive issue is the future of Sino-Taiwanese relations. As the domestic political situation in Taiwan is currently developing, there is a growing likelihood that its proclamation of full independence is only a matter of time. This does not mean, of course, that Russia should change its traditional Soviet stand on the problem of Taiwan; however, the development of nonpolitical, especially economic, relations with Taipei may be quite desirable for Moscow, which is now striving to overcome the present domestic economic crisis. But when a nongovernmental Russian delegation visited Taiwan in September 1992 and reached an agreement there to open a direct air service between Moscow and Taipei, this caused serious displeasure in Peking.[3]

Japan

The development of normal constructive relations with Japan is at least as important for Russia as the development of Russo-Chinese relations. The potential advantages that Russia can gain from the development of commercial, financial, investment, and scientific relations with Japan are quite obvious. It is the widely spread perception, however, that this potential cannot be realized unless the territorial problem between Russia and Japan—the issue of the southern Kuril Islands, which were taken from Japan by the Soviet Union through the San Francisco Peace Treaty in 1951—is resolved. Japan disputes this decision, insisting on its title to four of the islands.

This problem should obviously be resolved, but only on mutually accepted terms. One must not disregard not only Japanese arguments but also the fact that in a March 1991 referendum, a decided majority of the Russian population living on the Kuril Islands voted against ceding the islands to Japan. Since that time, the public mood in Russia—and not only in its Far Eastern regions—has constantly grown in favor of that stand. Thus, according to the results of a public opinion poll conducted in twelve major regions of Russia in August 1992, over 76 percent of the population said no to the possibility of handing over the southern Kuril islands to Japan. In November 1991, 71 percent of the respondents in a similar opinion poll gave negative answers.[4] It was small wonder, therefore, that President Yeltsin decided to postpone the official visit to Japan originally planned for September 1991 when he clearly recognized the state of the public mood prevailing in Russia. Foreign Minister Andrei Kozyrev proved to be right when he warned his Japanese counterpart Michio Watanabe during his visit to Tokyo in March 1992 that Japan's policy of refusing large-scale aid prior to the return of the islands might be counterproductive.[5]

Even if the disputed islands were to soon be handed over to Japan, this would not in itself change the existing cool attitude of Japanese business toward prospects of economic cooperation with Russia. The reason for such an attitude is not so much political but now largely an economic one—the growing incompatibility of the Japanese and Russian (especially its Far Eastern part) economies makes this cooperation less and less attractive for Japan. Therefore, while efforts should continue toward resolving the territorial dispute, in principle at least the new Russian doctrine should not be based on shaky assumptions and disregard of domestic public opinion.

The Two Koreas

Moscow's relations with the Republic of Korea are clearly rapidly developing. This is especially true as concerns trade and economic ties, though there is still much room for improvement.

What now limits the expansion of Russian-South Korean trade is not politics but purely economic constraints. So far, Russian exports have included mostly coal, pig iron, rolled metal, nickel, timber, and seafood. South Korean companies have expressed their interest in buying high-precision instruments, power generators, and metal-cutting tools and bearings as well as the latest Russian know-how in different fields of science and technology.

Moreover, South Korean interest in Russian machinery and equipment—particularly in power generation equipment and nuclear and space technology—makes Russia's chances of taking part in Asia-Pacific trade and economic exchanges very strong, not only as a supplier of raw materials but also as an exporter of high technology. It is worth noting here that while Soviet and Russian exports to Australia are very small, their structure is rather significant; over 75 percent of its value is represented by cars, tractors, metal-cutting tools, refrigerators, air conditioners, and cameras.

Politics is not only not an obstacle but rather a stimulating factor in Russian-South Korean relations. Thus Seoul recognized Moscow's favorable change of position on the issue of the denuclearization of the Korean Peninsula when the Soviet and then the Russian government refused to grant unconditional support to Pyongyang on this issue and demanded that its erstwhile ally accept its obligations under the Nuclear Non-Proliferation Treaty by opening its nuclear facilities to international inspection.

Seoul regarded as equally favorable the Soviet (now Russian) stand on the issue of the entry of the two Korean states into the UN when Moscow flatly refused to support Pyongyang's proposal of "two states—one seat" in the UN.

Moscow and Seoul are currently proceeding with preparations for signing a treaty on good neighborliness and cooperation originally proposed by former Soviet president Mikhail Gorbachev during his official visit to South Korea in April 1991 but later postponed because of the dissolution of the Soviet Union. When this treaty is concluded, it will not only promote bilateral Russian-South Korean relations but will make an important contribution to the legal framework being created in and around the Korean Peninsula, thus providing for more stable security.

If Russian–South Korean relations are improving, Russian–North Korean relations are definitely deteriorating. As a result, Russian–

North Korean ties in economic exchange have been reduced to the level of the mid-1970s, arms sales from Russia were stopped in 1991, and bilateral political relations have become very cool.

Any deterioration of Russian–North Korean relations could not be regarded to be in Russia's national interest, nor would it serve regional stability, since the decline of Soviet– and Russian–North Korean relations is regarded in Pyongyang as an unfriendly situation that plays into the hands of extremist elements in the local leadership. It is therefore highly imperative not only to extend the existing treaty of friendship and cooperation signed between the Soviet Union and North Korea in 1961 (this was in fact done automatically until 1996) but to supplement it with new protocols to update the treaty in accordance with new bilateral, regional, and global realities and to indicate to Pyongyang Moscow's willingness to maintain good relations with it.

This, however, does not mean that Russia should hesitate in opposing any moves by North Korea that may be considered detrimental to regional peace and stability. The central problem in this regard is the threat of nuclear proliferation in East Asia that may be triggered by the North Korean nuclear program if suspicions about its military character are proved to be correct. A scenario that may develop in this case is very easy to imagine: if South Korea and Japan feel threatened by the development of a military nuclear force in North Korea, they will probably start to produce nuclear weapons of their own, thus creating a highly explosive situation in Russia's immediate vicinity.

Even if the suspected North Korean nuclear military program is nothing more than a bluff, as some experts both in Russia and in the West believe it to be, since the country does not possess sufficient financial and technical resources for its implementation, it is in the national interest of Russia that the bluff be called off. The best way to allay existing fears and suspicions is, of course, to let the International Atomic Energy Agency (IAEA) thoroughly inspect all North Korean nuclear facilities, including a nuclear reprocessing center at Yongbyon. Thus Moscow welcomed the IAEA reports that stated that North Korea handed over to the agency a comprehensive list of nuclear facilities and that "contained more details of North Korea's nuclear industry than were necessary—and than the outside world knew of."[6]

Some analysts, mostly in the United States but also in Japan, Australia, Canada, and elsewhere, believe that regular IAEA inspections will not be sufficient to convince the outside world beyond any doubt of the absence of nuclear weapons production capacities in North Korea. They insist, therefore, that the IAEA should demand the consent of the North Korean government for intrusive or challenge inspections of its nuclear facilities. From the Russian perspective, such demands seem appropriate in principle, although to bring them to the North Korean government and expect its cooperation would better be done by means of diplomatic persuasion than by presenting ultimatums.

While the nuclear issue may cause immediate concern to Russian foreign policy and strategic planners, it remains only part of the larger problem of ensuring peace, security, and cooperation in the Korean Peninsula and of establishing an atmosphere in the region conducive to the eventual peaceful unification of the two Korean states. Speaking at an international conference held in Seoul in early November 1991, Sergei Rogov, who was at that time a head of the Far East Department of the Soviet Foreign Ministry, stated, "We [the Soviet government] firmly believe that a dialogue between Pyongyang and Seoul, as well as the overcoming of a politico-military confrontation between the two Korean states are central to achieving détente on the Korean Peninsula."[7]

This Soviet position toward a North-South dialogue and its role in peacekeeping and confidence-building efforts on the Korean Peninsula has basically been inherited by Russia and now constitutes one of the principal guidelines of Russian foreign policy in this part of the world. Moscow, therefore, reacted positively when North Korea and South Korea signed the Agreement on Reconciliation, Non-Aggression, Exchanges, and Cooperation between the South and the North in Pyongyang in February 1992. Along with another document that was signed simultaneously—a Joint Declaration on the Denuclearization of the Korean Peninsula—from Russia's perspective, this agreement created a legal basis for a concrete policy of building mutual trust and cooperation between the two Korean states.

From the Russian point of view, the success of such a policy is not only welcome but also highly desirable since the alternative is a continuation of the state of political and military confrontation on the peninsula. A failure to arrive at national reconciliation would not only further antagonize Pyongyang and Seoul but would negatively influence the positions of major outside powers.

U.S. Under-Secretary of Defense Paul Wolfowitz indicated what might happen in this case in his speech in Kuala Lumpur on 23 June

1992 when he stated, "North Korea's nuclear ambitions caused us to go back and reassess the security situation on the Korean Peninsula; we decided that because of the potential nuclear threat, it would be prudent to set aside for now the substantial phase two reductions [about 6,500 troops] programmed for Korea."[8] This revision of the withdrawal timetable of U.S. ground forces from South Korea would not only prolong the direct U.S. military presence in close proximity to Russian borders, a situation Russia hardly desires, despite the fact that U.S.-Russian relations have radically improved. It would also jeopardize chances of an early Korean unification since no North Korean government would voluntarily agree to such a unification unless there were a complete withdrawal of foreign troops from the Korean soil.

The unification of Korea is, of course, first and above all, a matter pertaining solely to the internal affairs of the Korean people. It is, however, in Russia's national interest to promote this process since the success of unification would mean the resolution of one of the most acute conflict situations in the Asia-Pacific region, where outside powers have been heavily involved. Moreover, a unified Korea might contribute positively to the state of international relations in East Asia, especially at a time when both Russia and the United States are in the process of reducing their military strength in the region for domestic reasons, and while Japan, acting under mounting domestic nationalist pressure, moves slowly but steadily from one stage to another in revising its postwar policies on security issues, that is, from increasing its defense expenditure in absolute and relative terms to expanding an area patrolled by its armed forces and to passing legislation allowing Japanese troops to be sent overseas for the first time since World War II. Korea, which had a painful experience with Japanese militarism in the past, is likely to become a natural ally of Russia in opposing the revival of any such militarism in the future and thus to become more influential in pursuing a policy to contain it when the country is unified.

Southeast Asia

As for relations with Southeast Asian countries, Russian interests there are connected first and foremost with prospects of trade and economic expansion. The previous model of Soviet relations with this part of the Asia-Pacific region is no longer valid; it was based on massive economic and military assistance to Vietnam, Laos, and Cambodia, while the scope of economic relations with the states of the Association of Southeast Asian Nations (ASEAN) remained negligible. Russia no longer wants to support one group of Southeast Asian countries against the other. Moreover, it is interested in maintaining an atmosphere of peace and cooperation in this area, which has now become very important both economically and politically.

In its relations with the states of Indochina, Russia is moving rapidly from unilateral assistance to the development of mutually beneficial relations. This has been made possible not only by the fundamental change in Moscow's stand on the issue of economic aid to its former friends and allies but also by the substantial recent growth in the economies of the Indochinese states, especially that of Vietnam.

As the result of domestic economic reforms, Vietnam has become not only self-sufficient in staple foods but also a large exporter of rice. Russia imports from 5 to 20 percent of its rice, natural rubbers, coffee, and vegetables from Vietnam. In return, Vietnam is a good market for Russian manufactured goods, especially machinery, equipment, and spare parts for industrial enterprises built earlier with Soviet assistance. This kind of commercial exchange and economic cooperation may become very beneficial both for Vietnam and for the Far Eastern regions of Russia because of an assured market for the type of commodities both sides can offer each other and also because of convenient sea lanes of communications between the two countries.

The development of large-scale trade, financial investment, and technological relations with the ASEAN countries may present even greater potential advantages and opportunities for Russia in its relations with these states. In addition to offering a rich source of raw materials, consumption goods, and modern technology, the ASEAN economies can also serve as an important alternative market to Japan and South Korea, thus presenting good commercial opportunities for potential Russian buyers.

Now that the ASEAN countries no longer regard Russia as an ideological or military threat to their interests, the main obstacles in the way of a speedy development of their economic relations with Russia are related to such issues as nonconvertibility of the Russian ruble and the low competitive levels of most Russian manufactured products. On the other hand, local ruling elites, especially in Malaysia and Indonesia, may seem interested now, as never before, in having good, stable, friendly relations with Moscow. This may be explained by their intention to retain a certain balance of great-power interests in Southeast Asia, especially now since the dissolution of the Soviet Union and the partial military withdrawal of the United States from the region. Russia should live up to this opportunity and make every effort to upgrade its relations with the ASEAN states. In the process it may not only improve its political image in this part of South Asia but also obtain firsthand knowledge about local markets as well as the opportunity to promote its own sales.

Oceania and the South Pacific

This region, though geographically quite far from Russia, should nevertheless be regarded by the current Moscow authorities as a very important part of the Asia-Pacific region for Russian national interests.

These interests are determined, first, by the role played by Australia and New Zealand as exporters of grain, meat, and other agricultural products to Russia. Moreover, smaller South Pacific nations may offer good opportunities for the Russian fishing fleet.

Second, Australia is the only country in the Asia-Pacific region that has a large Russian community. Since the defeat of communism in Russia, members of this community have expressed the desire to reestablish close links with the land of their forefathers—something no Russian government can overlook.

Third, Australia and New Zealand play an important role in regional economic organizations such as the Asian Development Bank, the Pacific Economic Cooperation Conference, and the Asia Pacific Economic Cooperation Forum. As Russia takes its first steps to join the world and regional economies, it would be worthwhile for it to engage the support of Australia and New Zealand in helping it to take part in these and similar economic organizations.

Conclusion

In conclusion, it is necessary to emphasize that while placing an accent on its new Pacific doctrine on bilateral relations with the regional countries, Russia should not abandon efforts to create a multilateral regional mechanism for maintaining peace and security in the Asia-Pacific region as well as nondiscriminatory multilateral regional economic cooperation.

This is in no way meant to suggest that Russia should devote its efforts to such suspicious schemes as the Asian collective security proposed by the Soviet government at the end of the 1960s. Instead, it should support proposals made by other Asia-Pacific countries that are aimed at avoiding military or economic conflicts and reducing international tension. Thus, for instance, it will be in Russia's interest to support peacekeeping efforts undertaken in the Asia-Pacific region either by the ASEAN states or by Australia or Canada. It would hence serve Russian national interests to support Canada in its initiative to establish a North Pacific Cooperative Security Dialogue that will help to engage countries of the North Pacific and East Asia in a multilateral dialogue on traditional and nontraditional security issues. So far, this initiative is in its preliminary stages, and Moscow may help to take it off the ground by extending formal support to it as well as by adding its own proposals on confidence building and cooperation in the region.

Since the end of the Cold War and progress recently achieved in resolving the Cambodian and Korean conflicts, however, regional security concerns seem to be generally on the decline in the Asia-Pacific region. Instead, economic issues have taken primary importance in global international relations. The contradictions that existed between former allies during the Cold War period have surfaced, and the world has begun to break up into rival trade blocs. The General Agreement on Tariff and Trade (GATT) system and free trade are now in more serious danger than ever before. This situation is highly detrimental to the interests of Russia.

It will therefore be imperative for Russia to support those countries in the Asia-Pacific region that raise their voices against the existing trend of dividing the regional economy into two or three major competing trade blocs. It will also be in Russia's interest to counterbalance the existing trend of dividing the world economy into competing regional blocs and to undertake active steps to support the GATT principles. Russia has no other alternative but to uphold the principles of regional cooperation, since if the Asia-Pacific region were to be divided between powerful economic blocs, it would be held in a subordinate position. By fostering regional cooperation, Russia would act as a responsible member of the international and Pacific communities. Further, a Pacific doctrine based on such principles would demonstrate to the outside world Russia's genuine interest in the Asia-Pacific region, thus averting suspicions of any ulterior motives in the new Russian foreign policy.

Notes

1. *Otkuda ishodit ugroza miru* (Whence the threat to peace) (Moscow, 1982), 15.

2. See, for instance, A. V. Vorontsov, *Otnosheniya mezhdu SSHA, Yaponiyei i Yuzhnoi Koreyei (vneshnepoliticheskiye aspecty)* (Relations between the United States, Japan, and South Korea: foreign policy aspects) (Moscow, 1985); V. Y. Leshire, *Osnovniye tendentsii yapono-amerikanskogo voenno-politicheskogo sotrudnichestva v 70-ye gody* (Main tendencies of U.S.-Japanese strategic cooperation in the 1970s) (Moscow, 1978); and V. M. Mazurov, *SSHA-Kitai-Yaponiya: perestroika mezhgosudarstvennyh otnosheni* (U.S.-China-Japan: reconstruction of interstate relations) (Moscow, 1980).

3. *Izvestiya*, 24 September 1992, 7.

4. *Izvestiya*, 7 September 1992, 6.

5. *International Herald Tribune*, 21 March 1992, 4.

6. *Economist*, 16 May 1992, 93–94.

7. *Soviet Russia, North Korea, and South Korea in the 1990s: Nuclear Issues and Arms Control in and around the Korean Peninsula* (Seoul, 1992), 28.

8. "Remarks by Honorable Paul Wolfowitz, U.S. Under-Secretary of Defense for Policy" (ISIS conference, Kuala Lumpur, 23 June 1992), 13.

Moscow, Cuba, and Central America

Anatoly Glinkin

Soviet Dilemmas in Central America

The end of the Cold War in the international arena and the peace settlement in Central America after many years of armed struggle have created a more propitious atmosphere than before for an objective analysis of the behavior of all states directly or indirectly involved in these events. The regional conflict in Central America emerged as a result of local and national contradictions that were strongly affected by the East-West confrontation. This created dilemmas for Soviet foreign policy.

Soviet involvement in Central American affairs began with the triumph of the Sandinista revolution in Nicaragua. Prior to 1979 Moscow had succeeded in establishing diplomatic ties with only one country in the region—Costa Rica. The inauguration of the Soviet Embassy in San José in November 1971, however, did not intensify relations between the partners. The cool posture of Costa Rica toward cooperation with Moscow may, at first glance, be explained by the fact that its government, because of its devotion to democracy, censured various aspects of Soviet international behavior and human rights violations in the USSR. Moscow's relations with other Central American countries were limited during many decades to the nonofficial ties of the Communist Party of the Soviet Union (CPSU) and Soviet public organizations with the Communist parties and leftist popular organizations in the region. Judging from a number of secret documents from the CPSU archives, published in Russia after the collapse of the August

1991 coup, there is every reason to assume that these channels could have been used by the Kremlin for financing the Central American left.

The victory of the Sandinista revolution heightened Moscow's enthusiasm. The general secretary of the CPSU, Leonid Brezhnev, in his report at the Twenty-sixth Party Congress, portrayed the overthrow of the Somosa dictatorship by the Nicaraguan people under the leadership of the Sandinista National Liberation Front (SNLF) as one of the outstanding revolutionary events during the late 1970s and as a new, eloquent testimony to the reinforcement of socialism and national liberation forces in the world arena.[1] Brezhnev and other Soviet leaders did not hesitate in adopting a decision to support Nicaragua. In conformity with their global strategy, the Soviet Union had to play the role of the bulwark of revolutionary and national liberation forces all over the world.

The USSR was among the group of more than thirty states that recognized the Nicaraguan Government of National Reconstruction during the first three days following 19 July 1979. Moscow and Managua agreed in October 1979 to normalize diplomatic relations that had been established in 1944. The first official Sandinista delegation visited the Soviet Union in March 1980 and signed a variety of agreements and protocols concerning trade, technical cooperation, civil aviation, and consular ties. In 1981–82 Moscow concluded further economic, technical, communications, and fishery agreements with Managua. Party-to-party ties between the CPSU and the SNLF had to be established.[2] In this way a solid treaty framework was laid down for a long-term multifaceted collaboration between the USSR and Nicaragua. According to the secrecy dogma, Moscow has never publicly acknowledged its military aid program to Managua, but the Stockholm International Peace Research Institute (SIPRI) registered the first deliveries of Soviet armaments to Nicaragua in 1981.[3]

The decision-making process in the Kremlin at that time was greatly influenced by the euphoria around the people's revolution in that small Central American country and by the impact of a wave of international solidarity with the "New Nicaragua." During the Brezhnev era, the Kremlin's Central American policy was inspired by optimistic expectations to gain a foothold in the strategically important region close to the southern flank of the United States. This could open new channels for strengthening Soviet influence over revolutionary developments in the region and consolidate interaction with its principal ally, Castro's Cuba, which had established close collaboration with the Sandinistas long before 1979.

In the specific conditions of the early 1980s, the following scenario appeared to be very attractive for the Soviet political and military establishment: the Havana-Managua axis was becoming a magnetic force for certain Caribbean countries (Grenada, Guyana, and Jamaica) in which, at that time, various experiments with so-called democratic, national, or cooperative socialism were being staged. From a long-term perspective, this tendency was expected to bring into being in the Western hemisphere a solid group of states of Socialist orientation opposing the United States. This perception also explained Moscow's interest in the outcomes of the civil war in El Salvador and the guerrilla fighting in Guatemala. The Soviet leaders further realized that close cooperation with Cuba in Central America could create some complications since Havana, in pursuing its own interests in the region, was undertaking various activities that were labeled export of revolution. Referring to the preeminence of the common interests of the Socialist world, the Cuban vice president, Carlos Rafael Rodrigues, stated, "This does not mean and cannot mean that our every day politics, guided by our own objectives and interests, become subordinate to the policy of other Socialist states."[4]

It was evident that Latin America as a whole and Central America in particular had been upgraded in the global and Third World strategy of the Soviet Union. In this connection, significant adjustment needed to be introduced into the theoretical and policy dimensions of Soviet Third World strategy to reflect both the inclusion of Latin America in its global scope and the recognition of its regional revolutionary potential and dynamics.

Did these adjustments go so far as to make possible the applicability of a broadly interpreted Brezhnev doctrine in Central America by the Communist empire, which during his tenure resorted twice to military intervention, first in Czechoslovakia and later in Afghanistan?

Several factors eliminated the probability of such an outcome in the 1980s. Soviet involvement in the ruinous arms race and Moscow's commitments to revolutionary and national liberation forces throughout the world had already turned into a backbreaking burden. The international community unanimously condemned the Soviet invasion of Afghanistan, and the USSR consequently found itself in isolation on the international scene. Moreover, the escalation of regional conflict in Central America could have triggered a direct confrontation between the two superpowers. Both the USSR and the United States remembered the Cuban missile crisis of 1962. In addition, Washington was not yet completely over the Vietnam syndrome, and Moscow had already begun to suffer from the Afghanistan syndrome.

The whole complex of global and regional factors called for Soviet restraint in Central America. In practice, the Kremlin had to avoid direct interference in the Salvadoran drama, thus confining itself to demonstrations of solidarity with the Revolutionary Democratic Front and the Farabundo Marti National Liberation Front. Moscow followed the same line concerning events in Guatemala, where the level of revolutionary activity was much lower. Hence Nicaragua was destined to become a key factor in Moscow's Central American strategy. No one could question the legitimacy of Soviet-Nicaraguan cooperation from the position of international law. The Sandinista government was a sovereign actor that maintained diplomatic relations with 112 foreign states including the United States.

So how justified were the assessments of U.S. political analysts who in the early 1980s raised alarm over the rapid growth of the Soviet threat and the appearance of a "New Cuba" in the region?[5] Was it true to the facts that Nicaragua was said to constitute "an unusual and extraordinary threat to the national security and foreign policy of the United States"?[6]

Analysis of the relevant documents and statistics demonstrates fundamental differences between the Soviet-Nicaraguan interaction during a decade of Sandinista rule and Moscow's collaboration with Cuba based on a privileged ally model. Because of limited resources, the Soviet Union could not economically support a "second Cuba" in the Western hemisphere. A massive Soviet presence in Nicaragua, in view of the U.S. proximity, moreover, could have been a dangerous game with an unpredictable outcome. From a military-strategic perspective, the Cuban fortress could satisfy the minimum requirements. After the beginning of the contra war against Nicaragua, the survival of the Sandinista regime became the major goal in Moscow's policy.

Soviet policy was clearly designed to avoid transforming the Nicaraguan issue into a U.S.-USSR confrontation. The Kremlin supported Managua diplomatically in the UN and provided financial and technical assistance to meet development needs in the areas of geological surveys, fishery, infrastructure, radio and telecommunications, mining, and processing industries. By the end of the first quinquennium of Sandinista rule, the Soviet Union, Cuba, and other socialist countries occupied only third place among foreign donors (24 percent of all loans and credits, amounting to $2.501 billion). The first place was occupied by Latin America (30 percent), and the second by multinational organizations (25 percent).[7] The distribution of Nicaraguan trade followed a similar pattern. Soviet bloc arms shipments to Nicaragua consisted mainly of defensive armaments such as BTR-60 armored personnel carriers, T-54 and T-53 tanks, 105-millimeter howitzers, antiaircraft guns and missiles, and Mi-17 and Mi-24 helicopters.[8] As some researchers have stated, "The major part of a limited number of modern sophisticated arms was bought by Sandinistas in Western Europe and not in the East."[9] Most probably, all these facts have led several analysts in both Latin America and the United States to the conclusion that the USSR pursued a low-profile policy in Nicaragua.[10] Diversified relations with the outside world fully corresponded to the nonaligned foreign policy declared by Managua.

The situation changed drastically during the second half of the 1980s. Gorbachev's perestroika did not immediately affect Soviet-Nicaraguan relations. As Daniel Ortega stated, the economic and military assistance from Cuba and Eastern Europe became crucial for the survival of the Nicaraguan revolution. According to available data from 1979 to 1989, Soviet material support for the Sandinistas amounted to $2.813 billion (including deliveries of nonmilitary goods worth more than $1 billion). The Socialist countries of Eastern Europe contributed $877 million, and Cuba contributed more than $600 million.[11] The Soviet Union became the main supplier of many goods that were vital to the Sandinistas, including oil and oil products. More than forty joint development projects were undertaken, among them an educational center in Managua and a hospital near Chinandega that became known throughout Central America. Soviet humanitarian aid arrived in Managua when the country suffered from natural disasters.

The new dimensions of Soviet-Nicaraguan collaboration did not constitute a Soviet offensive in Central America. The USSR filled the vacuum left by the withdrawal of a number of Western nations from Nicaragua. Moscow also undertook additional measures to meet the new requirements of the country, which was under permanent siege. Soviet assistance to Nicaragua, however, even during the most dramatic years of the escalation of regional conflict in Central America, was smaller than the Reagan administration's aid to its Central American allies.

In discussing the constraints of the superpowers' policies in Central America, a very important, often unacknowledged, factor should be mentioned—namely, the collective diplomatic efforts of Latin American powers aimed at the political settlement of the conflict in Central America.

First, the peacemaking activities began in this part of the globe earlier than in other hot spots. The Contadora Group created by Colombia, Mexico, Panama, and Venezuela succeeded in elaborating an integral conception for bringing about peace in the region. The Contadora Act for Peace and Cooperation in Central America was based on the principles of nonintervention and respect for freedom of opinion. Thus a clear and attractive alternative was set off against the use of military force. As a result, certain barriers were set in place against the escalation of tension and superpower interference in the region.

Second, during the course of the Contadora process, Latin American unity became stronger. In Central America there was consolidation of those forces that favored national reconciliation and termination of the bloodshed. There is no doubt that the Contadora process paved the way to the peace initiatives of the presidents of Guatemala and Costa Rica, which resulted in the signing by five Central American countries of the Esquipulas-2 or Guatemala Agreement: "Ways to Establish a Firm and Long-Lasting Peace in Central America."

Third, the proposals of the Contadora Group and the Guatemala Agreement were supported by the overwhelming majority of the international community. The socialist countries of Eastern Europe and many Western nations, including members of the North Atlantic Treaty Organization, Japan, the Nonaligned Movement, the Socialist International, the UN, and the Organization of American States (OAS) all gave it their support.

In such a situation, neither the Soviet Union nor the United States could brush aside the peace process initiated by the Contadora Group and its followers. Moscow and Washington were publicly obliged to disclose their positions. In a series of official declarations and statements, Soviet and American authorities expressed their support for the negotiation process and a peaceful settlement in Central America.

At first glance, their declarations could be interpreted as acknowledg-ment of a de facto obligation not to use military force in the region, although nothing was said to this effect in the documents.

A detailed analysis of these declarations, however, shows that both superpowers were preoccupied mainly with political rhetoric. No sub-stantial shifts in their Central American policy took place that could have paved the way for mutually acceptable compromises and con-structive interaction. Soviet diplomacy accentuated the ideologically biased approach of Managua and Havana toward the solution of regional conflict in Central America and stressed the urgent need to stop Washington's interference in the affairs of all countries of the Isthmus. The Reagan administration did its best to push forward its own plan to establish a negotiated peace in the region, though it had been rejected by Central American countries, the Contadora Group, and the Contadora Support Group (Argentina, Brazil, Peru, and Uru-guay). Herculean efforts would have been needed to build bridges of mutual understanding between Moscow and Washington.

Gorbachev's New Approach: From Confrontation to Cooperation

It is in the fields of foreign policy and diplomacy that Gorbachev's perestroika—the process of reform and transformation that swept through all spheres of Soviet life after 1985—was most successful. The transition to what was called the new political thinking allowed Gorbachev and his team to renovate the Soviet foreign policy radically and contribute to the solution of many complicated international prob-lems. Far-reaching changes have been made with respect to three cor-nerstones of Moscow's strategy in Central America: its conceptual base, relations with Soviet allies in this region, and dialogue with Washington. In the spirit of the principles of the new thinking, which consisted of such concepts as the removal of the ideological yoke from foreign policy and recognition of the right of every nation to choose its way, Mikhail Gorbachev was the first among Soviet leaders to make the unequivocal declaration that Moscow's principal objective in Central America was to reach a peaceful settlement of regional conflict on the basis of a Latin American decision. The new approach also explicitly rejected any claim to achieve a permanent Soviet military presence in this part of the globe.

The Soviet government's statement published in November 1986 read, "The USSR supports the constructive goals of the Contadora process to reach a Latin American solution to the regional crisis and is ready to contribute practically to the creation of favorable conditions for a just political settlement in Central America. With full responsibility the Soviet government . . . declares that the USSR has never established and is not going to establish military bases in Nicaragua."[12]

The Esquipulas-2 Agreement was met with satisfaction in Moscow. A statement made by the Soviet government spoke of a "resolution to respect the decision adopted by the five presidents . . . to promote efforts for the realization of this decision."[13] Soviet diplomacy followed this new line of conduct without deviations. During an official visit to the Republic of Cuba (2–5 April 1989), Mikhail Gorbachev, in his speech at the solemn session of the Cuban National Assembly, devoted much attention to the analysis of the international situation. He specifically dwelled on the foundations of relations with Latin American countries. "Our approach to the solution of the problems of Central America has always been constant," he stressed. "We are in favor of the Latin American decision."[14] He put forward a suggestion that all supplies of military hardware to the region, regardless of their origin, be stopped.

The new Soviet approach to the Central American conflict and a willingness to bring about practical results gave Moscow a good chance to speak a common language with Latin America's Big Three. In the course of then Soviet foreign minister Eduard Shevardnadze's visit to South America, as well as during Gorbachev's negotiations with the presidents of Argentina, Brazil, and Mexico from 1987 to 1991, the partners stressed in official communiqués that their positions concerning the Central American peace settlement were sufficiently similar if not identical.

Gorbachev's line could not have been successful without the mutual understanding and coordinated actions of the Soviet Union and its friends in the region. Gorbachev seemed to settle the first part of this problem during his visit to Cuba. The destiny of the Guatemala Agreement was intimately linked with the unbinding of the "Nicaraguan nod." The Soviet-Nicaraguan channel of communications at the top political level was functioning very intensively during the second half of the 1980s when Nicaragua was struck by the deep economic crisis and the armed opposition—the contras—launched large-scale military actions against Managua from the territory of Honduras.

Twice, in April 1985 and November 1987, Gorbachev had meetings with Daniel Ortega in Moscow. Their negotiations gave new impetus to bilateral relations. The leaders of the two states stressed the similarity of their assessments of the international situation and the Central American problem.

During his visit to Managua in October 1989, the year of the tenth anniversary of the Sandinista revolution, Shevardnadze advocated a new Soviet policy in Central America. Commenting at the press conference on the results of the negotiations with Ortega, he praised highly the Sandinistas' efforts to fulfill their obligations concerning further democratization in the country and holding free and fair general elections the following February. In his view, these actions of the Sandinistas constituted a real breakthrough in the implementation of the decisions approved at the last Central American summit. The Soviet foreign minister signaled to his counterparts that Moscow was unable to increase economic aid to Nicaragua and therefore the two countries should raise the efficacy of their cooperation.

In Shevardnadze's portfolio there were also a number of initiatives addressing third parties. In Managua he put forward a proposal that the Soviet Union and the United States act in the region as "co-guarantors of stability." The Soviet foreign minister stated that Moscow was ready to establish diplomatic relations with all Central American countries if they favored such a step.[15] These suggestions did not bring immediate results. They were regarded by all interested parties as a declaration of intentions and an invitation for active dialogue.

The problem of regional conflicts, including those in Central America, became an integral part of the agenda of Soviet-American negotiations after the two summit meetings between Gorbachev and Reagan, in Geneva and Reykjavík, where a good start was made on normalizing relations between Moscow and Washington. This topic continued to be debated by the presidents at working sessions of the foreign ministries and among foreign policy experts. The collective search for ways to clean up the Cold War relics at all so-called hot spots around the world turned out to be a challenge. At the postsummit press conference in Washington in December 1987, Gorbachev stated, "The discussion of regional problems has not been a light burden. . . . I would not say that we have made substantial progress in this area."[16] Several years were needed for the superpowers to find a way out of the many impasses set up by their rivalry in regional conflicts.

It was only in 1989 that the phenomenon of Soviet-U.S. parallel actions appeared in Central America. Following the U.S. Congress's vote to stop military aid to the contras and the Bush administration's shift in its Central American policy toward greater diplomatic emphasis, the Soviet government passed from verbally supporting the Contadora Group and the Guatemala Agreement to taking practical steps. Gorbachev responded to Costa Rican president Oscar Arias's call to stick to the new thinking in practice and announced that his country had ceased supplying arms to Nicaragua. Both powers also committed themselves to respecting the results of free elections in Nicaragua regardless of the outcome.

Some American analysts explained the U.S.-Soviet rapprochement on the Central American issue by the fact that Washington had been pressing Moscow until it began slowly to make concessions.[17] Though there is no reason to question this interpretation, such an explanation seems to play down the mightier factors of a global nature that were stimulating a full, across-the-board improvement in relations between the United States and the Soviet Union. It was also helpful that the Soviet diplomatic understanding and posture had been modified at that time by the realistic recognition of the role of traditional ties and interests between the United States and its southern neighbors. This stance did not mean that Moscow would keep silent in cases in which U.S. actions could be questioned in the context of international law or the UN Charter. For example, like most Latin American countries, the USSR condemned the U.S. intervention in Panama in December 1989.

By the beginning of the 1990s Moscow and Washington had succeeded in elaborating a coordinated position on the Central American settlement. In February 1990 in Moscow, Shevardnadze and Baker agreed on several concrete points:[18]

1. The paramount importance of carrying out in practice all provisions of Esquipulas-2 and later agreements;

2. No use of the territory of any Central American state for rendering support to irregular forces;

3. The halting of military aid to such forces from extraregional powers;

4. Effective international control over the electoral process in Nicaragua;

5. Confirmation of the commitment to respect the results of free and fair elections in Nicaragua;

6. Support of political settlement in Central America through negotiations; and

7. More active utilization of UN and the OAS mechanisms for monitoring the realization of peace accords in Central America.

Moscow and Washington undertook joint diplomatic demarches in 1991 to remove the delays and obstacles for successful implementation of the Guatemala Agreement. The two superpowers made a joint statement on El Salvador, which became the epicenter of regional tension after the success of national reconciliation in Nicaragua, and published a declaration about U.S.-Soviet interaction in Central America.[19] These coordinated actions by the White House and the Kremlin had a positive effect. They activated the UN secretary general's mediation efforts, speeding up the signing of a peace agreement between the government and guerrillas in El Salvador.

Moscow assessed the overall balance of changes in Central America with satisfaction. A decade of armed struggle in the region was over. Free from ideological constraints, Moscow was able to conduct a sensible diplomacy during the regime change in Nicaragua and to develop a businesslike cooperation and political dialogue with the government of Violeta Chamorro on the basis of mutual benefit. The USSR has since established diplomatic relations with Guatemala, Honduras, Panama, and El Salvador. As a successor state of the defunct USSR, Russia has inherited these ties. How soon will Boris Yeltsin's government benefit from this heritage?

Perestroika in Soviet-Cuban Cooperation

Soviet-Cuban relations presented a real challenge to Gorbachev's perestroika in the field of foreign policy. From the very beginning, Castro's regime enjoyed the status of most favored ally, which may be compared with the special relationship between the United States and Israel. From Moscow's perspective, the Soviet presence in Cuba constituted an important factor in the Soviet-American military-strategic parity. For thirty years the Soviet Union and Cuba maintained an exceptionally close collaboration notable for the extent of economic ties, interwoven international interests, and important military and security connections. Soviet aid to Cuba was estimated at $5 to $6 billion a year.[20] This economic assistance was sufficient not only to keep the Cuban economy afloat but also to make large-scale investments in the development of education, medical care, and the like. The cooperation between the Communist parties of the two countries was cemented by intimate personal contacts between the Soviet leaders (from Khrushchev to Gorbachev) and Fidel Castro. The thirty-year-long multifaceted Soviet-Cuban cooperation developed into an interdependent relationship, particularly in the economic sphere.

The cost volume of Soviet-Cuban trade amounted to 9 billion rubles. More than 70 percent of Cuban foreign trade turnover was directed at the USSR. Cuba placed sixth among the commercial counterparts of the Soviet Union. The Soviet Union was the only or main supplier of many goods that are vitally important for Cuba, including oil and oil products, cereals, metals, trucks and cars, and fertilizers. The USSR invested millions in the modernization of the Cuban economy and its sugar processing branch. The enterprises built or reconstructed with Soviet aid were producing practically all steel and rolled metal, sugar cane harvester combines, television sets and radios, 60 percent of cotton cloth, and 45 percent of electric power. In turn, the USSR had 30 percent of its needs in sugar, up to 50 percent in citrus fruits, and almost 20 percent in nickel-containing products supplied by Cuban exports. Cuban deliveries of some types of electronics, control and measuring instruments, medicine, and biological know-how were also valuable to the USSR.[21]

The only way out of the delicate situation in Soviet-Cuban relations produced by Gorbachev's reforms would be a patient dialogue based on full equality and not dramatizing the contradictions and different perceptions of world development or of the so-called new thinking. Any voluntaristic unilateral actions by such a great power as the Soviet Union would have proven to be inefficient and would hardly have coincided with perestroika. This was especially true in the case of Cuba since the Cuban question was a source of sharp disagreement between Moscow and Washington. The Bush administration linked the question of U.S. economic support for perestroika with the Soviet retreat from Cuba, but Gorbachev was not inclined to succumb to such pressure and desert Cuba.

The reshaping of Soviet-Cuban relations began in 1989 with Gorbachev's visit to Cuba. In the mass media at that time there were many guesses as to what happened, but three lines in a lengthy communiqué made it clear that Cuba and the Soviet Union would begin discussing the whole complex of their relations, based on the most favored ally model. The treaty on friendship and cooperation signed by the two leaders with all other measures included stipulated the active introduction of new forms of cooperation.[22] At that time, as had been the case during the first years of perestroika, high government-level talks were characterized by a wall of secrecy, which was often unnecessary and even counterproductive.

But the USSR's relations with Cuba were soon discussed publicly. This began on 1 March 1990 with the government's publication, on the demand of the people's deputies, of previously classified statistics concerning the cost of the USSR's cooperation with countries that had been its ideological, political, and military allies for many decades. These statistics revealed that the debt of sixty-one foreign countries to the USSR was about 85 billion rubles at the end of 1989.

Among the list of the debtor countries, Cuba occupied first place; its debt (15.5 billion rubles) was almost twice as large as that of Vietnam, the second-largest debtor.[23] These data provoked an acute public response in the Soviet Union and drew Cuban attention to the process of perestroika and its consequences for Third World countries that relied on Soviet economic assistance. Thus the discussion spread to the Soviet independent and government press, researchers, and the general public. In addition, this problem was raised at the meetings of democratic groups in Russia. The new impetus for the discussion came from the democratically elected president of Russia, Boris Yeltsin, and from the Russian Parliament. They had made the decision that from 1991 on, not a single ruble from the budget of the Russian federation would go toward financing any project or any type of economically burdensome relationship with the developing countries, including Cuba. Of course, this discussion was not limited to economic matters but dealt also with ideological and political issues, military collaboration, interparty cooperation, the role of the KGB, and other related concerns.

Many difficult questions with no simple answers were raised during this discussion. For example, during the course of talk about perestroika, a new military concept of reasonable defensive sufficiency was proclaimed. From the point of view of this concept, could large-scale shipments of military supplies to foreign countries be morally and politically justified? In the long run, how should relations with revolutionary movements, parties, and countries be shaped? Had they not unconditionally supported the Soviet policy, sometimes to the detriment of their own national interest, during many years of Cold War confrontation?

Another very important consideration was how to react when an ally with whom the USSR has had a traditional relationship of cooperation and friendship undertakes actions that are judged by the international community to be in violation of human rights. Is it acceptable from the moral point of view to refuse economic assistance to a small country that finds itself in a very difficult situation and continues to live under the conditions of a severe economic blockade imposed by its very mighty and influential neighbor?

During this discussion, a number of articles criticizing the Soviet-Cuban alliance were published in radical newspapers of the Soviet free press. In these articles one finds various references to Fidel Castro and his role in today's Cuba.[24] But this was only one side of the picture. Many Soviets have invested years of effort participating in the economic construction of Cuba, in the development of the Cuban educational system, and so forth. At the same time, thousands and thousands of Cubans were trained in the Soviet system of middle-level and higher education. There are Cubans who spent many years in Russia, married Soviet citizens, and have Russian children and grandchildren. Thus, in response to the sharp criticism of Fidel Castro, angry articles were published in Soviet periodicals and specialized journals by people who considered that to abandon Cuba would mean the betrayal of a nation that supported the Soviet Union.[25]

These facts provide some insight into the complex situation in the Soviet Union during the years of perestroika. The question of the future of Cuban-Soviet relations affected not only politicians but many rank-and-file people in both countries. When the inevitable public-debate exaggerations (such as the proposal to uncouple the Cuban car) finally ended, more rational approaches to restructure Soviet-Cuban relations came to the fore. Questions relevant to this issue were further discussed during visits by statesmen of various rank. During the period from 1985 to 1991, Soviet visitors to Cuba included Shevardnadze, then minister of foreign affairs; L. I. Abalkin, vice president of the USSR Council of Ministers; M. A. Moiseyev, the general staff chief of the Soviet armed forces; the delegation of the USSR Supreme Soviet; the secretaries of the Central Committee of the CPSU; and O. Baklanov and O. Shenin. In return, Cuban dignitaries visited Moscow. These included the vice-minister of foreign affairs, J. Viyera; and the delegation of the National Assembly of Cuba, headed by its president, J. Escalona.

The intensive flow of visitors from Moscow to Cuba demonstrated Gorbachev's wish to arrive at a final settlement with Cuba in view of a deepening economic crisis and political instability in the USSR. The imbalance in exchanges, as well as Castro's criticism of perestroika, reflected Cuba's reaction to shrinking Soviet aid to the country, which was experiencing, as Fidel Castro put it, "a special period in peace time."

On 29 December 1990, after six months of difficult negotiations, the Soviet and Cuban counterparts signed the documents on changes in commercial and trade relations between the two countries for 1991. Unlike the traditional five-year agreements, the new Soviet-Cuban trade accord was for one year and introduced drastic changes into the established practice of economic cooperation. From 1 January 1991 trade relations were to be based on current world prices and the settlement of accounts in hard currency. Moscow assumed obligations to go on supplying Cuba with the minimum of its economic needs, and Havana agreed to increase exports of Cuban commodities to the USSR.[26]

Despite its own critical financial position, the Soviet government consented to put off Cuban debt payments, due in 1991–95 (about 5.8 billion rubles), until after the year 2000. And in spite of disagreements and misunderstandings, the Soviet and Cuban governments succeeded until August 1991 in keeping under control the complex process of reshaping bilateral relations. They managed to regulate these in a planned manner and guaranteed step-by-step solutions of burning issues.

Russia, the CIS, and Cuba

The abortive coup d'état in Moscow in August 1991 and the collapse of the USSR in December 1991 brought to a close Cuba's position as a privileged ally. This was clearly to affect Cuba's trade and economy. After the collapse of the August 1991 coup, Gorbachev resigned as general secretary of the Communist Party of the Soviet Union and declared the dissolution of the Central Committee of the Communist party. Democratic forces immediately seized advantage of the new situation and managed the practically complete decommunization of the country.

In accordance with President Yeltsin's decrees, the CPSU's activities were suspended within the territory of the Soviet Union and were later banned in the Russian Federation. About five thousand party buildings throughout the country were closed, and the party media empire, with about eighty thousand people working in 144 publications and 81 publishing houses, was shattered. Local party organizations were dissolved. For all practical purposes, the party was put out of business, and party officials were out of work. For Castro, who had once spoken directly to Khrushchev or Brezhnev to obtain what he wanted, the situation was greatly altered. The system of intimate contacts between the Communist parties of the USSR and Cuba, the backbone of the Moscow-Havana alliance during the last three decades, completely collapsed in the last months of 1991.

Security ties between Cuba and the Soviet Union had still been close before the coup. Cuban general Juan Escalona had been to the Soviet Union in February 1991, and the head of the KGB, Vladimir Kruchkov, had visited Cuba at the personal invitation of Fidel Castro in May-June 1991. At the end of June, Carlos Aldana, the secretary of the Central Committee of the Communist Party of Cuba, paid a visit to Moscow and met with various Soviet leaders. After the defeat of the coup, the KGB was officially abolished, and it was declared that there would be no further involvement in secret operations in foreign countries. There were many indications that the previously close relationship between the Soviet and Cuban security services had come to an end.

The military relationship between the two countries was also under reconsideration. Since 1990 there had been no Cuban-based Soviet reconnaissance flights. Port calls by Soviet surface and submarine vessels were ending. Soviet military supplies to Cuba had been considerably cut back, and Moscow's and Havana's economic ties had been significantly modified from unlimited preferential cooperation to commercial exchanges. Gorbachev's call in September 1991 to begin pulling out the Soviet training brigade and military specialists from Cuba by January 1992 was a logical move in conformity with the military doctrine of reasonable defense sufficiency. After the end of the Cold

War confrontation between the USSR and the United States, Cuba had lost its strategic significance as a military bridgehead. There were other reasons that explained Gorbachev's step, particularly his efforts to improve further his country's relations with the Bush administration. Moreover, Gorbachev seemed to be still in shock after his detention in the Crimea when he made a spontaneous announcement about a forthcoming withdrawal of Soviet troops from Cuba in a way that was detrimental to the USSR's international image and offensive to Cuba. No previous consultations with Havana had taken place, though Article 2 of the treaty of friendship and cooperation signed by Gorbachev and Castro in 1989 provided for the "exchange of opinions on the most important issues of mutual interest." No wonder that on 12 September 1991, the Cuban ambassador to the USSR, J. P. Balaguer, handed an official note of protest to Gorbachev. The Cuban leadership, as was observed in the editorial published the following day by the newspaper *Granma,* was especially displeased with the fact that Gorbachev, in his statement, did not connect the withdrawal of the Soviet brigade from Cuba with the problem of the American military presence in the island and the liquidation of the Guantanamo base.[27] This controversy seriously complicated Soviet-Cuban negotiations on the technical aspects of the Soviet military pullout from Cuba. Nevertheless, by mid-1992 the majority of the Soviet civilian and military personnel stationed in Cuba had left the island.[28]

The most dramatic changes occurred in the area of economic ties. As Cuban trade minister Ricardo Cabrisas pointed out during his visit to the Ukraine in January 1992, the economy of Cuba had by this time become "virtually paralyzed" as a result of the suspension of supplies from Russia, other republics of the former Soviet Union, and East European countries.[29]

Russia and the other independent states that have emerged from the ruins of the USSR are experiencing an extremely difficult period of economic crisis, political turmoil, and interethnic conflict. Relations with Cuba consequently have had low priority. In abandoning old dogmas and ideological messianism (that is, the conquest of more and more areas for socialism), Russia, according to its foreign minister, Andrei Kozyrev, has set a course for pragmatism and for the achievement of the national interests of the Russian Federation.[30] It was concluded that Russian national interests will be mainly confined to the Northern Hemisphere and are to be geared toward three priority spheres: the USSR's former Union republics ("immediate foreign neighbors"); the community of Western democratic states with a market economy; and Russia's neighbors directly to the South, including Turkey, Iran, Pakistan, Afghanistan, China, and Japan. The setting of these priorities, however, does not mean that Yeltsin's government intends to withdraw completely from the Third World, especially since many countries in this area (India, Angola, and Cuba, for example) have been long-standing Soviet economic and political partners. As the legal successor of the Soviet Union, Russia does not ignore its part of the responsibilities in the sphere of foreign relations.

Facing the new realities, Castro's government has undertaken an active diplomatic campaign aimed at maintaining former ties and opening new markets within the former Soviet economic space. Havana has officially recognized Russia, Ukraine, the Baltic, and other republics as independent states. A Cuban mission has visited a number of the capitals of the newly independent states, and its head, Ricardo Cabrisas, has signed trade agreements with them. Kazakhstan will deliver a large consignment of petroleum to Cuba in exchange for 200,000 tons of raw sugar. Cuba and Tajikistan have agreed to collaborate in two areas: the sugar industry and health care. Lithuania and Cuba signed a five-year agreement on economic cooperation and a protocol on bilateral trade in 1992. Latvia will receive 50,000 tons of Cuban raw sugar in exchange for supplies of beef fat, cheese, and condensed milk. The Cuban-Ukrainian accord on trade and cooperation provides for creating joint ventures in the field of medical preparations and equipment and for developing commercial ties along traditional patterns. Ukraine will supply sulfur and metallurgical and chemical industry products to Cuba and in turn will receive medical preparations, raw sugar, and nickel from Havana.

The November 1991 visit to Moscow by a Cuban delegation yielded some results in Cuban-Russian relations. The sides have formulated "basic parameters for trade and economic relations," which include mutual benefit, use of the world price index for oil and sugar, parity and payment in dollars on a clearing basis. "Specific parameters" concern complex issues that have yet to be resolved. The USSR's legacy in economic cooperation with Cuba includes a nuclear power plant and thirty other construction projects. The investment in these projects, if calculated in hard currency, totals about 2.3 billion rubles. Russia cannot abandon such large investments. There are also serious concerns about Cuba's foreign debt to the former Soviet Union. The decision about how to manage this complex issue of collection and distribution of this debt will have to be coordinated between CIS member countries and the other former USSR republics.

After protracted preliminary negotiations, a breakthrough in Russian-Cuban economic relations took place on in Moscow on 3 November 1992, when a vice chairman of the Council of Ministers of Cuba, L. Soto, signed an agreement on trade and economic cooperation, an agreement on commercial navigation, and a protocol on commodity turnover and payments for 1993. According to these agreements, Russia will supply Cuba in 1993 with approximately 1.5 million tons of oil and oil products in exchange for 3.3 million tons of Cuban sugar.

The partners agreed to resume the construction of the nuclear power plant in Juragua, Cienfuegos, which was temporarily stopped on Castro's unilateral decision in September 1992, and to invite France or other countries to take part in financing this project by delivering Western-made equipment.

A. Shokin and L. Soto also discussed some aspects of military-technical cooperation between the two countries and concluded a specific barter arrangement by the terms of which Russia will maintain the huge Soviet electronic listening post and intelligence facility at Lourdes, near Havana, until a new accord is elaborated, while Cuba will receive from Moscow spare parts for military hardware made in the former USSR.

Political dialogue between the Cuban and Russian sides began through an exchange of messages between Russian president Boris Yeltsin and Cuban president Fidel Castro in January 1992. In their notes, the two statesmen discussed questions of principal concern affecting relations between the two countries. Russian foreign policy cannot ignore the well-known fact that Cuba is an influential member of the Nonaligned Movement and is very active in international organizations such as the UN. Yeltsin's government, however, has to take into account the fact that a number of Russian parliamentarians and human rights organizations strongly criticize regularly reported human rights violations in Cuba and suggest that economic sanctions and an arms embargo be used to exert pressure on Cuban authorities. With Russia's entry into the international arena as an independent state, its foreign policy places more emphasis than it did formerly on democratic principles, humanitarian problems, and human rights. At the Forty-eighth session of the UN Commission on Human Rights held in Geneva in March 1992, the Russian delegation backed a resolution condemning Cuba for human rights violations.

This move provoked sharp political battles inside Russia between the supporters of Kozyrev's civilized foreign policy and the hard-liners' opposition to Yeltsin's government. The latter also vigorously criticized the behavior of the Russian delegation to the UN in November 1992 for abstaining when a resolution censuring U.S. legislation on tightening the economic blockade of Cuba was to be voted on at the meeting of the General Assembly.

As for the key problem of today's Cuba—what is next for Cuba as a nation—it is most likely that the country will join the worldwide trend toward democratization. Russia shares with the U.S. a desire to see Cuba transformed (through a "velvet revolution") from a nation embracing the socialist model to one that upholds democratic principles.

Notes

1. *Materialy XXVI s'ezda KPSS* (Materials of the twenty-sixth congress of the CPSU) (Moscow: Politizdat, 1981), 4.

2. *Pravda,* 23 March 1980; 10 May 1982.

3. *World Armaments and Disarmament: SIPRI Yearbook, 1983* (London and New York: Taylor and Francis, 1983), 326.

4. Carlos Rafael Rodrigues, "Fundamentos estratégicos de la política exterior de Cuba" (Fundamental strategies in Cuban foreign policy), *Cuba Socialista,* no. 1 (December 1981): 32.

5. See Robert Leiken, *Soviet Strategy in Latin America* (New York: Praeger, 1982), and Jiri and Virginia Valenta, "Soviet Strategy in the Caribbean Basin," in Alan Adelman and Reid Reasing, eds., *Confrontation in the Caribbean Basin* (Pittsburgh: University of Pittsburgh Press, 1984), 242–65.

6. Mark Edelman, "Lifelines: Nicaragua and the Socialist Countries," in *NACLA: Report on the Americas* 19, no. 3 (1985): 48–50.

7. Ibid.

8. See *World Armaments and Disarmament: SIPRI Yearbook* (New York: Oxford University Press, 1985–90).

9. Augusto Varas, ed., *América Latina y la Unión Soviética: una nueva relacion* (Latin America and the Soviet Union: a new relationship) (Buenos Aires: Grupo Editor Latinoamericano, 1987), 71.

10. Ibid., p. 70; see also Eusebio Mujal-Leon, ed., *The USSR and Latin America: A Developing Relationship* (Boston: Unwin Hyman, 1989), 281.

11. See *Pravda,* 10 October 1989; *Envio* 11, no. 24 (March 1992): 16; *Barricada,* 12 June 1987.

12. *Pravda*, 17 November 1986.

13. *Pravda*, 7 August 1987.

14. M. S. Gorbachev, *Izbrannye rechi i stat'i* (Selected speeches and articles) (Moscow: Politizdat, 1990), 437.

15. *Pravda*, 19 October 1989.

16. M. S. Gorbachev, *Izbrannye rechi i stat'i* (Selected speeches and articles) (Moscow: Politizdat, 1988), 534.

17. Douglas W. Payne, Mark Falcoff, and Susan Kaufman Purcell, *Latin America: U.S. Policy after the Cold War* (New York: Americas Society, 1991), 15.

18. *Izvestiya*, 11 February 1990.

19. See *Pravda*, 18 March 1991; 1 August 1991.

20. *Nezavisimaya Gazeta*, 28 January 1992.

21. See A. D. Bekarevich and N. M. Kukharev, *Sovetskiy Soyuz-Kuba: ekonomicheskoye sotrudnichestvo* (Soviet-Cuban economic cooperation) (Moscow: Nauka, 1990).

22. *Pravda*, 6 April 1989.

23. *Izvestiya*, 1 March 1990.

24. A. Novikov, "Iz lichnoy zhizni Fidelya" (From the personal life of Fidel), *Komsomol'skaya Pravda*, 18 October 1990.

25. D. Z. Mutagirov, "Fenomen antikubizma v SSSR" (The phenomenon of anti-Cubanism in the USSR), *Latinskaya Amerika*, no. 4 (April 1991): 44–50.

26. *Izvestiya*, 1 March 1990.

27. *Granma*, 13 September 1991.

28. In 1991 there were in Cuba about 12,700 Soviet specialists: 2,800 military advisers, 2,100 KGB and intelligence officers, 2,800 soldiers, and 5,000 civilian specialists. About 3,000 men were in the training brigade. (*Izvestiya*, 13 September 1991).

29. *URYADOVYY KUREER* (Kiev) 49, no. 3 (January 1992): 7.

30. See "Preobrazhennaya Rossiya v novom mire" (A transformed Russia in the new world), *Mezhdunarodnaya zhizn'*, no. 3–4 (March-April 1992): 91–98.

Chapter 13 ▬▬▬▬▬▬▬▬▬▬▬▬▬▬▬▬▬▬▬▬

Moscow's Relations with Argentina and Brazil

End or Renewal?

Aldo C. Vacs

The disintegration of the USSR and the emergence of the loosely tied Commonwealth of Independent States (CIS) constitute a momentous change whose ultimate consequences are still very difficult to assess. It is clear, however, that these transformations have had a tremendous impact on former Soviet clients and allies such as Cuba, which has lost its main source of economic, military, and political support. The impact of the Soviet collapse on the rest of the Latin American region is more difficult to evaluate, but it is apparent that previous Soviet links with Latin American countries will undoubtedly be affected by Soviet disintegration and the need of the Latin American countries to establish new ties with a nascent constellation of independent and semi-independent republics. The result is likely to be even more complex relationships, the features of which cannot be conclusively assessed without distinguishing among particular national cases and waiting for more stable conditions to materialize in the former USSR.

It is possible, however, to begin to examine the potential consequences of these changes by limiting the scope of analysis to comparable Latin American countries and making some informed assumptions on their evolution and that of the former Soviet republics. This chapter therefore examines the relationship between the two largest and more developed South American nations—Argentina and Brazil—and the Soviet Union and its current successor states. These two South American countries present similarities in domestic economic and political development as well as in their position in the international system and in features of their foreign policy that facilitate analysis of their past and current relationship with the USSR and the CIS.

Soviet Relations with Argentina and Brazil: From the Russian Revolution to Gorbachev

Despite occasional fluctuations and setbacks, Soviet ties with Argentina and Brazil up to the rise of Gorbachev evolved in the direction of mutually beneficial economic and diplomatic links characterized by pragmatism and the gradual decline of the importance assigned to ideological factors. The cautious Soviet approach to Argentina and Brazil was shaped by the USSR's interest in developing economic relations that could help to alleviate its production problems, establishing a diplomatic and political presence befitting the Soviet role as a superpower while recognizing its incapacity to play a hegemonic role in South America, and facilitating tendencies toward nonalignment that could weaken these countries' ties to the United States and other Western powers without generating hostile reactions. In turn, the Argentine and Brazilian responses evolved from an initial wariness toward a more cooperative attitude as fear of Soviet-sponsored subversion subsided and opportunities for economic and political-diplomatic gains associated with normal ties with the USSR began to be appreciated.

The Soviet Union and Argentina: Economic Complementarities and Growing Cooperation

The initial Soviet approach to Argentina included a combination of commercial openings and diplomatic probes.[1] Commercial relations were established in the early 1920s and expanded as long as the Soviet interest in obtaining agricultural products matched the Argentine desire to find new markets for its products. Successive Argentine administrations distrusted Soviet political intentions—an attitude that was reinforced by pro-Soviet radical positions taken by the Partido Comunista Argentino (PCA; the Argentine Communist party), especially following the Comintern's leftist swing in 1928—and refused to establish diplomatic relations despite repeated Soviet entreaties. On the Soviet side, economic considerations outweighed the anticommunism of the Argentine military and conservative governments of the 1930s and 1940s, which was disregarded as the USSR tried with limited success to develop trade relations.

After a period of growing hostility during World War II, the rise of the Soviet Union to superpower status and Perón's coming to power in Argentina resulted in a more flexible and pragmatic attitude on both sides.[2] Shortly after Perón's presidential inauguration in 1946, Argentina established diplomatic relations with the USSR. The Peronist doctrine of the "third position," which called for Argentina's nonalignment in the confrontation between the superpowers, facilitated this step. Although Perón and the post-Peronist administrations supported U.S. positions on issues such as hemispheric defense, the Korean conflict, and the Cuban crisis and exhibited a strongly anticommunist position at home, diplomatic, and economic relations between the USSR and Argentina were not interrupted during the Cold War period as they were with other Latin American countries. On the economic plane, the signing of a Soviet-Argentine agreement on trade and payments in 1953 was followed by a rise in bilateral trade. Bilateral commercial relations were never interrupted after this, although the volume of trade fluctuated. Throughout these years the PCA remained a marginal player in Argentine politics, and its policies followed to some extent the ups and downs of bilateral relations, becoming more belligerent against governments that adopted strong anti-Soviet positions and more cooperative with administrations that maintained better diplomatic and economic relations with the USSR. Even when it was banned and persecuted, as under the military government of generals Onganía and Levingston (1966–71), the PCA remained an orthodox pro-Moscow party that supported all Soviet initiatives and praised the achievements of the Cuban revolution but refused to accept the armed road as a viable option in the Argentine context.

The early 1970s marked a turning point in Soviet-Argentine relations as Argentine economic problems (especially balance-of-payments deficits) and political changes (liberalization and democratization) led to the search for new customers for Argentina's exports of agricultural products and facilitated the rise of a so-called ideological pluralism that called for the elimination of anti-Soviet prejudices and the development of profitable relations with all countries regardless of the ideology held by their governments.[3] In 1971 the military administration of General Lanusse signed a trade and payments agreement with the USSR that gave most-favored-nation status to both sides and established that payments would be made in freely convertible currencies. Although initially the volume of trade increased slowly, this agreement created the conditions for civilian governments to deepen relations with the USSR without feeling threatened by domestic anticommunist groups interested in promoting military coups. The Peronist administrations of 1973–76 reinforced the trend toward closer economic relations and more cooperative diplomatic ties with the Soviet Union. Argentine exports of grains increased substantially during this period, and for the first time the USSR won a bid to participate in a major hydroelectric work (Salto Grande) planned by the Argentine government. This economic opening to the East was complemented by the revival of the third-position doctrine that led to Argentina's more active role in the nonaligned movement and more cordial diplomatic relations with the socialist countries. Meanwhile, the PCA supported Perón's presidential bid in 1973 and maintained its support for the Peronist administration as long as relations with the USSR remained cordial and productive.

Unlike previous military governments, the one inaugurated in March 1976 did not adopt an anti-Soviet foreign policy stance. On the contrary, the 1976–83 military administrations favored closer economic and diplomatic relations with the USSR.[4] On the economic plane, the Soviet Union was seen as a reliable customer for Argentina's exports of grains and meat in a global context of growing competition and increasing protectionism. Politically, friendly relations with the USSR gave the Argentine government its only important ally that blocked in international forums the condemnation of the military regime for its brutal human-rights violations. Moreover, the PCA was not outlawed but only suspended, and it proceeded to defend the "moderate" sectors of the armed forces, praising their liberal disposition and commending their decision to establish closer ties with the socialist countries. Meanwhile, the Soviet Union benefited from the opportunity to diversify its suppliers of grains, avoiding excessive reliance on the United States and its Western allies; to maintain its diplomatic presence in a region plagued by anti-Soviet military regimes; and to promote Argentina's trend toward nonalignment as the human-rights issue embittered relations between Argentina's military regime and the United States and Western Europe.

The friendly Soviet-Argentine relationship reached its climax in 1980, after the Carter administration decided to impose a grain sales embargo against the USSR following the Soviet invasion of Afghanistan. The Argentine government, after some hesitation, decided not to join the embargo and took the opportunity not only to sell most of its available grains to the USSR at a premium but also to sign medium-term commercial agreements for the supply of Argentine grains and beef. Argentine exports to the USSR skyrocketed, with the Soviets absorbing more than 80 percent of Argentina's grain exports in 1981 and remaining the most important customers of Argentine grains in the following years. Argentine imports of Soviet products remained, however, extremely low, and despite growing Soviet pressures, the balance of trade was extremely favorable for Argentina. The Soviets were able to participate in some hydroelectric projects and to sell some transportation equipment and heavy machinery but were not capable of making any noticeable inroads in the Argentine market, with most Argentine imports still coming from Western countries, Japan, and some Latin American nations.

At the same time, Soviet-Argentine political-diplomatic consultations multiplied, including treatment of such topics as disarmament, the use of UN peacekeeping forces, apartheid, and nuclear proliferation. Mutual support vis-à-vis accusations of human-rights violations throve in the UN Human Rights Commission, and violations occurring in each country were ignored by the other's government. The USSR began to supply the Argentine nuclear program with materials such as heavy water and enriched uranium, which had been denied by Western sources. Military missions were exchanged, and the number of military attachés was increased.

After December 1981, during the initial period of General Galtieri's administration, there was a brief Argentine attempt to minimize relations with the USSR and establish closer ties with the United States by expressing support for the Western powers; denouncing Soviet and Cuban actions in Eastern Europe, Africa, and Central America; and giving support to the Nicaraguan Contras. The Falklands-Malvinas crisis in April 1982, though, marked the end of this attempt as the United States supported Great Britain and the Argentine government turned toward the Soviet Union and its allies in search of diplomatic support.

The end of military rule and the inauguration of Raúl Alfonsín did not change the nature of Argentine-Soviet relations.[5] The PCA believed that the Peronists would win the elections and offered its support to their presidential candidate in the expectation of gaining some influence. The Soviet government and the Communist Party of the Soviet Union (CPSU), however, did not express any preference and congratulated Alfonsín and the Radical party after their victory. The Radical administration stated its interest in maintaining cordial relations with the USSR. Although Argentine exports to the USSR decreased slightly after 1982 (in part as a result of the lifting of the U.S. grain embargo), the Soviets established negotiations to renew the five-year grain supply agreement but pointed out their interest in increasing their exports to Argentina. In turn, the Argentine government offered to buy $500 million (U.S.) in Soviet products during the same five-year period. Meanwhile, as a result of democratization and the reemergence of federalism, Argentine provincial governments (including those of Mendoza, Chaco, Formosa, Santa Fe, and Corrientes) signed direct contracts for the purchase of Soviet transportation equipment and road construction machinery in exchange for the export in some cases of regional products (wine, sugar, tannin, petrochemicals, and the like).

The Soviet Union and Brazil: From Hostility to Rapprochement

Between 1917 and 1945, relations between Brazil and the USSR were plagued by distrust and outright enmity.[6] Limited opportunities for exporting Brazilian tropical products—coffee, sugar, and rubber—to the USSR together with radical positions taken by the Partido Comunista do Brasil (PCB; the Communist party of Brazil) after its creation in 1922 reinforced the Brazilian elites' hostility toward the Soviet Union and resulted in the rejection of any attempt to establish durable commercial or diplomatic ties.

In the 1920s the PCB remained a marginal actor in Brazilian politics, hampered by internal factionalism that reflected splits in the Soviet party and the Comintern and by its inability to make inroads among the urban and rural workers. Moreover, continuous state repression and the ultra-leftist strategy followed by the PCB made it impossible to cooperate with democratic middle-class groups such as the tenentista movement and the Prestes Column, who were dismissed as petit bourgeois, nationalistic adventurers.[7] In the early 1930s, however, the Soviets adopted a friendlier attitude toward Prestes, who, after a stay in Moscow, declared himself a Communist and was appointed a member of the Comintern's executive committee before returning to Brazil as the imposed leader of the PCB. In 1935, under the Comintern's influence, the PCB developed a two-pronged strategy: on one hand, it joined middle-class radical groups in organizing a popular front, the National Liberating Alliance (ANL); on the other, it began to plan an armed socialist insurrection. When the Vargas government banned the ANL, an ill-prepared uprising took place with the participation of civilian party members and a small group of military. The revolt was rapidly suppressed, and the party's organization was severely damaged and forced to go underground.[8] Carefully presented by Vargas and the military command, the 1935 mutiny attained a mythical status among the Brazilian military, who interpreted it as the treacherous slaughter of military officers by a band of Communists directed from Moscow that eliminated any possibility of establishing normal relations with the USSR.

Only in 1944, after Brazil had become the only Latin American country to send troops to fight with the Allies in Europe, the Vargas administration decided to establish diplomatic relations with the USSR and lift the ban on the PCB. The PCB in turn participated in the political campaign aimed to keep Vargas in power, but his overthrow by the military in October 1945 hindered the PCB-government rapprochement as well as the development of more cordial ties between Brazil and the USSR. The PCB participated in the first post-Vargas elections, gathering 10 percent of the votes, and this performance was sufficient to alarm Brazilian conservative groups. In 1947, taking advantage of the Cold War climate, the Dutra administration banned the PCB and expelled all Communists from elective offices. Afterward the government denounced attacks on President Dutra published in the Soviet press and used them as grounds to sever diplomatic relations with the USSR.

For a brief period beginning in the late 1950s, the Brazilian developmentalist and nationalistic civilian administrations of Kubitschek, Quadros, and Goulart promoted better relations with the USSR in the expectation that this move would offer new economic opportunities and help to counterbalance U.S. influence. In 1961 diplomatic relations were reestablished. Meanwhile the PCB remained banned but enjoyed a relative degree of freedom, which it used to expand its influence on the urban labor movement and the rural sectors, supporting some governmental measures such as wage raises and agrarian reform.

The inauguration in 1964 of the military government headed by General Castelo Branco resulted in a renewed repression of the PCB and a noticeable chill in relations with the USSR. The military regime embraced the strongly anticommunist doctrine of "national security," which called for the suppression of domestic Marxist groups, closer relations with the United States, consistent anti-Cuban and anti-Soviet positions in the diplomatic arena, and support for similarly oriented military governments in Latin America. Members of the PCB were jailed, tortured, and killed, and military repression increased as splinter groups that disagreed with the peaceful tactics supported by the PCB's leadership began to engage in armed actions. Diplomatic relations with the USSR were maintained at a very low level as the Brazilian government denounced the Castroite-Soviet influence behind subversive groups and the Soviet press depicted the Brazilian regime as a reactionary, subimperialist government whose economic accomplishments were the result of superexploitation of the working class.[9]

In the early 1970s, as the Brazilian economy expanded and modernized and the military government adopted a more flexible foreign policy strategy, relations with the USSR began to improve. Brazilian exports, including some nontraditional products such as soybeans, textiles, medicines, and shoes, as well as traditional agricultural products like coffee, cocoa, and sugar, increased rapidly, going from $23 million (U.S.) in 1970 to $158 million in 1973. Soviet exports to Brazil, especially oil, grew rapidly, going from $2.7 million (U.S.) in 1970 to $129.3 million in 1975. Meanwhile, the inauguration of General Geisel as president in 1974 was accompanied by the introduction of a foreign policy of "responsible pragmatism" that ended Brazil's automatic alignment with the United States and called for more diversified external relations, including closer ties with socialist and nonaligned countries. At the domestic level, the process of gradual political liberalization ("apertura") did not lead to the legalization of the PCB, but anticommunist repression subsided and the party was able to engage in political activities, supporting the opposition Brazilian Democratic Movement (MDB) and even electing some members to Congress under the MDB's ticket.

In the early 1980s, during General Figueiredo's administration, Soviet-Brazilian relations continued to improve. The Brazilian government refused to join the U.S.-sponsored grain embargo, and, going a step further than Argentina, declined to boycott the Moscow Olympics. Brazilian exports of agricultural and industrial products to the USSR increased rapidly, and in 1981 bilateral agreements established medium-term parameters for Brazilian exports to the USSR, calling for Soviet participation in hydroelectric and petrochemical projects in Brazil and setting the conditions for joint Soviet-Brazilian participation in hydroelectric and road construction projects in Angola, Ethiopia, and Peru. Trade balances remained favorable to Brazil, but by 1984, Brazilian exports of $402 million (U.S.) were accompanied by imports of Soviet products worth $153 million. In diplomatic terms, growing disagreements between Brazil and the United States over issues such as human rights, nuclear technology, foreign debt, and protectionism contrasted with growing harmony with the USSR on certain issues. These included relations with Angola, Mozambique, and Guinea-Bissau; support for the Palestinians in the UN; sales of weapons to Iraq, Iran, and Libya; and nonintervention stands on Nicaragua and Grenada. Meanwhile, the Soviet Union carefully avoided any hint of interfering in domestic Brazilian affairs, merely stating its support for the process of political liberalization. After the PCB split into two factions—a larger Euro-Communist organization headed by Giocondo Dias and a smaller pro-Soviet group led by Prestes after his return from Moscow in 1980—the CPSU refused to take sides in the dispute and maintained low-profile contacts with both factions, emphasizing the role played by the Communists in the transition to democracy and their support of the Democratic Alliance ticket that ensured the 1985 election of the first civilian administration since 1964.

Perestroika and Democratization: Soviet Relations with Argentina and Brazil in a Time of Change

Among the factors that modified the features of Soviet relations with Argentina and Brazil in recent years were the movement for economic, social, and political reform launched by Mikhail Gorbachev in the Soviet Union; the rise of democracy and the economic emergency in the Southern Cone of Latin America; and the relaxation of East-West tensions. Gorbachev's attempts to promote economic efficiency, raise productivity, and reduce external imbalances resulted in Soviet efforts to reduce the bilateral trade deficits, increase and diversify the volume of Soviet exports, and decrease the volume of imports from Argentina and Brazil. At the same time, Soviet political determination to reduce international tensions led to renewed attempts to establish more cooperative diplomatic relations with the two largest countries in South America, especially on issues such as world peace and disarmament. In Argentina and Brazil, the democratization processes of the early 1980s took place amid a persistent economic crisis that prompted the implementation of austere programs for economic adjustment. Thus while democratization facilitated the maintenance or reformulation of pragmatic foreign policies aimed at promoting closer diplomatic relations with the USSR, economic stabilization policies reduced the South American countries' capacity to import Soviet products and the chances for Soviet participation in public works and private ventures. The climate of international distension facilitated development of closer diplomatic ties, but the nature of the economic problems faced by both sides—foreign debt and financial flows, trade deficits, restructuring of domestic productive activities, reentry into the world economy under new conditions—diminished the chances of bilateral economic cooperation. In the context of declining East-West tensions, politically motivated commercial agreements were no longer a significant component of the Soviet approach to the Southern Cone countries. Simultaneously, the Latin American nations attempted to find a way out of the crisis through neoliberal economic policies that drove them closer to the Western developed countries. As a result, there was a decline in the volume of Argentine and Brazilian exports to the USSR and of Soviet economic participation in public works, which led to a commercial impasse and resulted in attempts to establish new forms of economic cooperation.

Soviet Foreign Policy toward Latin America under Gorbachev

After Mikhail Gorbachev became secretary general of the CPSU in 1985, the economic and political transformations under way in the USSR modified the characteristics of its relations with the Third World and Latin America as well as the Soviet interpretation of these links.[10] Gorbachev's call for perestroika or socioeconomic restructuring departed from the acknowledgment of a serious developmental crisis whose resolution required the implementation of radical policy changes and profound institutional innovations.[11] The economic restructuring advocated by the Soviet leadership included, among other objectives, the establishment of favorable conditions for a process of balanced economic growth directed to satisfy consumer demands; modernization, rationalization, and efficient operation of the public sector; the encouragement of private initiative in the context of a more flexible socialist economy; promotion of scientific-technological innovations to foster the intensive use of the factors of production; reinvigoration of the monetary aspects of the economy, especially concerning prices,

credit, and supply-demand relations; and reentry into the world economy, establishing more flexible and direct relations between Soviet
enterprises and foreign markets. In political-institutional terms, the
new approach emphasized the need for informative transparency—
glasnost—and popular debate on public policies, called for a revalori-
zation of Socialist democracy understood from a Leninist perspective,
promoted new forms of participation and self-management, and advocated the reduction of bureaucratic controls through decentralization.

Together with this reassessment of the domestic situation, Gorbachev and his supporters called for the introduction of "new thinking"
in matters of foreign policy. This notion acknowledged the existence of
"a contradictory but interconnected, interdependent and, essentially,
integral world" in which "the security of each nation should be coupled
with the security for all members of the world community."[12] This
endorsement of the notion of global interdependence encouraged the
abandonment of autarkic inclinations and the reentry of the USSR
into the world economy in order to secure the success of the economic
reform. Deepening and diversifying economic relations with the rest
of the world, and especially with the market economies, would make
it possible for the Soviet Union to obtain the resources (goods, technology, credit, and investment) necessary to accelerate the pace of restructuring and overcome the resistance opposed to the transformation by
entrenched interest groups. Successful implementation of this project
required the relaxation of international tensions to facilitate Soviet
access to new markets and technologies, to reduce Soviet military
expenditures and concentrate investment in consumer-oriented economic activities, and to diminish the drain on resources stemming from
the need to support Soviet allies in conflictive areas of the world.

Consequently, the new Soviet approach to international relations
emphasized the need to rise above ideological disagreements and
stressed the advantages of diplomacy over the use of force and military
superiority to resolve international problems.[13] The arms buildup and
military commitments in the Third World characteristic of the Brezhnev era were seen as wasteful and counterproductive as they escalated
the arms race, drained scarce resources, and limited the chances of the
USSR's obtaining foreign capital and technology from the Western
developed countries without securing for the Soviets any well-defined
strategic or political advantages. Even in the cases of so-called socialist-
oriented countries, it was considered appropriate to remind them that

socialism should be built through their own efforts, counting on only limited Soviet support.[14]

In reference to Latin America, Gorbachev emphasized that the USSR did not want to interfere in these countries' internal affairs to promote revolutionary changes:

> We do sympathize with the Latin American countries in their efforts to consolidate their independence in every sphere and cast off all neocolonialist fetters, and we have never made any secret of this. We much appreciate the energetic foreign policies of Mexico and Argentina, their responsible stances on disarmament and international security, and their contribution to the initiatives of the Six. We support the peace making efforts of Contadora Group, initiatives by Central American heads of state, and the Guatemala City accord. We welcome the democratic changes in many Latin American countries, and appreciate the growing consolidation of the countries of the continent which will help preserve and strengthen their national sovereignty.
>
> At the same time, I would like to emphasize once again that we do not seek any advantages in Latin America. We don't want either its raw materials, or its cheap labor. We are not going to exploit anti-U.S. attitudes, let alone fuel them, nor do we intend to erode the traditional links between Latin America and the United States. That would be adventurism, not sound politics, and we are realists, not reckless adventurers.
>
> But our sympathies always lie with nations fighting for freedom and independence. Let there be no misunderstanding on that score.[15]

In practice, this formulation led to attempts to develop and strengthen diplomatic relations with the largest countries in the region (such as Argentina and Brazil), appreciating the relative degree of autonomy of these countries' foreign policies and the agreement between them and the USSR on issues such as international security, regional peace, and nuclear disarmament. These intermediate powers also had the advantage, from the Soviet perspective, that their foreign policy initiatives, even if they clashed with U.S. views, could not be adjudicated to Soviet influence. This reduced the chances of a rise in superpower tensions. Moreover, their importance at the regional level was expected to increase the impact of diplomatic agreements eventually reached by the USSR. Reinforcing this trend, the new thinking also led to the formulation of Soviet initiatives aimed at expanding and diversifying its economic relations with those Latin American countries whose economies were considered complementary to those of the USSR while emphasizing the need to eliminate persistent Soviet trade deficits with some of them.

As the Soviet approach to the region became more pragmatic, it attempted to reduce the burden imposed on the Soviet Union by economic and military aid provided to Cuba and Nicaragua. The Soviet government made it clear that its priorities had changed and that the political considerations that motivated its past largess had been replaced by an approach heralding the gradual elimination of aid and subsidies. The proclaimed solidarity with these revolutionary governments was accompanied by recommendations for them to expand their range of economic relations and to avoid actions that could affect the emerging international détente. At the same time, the Gorbachev administration favored opening or deepening diplomatic relations with all Latin American governments, disregarding their political orientation. Besides developing closer relations with those countries with whom they already had diplomatic ties, the Soviets indicated their interest in establishing diplomatic relations with those countries with which they had never established such ties (Honduras, Paraguay, El Salvador, Belize) or countries that had broken them in the past (Chile).[16] Finally, to dispel any remaining misgivings, the Soviet government took further distance from the pro-Moscow Communist parties by stressing the diversity and decentralization of the international Communist movement, the USSR's respect for other countries' sovereignty, and its commitment not to interfere in their domestic affairs.

Argentina and Brazil: Democratization, Economic Crisis, and Foreign Policy

The Argentine and Brazilian transitions to democracy had different features and timetables, but in both cases democratization took place amid critical economic conditions: debt crisis, balance-of-payments difficulties, stagflationary signals, fiscal deficits, and a generalized perception that the political-economic models implemented by authoritarian regimes had exhausted their capacity to generate growth and ensure political order.

In Argentina, the restoration of democracy marked the end of an internationally discredited regime whose erratic foreign policies were initially replaced by the Radical administration with a more coherent strategy based on the principles of pluralist democracy and international morality, justice and law, self-determination and nonintervention in domestic affairs, defense of human rights and democratization at the international level, support for a more equitable international economic order, and promotion of disarmament and peaceful resolution of disputes.[17]

Concerning the USSR, the Alfonsín administration intended to maintain adequate relations to ensure the continuation of profitable economic exchanges as well as Soviet support for and consultation with Argentina on issues of common interest. The existence of these ties, however, would not prevent the Argentine government from defending the principles of self-determination, nonintervention of other countries in domestic affairs, and respect for human rights and from denouncing their violation anywhere in the world.[18] Moreover, the foreign relations minister, Dante Caputo, declared before taking office that, although Argentina would not practice "ideological discrimination in its commercial relations with the Eastern countries," it would try to diversify the direction of its exports "for national interest reasons, because the almost exclusive presence of a single customer creates as a matter of fact relations of dependence that are not convenient."[19]

Nevertheless, United States and Western European reluctance or inability to respond to the Argentine approach by promoting some kind of debt relief and opening its markets to Argentine products forced the Argentine government to reassess the importance of the Soviet market for its exports. Preserving and deepening profitable economic relations with the USSR became once again a priority for Argentine policymakers. At the same time, the innovative and dynamic political-diplomatic strategy pursued by the Soviet Union after the rise of Gorbachev contrasted with the confrontational approach followed by the Reagan administration concerning the Central American crisis and nuclear disarmament issues. The verification of the existence of similar viewpoints with regard to nuclear disarmament, world peace, and regional crises facilitated the exchange of visits by Argentine and Soviet dignitaries, the issue of joint declarations, and mutual support for the foreign policy positions held by the two governments.

The inauguration in July 1989 of the Menem administration, however, which took place amid domestic hyperinflation, social turmoil, and a realization that the Soviet crisis was reducing the volume of trade to minimal levels, led to a renewed emphasis on pro-Western features of Argentina's foreign policies.[20] The resolution of Argentina's domestic economic and social problems was the first priority and required an absolute consistency between domestic macroeconomic and social policies based on a free-market strategy and a foreign policy oriented toward profitable relations with the developed capitalist countries able to help solve trade, investment, and foreign debt problems. The application of this formula led to the reestablishment of diplomatic relations with Great Britain and many efforts to promote closer relations with the United States. In relation to the USSR, the Menem administration's policies were aimed at maintaining the existing level of cooperation, but the development of closer ties was not considered a priority as the capacity of a collapsing Soviet Union to help solve the Argentine crisis was judged very low.

In Brazil the process of democratic transition culminated in March 1985 with the inauguration of José Sarney, whose foreign policy program represented the continuation of the policies of "responsible pragmatism" implemented since the mid-1970s by the military administrations.[21] The foreign relations ministers appointed by Sarney and, after 1990, his successor, Fernando Collor, did not alter the general lines established by their predecessors.[22] The promotion of an autonomous foreign policy fitting Brazil's image as an emerging intermediate power was initially translated into renewed clashes with the United States on economic, military, and diplomatic issues; establishing or reinforcing ties with Latin American countries (diplomatic recognition of Cuba and integration accords with Argentina); deepening commercial ties with African and Middle Eastern countries; creating openings toward the European Economic Community (EEC); and active participation in international organizations and multilateral forums.

As in the Argentine case, resolving or lessening economic problems was the main priority for Brazil's democratic administrations. Since 1982, constraints imposed on the Brazilian economy by foreign debt obligations, a scarcity of new loans, and a decrease in foreign investment had left foreign trade as the only positive aspect of a critical balance-of-payments problem.[23] In relation to the USSR, these political and economic considerations resulted in attempts to deepen and diversify bilateral relations. In the words of the first foreign relations minister appointed by Sarney, Olavo Setubal, "Departing from the scarcely correct relationship established with this superpower, we established the foundation for a more mature and diversified relation. . . . not only the possibilities of economic cooperation, joint ventures, and commercial expansion increased . . . but we also started a more effective political dialogue with the USSR."[24]

The inauguration of Fernando Collor in March 1990 did not alter the essential features of Brazilian foreign policy but led to a growing emphasis on economic and diplomatic rapprochement with the United States and other developed market economies as well as on the formulation of more liberal economic policies.[25] Brazil's reentry into the international political economy under these conditions would indicate that the priority would be to establish closer relations with the Western industrialized nations that could help to lessen Brazil's socioeconomic problems by opening their markets to Brazilian exports, offering credits and investments, and considering the possibility of debt relief measures. In this context, the maintenance of profitable economic relations and cordial diplomatic ties with the USSR would have been very helpful, but considering the Soviet crisis, the attention and resources of the Brazilian government were more effectively concentrated on restructuring and deepening economic and political links with the Western developed countries.

The Bilateral Economic Impasse

Between 1985 and 1991 the Soviet decision to reformulate its foreign economic relations following the principles of competitiveness, efficiency, and reciprocity had a negative impact on bilateral trade with Argentina and Brazil. In the emerging context of détente, the political reliability of suppliers was no longer so important as the price, quality, and credit conditions they could offer. Meanwhile, the growing competition among agricultural exporters and the large size of the Soviet market gave Soviet traders considerable leverage in their negotiations with prospective sellers. This situation made it very difficult for Argentina and Brazil to ignore Soviet pressures for commercial concessions. At the same time, the domestic crisis and external imbalances that affected their economies hindered their chances of increasing the volume of Soviet imports or offering lower prices and acceptable credit terms to the USSR.

Between 1986 and 1990 most Soviet import and export exchanges with Latin America (excluding Cuba and Nicaragua) continued to take place with Argentina and Brazil. Argentine products (mainly grains, soybeans, beef, and fish) represented more than 50 percent of the total

Soviet imports from Latin America while Brazil contributed around 30 percent of the total. (Peruvian and Uruguayan exports represented 5 percent each.) During this same period, Soviet exports, mainly of machinery, manufactures, and oil, were mostly directed to these same countries, with Argentina absorbing 35 percent of the total and Brazil 21 percent (Peru took close to 20 percent).[26] But in absolute terms there was a precipitous fall in the value and volume of bilateral trade between Argentina and Brazil and the USSR. Argentina's exports to the Soviet Union declined from $1.2 billion dollars in 1985 to $208 million in 1986, rose to $640 million and $836 million in 1987 and 1988 respectively, and remained around $830 million in 1989 and 1990. Argentine imports of Soviet products rose minimally during these same years, from $14.5 million (U.S.) in 1986 to $23 million in 1989.[27] Brazil's exports to the USSR declined from $450 million (U.S.) in 1985 to $265 million in 1986, rose to $380 million in 1987, dropped to only $257 million in 1988 (their lowest point since 1980), and remained around $390 million in 1989. Meanwhile, Brazilian imports from the USSR dropped from $75 million (U.S.) in 1985 to $45 million in 1986, rose to $70 million in 1987, declined abruptly to $29 million in 1988, and increased slightly to $35 million in 1989.[28]

These depressed trade figures highlight the difficulties that plagued the economic relationships of Brazil and Argentina with the USSR during this period. Renewed Soviet emphasis on the notions of commercial profitability and reciprocity cut down trade with those countries reluctant or unable to promote their exports through subsidies and credits and unable to increase their imports of Soviet products. Departing from a comparison of prices and sale conditions, the Soviets concentrated their purchases in the United States and the EEC, which offered subsidized prices and credits, in contrast to the two Latin American countries, which asked for market prices and cash payments in hard currency. Moreover, the glut in the global oil market and the consequent decline in prices resulted in a substantial drop in Soviet hard-currency earnings and reductions in their import capacity. Finally, the restructuring of the Soviet economy faced many obstacles that, in the short term, made it difficult to expand the export of Soviet products to the Latin American markets. The sluggishness of the Soviet economy, the growing domestic demand, and a number of quality, distribution, and marketing problems reduced the volume, diversity, and competitiveness of the products offered by the USSR to the Latin American countries.

In Argentina and Brazil the persistent economic crisis reduced the levels of domestic investment, production, and consumption and had a negative impact on import capacity. Thus the chances of increasing or even maintaining the volume of imports from the USSR were nonexistent unless the recession could be overcome and new forms of economic exchange and cooperation introduced. Moreover, the stringent fiscal policies implemented by these countries lowered the level of public investment, which particularly affected interest in importing goods traditionally offered by the USSR such as hydroelectric equipment, road construction machinery, and transportation equipment.

In this regard the protracted discussions that preceded the renewal of the Argentine-Soviet grain supply agreement in 1986 and its ultimate fate are illustrative: Soviet negotiators made it clear that Argentine political reliability as a supplier was no longer the foremost consideration and that the accord would be renewed only if Argentina agreed to increase its imports of Soviet products during the next few years. Finally, the Soviets consented to renew the agreement only after Argentina promised to increase substantially its imports of Soviet manufactures.[29] Neither side, however, met the agreed targets: Soviet purchases remained well below the agreed-upon 4.5 million tons, while Argentine imports of Soviet goods never reached the expected figures.

A mutual recognition of these problems forced both countries to look for alternative methods to revitalize the economic relationship.[30] The most important of the new forms of economic cooperation promoted by the USSR were the creation of binational or multinational enterprises and the promotion of joint ventures.[31] The majority of these Soviet cooperative ventures with Argentine and Brazilian companies have taken place in the areas of food processing, fishing, railroad construction and modernization, and hydroelectric dam construction and equipment. In Argentina these joint ventures included partnerships established between the Soviet fishing company Sovrybflot and the Argentine firms Bajamar, Argenpez, and Pesquera Argentina del Sur, authorized by a bilateral five-year agreement to catch 180,000 tons of fish each year for the Soviet market; and a Soviet-Argentine consortium using Soviet technology to produce part of the equipment for the Piedra del Aguila hydroelectric power plant.[32] In Brazil these joint enterprises included the creation of a Soviet-Brazilian company to build a transnortheastern railroad in Brazil and automatize some of the Soviet railroads, a joint enterprise between Tyazhpromeksport and the Brazilian state enterprise Vale do Rio Doce to produce ferromanganese, the creation of a Soviet-Brazilian-British company to be located in Brazil to bottle and commercialize Soviet vodka for the Latin American market, and the joint production of electrical equipment by the Soviet Tekhnopromeksport and the Brazilian Usimec.[33] Some of these mixed corporations have operated in third countries—for instance, the binational company formed by the association of the Brazilian construction firm Odebrecht and the Soviet electrical power company Tekhnopromeksport also contracted to build the Capanga dam in Angola, the total cost of which is around $1 billion (U.S.).[34]

Argentine and Brazilian joint ventures operating in the USSR were less common. Since January 1987, however, when the Soviet government authorized the creation in the USSR of joint ventures with foreign capital participation, a number of projects have been considered by Argentine and Brazilian business groups. On different occasions, Soviet representatives underscored the opportunities offered by this new policy to Argentine and Brazilian investors, especially in the areas of food processing (dairy products and citrus), textiles, shoes, sports equipment, computers, and a series of consumer-related sectors.[35] The number of concrete operations, however, was limited by problems such as lack of experience, the inconvertibility of the ruble, technological dependence of the Latin American companies on Western corporations, scarcity of local capital, and bureaucratic obstacles on both sides. Thus in 1991 there were only five joint enterprises under way in the USSR with these countries (three with Argentine private participation and two with Brazilian), including an Argentine-Soviet firm using Argentine technology to produce gymnasium equipment and a Brazilian-Swedish-Soviet apple juice factory that employs Brazilian technology.[36]

Countertrade was also encouraged in an attempt to overcome hard currency shortages experienced by the USSR and its Latin American counterparts. Barter operations have included, for instance, the exchange of Brazilian soybeans for Soviet oil and the barter of Argentine wine for trolley buses and antihail equipment. A number of major obstacles, though, hindered the expansion of this kind of exchange, including in Argentina and Brazil a lack of familiarity with Soviet products, doubts about their quality, and a declining demand resulting from recession in the two South American countries. Exchange was hampered on the Soviet side by an inadequacy in several areas including marketing strategies; spare parts and after-sales maintenance; and technical, quality, and finishing standards.

After 1985 another innovative economic development was the establishment of direct commercial relations between Soviet enterprises and some local governments within Argentina and Brazil. Partial economic decentralization and the lifting of bureaucratic obstacles promoted by perestroika gave Soviet enterprises a chance to establish commercial relations with foreign partners without following the cumbersome state-to-state approach characteristic of the previous era. Meanwhile, in Argentina and Brazil, democratization had restored provincial and state autonomies suppressed by centralizing military regimes, giving local governments the opportunity to search for new economic opportunities abroad. Representatives of Soviet companies began to approach local authorities to offer their products and explore the possibilities of mutually profitable exchanges. In turn, local governments, whose economies were passing through critical times, appeared eager to promote the export of regional goods to the USSR. In Argentina economic contacts with the USSR multiplied as several provincial governors—from Mendoza, Buenos Aires, San Juan, Santa Cruz, Chaco, Santa Fe, Misiones, and Formosa—visited the Soviet Union and signed agreements for the exchange of regional products (wine, tannin, and foodstuffs) for machinery and manufactures (transportation equipment, road construction machines, and antihail equipment). In Brazil, similar contacts took place between the governments of the states of Rio de Janeiro and São Paulo and the governments of the Soviet Union and some of the Soviet republics.

It is important to point out that although these new forms of cooperation helped to diversify the contents and scope of bilateral economic relations, they were not enough to offset the decline in traditional forms of trade. In early 1991, Soviet economic relations with Argentina and Brazil were passing through their lowest point since the mid-1970s, and there were no clear prospects of recovery as long as the Soviet political-economic crisis continued and the Argentine and Brazilian economies remained stagnated.

Diplomatic Cooperation and Political Convergence

Between 1986 and 1991 Gorbachev's innovative approach to international affairs coincided with some of the initiatives advanced by democratic administrations of several Latin American nations. There was a noticeable shift in the nature of bilateral links as the Soviet Union and the two largest Latin American countries found new areas of agreement.

In 1984 Argentina had participated with Mexico, Greece, India, Sweden, and Tanzania in the creation of the Group of Six, a peace initiative of countries of the five continents that urged both superpowers to take decisive steps toward nuclear disarmament and the relaxation of world tensions. After 1985, in contrast to the relative indifference shown by previous Soviet leadership, the initiatives of the Six were welcomed by Gorbachev, who emphasized the Soviet interest in reducing international tensions and pointed out concrete steps taken by the USSR in this direction. The Declarations of New Delhi, issued by the Six in January and October 1985, offered Gorbachev an opportunity to emphasize Soviet support for these initiatives and contrast it with the Reagan administration's refusal to suspend nuclear tests.[37] Successive messages sent by the Group of Six calling for concrete measures to prevent an arms race in space and to promote nuclear disarmament, as well as proposals to verify the suspension of nuclear tests, were welcomed by Gorbachev and facilitated the consolidation of friendlier ties. In 1989 a declaration issued by the Six supported the dialogue between the superpowers, hailed the progress in reduction of strategic arsenals, and called for the construction of a world free of nuclear weapons. Gorbachev thanked the Six for their efforts and affirmed Soviet support for a number of their initiatives including complete elimination of nuclear and chemical weapons, suspension of nuclear tests, and continuous prohibition of nuclear weapons in space.[38]

Changes in the Soviet Union and the democratization of Argentina and Brazil also encouraged the multiplication of official visits as political-ideological obstacles and mutual suspicions were removed.[39] After 1985 missions headed by foreign relations ministers and presidents became more frequent and productive. In December 1985 Olavo Setubal became the first Brazilian foreign relations minister to visit the USSR.[40] This visit gave both sides an opportunity to discuss economic and political issues including the prospects of diversifying their trade relations and their respective positions on world peace and the Central American crisis. In January 1986 Argentine foreign relations minister Dante Caputo arrived in Moscow for an official visit.[41] During this visit a number of agreements were signed, including the renewal for five years of the grain supply agreement, an agreement on cultural and scientific cooperation, and a protocol establishing mechanisms for annual mutual consultations on bilateral and global issues.

In October 1986 Raúl Alfonsín arrived in Moscow. This was the first visit by an Argentine president to the USSR.[42] In his meetings with Gorbachev and Shevardnadze, Alfonsín praised the Soviet nuclear moratorium and other peace initiatives. The Soviets commended the role played by Argentina in the Group of Six and Contadora Support Group, supported the Brazilian-Argentine proposal to demilitarize the South Atlantic, and declared agreement with the Argentine demand for a political settlement of the Falklands-Malvinas issue. During this visit the system of bilateral diplomatic consultations between Argentina and the USSR that had been informally established in the early 1980s was institutionalized in a protocol that announced annual political consultation meetings between officials of the respective ministries of foreign relations to discuss bilateral and international issues of mutual interest. The accord created mechanisms for permanent consultation uncommon not only in the context of Soviet relations with Latin America but also in that of Soviet relations with the rest of the world. This agreement represented a remarkable new phase of diplomatic cooperation between countries with different political and socioeconomic systems.

In September-October 1987, Soviet foreign relations minister Eduard Shevardnadze visited Brazil and Argentina.[43] In Brazil, the joint communiqué issued by the end of the visit underscored the need to expand and diversify bilateral economic relations and affirmed Soviet-Brazilian agreement on such topics as global and regional peace, disarmament, and international security, including Soviet arms limitation proposals, the Brazilian proposal on the creation of a peace and cooperation area in the South Atlantic and Brazil's participation in the Contadora Support Group, preservation of the Antarctic Treaty, the condemnation of colonialism and racism, the need to find adequate solutions to the debt crisis, and support for an international peace conference on the Middle East and UN peacemaking initiatives. In Argentina the Soviet-Argentine joint declaration called for more diversified economic-commercial relations, the elimination of all nuclear and chemical weapons, a halt to nuclear testing, and prohibition of the militarization of space. It also underscored agreement on issues such as the demilitarization of the South Atlantic; a peaceful resolution of the Malvinas problem and the Central American, Middle East, and Persian Gulf conflicts; the importance of preserving the Antarctic Treaty; and the convenience of restructuring the international economic system to overcome the debt crisis and underdevelopment.

In October 1988 José Sarney arrived in the Soviet Union for the first official visit there by a Brazilian president.[44] During his stay both sides emphasized the friendly and cooperative nature of the bilateral relationship and signed a number of economic agreements for the exchange of machinery and equipment, the establishment of commercial credit lines, and the creation of joint ventures. In their declarations Gorbachev and Sarney praised the elimination of ideological prejudices and the rise of "international pluralism" that created an adequate framework for the development of creative economic and political relations between the East and the South. The visit culminated with the signing of a fourteen-point "declaration on principles for interaction concerning international peace and cooperation" that stressed the possibilities of political collaboration between countries with different socioeconomic and political systems and established a system of permanent bilateral consultations on diplomatic and economic issues similar to the one endorsed by Argentina.

While these visits and agreements unfolded, the shift in the Soviet approach to the Central American crisis removed one of the last points of contention and facilitated the strengthening of its diplomatic ties with Argentina and Brazil. Under Gorbachev the Soviets displayed a growing interest in promoting a peaceful resolution of the Central American crisis as their policy toward the region was gradually reassessed from a perspective that emphasized common global security and alertness to the risks of escalation of regional or local conflicts.[45] This Soviet approach coincided with Argentine and Brazilian interest in reducing regional tensions and securing a peaceful resolution of the crisis as shown through their participation in the Contadora Support Group.[46] Soviet representatives repeatedly praised the Argentine-Brazilian attitude and declared its support for Latin American efforts to resolve the crisis peacefully. In 1988 the Soviets supported the Alajuela summit initiatives, disregarding Nicaraguan objections to the elimination of the international commission for verification of compliance with the Esquipulas-2 agreement, and decided to suspend arms shipments to Nicaragua. Throughout 1989 the Soviets supported political accords on peace and democratization reached by the Central American presidents, denied new arms shipments to Nicaragua, objected to Cuba's transshipment of Soviet weapons to the Sandinistas, opposed the delivery of armament to the Salvadoran guerrillas by the Cubans and Nicaraguans, praised the agreement reached between the Sandinistas and the Contras on the suspension of military operations, and supported the celebration of free general elections in February 1990.

Reinforcing this trend toward growing consensus was the removal of the last ideological-political misgivings held by the Argentine and Soviet governments concerning the relations between the CPSU and local Communist parties. Throughout this period, Gorbachev made it sufficiently clear that the CPSU was not interested in interfering in the internal affairs of countries with which the USSR maintained normal diplomatic relations and that local Communist parties were free to design their political strategies according to their own diagnoses and analyses of domestic circumstances. In Argentina and Brazil, where the pro-Soviet Communist parties were accustomed to following the meanders of the CPSU's strategic and tactical decisions, this new situation forced a reassessment of domestic and international positions. Internal debate and attempts to follow an autonomous course resulted in most cases in acute factional struggles and organizational splits. Faced with a growing number of such intraparty feuds, the Soviet government and the CPSU did not offer support to any faction, preferring rather to preserve cordial relations with the Argentine and Brazilian administrations, especially after some groups within the PCA and the PCB began to praise the Cuban model and to reject the Soviet ideological and political shifts as contrary to Marxist-Leninist ideas and methods.

Between 1989 and 1991 Soviet diplomatic relations with Argentina and Brazil remained cordial, but there was a noticeable decrease in the number and importance of new developments. Although Gorbachev had accepted invitations to visit Argentina and Brazil, growing Soviet domestic problems and the installation of new administrations in these Latin American countries caused the tour to be postponed. Under Menem, Argentina's foreign policies discarded traditional Peronist nationalistic and nonaligned elements and aimed to establish closer links with the United States and Western European countries in order to receive economic and political help in solving the acute economic crisis. Although the results of this Western-centered foreign policy strategy were not very encouraging in economic terms, the Menem administration persisted in its application. Diplomatic relations with the USSR remained cordial, but the only noticeable developments were Menem's visit to Moscow in October 1990 and the signing of a "Declaration on Collaboration Principles" that included several points stated in previous Argentine-Soviet declarations such as support for international distension, peace, and disarmament; respect for self-determination; endorsement of the UN role; backing of democratization; and calls for an international effort to promote balanced economic growth and solve the debt crisis.[47] No concrete agreement was reached, however, on bilateral economic issues other than reiterating the importance of reducing the Soviet trade deficit, maintaining Argentina's role as a grain supplier, and establishing joint ventures and mixed enterprises. In Brazil under Collor, the development of closer relations with the USSR was a secondary objective as the growing crisis in the Soviet Union indicated that there were limited opportunities to increase the volume of exports and negligible chances of acquiring the kind of credits and technology that Brazil needed and that the USSR itself was trying to obtain from the developed market economies.

Argentina, Brazil, and the Collapse of the USSR:
A Provisional Assessment

In the last few years, changes in the USSR, Argentina, and Brazil led to a new, transitional phase in relations as the three actors engaged in the search for more advantageous approaches, modifying the pattern established in the 1970s and early 1980s. Since the mid-1980s the three countries have explored, with different degrees of success, the possibility of devising new forms of diplomatic and economic cooperation compatible with fundamental transformations in their domestic situations and in the international arena. By the early 1990s, however, bilateral relations had reached an impasse. In the Soviet Union, national and ethnic unrest, acceleration of the pace of political liberalization, the growing resistance of entrenched groups, problems associated with the implementation of perestroika, and transformations under way in Eastern Europe reduced chances to formulate and implement new foreign policy initiatives toward countries such as Argentina and Brazil that had very low priority in the design of a global Soviet strategy. In Argentina and Brazil, efforts to solve the economic crisis and attempts to consolidate the nascent democracies led to a surge of neoconservative governments interested in promoting capitalist modernization and developing closer relations with the Western developed countries. The Soviet role as a customer and diplomatic actor was appreciated, but there was no inclination to formulate innovative foreign policies toward the USSR that could jeopardize relations with the United States, affect domestic political stability, or divert scarce economic resources.

Economic Relations and Their Prospects

In this context, the acceleration and worsening of the Soviet economic and political crisis extinguished any hope that the impasse could be overcome in the short term or even in the medium term. As long as the socioeconomic and political crisis continued, the resources, will, and capacity to design new strategies to end the impasse were missing, and bilateral relationships experienced further decline. Well before the failed August coup and the disintegration of the USSR, the economic problems that plagued the country had made 1991 the worst year for Soviet trade with Argentina and Brazil since the late 1950s. As it was reported in the Soviet press, throughout the first eleven months of 1991 the volume of foreign Soviet trade had fallen off by 36.4 percent with imports falling by 41.7 percent, including an extraordinarily sharp decline in the volume of imported foodstuffs and consumer goods.[48] At the same time, the USSR was failing to pay some of its outstanding bills for purchases made the previous year, including Brazilian instant coffee and poultry.[49] The rapid decline in Soviet reserves of foreign currency and gold, together with the rapid devaluation of the ruble, made it clear that no recovery in the import capacity of the CIS or the republics would take place in the short term. It was not surprising, therefore, that during 1991 practically all the imports of grains by the central government (30 million tons) and the republics (7 million tons) were financed with credits obtained from the United States, Germany, the EEC, Canada, and France, among other states.[50] As a result, the countries offering the credits were the only ones that exported agricultural products to the USSR in 1991. By October 1991, Argentina and Brazil did not appear among the countries listed in a detailed roster that included exporter nations that had supplied 31 million tons of wheat, maize, barley, and soybeans to the USSR since the beginning of the year.[51] By early 1991 the inability of the two South American countries to offer credits to finance the purchase of their grains and the growing shortage of foreign currency in the USSR had resulted in the elimination of the most important component of bilateral trade relations.

Most experts seem to agree that in the 1990s there will be little growth in domestic agricultural production in the former USSR and that transportation, storage, and commercialization problems will continue to plague the agricultural sector.[52] Changes in agricultural policies associated with perestroika—for example, land leasing, the sale of part of the production at market prices, and partial payment in hard currency—did not have the expected results.[53] More radical— free-market-oriented—institutional and price reforms have been implemented since the emergence of the CIS, but it may take years for the CIS to reduce its grain import needs, especially if the transition to free-market agriculture takes place among economic and political turmoil, as was the case in 1991. According to some estimates, in the next few years the grain import needs of the former USSR will fluctuate between 25 and 40 million tons per year, depending on weather conditions, the effectiveness of agricultural policies implemented in different republics, and the capacity of intra-CIS trade to allocate grains stocks. It is also possible that, if market signals are heeded and a more efficient system of procurement is created, there will be a decline in Soviet imports of wheat and other grains for human consumption and an increase in the volume of imported high-protein livestock fodder, such as soybeans and oilseed cakes.[54]

This shift in import patterns might at some point benefit Argentina and Brazil, which have recently increased their soybean acreage and shares of the world soybean market, although there is some concern in both countries about the declining trend in soy prices and their own growing reliance on one particular export crop.[55] But even if the Soviet imports of soybeans and other primary products (linseed and sunflower cakes) from Argentina and Brazil resume in the future, massive purchases characteristic of those the USSR made in the late 1970s and early 1980s would not be repeated. Even if the goal of agricultural self-sufficiency remains elusive, the CIS and the former Soviet republics would not be able to sustain the huge trade deficits with Argentina and Brazil that the Soviet government condoned until 1985 for political-strategic reasons—such as to diversify suppliers and to overcome the impact of Western sanctions. Most likely, the Commonwealth and the newly independent republics will try to satisfy the domestic demand for foodstuffs by buying on credit or using their scarce foreign currency reserves in the most effective way: buying from those countries that offer the best price, quality, and credit conditions or from those that import Soviet products in satisfactory volumes. In these circumstances, export prospects for certain Argentine and Brazilian agricultural products will be affected by competition from the United States, Canada, and the EEC in terms of price and conditions of payment.

Thus the development of bilateral commercial relations will require less reliance on traditional forms of trade and will depend instead on the formulation of innovative and more dynamic approaches aimed at diversifying exchanges and establishing new forms of cooperation, particularly in more technologically advanced economic activities. Especially in the Argentine case, this is a very difficult proposition because the domestic recession and the decline of the industrial sector make it hard to increase imports and engage in new forms of cooperation. In Brazil, possibilities of establishing new forms of economic interaction with the CIS and the former Soviet republics are relatively more encouraging because of the higher level of modernization of the Brazilian industrial sector and the significant role still played in the economy by the public sector. As in the Argentine case, however, Brazilian and Soviet economic and political problems have created enormous uncertainty among public and private actors, reducing the incentives to explore new forms of economic cooperation or to invest scarce resources in such a risky situation.

Although the independence of several former Soviet republics and the decentralization of economic decisions and activities have multiplied the number of possible commercial and economic partners for Argentina and Brazil, actual establishment of profitable economic ties requires a degree of economic and political stability that has been absent up to now in the former USSR. The disintegration of the Soviet Union generated a growing political and economic uncertainty that led to the interruption of negotiations and the shelving of proposals for joint ventures that had been discussed between some of the Soviet republics and enterprises and Argentine and Brazilian governments and companies. In the Argentine case, no new joint enterprises were considered; the only developments included some exploratory contacts concerning the possibility of a Russian civil construction consortium that might join some Argentine companies to improve fresh water and sewage services in Mendoza province and trading construction materials for fruits and vegetables.[56] In the Brazilian case, conversations about establishing a joint enterprise including the Brazilian company Sabo to produce auto parts in Armenia were suspended; the fate of two Brazilian projects under way in Russia (the construction of a steel and iron plant and the establishment of a consortium to exploit natural gas) became uncertain; and the prospects of technological cooperation between the Brazilian state enterprise Vale do Rio Doce Company and Tyazhpromeksport on the lamination of metallic titanium remained unclear.[57]

The chances of resuming negotiations and establishing Argentine and Brazilian joint ventures in the CIS or the republics remain slim not only because of uncertainty resulting from the economic and political crisis but also because the shortage of hard currency makes it very difficult to remit profits abroad while payments in kind, which are sometimes offered as an alternative, require complicated international transactions before they are turned into foreign currency. Moreover, many of the previously named obstacles to the establishment of joint ventures continue to lessen the prospects for this kind of cooperation.

One novel trend that emerged after the collapse of the USSR and the worsening of the economic and political crisis has been an interest on the part of Argentina and Brazil in promoting the immigration of former Soviet citizens, especially scientists and technicians in the case of Brazil and 100,000 members of Russian minorities from the Baltic republics in the case of Argentina.[58] These initiatives may help to solve some of the problems faced by individual Soviet citizens and contribute to promote scientific and technological progress in Argentina and Brazil, but they are not going to contribute to the reestablishment of relations on a more solid economic and political foundation.

The Political-Diplomatic Situation

In the political-diplomatic sphere, relations between the CIS and independent republics on the one side and Argentina and Brazil on the other have remained cordial but inconsequential. The Argentine and Brazilian presidents expressed in a joint statement their "deep concern" about the August coup attempt and their confidence that "the values of democracy, peace and justice [would] not be affected."[59] Immediately after the reinstatement of the Soviet government, both Menem and Collor sent messages to Gorbachev and Yeltsin declaring their "profound satisfaction" with the reestablishment of constitutional order and their willingness to maintain and deepen bilateral ties. At the same time, Argentina and Brazil recognized the independence of Lithuania, Latvia, and Estonia and formally established diplomatic relations with the Baltic republics.[60] In December 1991 the Argentine and Brazilian governments, after expressing their esteem for Gorbachev, announced their recognition of the CIS as a continuation of the USSR and started to recognize and establish diplomatic relations with the new republics, including Ukraine, Moldova, Uzbekistan, Tajikistan, Georgia, and Armenia.[61] In turn, Yeltsin and the leaders of the republics expressed their satisfaction with the prompt recognition of their new status and announced their intention to develop and maintain friendly relations with their Latin American counterparts.

Although the cordial nature of these exchanges presages the development of cooperative ties, the new international situation created by the collapse of the USSR should not be assessed as completely favorable to the interests of Argentina and Brazil. As was the case with Gorbachev's foreign policies, the initiatives taken by the CIS and the republics to reduce international tensions are undoubtedly welcomed by Argentina and Brazil as positive contributions to global peace and security as long as they encourage a more effective participation of both countries in the discussion of global issues and facilitate the satisfactory resolution of regional problems. There is, however, also some apprehension on the part of Argentines and Brazilians over possible consequences that the collapse of the USSR and the cooperation between the CIS, the independent republics, and the United States might have on their ability to formulate and implement more independent foreign policies. In these new international circumstances, the elimination of traditional East-West tensions abets the reduction of the South American countries' autonomy and may force them to make political, strategic, and economic concessions to the United States and Western developed countries that would have been rejected in the 1970s and early 1980s, when a rapprochement with the Soviet bloc could be used to enlarge Argentina's and Brazil's margin of maneuver in the international arena. In this regard, current Argentine and Brazilian trends toward foreign trade and domestic market liberalization, acceptance of International Monetary Fund policy recommendations concerning the debt crisis, the lack of strong opposition to U.S. intervention in Latin America and the backing for U.S. action in the Persian Gulf, a more compliant attitude in nuclear proliferation matters, and support for Western initiatives in international forums all indicate a revival of the hegemonic role of the United States and other Western developed nations that results, in part, from the South American countries' inability to continue to play the Soviet card to counterbalance Western influence.

From the CIS perspective, the Latin American countries' rapprochement with the United States and the application of increasingly harsher programs of economic stabilization and adjustment have reduced the possibilities of developing closer political and economic ties. But the Latin American experiment in economic and political liberalization also had an interesting impact on debates established in the former USSR on the nature and direction of the political economic transformations under way.[62] On several occasions these Latin American experiences have been used by CIS analysts to support or criticize the process of economic liberalization and democratization initiated by Gorbachev and its expected outcomes. For some observers, the Latin American move toward the free market and liberal democracy is seen as evidence of the global inevitability of these trends and as justification of the need to implement similar policies in the former USSR to ensure a successful political-economic transformation. For others, the social costs and political problems associated with the implementation of these programs in Latin America are an object lesson on the need to avoid a repetition of such mistakes, especially those resulting from unleashing unrestrained market forces in societies traditionally characterized by a high level of state economic intervention. For other analysts, the recent Latin American developments tend to confirm their belief that there is a strong connection between economic and political liberalization, between free-market and liberal democracy. For still others, Latin American political-economic experiences of the 1970s and 1980s (especially those in Argentina, Brazil, Chile, and even Mexico) are used to justify the claim that restrictions should be imposed on democratic political participation, at least until the process of capitalist modernization is well under way. In all these cases the Latin American liberalization experience is conceived as a distant mirror that reflects—or anticipates—political-economic developments in the former USSR and that can be used either as a model for positive transformation or as an example of the type of transformation that should be avoided.

In conclusion, the prospects for relations between Argentina and Brazil and the states emerging from the disintegration of the USSR are uncertain because they depend on the evolution of a number of variables whose behavior is difficult to predict. If the situation in the CIS and the new republics becomes more stable and the economic crisis affecting them and Argentina and Brazil subsides, there will be opportunities for diplomatic collaboration and economic cooperation as they share similar interests in promoting the peaceful resolution of disputes and the creation of conditions for economic development into a more equitable international political-economic order. It is clear, however, that current global and domestic circumstances tend to lessen the chances of this scenario's becoming a reality in the near future. Only in the medium and long range might the gradual emergence of more stable and favorable international and domestic conditions facilitate the establishment of new relations characterized by new forms of mutually beneficial diplomatic interaction, economic collaboration, and political-ideological understanding.

Notes

1. On early Soviet-Argentine relations see Aldo C. Vacs, *Discreet Partners: Argentina and the USSR since 1917* (Pittsburgh: University of Pittsburgh Press, 1984), 3–12.

2. On Soviet-Argentine relations in the period 1945–70, see ibid., 12–23.

3. On the rapprochement with the USSR that followed these new developments in Argentina see ibid., 24–41, 66–71.

4. On the military governments's approach to the USSR in the period 1976–83 see ibid., 41–65, 71–90.

5. On Soviet-Argentine relations after 1983 see Aldo C. Vacs, "Democratization and Perestroika: New Challenges and Opportunities in Argentine-Soviet Relations" (paper delivered at the 15th Congress of the Latin American Studies Association, Miami, December 1989).

6. On Soviet-Brazilian relations see, for example, Stephen Clissold, *Soviet Relations with Latin America, 1918–1968: A Documentary Survey* (London, New York, and Toronto: Oxford University Press, 1970), 73–81, 151–56; T. Stephen Cheston, "Diplomatic Sideshow: A Study of Soviet Relations with Latin America, 1918–1936" (Ph.D. diss., Georgetown University, 1972); and Isabel Turrent, "Brazil and the Soviet Union: A Low-Profile Relationship," in Augusto Varas, ed., *Soviet-Latin American Relations in the 1980s* (Boulder, Colo., and London: Westview Press, 1987), 230–49.

7. On the CPB's origins, strategy, and activities see Leoncio Basbaum, *Uma Vida em Seis Tempos* (A life in six phases) (São Paulo: Alfa-Omega, 1976);

Astrojildo Pereira, *Formação do PCB, 1922–1928* (The formation of the PCB, 1922–1928) (Rio de Janeiro: Vitoria, 1962); and Ronald H. Chilcote, *The Brazilian Communist Party: Conflict and Integration, 1922–1972* (New York: Oxford University Press, 1974).

8. On the 1935 revolt see Helio Silva, *1935, A Revolta Vermelha* (1935, the red revolution) (Rio de Janeiro: Civilização Brasileira, 1969).

9. On the Brazilian "national security doctrine," see Maria Helena Moreira Alves, *State and Opposition in Military Brazil* (Austin: University of Texas Press, 1985). On the Soviet characterization of the Brazilian military regime see, for example, the debate on Latin American authoritarian regimes in "En torno al problema de los regímenes autoritarios de derecha contemporáneos" (Regarding the problem of contemporary right-wing authoritarian regimes) *América Latina* 3 (1976): 76–155.

10. Recent analyses of the Soviet approach to Latin America under Gorbachev can be found in Augusto Varas, "La Perestroika y las relaciones Unión Soviética-América Latina" (Perestroika and Soviet-Latin American relations), in Heraldo Muñoz, ed., *Las políticas exteriores de América Latina y el Caribe: Un balance de esperanzas* (The international relations of Latin America and the Caribbean: a balance of hope) (Buenos Aires: PROSPEL/GEL, 1988), 367–78; Fernando Bustamante, "Política exterior de la Unión Soviética hacia América Latina: la hora de la renovación" (Soviet foreign policy toward Latin America: the time of renewal), in Muñoz, ed., *Anuario de políticas exteriores latinoamericanas 1988–1989: A la espera de una nueva etapa* (Yearbook of the international relations of Latin America, 1988–89: awaiting the new era) (Caracas: PROSPEL/Nueva Sociedad, 1989), 335–56; Edme Dominguez Reyes, "La Unión Soviética y América Latina a finales de los ochenta: el fin de una era" (The USSR and Latin America at the end of the 1980s: the end of an era), in Jorge Heine, ed., *Anuario de políticas exteriores latinoamericanas 1990–1991: Hacia unas relaciones internacionales de mercado?* (Yearbook of the international relations of Latin America 1900–1991: toward market international relations?) (Caracas: PROSPEL/Nueva Sociedad, 1991); Nicola Miller, *Soviet Relations with Latin America* (Cambridge and New York: Cambridge University Press, 1989); Hugo Perosa, *Las relaciones argentino-soviéticas contemporaneas/2* (Contemporary Soviet-Argentine relations) (Buenos Aires: CEDAL, 1990), 146–51; and Roberto Russell, ed., *Nuevos rumbos en la relación Unión Soviética/América Latina* (New trends in Soviet–Latin American relations) (Buenos Aires: FLACSO-Grupo Editor Latinoamericano, 1990), 134. Among recent studies of Gorbachev's foreign policy toward the Third World see Francis Fukuyama, "Patterns of Soviet Third World Policy," *Problems of Communism* 36, no. 5 (September-October 1987): 1–13; Giovanni Graziani, *Gorbachev's Economic Strategy in the Third World* (New York and London: Praeger, Center for Strategic and International Studies,

Washington Papers, no. 142, 1990); Mark N. Katz, *Gorbachev's Military Strategy in the Third World* (New York and London: Praeger, Center for Strategic and International Studies, Washington Papers, no. 140, 1989); W. Raymond Duncan and Carolyn McGiffert Ekedhal, *Moscow and the Third World under Gorbachev* (Boulder, San Francisco, and Oxford: Westview Press, 1990); and Jiri Valenta and Frank Cibulka, eds., *Gorbachev's New Thinking and Third World Conflicts* (New Brunswick and London: Transaction Publishers, 1990).

11. Gorbachev's diagnosis of the Soviet crisis, his domestic policy recommendations, and his analyses of the international situation can be found in the speeches and messages collected in Mikhail S. Gorbachev, *A Time for Peace* (New York: Richardson and Steirman, 1985), *The Coming Century of Peace* (New York: Richardson and Steirman, 1986), *Toward a Better World* (New York: Richardson and Steirman, 1987), and *Perestroika: New Thinking for Our Country and the World* (New York: Harper and Row, 1987). Among the numerous studies of the transformations under way in the USSR since 1985, the following are worthy of mention: Abel G. Aganbegyan, *The Economic Challenge of Perestroika* (Bloomington and Indianapolis: Indiana University Press, 1988); Anders Aslund, *Gorbachev's Struggle for Economic Reform* (Ithaca, N.Y.: Cornell University Press, 1989); Padma Desai, *Perestroika in Perspective* (Princeton: Princeton University Press, 1989); Ernest Mandel, *Beyond Perestroika: The Future of Gorbachev's USSR* (London and New York: Verso, 1989); and Roy Medvedev and Giulietto Chiesa, *Time of Change* (New York: Pantheon, 1989).

12. Mikhail S. Gorbachev, *Perestroika*, 139, 142.

13. On the deideologization of Soviet foreign policy outlook see Sylvia Woodby, *Gorbachev and the Decline of Ideology in Soviet Foreign Policy* (Boulder, San Francisco, and London: Westview Press, 1989).

14. See Eusebio Mujal León, "La URSS y América Latina: Una relación en vías de desarrollo" (The USSR and Latin America: a developing relationship), in Roberto Russell, ed., *Nuevos rumbos,* 134.

15. Gorbachev, *Perestroika*, 188.

16. See Serguei Iskenderov, "La política de la Unión Soviética respecto a América Latina, hoy" (Soviet Policy toward Latin America today) (interview with Yuri Pavlov, chief of the Latin American Department of the Soviet foreign relations ministry), *Noticias de la Unión Soviética*, no. 10,375 (26 July 1989): 2–3; no. 10,376 (3 August 1989): 2–3.

17. For the foreign policy program of the Radical party see Unión Cívica Radical, *Plataforma de gobierno* (Government platform) (Buenos Aires: El Cid Editor, 1983), 25–31. Analyses from different perspectives of Radical foreign policy ideas and actions are found in Oscar Camilión, "Tres años de política exterior argentina" (Three years of Argentine foreign policy), Osvaldo

Díez, "Criterios rectores de la política exterior del gobierno de la UCR" (Foreign policy criteria of the UCR), and Juan Carlos Lohlé, "Lineamientos generales y distintos temas de la política exterior argentina" (General features and different themes in Argentina's foreign policy), *America Latina/Internacional* 4, no. 12 (April-June): 105–16; and Roberto Russell, "La nueva política exterior argentina: rupturas conceptuales" (The new foreign policy of Argentina: conceptual breaks), *Sumario* 1, no. 2 (April-June 1987): 30–44.

18. On this foreign policy "moral stand" see, for instance, the speech by the foreign relations minister, D. Caputo, before the UN Commission on Human Rights, Geneva, 27 February 1984, in República Argentina, *Discursos del señor Ministro de Relaciones Exteriores y Culto, Dr. Dante Caputo/Diciembre 1983-Diciembre 1986* (Speeches of Dr. Dante Caputo, minister of foreign relations: December 1983-December 1986) (Buenos Aires, 1987), 13–17.

19. Interview with Dante Caputo in *La Nación*, 10 November 1983, quoted in Mario Rapoport, "Argentina: Las relaciones con la Unión Soviética: Balance y perspectivas" (Argentine-Soviet relations: balance and perspectives), *América Latina/Internacional* 2, no. 5 (July-September 1985): 95.

20. See Roberto Russell, "Cambio de gobierno y política exterior: las primeras tendencias de la gestión peronista" (Change of government and foreign policy: the first tendencies of the Peronist demarche), *América Latina/Internacional* 7, no. 24 (April-June 1990): 333–41; "Cavallo Cites Progress in Relations with U.S." (interview with Foreign Minister Domingo Cavallo), *La Prensa*, 19 August 1990, in *Foreign Broadcast Information Service—Latin America* (22 August 1990): 46–48; and Vacs, "Abandoning the 'Third Position,'" *Hemisphere* 4, no. 1 (Fall 1991): 28–29.

21. On the evolution of the Brazilian military regime's foreign policy since 1974 see Sonia de Camargo and José M. Vásquez Ocampo, *Autoritarismo e democracia na Argentina e Brasil (uma década de política exterior, 1973–1984)* (Authoritarianism and democracy in Argentina and Brazil: a decade of foreign policy, 1973–1984) (São Paulo: Convivio, 1988), 22–188; Monica Hirst, "Democratic Transition and Foreign Policy: The Experience of Brazil," in Muñoz and Joseph Tulchin, eds., *Latin American Nations in World Politics* (Boulder, Colo., and London: Westview Press, 1984), 216–29; Monica Hirst, "Transición democrática y política exterior" (Democratic transition and foreign policy), in Monica Hirst, *Las relaciones internacionales del Brasil* (Brazil's international relations) (Buenos Aires: FLACSO, Serie Documentos e Informes de Investigación, no. 93, April 1990), 3–34; Celso Lafer, *O Brasil e a crise mundial* (Brazil and the world crisis) (São Paulo: Perspectiva, 1984).

22. On the foreign policies of the "New Republic" see Manfred Wilhelmy, "Brasil: el difícil comienzo de la Nueva República" (Brazil: the difficult beginning of the new republic), in Muñoz, ed., *Anuario de políticas exteriores latinoamericanas 1985* (Yearbook of the international relations of Latin

America, 1985) (Buenos Aires: PROSPEL/Grupo Editor Latinoamericano, 1986), 49–91; Monica Hirst, "La política exterior de Brasil en 1986: continuidad y cambio" (Brazil's foreign policy in 1986: continuity and change), in Muñoz, ed., *Anuario de políticas exteriores latinoamericanas 1986*, 43–68; Monica Hirst and Magdalena Segré, "La política exterior de Brasil en tiempos de crisis" (Brazil's foreign policy in times of crisis), in Muñoz, ed., *Anuario de políticas exteriores latinoamericanas 1987*, 35–50; Monica Hirst, "Política exterior de Brasil en 1988: los avances posibles" (Brazil's foreign policy in 1988: possible progress), in Muñoz, ed., *Anuario de políticas exteriores latinoamericanas 1988–1989*, 32–48; Magdalena Segré and Héctor Bocco, "La política exterior de Brasil en 1989: el último capítulo del gobierno Sarney" (Brazil's foreign policy in 1989: the last chapter of Sarney's government), *América Latina/Internacional 7*, no. 23 (January-March 1990); Segré and Bocco, "Brazil: el primer año de consolidación democrática: Un balance preliminar" (Brazil's first year of democratic consolidation: a preliminary balance sheet), in Heine, ed., *Anuario de políticas exteriores latinoamericanas 1990–1991: Hacia unas relaciones internacionales de mercado?* For the positions of Brazil's successive foreign relations ministers between 1985 and 1991 see, for instance, Olavo Setubal, "Uma diplomacia para resultados" (Diplomacy for results) (inaugural speech as minister of foreign relations, 15 March 1985), in Olavo Setubal, *Acão política e discurso liberal* (Political action and liberal discourse) (Rio de Janeiro: Nova Fronteira, 1986), 202–14; Roberto Costa de Abreu Sodré's speech before the 41st session of the UN General Assembly (22 September 1986) in Brazil. Presidência da República. *III Encontro governo-sociedade: o Brasil na virada do século* (The third government-society meeting: Brazil at the turn of the century) (Brasília: Presidência da República, 1986), 1–12; and Francisco Rezek's interview in *O Estado de São Paulo*, 19 August 1990, reproduced in *Foreign Broadcast Information Service—Latin America* (21 August 1990): 22–25.

23. On the Brazilian external economic situation and perspectives see Paulo de Tarso Flecha Lima, "Dados para una reflexão sobre a política comercial brasileira" (Data for reflection on Brazil's commercial policy); and Rubens Ricupero, "Comercio exterior brasileiro: competitividade e perspectivas" (Brazilian commerce: competitiveness and perspectives), in Gelson Fonseca, Jr., and Valdemar Carneiro Leão, eds., *Temas de política externa brasileira* (Themes in brazilian foreign policy) (Brasilia: Fundação Alexandre de Gusmão/IPRI-Editora Ática, 1989), 11–52.

24. Olavo Setubal, "A nova política externa" (The new foreign policy) (article published in *Folha de São Paulo*, 5 January 1986), in Olavo Setubal, *Acão política e discurso liberal*, 220.

25. On the Collor administration's initial foreign policies see Maria Regina Soares de Lima, "Brasil: Política Exterior y los Desafíos de la Decada" (Brazil's foreign policy and the challenges of the decade); Monica Hirst, "Brasil: Prim-

eras impresiones sobre la política exterior del nuevo gobierno" (Brazil: first impressions on the foreign policy of the new government) *América Latina/ Internacional* 7, no. 24 (April-June 1990): 341–46; and Rezek's interview in *Foreign Broadcast Information Service-Latin America* (21 August 1990).

26. See *Foreign Trade* (Moscow), various issues 1987–90.

27. Data obtained from the Instituto Nacional de Estadísticas y Censos (Buenos Aires), March 1990.

28. International Monetary Fund, *Direction of Trade Statistics: Yearbook 1989*, 396; Allan P. Pollard, ed., *USSR: Facts and Figures Annual, Volume 15, 1991* (Gulf Breeze, Fla.: Academic International Press, 1991), 352.

29. The renewed grain supply agreement established that the USSR would buy a minimum of 4 million tons of Argentine corn (70 percent) and sorghum (30 percent) and 500,000 tons of soybeans. Argentina was committed to buy during the five years $500 million of Soviet products (including the turbines for the Piedra del Aguila hydroelectrical complex). See Vacs, *Democratization and Perestroika*, 24–31.

30. On the characteristics of these attempts see the excellent analyses by Fernando Bustamante, "Política exterior de la Unión Soviética hacia América Latina" (The USSR's foreign policy toward Latin America), in *Anuario de políticas exteriores latinoamericanas;* and Fernando Bustamante and Boris Yopo, "América Latina en la nueva política exterior de la Unión Soviética" (Latin America in the Soviet Union's new foreign policy), in Russell, ed., *Nuevos rumbos,* 141–74. For a Soviet perspective see, for instance, Piotr Yakovlev, "Problemas y perspectivas de la colaboración del Este con el Sur: el ejemplo de la relaciones soviético-argentinas" (Problems and perspectives in East-South colaboration: the example of Soviet-Argentine relations), in ibid., 203–11.

31. Because of their technological features and economies of scale, these cooperative undertakings reinforce the trend toward closer relations between the USSR and the relatively most developed countries in the Third World. On the Soviet interest in organizing joint ventures and mixed enterprises with Latin American counterparts see, for instance, Graziani, *Gorbachev's Economic Strategy,* 86–92; and Cámara de Comercio Argentino Soviético, "Empresas mixtas en la URSS: Como formarlas?" (Mixed enterprises in the USSR: how to create them), *Boletín* 4, no. 1 (March-April 1990): 10–12.

32. *Foreign Broadcast Information Service-Latin America* (20 August 1990): 36; (2 May 1986): 1.

33. Bustamante and Yopo, "América Latina en la nueva política exterior," 154–55; and Varas, "La 'Perestroika' y las relaciones," 375–76.

34. Hirst and Bocco, "Brasil-Unión Soviética: Parámetros para un nuevo diálogo" (Brazil and the Soviet Union: parameters for a new dialogue), in Russell, ed., *Nuevos rumbos,* 225.

35. See, for instance, declarations by Soviet representatives visiting Argentina and Brazil in *Foreign Broadcast Information Service—Latin America* (1 May 1990): 37; (27 June 1990): 45–46; (29 June 1990); (27 August 1990): 1.

36. *Foreign Broadcast Information Service—Latin America* (1 May 1990): 37–38; (23 August 1990): 30–31; and *Foreign Broadcast Information Service—Soviet Union* (16 October 1991): 41–43. The capital of the three Argentine-Soviet joint enterprises was 4.063 billion rubles, but the share of Argentine participation was very low, less than 3 percent of the capital. No similar information is available on Soviet-Brazilian joint ventures.

37. See Agencia de Prensa Novosti, comp., *Iniciativas del "Grupo de los Seis de Nueva Delhi" y la posición de la URSS* (The New Delhi Group of Six initiatives and the Soviet position) (Moscow: Novosti, 1987) for the messages exchanged between the group and the Soviet government.

38. See "Los Seis llaman a comenzar desarme nuclear" (The "Six" call for the beginning of nuclear disarmament) and "Respuesta de Gorbachev a mensaje de los Seis" (Gorbachev's response to the Group of Six), *Noticias de la Unión Soviética*, no. 10,355 (21 June 1989): 1–3.

39. On the exchange of visits between Soviet authorities and Argentine and Brazilian authorities see Perosa, "Los viajes al máximo nivel: La diplomacia directa como factor de consolidación de las relaciones de Argentina y Brasil con la Unión Soviética" (Trips at the highest level: direct diplomacy as a factor in the consolidation of Argentine-Brazilian relations), in Russell, ed., *Nuevos rumbos*, 247–76.

40. *Folha de São Paulo*, 12 December 1985, 13 December 1985.

41. Speech at the luncheon offered by Soviet foreign minister Eduard Shevardnadze to Dante Caputo (Moscow, 29 January 1986), in República Argentina, *Discursos del señor ministro de Relaciones Exteriores*, 150–56.

42. On Alfonsín's visit to the USSR see *Clarín*, 14 October 1986, 15 October 1986, 16 October 1986.

43. On Shevardnadze's visit to Brazil and Argentina see Agencia de Prensa Novosti, *En aras de la paz y la cooperación: Visita oficial del ministro de relaciones exteriores de la Unión Soviética, Eduard Shevardnadze, al Brasil, la Argentina, Uruguay y estada de trabajo en Cuba* (Toward peace and cooperation: official visit by Soviet foreign minister Eduard Shevardnadze to Brazil, Argentina, and Uruguay, and stay in Cuba) (Novosti, 1987).

44. On Sarney's visit to the USSR and recent Soviet-Brazilian relations see Perosa, "Los viajes al máximo nivel," in Russell, ed., *Nuevos rumbos*, 247–76; and Hirst and Bocco, "Brasil-Unión Soviética: Parámetros para un nuevo diálogo," in ibid., 213–29.

45. On the Soviet policy approach to the Central American crisis in the late 1980s see, for instance, Agencia de Prensa Novosti, "Conflicto Centro-

americano: Etapa Salvadoreña" (Central American conflict: the Salvadorean stage) (interview with Yuri Pavlov), *Noticias de la Unión Soviética*, No. 10,281 (20 February 1989); *Izvestiya*, "América Central: No a los conflictos regionales: Eduard Shevardnadze, ministro de Relaciones Exteriores de la URSS, responde a preguntas de '*Izvestiya*' sobre los resultados de la cumbré de los presidentes de cinco Estados de América Central" (Central America: no to regional conflicts: Eduard Shevardnadze, Soviet minister of foreign affairs, answers *Izvestiya*'s questions about the results of the summit of five Central American heads of state), in *URSS: Documentos, materiales, información* (USSR: documents, material, and information), Sección de Prensa de la embajada de la URSS, Buenos Aires (11 August 1989); and Agencia de Prensa Novosti, "Gorbachov en la Asamblea Nacional: 'La influencia moral de la Revolución Cubana'" (Gorbachev in the National Assembly: the moral influence of the Cuban Revolution), in *USSR: Documentos, materiales, información*, Sección de Prensa de la embajada de la URSS, Argentina (5 April 1989): 3–5. On the impact of U.S.-Soviet diplomatic understandings on this approach see Michael Kramer, "Anger, Bluff—and Cooperation," *Time* 135, no. 23 (4 June 1990): 18–23. For two different Soviet perspectives on the role of the USSR in Central America see Vladimir I. Stanchenko, "The Triangle United States-USSR-Latin America and the Soviet Role in Central America," in Margarita Balmaceda, ed., *Nuevas tendencias en las ciencias sociales y la sociedad soviéticas* (New tendencies in the social sciences and Soviet society) (Buenos Aires: EURAL, Serie Documentos de trabajo, no. 33, 1990), 99–112; and Vladimir Sudarev, "Los conflictos regionales y el problema del desbloqueo" (Regional conflicts and the problem of bipolarity), *América Latina* 4, no. 89 (April 1989): 4–13.

46. On the Argentine approach to the Central American crisis see, for instance, Roberto Russell and Juan Tokatlian, *Argentina y la crisis centroamericana, 1976–1985* (Argentina and the Central American crisis: 1976–1985) (Buenos Aires: FLACSO, Documentos e informes de investigación 36, 1986); and Vacs, "A Delicate Balance: Confrontation and Cooperation between Argentina and the United States in the 1980s," *Journal of Interamerican Studies and World Affairs* 31, no. 4 (Winter 1989): 23–59. On the Brazilian foreign policy stance on Central America see, for example, Sônia de Camargo, *Autoritarismo e Democracia*, 148–56.

47. *Clarin—edicion internacional*, 22–28 October 1990.

48. See *Foreign Broadcast Information Service—Soviet Union* (17 December 1991): 30.

49. See *Foreign Broadcast Information Service—Latin America* (17 December 1991): 34.

50. On the grain shortage and import problems see *Foreign Broadcast Information Service—Soviet Union* (19 November 1991): 37–38. For a de-

tailed breakdown of the creditor countries, the size of the credits, and the goods supplied see ibid. (5 December 1991): 31–32.

51. See *Foreign Broadcast Information Service—Soviet Union* (8 November 1991): 31.

52. See, for instance, Aslund, *Gorbachev's Struggle,* 96–101; and U.S. Congress, Joint Economic Committee, *Agricultural Reforms in the Soviet Union and China* (hearing before the Joint Economic Committee, Congress of the United States, 7 September 1989).

53. On the continuous Soviet agricultural problems under Gorbachev see, for example, Roy D. Laird and Betty A. Laird, "Glasnost, Perestroika, and Gorbachev's Rural Policies: The Built-in Contradictions of Soviet Socialism," *Studies in Comparative Communism* 23, no. 2 (Summer 1990), 115–24.

54. In this regard see, for instance, the article by B. Chernyakov and O. Ovchinnikov published in *Izvestiya* (23 July 1991) and reproduced under the title "Call to Rethink Import Food Policy" in *Foreign Broadcast Information Service—Soviet Union* (28 August 1991): 61–63.

55. See U.S. Senate, Committee on Agriculture, Nutrition, and Forestry, *Soybeans and the World Market,* Joint Hearing, 18 March 1988 (Washington, D.C.: U.S. Government Printing Office, 1988); Jorge Ingaramo, "La agricultura argentina en el mundo y una gran pregunta: más o menos soja?" (Argentine agriculture in the world and a great question: more or less soy?), *Cronista Comercial,* 1 April 1990, 13.

56. *Foreign Broadcast Information Service—Latin America* (4 December 1991): 35.

57. See *Foreign Broadcast Information Service—Latin America* (23 August 1991): 25; (27 August 1991): 48–49; (19 September 1991): 25.

58. See, for example, *Foreign Broadcast Information Service—Latin America* (10 September 1991): 31; (9 December 1991): 33; (21 January 1992): 35–36.

59. See *Foreign Broadcast Information Service—Latin America* (20 August 1991): 23.

60. See *Foreign Broadcast Information Service—Latin America* (27 August 1991): 33; (2 October 1991): 22.

61. See *Foreign Broadcast Information Service—Latin America* (27 December 1991): 17, 27–28.

62. See, for example, Margarita M. Balmaceda, "Latin American Studies and the Search for a New Political Model in the USSR," and Lawrence S. Graham, "The Implications for Economic and Social Policy of the Transitions in Eastern Europe and Latin America" (papers delivered at the 16th International Congress of the Latin America Studies Association, Washington, D.C., 4–6 April 1991).

Chapter 14 ━━━━━━━━━━━━━━━━━━━━━━━━━━━━

Russia and the Middle East

Continuity and Change

Irina Zviagelskaya and Vitaly Naumkin

Russia appeared as an independent political actor in the international arena only recently, after the collapse of the Soviet Union. As a republic of the Soviet Union, it had played a limited role in foreign policy since the Soviet Union functioned as a unitarian state. Despite all slogans and pronouncements of confederation, the republics that comprised the USSR were deprived of any sovereignty. Even Russia, which had been the backbone of the empire, had to identify its interests completely with those of the Soviet Union.

Under these circumstances the Russian foreign ministry played only a symbolic role, as it was subordinated to the central authorities who represented the Soviet state in the international arena. Any hint of specifically Russian interests that might differ from those of other republics (because of Russia's history, level of development, traditions, and ethnic makeup) would have been perceived as heretical.

Efforts had failed to find a new model for the disintegrating union that would recognize the sovereignty of the republics and at the same time preserve a relatively strong and influential center. It was already too late for renovation. As the last leader of the Soviet Union, President Mikhail Gorbachev, stated in his address to the Mideast Peace Conference in Madrid, "Of late the world has been confronted by yet another crisis of tremendous proportions. What I have in mind is my own country. It became inevitable as a result of latent contradictions building up over a long period of time. A great country is going through a great transformation. It is a painful and arduous process which has brought about personal tragedies and interethnic and regional conflicts. Much in the world depends on how our crisis will be resolved."[1]

The dramatic developments in the Soviet Union have brought Russia into focus. In 1991 it was the newly elected Russian leadership that headed the crusade against the central authorities. The coup d'état of August 1991 gave a new impulse to the rivalry between the two presidents, Yeltsin and Gorbachev, speeding up the disintegration of the state. The Soviet Union ceased to exist. It was replaced by the Commonwealth of Independent States, which was a vague structure, unable to shoulder the burden of the foreign heritage of its mighty predecessor. At that time only Russia could put forth the claim of being the legitimate successor of the Soviet Union, ready to take responsibility for its debts and other international commitments.

Given its new status, Russia now faces the challenge of formulating its national interests and working out an appropriate political course. Because of its special role, it will have to preserve a measure of continuity in its approaches to international issues. Its own capabilities, however, which cannot be compared equally to those of the late superpower, will dictate changes in its political behavior. Especially with regard to the Middle East, Russia will have to tread on unknown ground in many respects, despite a long history of Soviet interaction with the states of that region. According to Mr. Shuikov, a secretary of the Supreme Council Committee on Defense and Security, Russia has no foreign policy toward the Muslim East but is making concerted efforts to create such a policy.[2]

Soviet interests in the Middle East, which do not fully coincide with Russian interests in the area, were never properly formulated. There was apprehension about what these interests should be and consequently what measures should be taken to secure them.

This essay will deal with Soviet and Russian Middle East policy by identifying key factors according to which the framework of this policy has been formulated. It will then look into the implications of the Soviet collapse for Middle East policy and the new and emerging dynamics. For the purpose of analytical clarity and differentiation, the region will be dealt with within two operative theaters, the Arab-Israeli theater and the Persian Gulf theater. Though both regions are constituent parts of the total polity, each presents Russia with its own specific challenges and opportunities. Finally, the study will address the elements of continuity and change in Russia's policy.

Moscow and the Middle East: A Conceptual Framework

Geostrategy

Geostrategic considerations dominated Moscow's political thinking during the days of the USSR. In the context of the acute Soviet-American confrontation, the importance of the Middle East was determined first and foremost by its proximity to Soviet borders and by the prospect of a U.S. military buildup in the area that would pose a threat to the USSR. As one American scholar has stated, "The Soviets have thought of the region as contiguous to their borders and therefore, as an area to be kept free of military threats. For the same reason of proximity to the Soviet Union, the United States has sought to project power from bases and facilities in the Middle East."[3] There is no doubt that the leadership of both countries sought to achieve reliable security, but as their evaluation of the nature of the threat was not free of ideological tenor, military and/or political presence often became an end in itself.

The USSR viewed the division of the world into two sociopolitical systems as evidence of the sure success of socialism. The systems were considered to be not only mutually antagonistic but also autonomous. This approach ignored the interdependence of various actors in international relations and made it possible practically to disregard the adversary's interests. The result was an intense Soviet-American rivalry in different regions including the Middle East.

The USSR's approach to the newly free countries was not formed under the exclusive influence of ideological dogmas. While ideology played a negative role, Soviet policy toward the Middle East, even at the height of the Cold War, was nevertheless pragmatic and had undergone a certain ideological evolution to become more in line with reality. Initially, Communist parties were considered the only reliable pro-Soviet forces. This, however, did not prevent Stalin and his entourage from ruthlessly exterminating their "class friends" or closing their eyes to their tragic fate in many countries. In the early 1950s Soviet leadership had volubly cursed the national movements, especially those in which the army, regarded as an instrument of oppression, was the leading political force. Later it became clear that in the Arab countries, beginning with Egypt, it was the nationalists who were the real political force to be dealt with. The pendulum of Soviet policy had swung to the other side—not the attitude of the authorities to Communists inside the country but their attitude toward the West had become the criterion for the choice of local allies.[4]

It would be wrong to believe that it was only the Soviet leadership that initiated or imposed cooperation with the Arab radical regimes. These regimes were themselves interested in having the support of a superpower in the struggle against their regional rivals or at least to balance American influence in the region.

Mention should also be made of the Soviet development model. Not all Arab nationalists found it appealing or acceptable. It is known, for instance, that Nasser spoke quite critically of it. However, the example of the USSR for many years served as a touchstone for local radical nationalist forces. Soviet totalitarianism and authoritarianism, so repulsive to a Western democrat, were regarded in a completely different light in the East. This was especially true in the 1960s, when the Soviet political and economic system had not yet demonstrated its insolvency. The signs of crisis, perhaps visible to economists, evaded the attention of nonspecialists and were regarded as individual errors against which no economic organism was ensured. The desire of the Arab countries for a strong centralized power was the result of the influence of traditions, the level of their economic development, and characteristic features of their political culture. As Georgy Mirsky states,

> A society with an incomplete process of class differentiation, multitude of economic forms, prevalence of small producers, hardly or not at all involved in the system of capitalist commodity production, such a society is a favorable medium for a mighty state power. Diversity; the torn and heterogeneous nature of that society; the precariousness of the pyramid, the bottom of which has not yet left the precapitalistic social relations while the top has already adopted the way of life and thought of the second half of the 20th century; the weakness of "internal cohesion" between the components of the nation in the state of formation—all that . . . strengthens authoritarian tendencies.[5]

Thus copying individual elements of the Soviet model or even copying it whole was not always the result of the desire of Soviet leaders to impose it on their local allies. In the least developed countries of the Middle East, however, which were greatly dependent on the

Soviet Union, attempts to plant the Soviet model were, in fact, made. For instance, a vanguard-type party was established in South Yemen.[6] It was an experiment that failed under the pressure of local conditions and was finally buried after the unification of the two Yemens. Behind this ideological crusade was primarily the desire to establish a military and political presence in vital parts of the region.

In actuality, none of the existing regimes in the Arab world could have been unequivocally numbered among the USSR's allies. Consequently, it was necessary ideologically to justify choices made on the basis of pragmatic considerations. Thus the theory of the noncapitalist path of development or of socialist orientation was developed. It was based on the Marxist premise about the probability of the transition to socialism in countries where the capitalist mode had not become dominant.[7]

At the time of its birth, in the 1960s, the theory was highly simplistic. It assumed that the assistance of the socialist countries and the establishment of a one-party system were sufficient prerequisites to ensure the onward advance of developing countries to socialism. As time passed, it became obvious that no such process was taking place. Moreover, developments in Egypt under Sadat were considered by party theorists as a rollback caused by the machinations of imperialists and internal reactionaries. Egypt's denationalization and the opening of its doors to Western capital were strongly condemned in Moscow, which was further outraged by Sadat's denunciation of the Treaty of Friendship with the USSR.

Soviet ideologues began a search for criteria that would define socialist-oriented countries and at the same time preserve the ideological lining of Moscow's political course in the Third World. For this purpose a document describing common characteristics of Socialist-oriented countries was introduced. The fact that formulating this description was not an academic exercise but rather a political task is evidenced by its incorporation into the report of the Central Committee of the Communist Party of the Soviet Union (CPSU) to the Twenty-sixth Party Congress. The Socialist country may be recognized in part by the following:

the gradual liquidation of the positions of imperialist monopolies, indigenous big bourgeoisie and feudal elements, and the restriction of the activities of foreign capital. . . . the provision of the people's state with

command heights in economy and switch-over to a planned development
of forces of production, and promotion of the cooperative movements
in the countryside. . . . the enhancement of the role of the working people
in public life, and gradual strengthening of the state apparatus with
national cadres devoted to the people. . . . the anti-imperialist character
of these countries' foreign policies. Revolutionary parties expressing the
interests of the broad masses of the working people become stronger
there.[8]

An outstanding role in that enumeration was given to anti-imperi-
alism, which, because of the USSR's global confrontation with the
United States, was associated with the anti-Americanism of certain
regimes and movements.

In the context of the Arab-Israeli conflict, geostrategic considerations
with an ideological imprint resulted in the efforts of the superpowers
to divide the participants into Soviet and American allies. This precluded the cooperation of the two powers in reducing the conflict with
some short-lived exceptions such as the Geneva peace conference of
1973–74.

Economic Relations

Interest in economic cooperation with the states of the region was
greatly overshadowed by the goal of countering American influence.
As the choice of local partners was dictated by the rules of a zero-sum
game, Soviet-Arab cooperation was reduced mainly to either military
collaboration with certain Arab regimes or technical assistance to them.
The Soviet leaders did not have economic benefits in mind but rather
the goal of winning Arab support for their regional and global policy.

Domestic Considerations

Though there were about 60 million ethnic Muslims in the country,
this domestic factor never had a significant impact upon Soviet-Middle
East policy making. The Soviet attitude toward the Muslim population
was dictated by the myth of the creation of a Soviet people, a completely
new entity. Differences in culture, traditions, and religion among various ethnic groups were considered by Party theoreticians to be irrelevant and doomed to end in the process of the socialist renovation of
society. Further, the Soviet totalitarian regime suppressed any search
for national identity, denouncing this as part of a nationalist, separatist

current. The historical, cultural, and ethnic ties that link the Soviet Muslims to the peoples of the Middle East were ignored by Moscow.

The Jewish factor also made only a minor impact on Soviet policy in the area. Jewish immigration to Israel was not viewed as a reaction to national suppression. Jews suffered no more than other ethnic minorities in the USSR. Consequently, immigration was seen as a result of American and Israeli plotting. It cannot be denied that Israel and the United States were for their own ends interested in a large-scale Jewish immigration, but this stemmed first and foremost from domestic factors.

The emigration issue became a card in the global game between the two superpowers. When the Soviet government sought to improve relations with Washington, it would turn on the tap, and when relations got worse, the tap would be turned off again.

The Soviet Union and the Arab-Israeli Conflict

None of the achievements and failures in the Middle East were regarded in Moscow as having an importance of their own. Before 1985 Soviet Middle East policy was subordinated to the USSR's global rivalry with the United States. A good example of such subordination is evident in the history of Soviet-Israeli relations. The USSR was among the first to recognize the state of Israel and, through what has come to be known as the Czech deal, assisted the new nation with arms during the 1948–49 war.

The main determining factor in Soviet policy in that period was the wish to weaken Great Britain's position in the region. As Yaacov Ro'i stated, "The Soviet decision to support the Jewish State had been partly based on a negative evaluation of the chances of an effective Arab struggle against Britain."[9]

The pro-British Arab regimes at the time were regarded as a greater evil than the Israeli Zionists, though the latter, too, had been treated by the Soviet leaders with ideological hatred from time immemorial. Social-Zionists were considered to be enemies of the international struggle of the working class, and like all apostates, in the days of Stalin and his clique, they were considered no better than imperialists. Speeding up the collapse of British colonialism, however, occupied a higher place in the scale of Soviet foreign policy priorities.

Support for Israel was motivated by the requirements of the moment and could not be lasting, as was soon evident. On the one hand, "the doctors' plot" in the USSR inspired anti-Semitic trials in a number of other East European countries, and on the other, the development of Israeli-American ties added a sharp strain to Soviet-Israeli relations. Even before the official 1967 break in relations, political contacts were limited and cooperation was minute.

Israel had often been perceived in Moscow as a puppet of the United States. A resolution of the CPSU Central Committee Plenum of 21 June 1967 pointed out that "Israel's aggression is the result of the most reactionary forces of international imperialism, particularly the U.S., against a detachment of a national-liberation movement."[10] The perception of the nature of the Arab-Israeli conflict as first and foremost a class struggle was maintained in official assessments for a long time.

These perceptions of the conflict made Soviet Middle East policy somewhat ambivalent. After the Six Day War, the Soviet leaders continued for some time to differentiate between political struggle and military stability and eagerly welcomed the former if it could lead to a further radicalization of the Arab world. The conflict had been consequently regarded as fertile ground for the emergence and development of leftist currents. The interest in conflict reduction became clearly manifest only in the early 1970s when the USSR realized that periodical eruptions of hostilities in the region were detrimental to its national interests. An absence of diplomatic relations with Israel and traditional support for Arab radicals motivated by ideological reasons, however, could not but substantially curb Soviet abilities to mediate. Diplomatic efforts were further limited by the Soviet-American rivalry, which led to mutual suspicions and precluded the cooperation of the two powers in conflict reduction.

The Gorbachev Era

After 1985, with a new détente gaining momentum, Moscow tried to prevent its Middle East course from becoming a spoiler of Soviet-American understanding. Middle East policy was subordinated again, this time to cooperation with the United States and the West as a whole.

Relations with the West were at the top of the list of Soviet international priorities. Their importance was dictated both by the Soviet Union's poor economy, which could no longer endure an arms race, and by a new orientation in favor of domestic economic and political reform. Consequently, Middle East issues were looked upon mainly within the context of their relevance to the Soviet Union's central goal, which was national and economic revival.

The Soviet government maintained close collaboration with the West during the Persian Gulf crisis of 1990–91. For the USSR, the Iraqi aggression posed a serious dilemma that resulted in a hot debate within the country. While the reformists were ready to extend every possible support to the United States, with some even considering a dispatch of Soviet troops to the Persian Gulf, the conservatives took a pro-Iraqi stand. The central issue was not so much the Persian Gulf situation, dangerous as it was, but rather the issue of foreign policy reorientation, particularly in the Middle East. Pragmatism took priority over the traditional East-West rivalry in the region. The liberation of Kuwait, though leaving many regional problems unresolved, opened the door for the Middle East Peace Conference, where Moscow had its special seat.

The Soviet Union had traditionally been an active participant in the Middle East settlement. Though its position as mediator had been considerably complicated by its exclusive linkage with Arab radicals, its interest in reducing the conflict prompted the USSR to use its own channels to try to lure Arabs away from extremism. Much was done in this respect vis-à-vis the Palestine Liberaton Organization (PLO). At the same time, while the Arab allies showed no inclination to take a realistic stand, Soviet diplomacy continued officially to support their demands, which was a strategy not necessarily in line with the task of finding a peaceful solution to the conflict. All this made the Soviet posture both inert and rigid. Thus the USSR responded coldly to the Fahd Plan of November 1981 despite the fact that it did not contradict Soviet approaches and even despite Soviet interest in normalizing relations with Saudi Arabia. This occurred because the radical regimes, particularly Syria, had rejected Saudi proposals, not wanting to yield to the Saudis the leadership of the Arab world. The Fahd Plan later became the basis of the common Arab platform elaborated at Fez in September 1982, which was favorably received by the Soviets.

Mention should also be made of the Soviet reaction to the Amman agreement reached by King Hussein and Yasir Arafat in February 1985, envisaging a joint settlement strategy. It was negatively assessed in the press not only because of fear that the United States might use the opportunity to revive the peace process without the USSR's participation but also because of the attitude of the radical leftist forces in the PLO, who bitterly criticized Arafat and thus forced him to denounce the document.

Soviet policy in the conflict was far from balanced, but its support of the Arab radicals had its limitations. Politically, the USSR, irrespective of the state of its relations with Israel, never questioned Israel's right to exist. Indeed, it was highly critical of the extremist calls for its destruction. Militarily, as a leading supplier of arms to the Middle East, the USSR never delivered the most sophisticated offensive and destructive weapons to its allies, despite their repeated requests. However, the Soviets did have a clear-cut Middle East policy based on certain principles that made the Arabs regard the Soviet stand in the Arab-Israeli conflict as a reliable counterweight to American policy in the region.

The peculiarity of the Middle East situation is that the partial withdrawal of the USSR from the region did not mean a loss of prestige and authority. The repudiation of the old ideological concepts made it possible to carry out a much more balanced regional course. Diplomatic relations were established with Israel, and contacts with this country acquired a previously unheard of dynamism. Diplomatic relations with the Arab world, particularly with the Gulf Cooperation Council (GCC) states, were expanded. This provided Moscow with new opportunities for mediation in the Middle East conflict.

The Soviet Union came to the Madrid Peace conference significantly weakened by its domestic turmoil. *Izvestiya* reporter Stanislav Kondrashov called the Soviet performance in Madrid "the last tango."[11] According to him, it was the United States who had made the conference possible, while the Soviet role was marginal. The American president gave his Soviet counterpart a chance to preserve his country's image as a superpower, an indispensable participant in the peace process, at a time when the USSR had lost this status. The Middle East proved once again that the nature of American-Soviet interaction had changed dramatically. The two countries were no longer adversaries or equal partners; the former Soviet Union was desperately seeking the patronage of the United States.

It is true that since the Persian Gulf War, the United States has acquired strong positions in the region. Without the swift victory in the Persian Gulf, there probably would not have been a peace conference. By demonstrating its indispensability for Middle East security, the United States got an opportunity to use coercion safely to bring reluctant actors to the negotiations. At the same time, it is equally true that Soviet policy during the Persian Gulf crisis and afterward proved that regardless of all domestic limitation, Moscow had remained a player on the Middle East scene, and its participation in the Peace Conference was welcomed by regional actors.

Russia and the Peace Process

Soviet commitments to Middle East stability were inherited by Russia, which became a cochair at the Moscow Organizational Meeting for Multilateral Negotiations on the Middle East in January 1992. Russia's priorities have, however, vividly changed. The first priority mentioned by Russian foreign minister Andrei Kozyrev in his opening remarks was the domestic situation, and here the need to ensure Russia's economic interests is critical. Moscow desires for this reason to develop mutually advantageous economic cooperation with all countries in the region. This is impossible in the absence of peace and stability in the area. The foreign minister also stressed Russia's intentions to move rapidly from partnership with the United States and its allies to friendly relations with them.[12]

With its newly acquired international status and an interest in stability and economic cooperation, Russia must contribute to the Arab-Israeli settlement. It has yet to come out with any ideas that would differ from those of the Soviet Union of the 1990s. It supports the right of the Palestinian people for self-determination but believes that there should be a stage-by-stage approach, including a form of Palestinian autonomy for a certain period of time.

Further developments in the region showed that Russia still played some role in the peace process, though this role was inevitably limited by the country's real potential. The elections in Israel and the victory of the Labor party, with Yitzhak Rabin at its head, have paved the way for negotiations, thus demanding more attention from the cochairs of the conference. Moreover, the gradual progress in Russia's relations with Israel during 1992, combined with preservation of the old ties with the Arab countries and the PLO, made it possible for Russia to act as a mediator who was equally acceptable to all sides in the conflict.

Changes in Russia's Middle East policy were accompanied by a growing political debate over them. Russian radical nationalists claimed that the government's policy led to severing all bonds with old Arab friends and that new relations with Israel were being built at the cost of old Russian-Arab connections that were more vital to Russian interests. Indeed, some "Atlantic-biased" politicians gave ground to accusations of this kind by unreasonably stressing the new Russia's total break with the old foreign policy, including close ties with the Arab world. At the end of 1992, however, a transitional period in Russian foreign policy, a balanced and pragmatic attitude toward all Middle Eastern countries prevailed. There was more talk of Russia's Eurasian character. Russia's relations with the Arab world, especially the Arab moderates, became an important part of Russian foreign policy, which was evidenced by a noticeable increase in diplomatic and trade activity. While having set its relations with Egypt, the Persian Gulf states, and other Arab moderates as a new priority in the regional policy, the Russian government decided also to maintain, albeit at a reduced level, its relations with the former clients of the USSR among the Arab radicals, which still carry considerable weight in the system of Middle East politics. This political balance certainly enhances Russia's appeal to the world community as a possible mediator in the region. Russia also took into consideration the fact that the Arab radical regimes are among the heaviest debtors of the former USSR.

Moscow and the Persian Gulf

Within the context of contemporary history, the Soviet experience in the Persian Gulf is rather recent. Except for Iraq, with which Russia had a relationship of long standing, Moscow has made a very recent entry into this region.[13] The three decades since the 1958 Iraqi revolution have been difficult, complex, and eventful.

The first two years following the 1958 revolution marked the rapid growth of relations between the Soviet Union and Iraq, despite some occasional rough spots. The Soviet Union's desire to have better relations with Iran was thwarted by the alliance between the United States and the shah, which sought to oppose Soviet interests in this country. But in 1961 the USSR initiated and expanded relations with Kuwait, the first of the Persian Gulf oil monarchies to do so. By the end of the 1960s the Soviet Union supported the radical regime in South Yemen, providing vast economic and military aid to Aden. But the role of this regime was rather marginal and could not lead to the substantial growth of Soviet influence in the region. At the same time, Moscow continued to build close cooperation with Baghdad, followed by the signing of the Treaty of Cooperation with Iraq in 1972.

The 1970s were marked by the escalation of Soviet-American rivalry. Much of Soviet behavior in the region, as in the rest of the Middle East, was dictated by this rivalry and confrontation. Geopolitical, pragmatic interests usually dominated over ideological concerns. The Soviet leadership was nevertheless ready to act to promote "revolutionary change" in the world if this change was not contradictory to its national interests. Thus the repression of Iraqi Communists by the Ba'thist regime did not have a serious impact on Moscow's relations with Baghdad, which remained one of its main sources of hard currency.

With the beginning of the Iran-Iraq War in 1980, the Soviet Union faced a difficult dilemma: to support Iraq would be seen as an unjust act that would threaten Soviet-Iranian relations; to cut ties with its ally would create doubts about Moscow's reliability. Both regimes were ideologically hostile to Communism. At the same time, however, their enmity toward the United States made them very important for the Soviet Union. Thus the Soviet Union balanced itself between the warring sides, trying to reconcile them and promoting the idea that the continuation of the war was to the advantage of neither country.

In 1981 Iraq was the leader among the Soviet Union's partners in commerce and trade from the Near East and North Africa. It moved into second place, after Libya, among the Arab countries in 1982–86 and advanced to second position after India in commodity turnover among all Third World countries in 1987–88.[14] In structure, Soviet trade and economic relations with Iraq revealed two characteristics. First, Iraq was an important market for Soviet arms, exports of which were estimated at about $10 billion between 1982 and 1987.[15] Second, a major portion of Soviet exports to Iraq consisted of plant equipment and transport vehicles, accounting for 94.3 percent in 1987–88, with aircraft topping the list at 41.3 percent in 1988. Up to the end of 1989 the USSR assisted Iraq in the construction of ninety-eight projects, of which ninety-two became operational.[16] Chief among these were oil field enhancement facilities, a petroleum product pipeline, and thermal and hydropower plants.

Soviet relations with the GCC states were hindered by the Soviet military intervention in Afghanistan, which Saudi Arabia regarded as a threat to its interests. The traditional orientation of the GCC states toward the West and fear of the potential expansion of communism also prevented any serious improvement of relations with Moscow. But the first war in the Persian Gulf made these states more interested in maintaining some level of relations with the Soviet Union. Thus, despite the fact that Saudi Arabia was giving substantial aid to the Afghan resistance, and, along with some other Persian Gulf monarchies, was reluctant to establish diplomatic relations with Moscow, the first half of the 1980s stands out because of a considerable increase in Soviet commodity turnover with the Persian Gulf countries through expanded imports. But a crucial factor is that at the time, Saudi Arabia and Kuwait were supplying oil to the USSR to make up the deficit in Iraqi shipments, the latter being unable to continue to fulfil its obligations to the Soviet Union because of its war with Iran. The principal Soviet export items included timber, cement, gas, and pipes; while oil, petroleum products, and wheat (from Saudi Arabia) were the main imports.

Gorbachev and the Persian Gulf

The period of deep reforms in the Soviet Union under Gorbachev's rule drastically changed the essence and policy of the Soviet regime. The Soviet Union would no longer regard the Persian Gulf as an arena for confrontation and competition with the United States. The deideologization of Soviet foreign policy put an end to the idea of promoting "revolutionary change" in the Third World. More attention was paid to relations with neighboring states, and Soviet-Iranian relations improved as a result.

The changing nature of the Soviet Union allowed for a rapprochement between Moscow and the Arab monarchies of the Gulf. Diplomatic relations were established with Oman and the United Arab Emirates (UAE) in 1985 and with Qatar in 1988. Diplomatic relations with Saudi Arabia and Bahrain, however, were nonexistent until the Persian Gulf crisis.

The Soviet Union's historically poor trade and economic relations with the Arab states of the Persian Gulf (with the exception of Iraq) were due primarily to objective reasons: the poor competitiveness of Soviet goods in these nations' markets and the fact that the Soviet Union was not producing the goods these states needed. As a result, several Arab states—Iraq, Egypt, Libya, Syria and Algeria—accounted for 90 percent of commodity turnover and 85 percent of technoeconomic cooperation with the USSR. Commodity turnover with the GCC states made up 0.9 to 1.9 percent of the Soviet Union's total turnover with the Arab community, with exports from the USSR the main item.

In 1987, for the first time on record, a consortium of Kuwaiti banks offered the USSR a loan of $150 million, followed in May 1990 by a second loan of $300 million.[17] The parties agreed to create three joint ventures for the construction of oil industry projects in the USSR and third countries. The Soviet Union's duties under the agreement concerned geological exploration, assessment of reserves, estimating cost-effectiveness of oil fields, and assessment of project costs and project lead times; while Kuwait assumed obligations for project financing, recruitment of modern technologies, and provision of markets for product sales from the three joint ventures.[18] Thus far, however, none of the agreed-upon points has been implemented. Both sides have expressed their desire to have an agreement that would protect mutual investment. In an interview with a Soviet newspaper, the Kuwaiti ambassador to Moscow called for raising economic relations between the two countries to the level of their political relations and went on to suggest forming Soviet-Kuwaiti joint ventures in third countries.[19]

At the same time, the United States began to look differently at Soviet moves in the Persian Gulf. Washington was no longer motivated by the desire to contain the Soviet Union, especially after the withdrawal of Soviet troops from Afghanistan. Prior to this, the United States had consistently expressed concern over the Soviet Union's ability to maintain good relations with both Iran and Iraq. When the Soviet Union offered to mediate the conflict between Iran and Iraq and made diplomatic moves in this direction, not only did the United States not oppose the idea of mediation, as it would have done two or three years earlier, but it showed an understanding of the USSR's move. Media reports in May 1990 revealed that the mediation proposal would be discussed by Soviet deputy foreign minister Vladimir Petrovsky during his visit to Tehran. He observed, "The Soviet Union is among the few countries which have normal, good relations both with Iran and Iraq, providing us ample opportunity to offer our good offices to both sides. We stated in Iraq that our assistance could possibly take various forms including the use of our territory as the venue for negotiations—whether with our immediate involvement or without it, on a bilateral basis, is up to the sides to decide."[20] The Soviet Union also stressed that it had no intention of interfering with the efforts of the UN secretary general and the sides themselves.

Soviet-Iraqi trade and economic cooperation after 1989 came up against some serious limitations: difficult financial periods in both countries, restricted Soviet technoeconomical potential, and tense competition with third countries. Plans for an increase in trade and economic ties with Iraq took into close consideration that country's unwillingness to agree to turnkey projects. New contracts would need to make provisions for technology transfers and maximize the involvement of local building and other companies in the construction of specific projects. In 1990 a long-term pilot program for Soviet-Iraqi cooperation was set up. It was oriented toward the modernization of previously constructed projects; the erection of new ones on a compensation basis through product deliveries into the USSR, Iraq, and third countries; the formation of joint ventures with the participation of Iraqi capital; and shared efforts on third-country markets.

The improvement of Soviet relations with the GCC states manifested itself through the improvement of ties between Muslim communities. In 1990 Soviet Muslims set out on the first mass hajj to Mecca; in the past, only a few dozen had been able to make the pilgrimage. Fifteen hundred people from many Soviet cities were flown on chartered Aeroflot planes to Jidda, along with a consular group going to Saudi Arabia with the pilgrims for the duration of their sojourn there. Visits by Saudi businessmen to the Soviet Union became ordinary.

At the same time, not all Islamic forces in the Arab world expressed contentment with the death of their old enemy, communism. Concerns about "the rise of Zionism" in the Soviet Union and Eastern Europe and the beginning of an "era of American hegemony" were commonly expressed in some publications. Egyptian writer Fahmi Howeidi told a conference organized by the London-based Center for Studies on the Future of Islam and attended by forty scholars and political leaders from ten Arab countries that "the collapse of Communism will weaken, not strengthen, the Muslim world."[21]

The 1990 Persian Gulf crisis created a new dilemma for the Soviet Union. Moscow's policy reflected the reality that cooperation with the United States was to remain a key foreign policy trend for the Soviet Union. At the same time, Soviet foreign policy was under the pressure of domestic political struggle. This struggle dictated Gorbachev's moves, which were undertaken independently of those of the Western powers, and precluded his use of force, which might have had a negative impact on the political situation in Russia.

From the very beginning of the crisis, the Soviet stand against the Iraqi occupation of Kuwait was met with satisfaction in the GCC states. The Soviet stand against Iraqi aggression paved the way for the restoration of diplomatic relations between Moscow and Riyadh and the establishment of diplomatic relations between Moscow and Bahrain. Intensive political consultations began between the Soviet Union and the GCC states at the bilateral level as well as in the UN.

At the same time, there were still some problems that were spoiling the new climate of Soviet-Kuwaiti understanding and cooperation. Before the invasion, for example, Moscow had not responded to a Kuwaiti request to buy some Soviet military equipment. This position was later criticized by official Kuwaiti representatives.

Soviet peace initiatives conducted with the help of Gorbachev's special envoy Yevgeny Primakov aroused mixed feelings in the GCC states. Hopes for a quick solution of the crisis were mixed with suspicions regarding the Soviet Union's real intentions. The leadership of the GCC states was sure, however, that Moscow would not jeopardize its good relations with Washington and the West. Primakov's mission finally contributed to the expansion of cooperation between Moscow and the Persian Gulf capitals. In a symbolic gesture, after the end of the crisis the same envoy was sent to the Middle Eastern capitals once more to discuss economic cooperation. As the result of this mission, these states agreed to provide some economic and financial support to the Soviet Union. The Kuwaiti ambassador to Moscow told a Soviet journalist during the crisis, "We have no doubts about the sincerity of intentions of the Soviet Union and thank him for the support and help in preserving the independence and sovereignty of Kuwait. The peace plan which was put forward by Moscow has not given any result because of the position of Saddam Hussein; it is his sincerity that we cannot believe. But our relations with the USSR cannot be complicated because of that; their basis is very solid."[22]

Russia, the CIS, and the Persian Gulf

The collapse of the Soviet Union created a new reality, which manifested itself in the emergence of new independent states with different interests, problems, approaches, and policies toward the region. The system of new relations between these republics and all the Middle Eastern countries, including the Persian Gulf states, was just beginning to develop in the first months of 1992.

The main interest of the GCC states has been directed toward developing relations with Russia and the Islamic republics of the former USSR. Among the factors pushing the GCC states toward close cooperation with the Islamic republics—within the Commonwealth—is the fast rapprochement between these republics and neighboring states, especially Turkey and Iran.

One of the signs of the new geopolitical situation in the region has been the effort, beginning in 1990, to create the Black Sea Community, which was officially established in Istanbul on 2 February 1992. The establishment of this organization of states strengthened the role of Turkey in the region. Though it has no access to the Black Sea, Azerbaijan became a member of the community. A group of Central Asian republics and Azerbaijan have also joined Turkey, Iran, and Pakistan in the Economic Cooperation Organization (ECO). A third economic alliance, the Caspian Sea Group, was formed as well; it includes Russia, Iran, Kazakhstan, Azerbaijan, and Turkmenistan.

The active diplomatic role of Iran in this region has caused some fears in the West, and Western leaders explicitly began to encourage Turkey, as a democratic and secular state, to exert more influence on the Central Asian and Transcaucasian republics. This was demonstrated during Turkish prime minister Suleiman Demirel's visit to the United States in February 1992. Some Arab states have expressed their concern with the activities of both Turkey and Iran, arguing for a larger role for the Arab states.

Different views on this question were expressed during a seminar on 22–23 February 1992 in Cairo that was organized by the Al-Ahram Center for Strategic and Political Studies. Retired ambassador Salah Bassiouni stated at this gathering that he regarded the expansion of the ECO as a revival of the economic Central Treaty Organization, insisting that what had actually happened was the formation of "a new geopolitical space." He and some other participants expressed their concern about all new economic alliances, such as the ECO, the Black Sea Community, and the Caspian Sea Group, and the possible hegemony of Turkey and Iran in this region. The Arab countries, they urged, especially Egypt and the GCC states, should compete with Turkey and Iran in the Southern belt of the former USSR.

Another opinion, expressed by political analyst Ali Dessouki and supported by some of the other participants, was based on two assumptions. The first assumption is that the neighboring countries are going to play a legitimately important role for the Central Asian and Transcaucasian states because the borders they share make economic, cultural, and even political cooperation between them natural. The second is related to religious and ethnic ties between these states and Turkey, Iran, and Afghanistan. Religion and ethnicity are not factors in the relations between the Central Asian states and the Arab regimes, including the states of the Persian Gulf, which are neither geographically nor ethnically in the same position as Turkey or Iran. This group of analysts consequently concludes that the special role played in these republics by Turkey and Iran must not be regarded by the Arab states as a challenge that should be met and opposed. At the same time, they believe that the Islamic republics of the former Soviet Union need technology and money, which could hardly be provided by either Iran or Turkey.

Thus the logical partner for these republics is the Western world, which in its turn regards Turkey as the main channel for exerting Western influence in the East. In a rather quick response to the new realities, Saudi Arabia and Kuwait—having established relations with Russia—decided to develop official relations with the Islamic states that are members of the Commonwealth. In February 1992, Saudi foreign minister Saud Al-Faisal visited these states for this purpose, and a decision was made to support these republics financially.

At the same time, the newly independent states were not inclined to diminish their relations with neighboring states, including Afghanistan. While Turkmenistan president Niyazov met with Al-Faisal, his foreign minister, Kuliev, was meeting with the foreign minister of Afghanistan. During this time diplomatic relations were established between Turkmenistan and Afghanistan, and an exchange of visits between President Niyazov and Najibullah was agreed upon.

It is important to mention here that there were two main factors constraining Saudi desires to develop relations with the Central Asian and Transcaucasian states. The first was a lack of confidence in the former Communist leaders who were still in power in these states.

The second was the friendly relations between some of these states and the former government of Kabul—although these relations were merely pragmatic, being based primarily on commercial interests. Some Persian Gulf states openly demonstrated their concern over the position of Uzbekistan, Tajikistan, and Turkmenistan toward the Kabul government.

In February an official Kuwaiti delegation also visited these republics with the mission of establishing diplomatic relations. Possibilities for economic cooperation were explored by Kuwait as well as by Saudi businessmen and experts.

Businessmen from the GCC states, however, have not rushed into Central Asia and Transcaucasia. Most of them still believe that these republics are not ready for real economic cooperation and cannot provide good conditions for investment. Relations have, as a result, been confined mostly to trade protocols and agreements on providing aid in the religious sphere (religious education, building of mosques and religious schools, and the like). Arab businessmen have seen more opportunities for themselves in Russia, where Kuwait has made some efforts to start active economic and trade cooperation, including investments. The GCC states are also interested in developing closer ties with Kazakhstan, which is rich with resources and more open to cooperation than the other Southern states of the Commonwealth. Even before the collapse of the Soviet Union, a joint Kazakh-Saudi bank was created there with the participation of the al-Baraka Group. A bank was then opened in Tatarstan. Early in 1992 a group of Arab bankers also started a project to open the Caspian Bank in Baku (Azerbaijan).

Russia has continued with efforts to improve relations with the GCC states. In April-May 1992 Russian minister of foreign affairs Andrei Kozyrev visited the Arab states of the Persian Gulf. This was the first visit to the region by a Russian foreign minister. Kozyrev was accompanied by a number of Russian businessmen. Apart from political consultations, during which he discussed with his counterparts the Middle East peace process and the situation in the Persian Gulf, the Russian side paid much attention to widening economic cooperation with the GCC states. In the UAE the foreign minister raised the question of selling weapons to this state, and negotiations were subsequently held to discuss possible deals. This visit contributed to improving relations between Russia and the GCC states. It was followed by new steps on the part of the states to provide financial help to Moscow. It did not, however, lead to any substantial growth in economic cooperation because private companies in the Persian Gulf were afraid of possible risks that might result from investment in Russia and the other states of the CIS.

Though this region was obviously not at the top of the list of Russian foreign policy priorities, and the government of Russia was not disposed to be involved in more activities, it still tried to be more active there. It has been commented in the Supreme Council of Russia and in the mass media that Russia should conduct its own policy in this region and that it has something to offer the Persian Gulf states to meet their security needs.

By the end of 1992 the United States had signed agreements with the main GCC states under which it was allowed to store military equipment, stage aircraft, and bunker ships and to exercise with GCC military forces. This certainly served to enhance the ability of the United States to deploy its forces there rapidly. Most politicians and observers in Russia did not see this situation as a threat to its national interests but, on the contrary, regarded it as favorable. The Russian government, however, was making an effort not to allow its relations with the Arab countries to be affected by its growing cooperation with the West, especially the United States.

In August 1992 the Russian government decided to send two military ships to the Persian Gulf as part of a peacekeeping naval force created by UN Security Council resolution. This demonstrated closer cooperation between Moscow and the Western powers, particularly the United States, in the situation in the Persian Gulf.

At the same time, Russia voted for the resolution allowing the Western powers to use force against Iraqi airplanes if they flew over the southern regions of Iraq. Some political forces in Russia criticized this stand by saying that it would have been more logical for Russia to abstain from voting, keeping in mind its specific relationship with the Arab states, including Iraq. This time, however, public opinion in Russia was not much concerned with the government's political moves in the Persian Gulf.

During the following months, Russia's relations with the Persian Gulf states were further developing, as was reflected in growing diplomatic activity and increased trade.

The government's attitude toward regional problems had also shown some new trends, especially in 1993. One of these was the transition from unqualified support of U.S. policy to the development of a more independent political course, which was to represent Russia's diverse national interests as well as its historical ties. At the time of the "new Iraqi crisis" Russia expressed its anxiety over the development of the situation in the region and refused to support the allies' military actions. Russian officials, however, also spoke of the Iraqi regime's responsibility for what was happening and of the necessity for Iraq to comply with the UN resolutions. The official comments were that Russia was entitled to its partners' willingness to coordinate their actions with those taken by Russia. There was also talk that any reaction to violations of the UN sanctions should be proportionate to the nature of Iraqi violations and agreed upon by the UN Security Council. Moscow expressed its intention to develop its relations with Iraq, and President Yeltsin spoke about his wish that in the future Iraq would start paying in oil its old debts to the USSR. This attitude was a concession to the Russian radical nationalists as well as a reflection of the Russian government's determination to pursue a more balanced regional policy than that of the immediate postcoup months. The Russian Parliament circulated the question of financial losses suffered by Russia in its support of the sanctions against Iraq and Libya and of compensation of these losses by the West, which should have taken into consideration Russia's economic problems.

Despite these new trends in its regional policy, Russia kept in view its desire to further develop cooperation with countries where this cooperation promised to be most profitable financially. Here a new angle was that Russia shed its former post-Soviet idealistic notion of arms trade as a purely Communist activity and decided to make up for lost time. The Russian approach to arms trade was declared to be completely devoid of any ideological preferences, though the government stated that it would promote arms trade with countries in which the arms were needed for defense only and arms sales would not create new tensions or violate international laws such as the law against the proliferation of weapons of mass destruction. An example of this new approach was Russia's participation in the Abu Dhabi military exhibition of February 1993, where some of the latest Russian weaponry was on display for the first time. Other examples were Russian minister of defense Pavel Grachev's visits to a number of the Persian Gulf states declaring Russia's readiness to provide these states with air-defense systems and components. The new trend in Russia's policy was also reflected in its willingness, in spite of strong U.S. objections, to sign a large arms-sale package with Iran that included the sale of three K-class submarines.

Russia and the CIS: Elements of Continuity and Change

While the general framework of the future Russian foreign policy in the Middle East will continue to be shaped by Russian perception of security and threat, economic considerations, and domestic priorities, there are obvious changes in the content of this framework that are influencing Moscow's policy-making and its decisions.

Because of the proximity of the Middle East to Russian frontiers, geostrategic considerations make the countries of that region important to Russia. The traditional perception of threat from the Middle East, however, has drastically changed. The old ideological coloring of Soviet Middle East policy has vanished: Russia has no intention of engaging again in a rivalry for spheres of influence. It is no longer the United States and its allies but rather political and military instability in the region in general and large-scale hostilities in particular that could threaten Russia. If conflict should erupt, even a medium-range missile might accidentally hit its territory, and the ecological consequences of a war would be disastrous.

Geostrategic concerns have acquired additional dimensions with the disintegration of the Soviet Union. The countries that formerly comprised the unitarian state are now independent international actors starting diplomatic activities of their own. Some of them, including the new states in Transcaucasia and Central Asia, gravitate toward certain Middle East countries, such as Iran, Turkey, and the Arab states, because of ethnic, religious, and historical ties as well as geographic proximity. The disintegration of the Soviet Union has given birth to the idea of an expanding Middle East. According to this perception, the former Muslim republics of the USSR will sooner or later become an integral part of the region, cutting their ties with Russia and other non-Muslim states to a minimum. Such a notion is far from reality. Along with the trend of developing good relations with neighboring states, there are strong incentives for the preservation of close links between Russia and the former Southern tier of the empire. In order to strengthen these links Russia must give priority to the development of relations with these republics. Nevertheless, the Russian minister of foreign affairs started official visits to the newly independent states much later than the American secretary of state. It is obvious that current relations with the Southern republics are demanding from Russia much more tolerance, understanding, and knowledge of local traditions. This experience will no doubt be useful in Russia's relations with Middle East countries.

The Middle East cannot be downgraded to an insignificant or subordinate position in Russian policy, because developments in that region might also affect Russia's relations within the CIS. The attitude of President Akayev of Kyrgyzstan to the decision-making process during the Persian Gulf crisis is quite telling. That conflict, in his opinion, was relevant to the states of Central Asia and Kazakhstan, where many Muslims live, yet neither these republics nor their neighbors could participate in the formation of Soviet policy toward the Persian Gulf.[23]

While the new states are developing their own relations with the countries of the area, Russian policy, reflecting first and foremost its national interests, should not ignore the positions of other CIS members. This is becoming more important since despite all obstacles, the CIS has proven to be indispensable for its members, at least for the time being.

Further, Middle East issues form a wide agenda for Russian-American interaction. The understanding between the two powers does not eliminate the asymmetry of their respective priorities in the area and of their capabilities to pursue a particular political course. Some tensions might appear, for example, over the issue of arms deliveries, though there are more opportunities to overcome possible frictions than ever before.

Russia's economic interests in the region, having been released of any ideological considerations, are now acquiring a special importance. The question of economic revival along the lines of a market economy presupposes that the foreign policy of the country should also be oriented to this goal. This means that the Russian approach to collaboration with various countries will be dictated by pragmatism, by a wish to make relations with them mutually beneficial.

The domestic ethnic-religious factor also has a profound impact upon Russia's Middle East policy, as even inside the Russian Federation there are millions of Muslims and non-Muslims who are ethnically close to the peoples of the area. A search for national identity contributes to a growing interest among them in renewing ties with their brothers abroad. The Middle Eastern states themselves, and certain influential ethnic groups inside them, are eager to make use of the new opportunities. The interaction between the autonomous republics of Russia and neighboring countries is acquiring political dimensions as well. For example, a domestic conflict between the Russian and the Chechen authorities, who were elected at the end of 1991, immediately drew the attention of certain ethnic and Muslim communities abroad. Observers from Iran and Syria attended the presidential elections. Anxiety was felt among the Chechen clans in Jordan. President Dudaev himself made reference to forces in Turkey that, according to him, were ready to extend their support to the republic.[24]

The quest for sovereignty, which in the former Soviet Union often manifests itself within an ethnic framework, demands much more flexibility from the Russian authorities in dealings with the autonomous subjects of the Federation, which are becoming increasingly open to the outside world. It should be mentioned that the quest of the autonomous republics for sovereignty is determined by a certain congenital resistance to the central authorities. President Yeltsin's victory during and after the coup was a kind of mixed blessing. On the one hand, it demonstrated that the central government might become a real threat for the republics. On the other, his own successful struggle has set an example to be followed not only by the former subjects of the USSR but also by certain republics of the Russian Federation. The signing of the Federative Treaty has slowed down the process of secession, but in the event that the Russian authorities do not pay enough attention to the demands of the autonomies, some of these might join the Chechen republic and Tatarstan, which have refused to sign the treaty.

The relationship between the Russian domestic situation and developments in the Middle East are well illustrated by the recently adopted emigration policy. According to democratic principles, those people who want to leave the country for any reason should be allowed to do so. Economic and political instability in Russia is a strong factor in the wish of millions of people to go abroad. The task is easier for those ethnic groups who, like the Jews, have a place to go to.

On the one hand, the new policy has brought Moscow some political benefits. It was perceived in the West as a sign that Moscow was sincere in its desire to carry out democratic reforms. With economic

cooperation with Israel gaining momentum, Russian Jews might become a useful link between the two countries. On the other hand, in
the Middle East, many Arabs tended to believe that a massive Jewish
immigration into their area would be a national disaster. Given Israel's
settlement policy in the Occupied Territories and the very slow and
unstable negotiation process, they claimed that in several years there
might not be any territory left even for a Palestinian self-rule. It is
obvious that no administrative measures can be used to regulate the
exodus of Russian citizens. The problem (which is painful for the
country itself) can be solved only if Russia manages to overcome
economic and political difficulties and if all ethnic groups are given
equal opportunities to realize their national aspirations.

It is quite understandable that the Russian leaders are trying to
consolidate relations with the West. Simultaneously, the importance
of the Eastern dimension for Russia is increasing. Russia's intention
to move consistently toward the East was confirmed by President
Yeltsin in an interview. "The former Soviet Union, unfortunately,
developed its ties, say with Iran, on the basis of its anti-Western stand.
This had caused great harm to our relations, including economic ties.
Now we want to have closer cooperation with China, Turkey, and
Iran, to say nothing of Japan, India, Korea."[25]

Russia is obviously searching for a proper balance between its Western and Eastern policies, while the Middle East is getting even closer
to its borders. Historically and geographically, Russia has always been
a kind of bridge between the West and the East, and this role has been
enhanced by the ethnic makeup of the country. Good relations with
the West do not make the Middle East dimension of its foreign course
less significant. With its regional policy not yet clear-cut, it seems
obvious that the formulation of Russian national interests in the area
will necessarily reflect a measure of continuity in the regional course
of the USSR's legitimate successor as well as changes dictated by its
own international status.

Notes

1. Address by Soviet president Mikhail Gorbachev to the Mideast Peace
Conference in Madrid, published in *Federal News SVC,* 30 October 1991, 3.

2. *Moscowskie Novosti,* no. 15 (April 1992).

3. William B. Quandt, "U.S.-Soviet Rivalry in the Middle East," in *East-*

West Tensions in theThird World, edited by Marshall D. Shulman (New York: Norton, 1986), 20.

4. "Revulytsionny protsess na Vostoke" (Revolutionary Process in the East), in R. A. Ulianovski, ed., *Istoria i sovremennost* (History and the present time) (Moscow: Nauka, 1982), 22.

5. G. I. Mirsky, *"Trety mir": obshchestvo, vlast, armiya* ("The Third World": society, power, army) (Moscow: Nauka, 1976), 374–75.

6. *Politicheskie Partii* (Political parties) (Moscow: Politizdat, 1986), 191–92.

7. V. I. Lenin, *Collected Works*, vol. 31, 4th ed. (Moscow: Politizdat, 1982), 244.

8. *Materialy XXVI svezda KPSS* (Materials of the twenty-sixth congress of the CPSU) (Moscow: Politizdat, 1981), 12.

9. Yaacov Ro'i, *Soviet Decision Making in Practice: The USSR and Israel 1947–1954* (New Brunswick and London: Transaction Books, 1980), 400.

10. *Vneshniaia politika Sovetskogo Soiuza i mezhdunarodnie otnosheniya 1967: Sbornik documentov* (The foreign policy of the Soviet Union and international relations, 1967: a collection of documents) (Moscow: Mezhdunarodnie otnosheniya, 1968), 160.

11. *Izvestiya*, 30 October 1991.

12. Remarks by foreign minister Andrei V. Kozyrev at the opening of the Organizational Meeting for Multilateral Negotiations on the Middle East, Moscow, House of Unions, 28 January 1982, Russian Ministry of Foreign Affairs.

13. The Soviet Union had relations with Yemen since 1928 and more short-lived relations with Saudi Arabia from 1926 through the late 1930s.

14. *External Economic Relations of the USSR in 1988* (Moscow, 1989), 10–14.

15. *Argumenti i facti*, no. 21 (1990).

16. Based on data from the Ministry of Foreign Economic Relations of the USSR.

17. *Arab Times*, 8 May 1990.

18. *Arab Times*, 8 May 1990; 18 February 1989.

19. *Izvestiya*, 2 June 1990.

20. *Izvestiya*, 25 June 1990.

21. *Arab Times*, 6 May 1990.

22. *Izvestiya*, 25 February 1991.

23. Bozdag Abidin, "Kurzbiographen. Askar Akayev," *Orient*, no. 3 (Hamburg, September 1991): 343.

24. *Izvestiya*, 1 November 1991; *Literaturnaya Gazeta*, 13 November 1991.

25. *Izvestiya*, 15 July 1992.

Chapter 15 ████████████████████████████

The Dynamics of Russian-Afghan Relations

A View from Moscow

Yuri V. Gankovsky

At the time of the writing of this paper, the final chapter of the Afghan saga has yet to be written. This paper will first address the Soviet experiment in its historical context and then will discuss the dynamics of the intervention itself—Moscow's decision making and the Russian mission—and the future implications of the Soviet withdrawal.

Historical Background

The historical relationship between Russia and Afghanistan can be viewed through several stages. The first developed from the mid-fifteenth to the early eighteenth centuries. During this stage, commercial relations maintained through Central Asian merchants prevailed, although these were highly irregular. In 1764 an attempt was made by the government of Catherine II to establish direct diplomatic relations with Afghanistan, which was then under the reign of Ahmad Shah Durrani. But it failed because of historical circumstances.[1]

After the downfall of the Durrani Empire at the beginning of the nineteenth century, Afghanistan broke up into several independent principalities, of which Kabul, Qandahar, Herat, and Peshawar were the largest. In the mid-nineteenth century the state of Afghanistan emerged from the unification of some of those same principalities. From 1830 up through the early 1900s Afghanistan's policies, both domestic and foreign, were determined by the rivalry between tsarist Russia and Great Britain in their efforts to control the resources of the Middle East and Asia.[2] This period marks the second stage of relations between Russia and Afghanistan.

In October 1835 the ruler of Kabul, Amir Dost Muhammad Khan, sent a letter to the tsar of Russia, Nicolas I. This diplomatic move was aimed at establishing friendly relations between Afghanistan and Russia. The Russian government accepted Kabul's offer to establish diplomatic relations and in May 1835 appointed Ivan V. Vitkevich Russia's representative to Kabul. In December 1837 Vitkevich arrived in the capital of Afghanistan.

Vitkevich had to inform Amir Dost Muhammad Khan "that, due to the long distance between Russia and Afghanistan, the former could not render him effective aid, but did nevertheless have sincere sympathy for him." Vitkevich was further instructed to discover opportunities for expanding trade between the two countries.[3] The architects of British colonial policy, however, managed to create obstacles that hampered the establishment of diplomatic relations between Afghanistan and Russia.

In 1873 the Russian minister of foreign affairs, Alexander M. Gorchakov, officially assured the British that it regarded Afghanistan "beyond the field of Russian influence." And, as the result of an agreement between Russia and Britain, the Amu Darya River was recognized as Afghanistan's northern frontier.[4] In spring 1878, however, the Russian government sent a diplomatic mission, headed by general Nicolas G. Stoletov, to Afghanistan.[5] The British used this event as justification for starting a war. In November 1878 the British army invaded Afghanistan.

The Russian government preferred an independent Afghanistan over a British colony for a neighbor. For this reason, tsarist authorities helped Sardar Abdurrahman Khan take possession of the Kabul throne. (Sardar Abdurrahman Khan had lived for more than ten years in Russia's Central Asian domains and had received grants from the tsarist government.) In September 1880 Sardar Abdurrahman Khan became amir of Afghanistan.

Amir Abdurrahman Khan sought independence for his state and thought that the rivalry between Russia and Great Britain could be used as a means to achieve this goal.[6] In the early 1900s Afghanistan maintained control over its domestic affairs. Its foreign policy, however, was still determined by Great Britain.

Political and economic circumstances influenced the Afghan authorities to maintain contacts with Russia. These relations, however, were limited to trade because of the realization that other interactions could evoke an immediate conflict with Britain. In the period between 1911 and 1915 trade with Russia accounted for approximately 40 percent of Afghanistan's entire foreign trade.[7]

On 31 August 1907 Russia and Britain agreed to divide their spheres of influence in Asia. As a result it was agreed that Afghanistan should reside outside Russia's sphere of influence. Furthermore, it was agreed that both Britain and Russia would have equal trade opportunities in Afghanistan. This agreement weakened Afghanistan's position and eliminated the possibility of its using the rivalry between Russia and Great Britain to its advantage.[8] The viceroy and governor general of India, Lord Minto, informed Amir Habibullah Khan of the Anglo-Russian agreement in a letter dated 10 September 1907. Amir Habibullah Khan rejected the agreement.

Russian-Afghan relations in the nineteenth and early twentieth centuries were neighborly. Russia never waged wars against Afghanistan. The only short-term conflict was in March 1885 (it later became known as the Tash-Kepri Bridge Conflict) and was provoked by Britain.[9] Russia's government never rendered help to the rebellion leaders who fought against the amir of Kabul. When in 1888 the governor of northern Afghanistan declared himself the independent ruler and turned to the Russians for help, his appeal was declined.

The third stage of relations begins after the revolution of 1917. On 28 February 1919 Amir Amanullah Khan declared Afghanistan independent and sovereign in its domestic and foreign affairs. According to the Afghan historian Mir Ghulam Muhammad Ghubar, "Afghanistan realized that no danger from the North [Russia] was threatening the country in the political and armed fight against Britain."[10] On 17 April 1919 Amir Ammanullah Khan informed Moscow about the restoration of Afghanistan's independence. The government of Soviet Russia recognized this independence and informed the amir that it had annulled all treaties and agreements (including the Anglo-Russian agreement of 1907) that infringed upon the sovereignty of Afghanistan. In March 1919 the Soviet government, following V. I. Lenin's instructions, sent a memorandum to the leaders of the Paris Peace Conference demanding recognition of Afghanistan's sovereignty.

The first document concerning Soviet-Afghan relations was the

Treaty of Friendship, concluded on 28 February 1921. The preamble to this treaty stated that it was concluded "with a view to consolidating friendly relations between the Soviet Union and Afghanistan and protecting Afghanistan's genuine independence."[11] Paragraph 10 stated that for "the strengthening of friendly relations between the high Contracting Parties the Government of the Russian Socialist Federative Soviet Republic agrees to render Afghanistan financial and other material assistance."[12] Russia itself was in dire straits at this time, but the Soviet Union nevertheless granted a number of commercial privileges to Afghan merchants, and in 1925 the free import of Afghan goods was allowed. An important event in the history of Soviet-Afghan relations was Amir Amanullah Khan's visit to the USSR in 1928 at the invitation of the Soviet government.

The second document to underline relations between the USSR and Afghanistan was the Treaty of Neutrality and Mutual Non-Aggression of 24 June 1931. This treaty emphasized that friendly relations between the two states were based on complete equality and mutual respect. Paragraph 3 stated that the parties would not tolerate any acts on their respective territories that might be detrimental to either of them. The treaty also included a paragraph stating that each party retained a free hand in taking steps to establish any kind of relations with third parties, provided these relations did not contradict provisions of the treaty.[13] In December 1975 a protocol was signed that extended the treaty for another ten years.

In 1950 and 1956 important Soviet-Afghan trade and economic agreements were signed. These agreements determined the principal trends of the economic and technical cooperation between the USSR and Afghanistan. The Treaty on the Development of Economic Cooperation, signed on 14 April 1977, dealt with economic and technical cooperation and trade between the two countries. This treaty was scheduled to culminate in 1989.

In all, seventy-three industrial projects were constructed with Soviet assistance. In 1975 more than 60 percent of Afghanistan's output of public sector goods was produced by the industries built with Soviet aid. The power stations built with Soviet aid generated 60 percent of all the electricity in Afghanistan. In addition, more than 70 percent of automobile highways with asphalt and concrete surfaces were built with Soviet aid. The Soviet Union also assisted Afghanistan in agricultural development.[14] Of important economic significance was the discovery of rich deposits of natural gas by Soviet geologists in Afghanistan's northern provinces.

The volume of Soviet-Afghan trade was steadily growing. In 1972 it was 69 million rubles, and by 1976 it had reached 154 million rubles. Moreover, since the beginning of the twentieth century, the Soviet Union has constantly rendered military assistance to Afghanistan.

Appraising the relations between the USSR and Afghanistan, the American ambassador in Kabul, Theodore L. Eliot, Jr., informed Washington on 30 January 1978 that relations with its northern neighbor were most important for Afghanistan and would continue to be both significant and profitable. The Soviet Union avoided any interference in the domestic affairs of Afghanistan and remained the main source of assistance to the country. (The USSR provided Afghanistan with more than $1 billion during the past twenty-five years, while the United States gave less than $500 million.)[15]

After the overthrow of Muhammad Daoud's government on 27 April 1978, many specialists worldwide discussed the possibility of Soviet involvement. (One well-known specialist wrote, "Had the Soviet embassy, in particular Ambassador Puzanov, planned the coup?")[16]

The Economic and Social Development of Afghanistan

In spite of some definite success in the economic development attained after 1919, Afghanistan on the eve of the April 1978 coup was one of the world's poorest countries. In 1977 Afghanistan's per capita national income was a mere $162, and its modern branches of industry were producing only 3.3 percent of the total GNP. Although nearly 70 percent of the workforce was engaged in agriculture, more than half of the arable land was left uncultivated. This was due to the extremely low level of production and persisting vestiges of precapitalist relations of production.[17] A great number of farmers were deeply indebted to moneylenders, paying them annual interest of up to 45 percent, and about one-third of peasant families had no land of their own. In addition, close to 2.5 million people in the country were nomads or seminomads.[18]

Archaic feudal and semifeudal forms of land ownership, unrestrained usury that brought misery to millions of peasants, and overpopulation led to further impoverishment of the peasants. In 1977 there were more than 600,000 peasant families that either worked for landowners as sharecroppers or owned plots of land smaller than an acre. About 40,000 landowners owned the greater and best part of all cultivated land.[19]

About 88 percent of the population was illiterate, and only 28.8 percent of children attended schools, 70 percent of which were in a dilapidated state. There were only seventy-one hospitals with a total of 3,600 beds for 16 million people, and 84 percent of the physicians were employed in Kabul.[20]

Various regions in Afghanistan were at different levels of development. For instance, Badakhshan, Hazarajat, Kunar, and regions populated by the Pashtun tribes in the South and Southeast lagged far behind Kabul and Herat, among others, in economic, social, and cultural development. Other indications of underdevelopment included the fact that numerous groups among the rural and urban population were (and continue to be) closely linked with precapitalist economic structures. The Pashtuns, Baluchis, and Brahuis, from the southern regions, among others, have retained many traditional features such as communal and patriarchal (tribal) social organization. As a result, the so-called traditional leaders, such as tribal khans, maliks, and sardars, along with the Muslim ulama, still enjoyed considerable influence among the local population.

The uneven development of various regions was compounded by the national (ethnic) heterogeneity of the population and the age-old tension between the upper strata of the Pashtuns and the national-ethnic minorities, particularly in the northern and central parts of the country. In some regions, as in Hazarajat and Badakhshan, ethnic tensions were aggravated by sectarian differences between Sunnis (Pashtuns) and Shiites, as well as the Ismailites who made up a significant part of the population of Hazarajat and Badakhshan.[21]

The traditional system of state administration, with its characteristic red tape, bribery, and corruption, offered the ruling class ample opportunity to plunder the country. The big bourgeoisie and the landowners were transferring a large part of their income abroad. The ruling elite was no better.[22]

Mounting discontent was expressed in several ways. Spontaneous protests by the population and rebellions among the Pashtun tribes flared up now and again, resulting in a number of clashes with the army. The situation was further aggravated by frequent instances of robbery and terrorism. In 1977 and at the beginning of 1978, the political situation in the country grew explosive.

Scholars who studied Afghanistan had no doubt that the country was on the eve of a revolutionary coup. One of the famous American scholars, Louis Dupree, had foreseen the inevitability of the Afghan revolution. In 1977 he wrote in the epilogue to his book *Afghanistan,* "The major constraint to Afghanistan's development is its current bureaucratic system, but if its leadership can intensify the involvement of the competent (and partly idle) Afghan technocratic class, Afghanistan just might pull off its gamble to develop through the evolutionary process. If not, comes the revolution."[23] Unfortunately, he was ignored.

The revolution took place on 27 April 1978. Whether the events of 27 April constituted a revolution or a military coup, they undoubtedly marked the beginning of an Afghan tragedy and of a war that has lasted for more than fifteen years. It can be argued that the coup in 1978 was the result of the social, political, and economic development that took place during the ten years preceding the coup.

The Soviet Invasion of Afghanistan

Any clear, exact, or comprehensive answer to the question of why the Soviet Union invaded Afghanistan in 1979 has yet to be found. This is due to the fact that the sources and materials necessary for an analysis of this magnitude have not been made available to scholars and specialists of the region. It is known, however, that in spring 1979 Nur Muhammad Taraki, the leader of the Kabul regime, asked A. N. Kosygin to bring Soviet troops to Afghanistan. The Kremlin refused.[24] Thus it is relevant to ask what was behind the Soviet decision to intervene.

The foreign policy of the Soviet Union was frequently based on the principle that what was bad for the United States was good for the USSR, a tenet that in reverse was the basis of many U.S. policy decisions. In practice, such an approach produced a situation o uncoordinated political, economic, and military action, which was conducive, so the Soviet leaders assumed, to the attainment of a political breakthrough or change in the balance of power in a given region. The foreign policy of the Soviet Union was both fragmented and pragmatic. And, contrary to the belief of foreign Sovietologists (or Kremlinologists), it was not driven by the imperative to "seize" new territory or to acquire a warm water outlet to the Indian Ocean. Certain Soviet actions were even conducted in circumstances that could have had political or military repercussions. All of this, once again, attests to the fragmented nature of Soviet foreign policy and the incompatibility of theory and practice.

On 4 May 1989 this author conducted an interview about the problems of Afghanistan that was printed in the newspaper *Izvestiya*.[25] This interview drew attention not only beyond the boundaries of the USSR but within its borders as well. It elicited letters from many Soviet cities, including Moscow, Leningrad, Odessa, Petrozavodsk, Baku, Sebastopol, Bukhara, and Ferghana. In response to these letters it was stated that

> it would have been highly useful to publish in Moscow a "White Book" on the war in Afghanistan and about our participation in it. Such a book would not only answer the questions justly disturbing our people but would also put an end to speculation based not only on lack of information but on the frank desire to damage the prestige of our country and to create doubt in the sincerity of the present Soviet leadership as well. It would be relevant to include in this "White Book" the documents of 1979, which concern the introduction of Soviet soldiers in Afghanistan, as well as accounts of the Soviet Embassy in Kabul since 1977. Information on the military and political situation in Afghanistan, which has been sent from Kabul to Moscow since April 1978, as well as other documents, should be included. It would also be advisable to decipher the pseudonyms of those authors who sent information to Moscow. The "White Book" must be published as soon as possible, in an effort to avoid the possible disappearance of documents.

In 1989 apprehensions about the possibility of liquidation or the disappearance of documents related to the events in Afghanistan were discussed. These apprehensions were confirmed in an article written by V. Kazak, head of the Department of the Military Procurator's Office of Turkestan Military District. In this article he stated that "the archives of the military detachments which left Afghanistan have been destroyed."[26] The answer to the *Izvestiya* readers was not published, and the "White Book" has yet to be printed.[27]

The final decision to send troops to Afghanistan was made on 12 December 1979. It is widely believed that the military figures who headed the Soviet Defense Ministry in 1979 were mainly responsible for deploying the contingent of Soviet military forces. It is known, however, that N. V. Ogarkov, S. F. Akhromeev, and V. I. Varennikov were against the introduction of Soviet military forces in Afghanistan but were unable to convince D. F. Ustinov, the minister of defense, not to send troops. In 1980 Sokolov, Akhromeev, and Varennikov declared after a trip to Afghanistan that there was no military solution to the Afghan problem. At this time they convinced Ustinov of the correctness of their opinion, and in early 1981 Ustinov suggested that it was necessary to withdraw the 40th Soviet Army from Afghanistan. This suggestion, however, was declined.

In 1980 Soviet generals said and wrote that there was no military solution to the Afghan problem. On 30 January 1980, three weeks before energetic antigovernment actions in Kabul began, a letter was sent to the head of a group of Soviet advisers working in Afghanistan. It stated the following:

> One of the important (perhaps the most important) tasks of Babrak Karmal's administration is widening and strengthening the social basis of the new regime. Though Karmal has been in power for more than a month, nothing has been done in this respect. This may lead to a further deepening of the social and political crisis in Afghanistan. Almost nothing has been done to improve the material conditions of the masses either. If things go on like this, if no political decision is attained to solve the problems of the country, then in two or three months a civil war will break out with all ensuing consequences.[28]

There was never a response. The analysis of specialists and scholars, as a rule, was not taken into consideration.

The Soviet Mission

Although there were nearly 110,000 soldiers and officers in the 40th Soviet Army, they were unable to control the mountainous country fully. Afghanistan's territory is much larger than the territory of France, the largest country in Western Europe. It is also necessary to take into account the fact that there are no railways there and only a few highways. For this reason, Soviet military forces had limited tasks. These included (1) not allowing the opposition forces to capture Kabul and other important administrative centers of the country; (2) ensuring the defense of two or three significant strategic points (the mountain pass of Salang, which connects Kabul with the North, and two airfields,

Baghram and Shindand); and (3) ensuring the defense of the country's economic centers, particularly in northern Afghanistan.

All these tasks were fulfilled. Moreover, the presence of the 40th Army resulted in the reconstruction of the Afghan army. Because of Hafizullah Amin's repression, in November 1979 there were only 40,000 soldiers in the Afghan army. By February 1989, when the Soviet army withdrew from Afghanistan, the Kabul regime had 160,000 soldiers and officers in its army, around 100,000 soldiers and officers in "the policy," and approximately 40,000 in security forces and frontier troops. It is necessary to point out that "the policy" is the "number-two army" because of its specialization in artillery, tanks, and helicopters.

In 1987 the Soviet Union decided to withdraw from Afghanistan, and in February 1989 the task was carried out. In 1986 a number of Soviet specialists in international affairs predicted that the Soviet army would remain in Afghanistan for years to come. In November of that same year the following statement was made to a group of Indian scholars in New Delhi: "After the interference in the affairs of Afghanistan is stopped, the Soviet Army will remain there for about two years. If we see that everything is all right in Afghanistan, we shall withdraw our soldiers. But if the interference continues, we will not withdraw our army. We shall stay in Afghanistan forever."

This was stated on 24 November 1986 at the Indian Center of international affairs, New Delhi, during a meeting between Gorbachev's advisers, who accompanied him when he visited India, and Indian experts including, among others, Subramanian, Bhavani Sen Gupta, Nihkil Chakravarti, Kunwar Rajendra Singh, Air Commodore Jasjit Singh, and Rajiv Sikri. The Geneva Agreement was signed on 14 April 1988. Many specialists, political figures, and military experts predicted that the Kabul regime would fall shortly after the Soviet withdrawal. The regime managed, however, to survive the initial shock of Soviet withdrawal and in fact continued to control Afghanistan's main economic, political, and strategic centers.

Afghanistan after the Soviet Withdrawal

In 1991 the Kabul government controlled 30 percent of Afghanistan's territory. It is important to stress that the government controlled all the important administrative centers as well as the main strategic and economic centers of the country. Another 30 percent of Afghan territory was controlled by the leaders of opposition groups based in Peshawar, Pakistan. Many of these leaders emigrated from Afghanistan and established their organization in Pakistan long before April 1978, during the rule of Muhammad Daoud (July 1973-April 1978) and even under King Zahir Shah. An additional 30 percent of Afghanistan's territory was controlled by the local commanders inside Afghanistan. Iranian-backed Shiite leaders controlled the remaining 10 percent of Afghanistan's territory.

In the early 1980s the Pakistan-based leadership forced many of the Mujahideen leaders who had led the fight against the Kabul regime to submit to the directives of the Peshawar government. In addition, the presence of Soviet troops temporarily united several diverse opposition groups. After the Soviet Union withdrew its forces from Afghanistan, many local leaders began to act more independently.

A significant portion of Afghanistan's population supported neither the Kabul authorities nor the Mujahideen. Each region in Afghanistan listens to and supports its own local leader. By the time the Najibullah regime collapsed in 1992, the country had already started to become divided into independent and semi-independent principalities. The process of disintegration gained momentum when Mujahideen factions engulfed the country in a protracted and bloody civil war almost immediately after their victorious arrival in Kabul.

Prospects for Peace

Contrary to general expectation, no real progress has been made in resolving the Afghan conflict since the final Soviet withdrawal. If one proceeds on the assumption that the long-term interests of Russia, the Commonwealth of Independent States (CIS), and the international community will be met by the preservation of Afghanistan as a united state, it is necessary to contribute actively to ending the civil war. This demands decisive changes in Russia's and the CIS's policy toward Afghanistan. Though Russia had some contact with the former Afghan opposition, they were limited to humanitarian issues connected with the release of prisoners of war. Such a policy must be altered. The Afghan leaders must be looked upon as serious partners in the negotiations. Relations with them must be considered an important part of the problem of Afghan regulation.

The fact is that today opportunities for Moscow to directly influence the situation inside Afghanistan are limited. Yet Russia's national interest and the security interests of the new states in Central Asia demand a more active Russian-CIS policy toward Afghanistan. This policy should promote or initiate an internationally viable scheme for ending the Afghan civil war and consolidate a stable government in Afghanistan.

The main aim of settling the Afghan problem is to help the Afghans become masters in their own house so that they will be able to solve their problems in accordance with their political traditions. The best way to achieve this is to ensure that there will no longer be any external interference in Afghanistan's domestic affairs. In the absence of a stable, independent, and united Afghanistan, Russia, the Central Asian states, and the international community will find themselves faced with another Lebanon along the southern border of the former Soviet Union, one that is even more dangerous and destabilizing than the original.

The Foreign Policy of Russia and the CIS

The question has been raised as to whether or not Russia's foreign policy has been affected by the events leading to the fall of Najibullah's government in Afghanistan. At present, Russian foreign policy is at a crossroads. This is due first of all to the internal problems of the Russian Federation. It is necessary to take into account that the weakness of the Russian economy and the increasing political instability have created great difficulties for the Russian Federation in the sphere of foreign policy. It is obvious that Russia has not set clear and concrete aims for Asia. Nor are there concrete definitions. The absence of definite aims and concrete definitions will lead to contradictions in any decisions made by Russia, the result of which will be the dissipation of resources. These difficulties will not be eliminated in the near future. Moreover, the aspiration of the republics of the CIS for an independent foreign policy creates a new and difficult problem, namely that of coordinating their activities.

One can argue that among the large and complicated domestic and foreign policy problems that Russia must solve, the problem of Afghanistan occupies a very modest place. Yet the events that are taking place in Afghanistan definitely influence Russia's foreign policy. Specifically, the negative repercussions of Afghan dynamics on the security of the new Central Asian states will remain a major concern for Russia. The presence of ten million Russian "minorities" in these states will make Russia's impartiality tenuous at best. But the nature and scope of Moscow's reaction to that factor remains uncertain.

The ensuing civil war in the republic of Tajikistan and the instability of its borders, over which there has been a constant flow of arms and men from Afghanistan since the collapse of the USSR, clearly point to the interdependence of Central Asian security and Afghanistan's stability. Unstable borders, cross-border ethnic affiliations, and aspirations among the newly independent states of Uzbekistan, Tajikistan, and Afghanistan have become major sources of concern in the Central Asian capitals and Moscow. Russian border troops, upon the request of the leaders of Tajikistan and the other Central Asian states, have been deployed along the Tajik-Afghan border to interdict the flow of arms and men. Russian diplomatic personnel have been airlifted from Kabul, as the capital of Afghanistan has become the scene of an unprecedented civil war between the victorious warring factions of the Mujahideen. The interim "Islamic" government in Kabul ironically enjoys less power and authority than the previous pro-Soviet regime. The withdrawal of Soviet troops and the end of Russia's traditional influence in Afghanistan may not be the last page of the Russian-Afghan saga. The reverberation of the Soviet collapse and the emergence of weak, unstable, and ethnically mixed states of Central Asia on the border of Afghanistan on the one hand and the presence of a large Russian minority in Central Asia on the other will continue to force a degree of political and security interest and interaction between Russia and Afghanistan for the foreseeable future.

Notes

1. For more detailed analysis see Yu. V. Gankovsky, "Missiya Bogdana Aslanova v Afghanistan v 1764" (Mission of Bogdan Aslanov to Afghanistan in 1764), *Soveskoe Vostokovedenie*, no. 2 (1958); "Torgovye otnosheniya mezhdu Rossiyai i Afghanistanom vo vtoroi polovine 18-go voka" (Commercial relations between Russia and Afghanistan in the second half of the eighteenth century), *Problemy Vosokovedeniya*, no. 1 (1959); and Gankovsky, ed., *Rossiya i Afghanistan* (Russia and Afghanistan) (Moscow: Nauka, 1989), 11–38.

2. For more details see V. M. Masson and V. A. Romodin, *Istoriya Afghanistana* (History of Afghanistan), vol. 2 (Moscow: Nauka, 1965); H. Rawlinson,

England and Russia in the East (London, 1875); and Sayid Qasim Rishtiya, *Afghanistan der gerne nozdehom* (Afghanistan in the nineteenth century) (Kabul, 1951).

3. Instruction to I. V. Vitkevich, 14 May 1837, in *Materialy, sobrannye Kavkazskoi archeographicheskoi komissiyei* (Reports of the Caucasian Archaeographic Commission), vol. 8 (Tbilisi, 1881), 344. For more details see Gankovsky, *Russiya i Afghanistan, 39–55.*

4. See N. A. Khalfin, *Rossiyskaya politika v Srednei Azii* (Russia's policy in Central Asia) (Moscow: Nauka, 1960).

5. I. L. Yavorsky, *Puteshestvie rossiyskogo posol'stva v Afghanistan* (The travel of the Russian mission in Afghanistan) vols. 1–2 (St. Petersburg, 1883).

6. Abdurrahman Khan, *The Life of Abdurrahman, Amir of Afghanistan,* vols. 1–2 (London, 1900).

7. Gankovsky, *Russia and Afghanistan,* 121–64.

8. A. E. Snesarev, *Anglo-russkoye soglashenie 1907 goda* (The 1907 Anglo-Russian Agreement) (St. Petersburg, 1908).

9. G. Forrest, *The Life of Lord Roberts* (London, 1914), 140; and Gankovsky, *Russia and Afghanistan,* 104–9.

10. M. G. M. Ghubar, *Afghanistan der masire tarih* (Afghanistan: its historical road) (Kabul, 1967), 755. Also see L. W. Adamec, *Afghanistan, 1900–1923: A Diplomatic History* (Berkeley and Los Angeles: University of California Press, 1967).

11. *Sovetsko-Afghanskiye otnosheniya 1919–1969: Dokumenty i materialy* (Soviet-Afghan relations, 1919–1969: documents and materials) (Moscow, 1971), 28.

12. Ibid.

13. For more details see L. B. Teplinsky, *SSSR i Afghanistan* (The USSR and Afghanistan) (Moscow: Nauka, 1982), 82–102; and *Istoriya sovetsko-afghanskih otnosheni 1919–1987* (History of Soviet-Afghan relations, 1919–1987) (Moscow: Mysl, 1988), 108–30.

14. Yu. M. Golovin, *Afghanistan* (Moscow: Nauka, 1962), 145–64; and V. Glukhoded, "Economy of Independent Afghanistan," in *Afghanistan: Past and Present* (Moscow: Nauka, 1981), 222–45.

15. 30 January 1978, no. 0820. From the U.S. embassy in Kabul to the secretary of state, Washington, D.C., confidential theme: Afghanistan in 1977, foreign policy estimation, in Gankovsky, ed., *Sekretnaya perepisku gosdeparta-menta SSHA po Afghanistanu* (Confidential correspondence of U.S. foreign policy departments on Afghanistan) (Moscow: Nauka, 1986), 11.

16. Oliver Roy, "The Lessons of the Soviet-Afghan War," *Adelphi Papers,* no. 359 (Oxford, 1991): 11.

17. See N. M. Gurevich, "Problems of Agricultural Production in Afghanistan," in *Afghanistan: Past and Present* (Moscow: Nauka, 1981), 157–77.

18. *The First Seven Year Economic and Social Development Plan: 1976-1983,* vol. 1 (Kabul, 1976), 100–101; *Afghan Agriculture in Figures* (Kabul, 1978), 1–2, 21, 105.

19. For more details see A. D. Davydov, *Socialnoekonomicheskaya strutura derevni Afghanistana* (The socioeconomic structure of the countryside in Afghanistan) (Moscow: Nauka, 1976).

20. *First Seven Year Economic and Social Development Plan,* 205–12, 227–29.

21. The borders of contemporary Afghanistan were defined in 1893–95. The territory of Afghanistan is 650,000 square kilometers; the population is 16.5 million. The Afghans—or the Pashtuns, as they call themselves—comprise 52 percent of the population. About 40 percent of all Pashtuns live on the territory of Afghanistan. About 14 million Pashtuns live in Pakistan. In Afghanistan, particularly in the northern provinces, there have always been many Tajiks, Uzbeks, and Turkmen. Tajiks comprise about 20 percent of the population of the country, Uzbeks 10 percent, and Turkmen 3 percent. Hazaras, Baluchis, Brahuis, Punjabis, and so-called Nuristanis (Kati, Ashkun, and others) live in Afghanistan as well. For more details see J. Pstrusinska, "Afghanistan 1989 in Sociolinguistic Perspective," *Central Asian Survey,* no. 7 (1989). (A general census of the population based on contemporary scientific foundation has never been conducted in Afghanistan. For this reason any available information on this country is the result of either investigations by scholars or inventions of Afghan authorities.)

The most widespread religion in Afghanistan is Islam, particularly Sunnism (80–85 percent of the population). The Shiite population (15–20 percent of the population) is composed primarily of Hazaras and some Tajiks. Among the people living in the northeastern part of Afghanistan there are many Ismailis, followers of Agha Khan. Among the Punjabis there are many Sikhs, as well as Hindus.

The largest social group in Afghanistan are the peasants; they make up 80 percent of the population. Workers comprise 3 percent; employees 3 percent; artisans and traders 12 percent; ulama (Muslim theologists, traditional Muslim intelligentsia) 1 percent; landlords and rich businessman less than 1 percent. For further details see Louis Dupree, *Afghanistan* (Princeton: Princeton University Press, 1980); and Gurevich, *Afghanistan.*

22. See Gurevich, *Afghanistan,* 120–21.

23. Dupree, *Afghanistan* (Princeton: Princeton University Press, 1980), 768.

24. Telephone conversation between A. N. Kosygin and N. M. Taraki, 18 March 1978. *Moskovskie Novosti,* no. 23 (Moscow, 7 June 1992): 12.

25. *Izvestiya,* 4 May 1989.

26. *Izvestiya,* 16 April 1991.

27. This author has recently coauthored a book titled *Lessons of Afghanistan*

(now in print in Karachi) with Geogiy M. Konienko, former foreign minister Eduard Shevardnadze, Lieutenant General (ret.) Leonid V. Shebarshin, and former Soviet advisers who worked in Afghanistan—Eduard K. Kolbenev, Mavlon Makhkamov, and Oleg I. Zarov, among others. In the supplement to the book there are a number of very interesting documents that have never before been published.

28. Author's personal archives.

Chapter 16

The Collapse of the USSR and the Northern Tier States

Shireen T. Hunter

Introduction

For forty years the Cold War and the East-West competition for global leadership shaped the character of the international political system, its rules of conduct, and interstate relations. The end of the Cold War, the disintegration of the Soviet Union's external and internal empires, and the seeming transformation of East-West enmity into cooperation and friendship will inevitably transform the character of the international political system and interstate relations in a fundamental way.

Given the short period of time that has elapsed since these events occurred, and because the future of states that once formed the Soviet Union, including Russia, remains uncertain, the final shape and character of the emerging international system is not yet clear. Nevertheless, these happenings have already produced considerable changes in the international system and in the positions and policies of many countries.

One of the most important immediate systemic consequences of the end of the Cold War has been the emergence of an ideological and paradigmatic vacuum for the definition and management of international affairs that the East-West competition provided during the Cold War era. This vacuum in turn has led to a search for a new overarching paradigm that could define and manage all aspects of international relations. Yet such a paradigm is unlikely to be found anytime soon, although a number of broad themes such as those related to the North-South debate or new global environmental concerns could become more important and influential. Nevertheless, in the Islamic world, particularly the Middle East, some observers and experts have been pointing to Islam, especially the more politicized and militant brand, as the most likely successor to communism and to a looming confrontation between Islam and the West as the new defining paradigm that could replace the East-West competition of the Cold War years. This time, however, Russia and the European members of the former socialist bloc are expected to be in the Western camp now that they have rediscovered their Christian roots and embraced Western political and economic values. In fact, observers such as Bernard Lewis and Samuel Huntington have talked about a clash of civilizations between the Islamic and Christian worlds.

For forty years the Cold War and the East-West confrontation pervaded all aspects of international life. Thus the systemic changes triggered by the transformation of the Soviet Union will affect international relations in all its dimensions and the fate of all countries, big and small, rich and poor. The Third World nations, however, which for four decades were the objects of East-West competition and were deeply affected by it, will feel the impact of these changes more intensely in both a negative and a positive sense. At this point, though, it is still impossible to predict what the final balance between negative and positive effects from these changes will be for these states.

Among the Third World countries, those states which lie in proximity to the former Soviet Union and now its successor states—most notably the so-called Northern Tier countries of Iran, Turkey, Pakistan, and Afghanistan—will be particularly affected by the changes. This is so because even in the pre-Cold War era these countries operated under systemic conditions of bipolarity similar to those prevalent during the Cold War. This situation was created by the acute rivalry between imperial Russia and Britain.

The final shape of the new international system will not become clear as long as the political fate of the former Soviet Union, the ultimate character of relations between its constituent parts—especially Russia—with its former rivals, and the future course of relations among the Western allies remain clouded. But before the characteristics of the new system are more clearly evident, it will be very difficult to assess its impact on and implications for the Third World, particularly the Northern Tier countries. What can be done at this stage is the following: (1) to analyze the impact that recent events have already had on the international system, on the Third World, and on the Northern Tier countries; (2) to discuss possible scenarios for the evolution of events in the former Soviet Union, especially Russia, including the most likely character of its future relations with its former adversaries; and (3) to assess the likely evolution of relations among the Western allies.

Before doing so, however, it is useful—indeed necessary—to recall briefly the basic characteristics of the international political system during the Cold War era and the consequences of that system for the Third World, especially the Northern Tier countries. This analysis will create a benchmark against which to assess the impact of recent developments and to make some educated guesses about potential future changes.

The Cold War International System

The international political system that emerged at the end of World War II had several salient characteristics that distinguished it from previous systems.

The most important feature of the new system was its bipolarity at the strategic, economic, and ideological levels, although by the 1960s this bipolarity suffered some erosion, first on the strategic level and later on the economic and ideological levels. The erosion began as a result of the acquisition of significant nuclear capability by Britain, France, and China. The growing Sino-Soviet rift beginning in the late 1950s eroded the ideological bipolarity. The economic recovery of Japan and Europe and the emergence of a number of newly industrialized countries ended the economic bipolarity by the late 1960s. Despite this erosion, however, the system's underlying strategic and ideological bipolarity remained in place until the disintegration of the Soviet Union.

Another significant distinguishing characteristic of the postwar system was the all-encompassing nature of the competition between the two principal protagonists and their allies. The new competition was no longer solely about capturing territory, controlling economic and strategic resources, or carving out exclusive spheres of economic and political influence. It extended, rather, to determining the principles that would shape and govern the social and political life of the world's peoples and states and that of the international community and its institutions. In this respect, it resembled the religious battles of the past for the soul of humanity. The difference this time was that two secular-materialist religions were the main protagonists.

This all-encompassing character of the East-West competition and the fact that at the end there could only be one victor made the new competition essentially a zero-sum game. One side's gain was always the other side's loss. This aspect of the Cold War rivalry was tempered by the imperatives of preventing a nuclear holocaust; hence the emergence of notions such as "peaceful coexistence," "détente," and so on. Such notions, however, applied only to the means of conducting the competition and did not eliminate the quest for ideological victory that was the ultimate goal of this competition.

The result of this situation was that no aspect of international life could remain untouched by the East-West competition. Indeed, the underlying competition shaped all states' perception of external realities and largely determined their behavior in regard to others, depending on where they stood in respect to the East-West competition. Even those countries that chose to reject both ideologies and both political camps—such as the so-called nonaligned countries—did so under the impact of this basic competition. Their choice too was determined by the Cold War paradigm.

The Cold War also affected the evolution of post–World War II international organizations. By and large, its impact was negative. It prevented the maturing of these international institutions, notably the UN, into effective multilateral security instruments. The UN became another arena of Cold War competition, with each superpower trying to use it as an instrument of its policy and a means of undermining its rival. This practice, with the excessive use or threat of use of the veto power, effectively paralyzed the UN and distracted it from its original purpose while also undermining its credibility as an effective global instrument for the settlement of disputes.

Impact on the Third World

The above-noted characteristics of the international system during the Cold War era had far-reaching consequences for the bulk of humanity, rather conveniently lumped together under the title Third World. Some of these consequences were positive, some were negative, and some were mixed, combining both positive and negative elements.

On the negative side, the Cold War further opened the Third World countries to great power interference and manipulation, which sometimes led to outright war, as was the case in Korea, Vietnam, Cambodia, and Afghanistan, and to a score of smaller conflicts, such as those in Nicaragua and El Salvador among others. The material and human losses suffered by the Third World countries as a result of these conflicts have been horrendous. The one million dead and six million refugees of the Afghan war give an indication of the Cold War's costs to the Third World nations. In addition, interferences by great powers distorted the natural political evolution of many Third World countries. They contributed to the defeat of fledgling democratic experiences, as in Iran in 1953 and in Guatemala in 1954, and led to the establishment of authoritarian regimes of the Left or the Right.

Paradoxically, however, the East-West competition and its zero-sum dimension exerted a disciplining influence on the great powers that prevented some of the intra–Third World disputes from escalating into larger conflicts. This happened because the two superpowers restrained their respective clients, lest their disputes trigger a direct superpower confrontation with all the risks that would entail. Moreover, the superpowers themselves were weary of direct military intervention in the Third World because of the fear of confrontation. This superpower reluctance, in turn, gave the Third World countries some measure of protection against superpower interference.

The zero-sum character of the Cold War and the superpower desire to avoid direct confrontation benefited the Third World in other ways. During the Cold War years, for instance, there was an emphasis on preventing large-scale territorial changes and the disintegration of national units, lest such events should benefit the rival camp. Thus there was an emphasis on the inviolability of existing borders, on the sovereignty of states, and on the principle of noninterference in the internal affairs of countries, even if the great powers frequently engaged in covert operations within Third World nations.

As a result, the balancing impact of superpower rivalry helped to preserve the territorial integrity of a number of Third World states. The superpower competition also afforded Third World countries a modicum of independence and helped them avoid descending to the state of pure clientship. The Cold War also helped speed up the process of decolonialization in Africa and in Asia as the colonial powers felt that if they held on to power too long, this might benefit the socialist camp. Moreover, the socialist countries provided assistance to a number of anticolonial movements, albeit for their own selfish reasons. Also on the positive ledger, the East-West competition was a spur to

Third World economic development and to the flow of financial and technical resources to these countries, though the imperatives of Cold War competition distorted the context and direction of external aid, often precipitating the misuse of foreign assistance by the recipient countries for purposes such as building large armies rather than spending it on economic and social development.

Nevertheless, in this respect also the balance for the Third World countries was positive. Without the Cold War and the East-West ideological battle, it is unlikely that the rich and industrially developed countries of both the East and the West would have had much interest in the advancement of the Third World nations.

Indeed, the North-South debate was largely a by-product of the East-West competition. The West was interested in the North-South debate because it feared that the South's poverty would open up opportunities for the East to establish its influence. The East, meanwhile, used the vulnerabilities of poor countries to make political and ideological inroads and to undermine Western positions. Paradoxically, however, the military cost of the Cold War diverted resources, both those of great powers and those of the Third World nations themselves, that ideally should have been spent on the development of the South and the improvement of its peoples' living conditions.

Impact of the Cold War on the Northern Tier Countries

Among the areas that constitute the so-called Third World, the Middle East–South Asia region, especially the Northern Tier countries (because of their proximity to the Soviet Union), were particularly affected by the Cold War and the post–World War II international system. Indeed, as was noted earlier, the Northern Tier countries, especially Iran, had lived under similar circumstances before because of the acute Anglo-Russian rivalry for predominance in these regions in the context of what was dubbed the Great Game.

This Anglo-Russian rivalry had extremely negative consequences for these countries, especially Iran. Yet for most of the nineteenth century and part of the twentieth, the Anglo-Russian rivalry and the determination of both sides to prevent their rivals from gaining control over these regions kept them (again notably Iran) from total disintegration and colonization. Anglo-Russian rivalry also delayed the collapse of the rapidly decaying Ottoman Empire. Yet since Anglo-Russian rivalry, like all other great power rivalries of pre–Cold War days, lacked an ideological content, the possibility of English and Russian collusion at the expense of the objects of their rivalry was always present and strong. The 1907 Anglo-Russian agreement to divide a vast region extending from Tibet to the Persian Gulf, with each country taking an area as its sphere of influence, was a clear expression of this threat.

The advent of the Cold War and the acute superpower rivalry, therefore, was not a totally novel phenomenon for Northern Tier countries. In fact, in some respects the zero-sum character of Cold War competition, by eliminating the possibility of superpower collusion, was an improvement for these states over the previous imperial rivalries, with the ever-present risk of collusion. Soon after the end of World War II, Turkey became a full-fledged member of the new Western military alliance, the North Atlantic Treaty Organization (NATO). The country's new position of trusted ally and its location on the southernmost flank of NATO constituted a great improvement over its previous position as the so-called sick man of Europe.

The consequences for Iran were far more mixed, with an overbalance perhaps on the negative side, especially with regard to its domestic evolution and political maturation. A particularly good example of the negative domestic consequences for Iran is the Mossadegh period, when East-West competition opened the country to undue interference by the great powers. Yet paradoxically the Cold War contributed to Iran's maintaining its territorial integrity and a modicum of independence. For example, without the onset of the Cold War, it would have been much more difficult to secure the withdrawal of occupying Soviet troops from Iran in 1946. Similarly, without the imperatives of the Cold War, the risk of direct superpower intervention in Iran in the 1980s, especially during the Iran-Iraq War, would have been stronger. Certainly the West, and especially the United States, would have been tempted to take more severe punitive actions against Iran in this period had it not been concerned that such actions could benefit the Soviet Union by pushing Iran to seek protection from Moscow.

Meanwhile, the Soviet Union, despite its treaty with Iraq, showed restraint in dealing with Iran lest undue pressure should provide an opportunity for the West to regain its lost position there. The later behavior of both the Soviet Union and the United States toward Iran proves the validity of the above observation. Indeed, by 1987, as U.S.-Soviet relations began to improve, the United States and its Western allies became much bolder in their approach toward Iran because they did not have to be concerned about Soviet reaction. For example, the reflagging operations of Kuwaiti tankers by the United States in 1987–88 would have been unthinkable in the Cold War era. Similarly, the East-West competition also enhanced Pakistan's strategic value to the competitors and resulted in political and material gains. In the 1980s, however, close involvement in the Afghan War—a by-product of the Cold War—produced a series of new domestic problems for Pakistan. As a full-fledged member of NATO, Turkey benefited most from the Cold War as Western powers poured financial resources into that country and put a high premium on maintaining its internal stability.

By and large, though the Cold War had mixed results for these states, especially Iran and Pakistan, it increased their leverage over the great powers and allowed them some room for maneuver by manipulating superpower rivalry. In addition, the Cold War (and, before it, the emergence of the Bolshevik state in Russia) helped these countries, especially Iran and Turkey, submerge their past rivalry and embark on a process of reconciliation. The fear of possible gains for the Soviet Union prevented them from exploiting each other's weaknesses and difficulties, at least in an exaggerated fashion. For instance, one of the reasons that Turkey tried in the 1980s to maintain reasonable relations with Iran, despite the two countries' significant ideological and other differences, was that Turkey feared Iran might fall under Soviet influence, which would have been a threat to Turkish security interests.

The Immediate Effects of Recent Changes

The international system of the Cold War era clearly no longer exists. Yet the shape of the emerging new system is not clear either. In fact, the current situation is one of transition, or what could be characterized as systemic interregnum.

A salient characteristic of this transitional period is the simultaneous persistence of some of the Cold War era institutions and modes of thinking; the resurfacing of pre–Cold War and even pre-1919 national, territorial, and other disputes and problems; and the emergence of new tendencies in modes of international thinking and action that may become dominant features of whatever new international political system ultimately succeeds the one that was prevalent in the Cold War era.

It is widely assumed that the current international system is unipolar, with the United States being the only remaining superpower. Yct, as far as nuclear balance is concerned, Russia, which has the bulk of the former Soviet Union's nuclear arsenal, is still a rival of the United States. Thus at the nuclear level, at least, the system is still almost bipolar. Its bipolarity is reflected in the fact that, as in Cold War days, the main issues related to nuclear and conventional arms control are handled by the United States and Russia, the main successor to the former Soviet Union, although two other former members of the Soviet Union, Ukraine and Kazakhstan, have in the last two years become partial players in the nuclear game.

By the same token, the raison d'être of NATO, namely the defense of Europe against possible Soviet invasion, has disappeared. Yet the institution itself continues to exist, although it is trying to redefine itself, its membership, and its new security role in an era without the Soviet threat. Meanwhile, a series of old problems have reemerged. Fears and rivalries that had been submerged by more urgent concerns caused by the Cold War and the rigidity of alliances and attitudes that were a feature of the Cold War days are resurfacing, albeit in different forms.

In Europe, for instance, a whole series of ethnic and territorial disputes is coming to the fore, as most dramatically illustrated by the unraveling of Yugoslavia. In Eastern Europe there are at least seventeen territorial and ethnic disputes. Whether any of these other disputes will degenerate to the level of that in Yugoslavia is hard to predict. But the risks, while they should not be exaggerated, certainly exist. Once more Europe and the United States are becoming concerned about Germany's growing power and how it may be used in the future. The alliance between the Western industrial nations and Japan is under growing strain, as economic, trade, and other differences are coming to the fore in the absence of the Soviet threat,

A similar phenomenon is observable in the case of the so-called Northern Tier countries, most notably Iran and Turkey. For instance, the emergence of several independent Muslim republics out of the ashes of the Soviet Union, regions that historically have been under the cultural and political influence of Iran and Turkey, has somewhat rekindled the old Ottoman-Persian competition. The disappearance of the common fear of the Soviet Union, which had helped Iran and Turkey submerge their ideological and other differences, has sharply brought to the fore both the old and the new competitive dimensions of their relations. Issues of ethnic and nationalist separatism and irredentism have also become more acute. If unchecked, these problems may become a source of heightened regional tension, conflict, and even outright war. The situation in the Transcaucasus is most ripe for triggering such conflict, but risks also exist in other areas.

Yet the consequences of recent changes for the character of relations among the Northern Tier countries need not be negative. The transformation of the Soviet Union could open up new opportunities for expanded economic and other cooperation among the Northern Tier countries and the new successor states in the Asian parts of the former Soviet Union. Given the intensity of regional rivalries and the manipulation of regional differences by outside powers, the cooperative potential of recent events may not be realized in the near future.

For its part, the UN, although no longer paralyzed by the Cold War and superpower abuse of the veto power, has not yet developed the instruments and resources necessary to prevent these problems from degenerating into large-scale conflicts. Nor is that agency in a position at this point to perform effectively the peacekeeping and peacemaking functions entrusted to it by its charter.

Meanwhile, certain changes have taken place in the shape of the international system within which the balance of power and influence is totally novel. These changes have already had significant implications for the Third World, especially the Northern Tier countries. Should they take root and form the principal features of the emerging international system, their impact on these states would become even more pronounced.

Systemic Impact of Soviet Events and Consequences for Third World Nations

The following are some of the more important systemic changes that have already taken place as a result of the Soviet Union's disintegration, along with their consequences for the Third World countries in general and for the Northern Tier countries in particular.

First, because of the disintegration of the Soviet empire and the discrediting of communism as an alternative to the Western secular democratic and free-market-oriented system, the Western industrial countries collectively have become the only base of global financial and technological resources, and thus they have seen their global political weight and influence also enhanced.

Second, the Western ideology of liberal democracy and free-market economy is also now without rival except in the Islamic world, where a highly political and politicized Islam is offered by some as an alternative both to defunct socialism and to seemingly victorious Western liberal democracy.

Third, although Western industrialized nations—which include Japan—have disagreements among themselves in regard to economic and trade matters, and although they are competitors for markets in the Third World, they share a great deal of commonality of economic interests.[1] This derives from the fact that the economies of principal industrial countries are very interdependent. Moreover, these countries want to maintain their leadership position within existing international financial and other institutions, and all of them have a stake in the existing economic system because it favors them. Thus they are unlikely to allow their competitiveness and minor differences to undermine either their dominant position or the current economic system.[2]

As a result, Third World countries will not be in a position to manipulate their differences to their own advantage as they did during the East-West conflict. They also share common interests in regard to such issues as energy supply and price. This latter point has special significance for a number of Third World countries, namely the oil producers, including Iran. What this means is that, despite their differences and competition, the Western industrial nations are likely to act more or less as a bloc vis-à-vis other countries in setting the rules and conditions for access to financial and technological resources. The ability to do this would, in turn, provide these countries with significant economic and political leverage over others, notably the Third World countries. The effects of this concentration of economic and technological power on the ability of these countries to force Third World states to undertake economic and political changes have in fact already been apparent in the last few years.

Moreover, with the elimination of the Soviet threat, the end of the East-West ideological competition for the Third World, and additional financial demands created by the needs of Eastern Europe and the states of the former Soviet Union, the economic needs of the Third World are likely, as a rule, to receive less attention. This rule will not, however, apply to the same degree to all Third World states. A number of them, notably those in the Middle East, will be favored because of concerns over the challenge of militant Islam. For instance, since the emergence of the Islamic challenge in Algeria, European and other countries seem more willing to help ease Algeria's debt and other financial problems. The Europeans' fear of the consequences of economic and political turmoil within other Maghreb countries is also prompting them to accord these countries preferential treatment. Other Third World countries deemed strategically important will receive preferential treatment as well. Meanwhile, less important countries or those viewed as hostile are likely to be starved of resources, either as punishment or because of sheer neglect.

The future of Russia and the other two main Slavic republics of the former Soviet Union is not yet clear, but in all likelihood, once they overcome their current economic problems, they will become part of the existing industrial and technological elite. They are thus likely to behave in a more or less similar fashion in relation to Third World countries.

But if Russia fails to resolve its problems, or if it becomes disenchanted with the West, it may behave differently. Even under those circumstances, though, given its economic limits, it is unlikely that Russia can play the kind of role as counterweight to the West that it played during the Cold War years.

At the political and ideological level too there is a great deal of convergence of interests among Western countries in the sense that they all espouse secular democratic political systems and that they are likely to insist on the adoption of similar principles and systems by Third World countries. Thus they are likely to favor those Third World states that adhere to these principles, even if only in words.

Moreover, their reaction to those countries that openly and aggressively challenge these ideals is likely to be very negative. This latter point will probably come to the fore in the Middle East in a new kind of competition, and possibly even conflict, between militant and politicized Islam on the one hand and, on the other, those who espouse Western secular political ideas, including some countries whose populations are predominantly Muslim.

Most of the existing governments and political elites of the former Soviet Union, including perhaps those of its Islamic parts, are likely to side with the West, largely because of their acute financial and technological needs. It should be noted nevertheless that many of the current governments may not be in power long and that the successor regimes may adopt different attitudes. But even the successor regimes will inevitably be affected by their economic and technological needs and will have to adapt their foreign policies to these needs. Western countries—which in this definition include Japan, several East Asian nations, Russia, and the Slavic republics—are likely, however, to face a number of serious dilemmas in dealing with the Islamic challenge. This problem could become acute if the Islamic forces tried to gain power through the electoral process, as was the case in Algeria in 1992. These states are likely to compromise their democratic principles if their application would mean victory, or at least more influence, for the Islamic forces. This attitude, however, would undermine the Western world's moral and political credibility and turn the majority of the peoples in the Islamic world against them. It also risks increasing rather than decreasing the threat of regional instability because the Muslim elements, if denied a share in power through legitimate means, could resort to violent means. The Northern Tier countries will be particularly affected by the phenomenon of Western-Muslim conflict.

Among these countries, Turkey will be the principal beneficiary of the trends triggered by the transformation of the Soviet Union because it is a secular state with a Muslim population, close Western ties, and good relations with Israel, at least in the short term.

Turkey has already become the West's favored partner with respect to the Muslim parts of the former Soviet Union, the Balkans, and the southeastern parts of Europe. It is also likely to perform a larger political and security role in the Persian Gulf and in the Middle East than the other states. The extent and significance of its security role in the latter regions will to some extent depend on the evolution of NATO and its post–Cold War mission and defense strategy.

With the end of the Cold War, many NATO countries believe that the principal challenges to their security will emanate from the Middle East-Persian Gulf region. They have been talking therefore about revising NATO strategy and force deployment in order to enable it to meet these challenges. Should this happen, Turkey will become the principal NATO outpost in the Middle East. This event would restore Turkey's past strategic significance, which was eroded by the end of the Cold War, improvements in U.S.-Soviet relations, and the disintegration of the Soviet Union.

Moreover, there is an effort to link the Muslim parts of the former

Soviet Union to European security institutions such as the Conference on Security and Cooperation in Europe (CSCE). Indeed, all former Soviet Muslim republics are now members of the CSCE, as well as a new forum, the North Atlantic Cooperation Council. In this respect, too, Turkey is likely to become the main conduit for the West and the linchpin of Western links with these areas. Russia and other Slavic republics favor Turkey as the main influence in the Muslim parts of former Soviet Asia because they are also concerned about the impact of militant Islam on the Russian communities in these areas as well as those in parts of Europe.

Excessive Turkish ambition, an unduly high Turkish profile, and most of all the espousal of a pan-Turkic policy, however, will not be without risk and possible costs to Turkey. Such a policy on Turkey's part will inevitably lead to the resurfacing of anti-Turkish sentiments and possibly even the formation of an unofficial anti-Turkish coalition. It will certainly lead non-Turkic peoples in the region to draw closer together. Russian concerns would also grow about the reemergence of Pan-Turkism and excessive Turkish influence.

Similarly, the weakening of NATO and the development of a European defense force that excludes Turkey will inevitably diminish Turkey's influence. In addition, developments within Turkey itself will have a tremendous impact on its future role, including its position as the favored partner of the West. A rise of both Islamic sentiment and extreme nationalist and pan-Turkic tendencies will inevitably complicate Turkey's relations with the West. Yet if Turkey does not become part of the European Community within a reasonably short period of time and turns increasingly eastward, the risk of the rise of Islamic and nationalist tendencies will increase.

Iran, by contrast, will be negatively affected by these events, at least in the foreseeable future. This will be so because the new constellation of international power views Iran, because of its espousal of militant Islam, as the primary challenge, especially in an ideological sense, to their views and their vision for the future of the Middle East and the former Soviet Asia. The Western portrayal of Iran as a serious threat to its interests from the Transcaucasus to North Africa and the declared intention of the West, especially the United States, to prevent Iran from having influence in the former Soviet republics, despite a three-thousand-year history of Iranian interaction with these lands, illustrate this tendency.[3]

Moreover, the end of the Cold War and the disintegration of the Soviet empire have eliminated Iran's historic value as the most formidable buffer between Russia—and later the Soviet Union—and the Persian Gulf with its vast oil resources. This development in turn has eroded Iran's bargaining position and eliminated great powers' incentives to maintain Iran's territorial integrity as a buffer against Soviet advances. In fact, after recent changes, Iran's size, resources, and overall power potential and importance may become a liability for it as it increasingly will be viewed as a competitor by the West and by other countries. Thus Iran faces an enhanced risk that others will try to prevent its economic reinvigoration and undermine its regional position. Already a number of regional countries, including those who claim friendship with Iran, are marketing themselves to the West as counterweights to Iran.

Should the occasion permit, the idea of dividing Iran, as was envisaged both in the 1907 Anglo-Russian treaty and in the Molotov-Ribbentrop Agreement of 1941, may even resurface. This, however, will not be easily accomplished. In fact, Iran's disintegration would have ramifications far beyond itself and would threaten the integrity of other countries, notably Turkey. Thus it is unlikely that others will embark lightly on such a course. But the risk is real. Certainly no one in the West would try to prevent Iran's breakup if it were to happen without threatening the integrity of other countries deemed important to Western interests, again notably Turkey.

In general, the end of the East-West competition has diluted, if not totally eliminated, aversion to massive territorial changes on the part of the great powers. Thus many observers now say that the twenty-first century may be that of nation breaking as the twentieth century was that of nation building.[4] An extension of this approach is that the new constellation of power is likely to focus more on the rights of individuals and minorities within states and to pursue a more intrusive policy in this regard. This, however, will be done selectively and whenever it is considered in the interests of the great powers. This trend is illustrated by the West's handling of Iraq and the rights of its minorities.

In other words, unlike the way it was in the past, when state sovereignty was the dominant principle of international relations, the rights of individuals may become more significant. If this principle is used properly, this situation should not be alarming to Third World states. But if it is abused and applied selectively, as is likely to happen, it can degenerate into nothing more than a means of pressure and interference by the great powers, and it will be highly destabilizing and damaging to the Third World countries.

The case of Pakistan is more ambiguous. Pakistan certainly is not a Western-style secular democratic state as Turkey is, at least superficially. The Pakistani brand of Islamic state is viewed as more tame and thus less threatening to Western interests than that of Iran. Moreover, Pakistan has long been a strategic ally of the West and a close friend to such key Western allies as Saudi Arabia. And given Pakistan's economic weakness, its power potential, unlike that of Iran, is not significant. As a result, Pakistan is not viewed by the West as a potential rival, at least in certain regions, as Iran is seen in the Persian Gulf and in Central Asia. Thus it is likely that the great powers may use Pakistan, as well as other Muslim countries such as Egypt and Saudi Arabia, as a model for the former Soviet Muslim states of an Islamic alternative, which would be less threatening and more accommodating than the Iranian model. Because of the erosion of Pakistan's strategic significance and its acute economic and financial problems, the great powers are in a strong position to pressure the country into accepting and following their positions.

Pakistan is in fact marketing itself to the West as a counterweight to Iran in Central Asia while at the same time courting Iran. Another consequence of the end of the Cold War is that local conflicts in the Third World, except in sensitive areas, will not receive much attention. This may not be altogether too negative a development, as in the past great power involvement tended to prolong such conflicts. But total disregard could also sap the energies of many Third World states and further hinder their development.[5]

U.S. Preponderance

During this systemic transition period, the United States is likely to play a preponderant role internationally and, in particular, in the Middle East–Persian Gulf region. Thus U.S. preferences and priorities are likely to have a significant impact on the course of events in these regions. What is less certain, however, is the outcome of the handling of this region by the United States . By no means can the United States be sure of total success; U.S. policy mistakes could very well undermine the United States' own interests and position in this area. They may also generate more regional instability, as has often been the case in the past.

The United States has significant domestic economic and social problems, and its economic power has declined in relative terms. Yet, for a variety of reasons, it is likely to play a leadership role internationally, at least until the end of the 1990s.

First, the United States is now the only country with economic and military power of global reach. It is both a Pacific and an Atlantic power; and through its allies it is also a Middle East, Persian Gulf, and South Asian power.

Second, currently there is no other power that is willing to perform the kind of leadership role that the United States has played in the past within the Western world and now seems ready to assume internationally. Europe is preoccupied with the challenges produced by the end of the Cold War and the transformation of the Soviet Union, plus the difficulties of European integration.

In addition, Soviet events have created new problems and tensions within the European Community that may slow the process of European integration. Thus in the near future Europe is unlikely to be able to act as a single power and to become an alternative to U.S. global leadership. Moreover, insofar as the Middle East–Persian Gulf region is concerned, there is a very large degree of commonality of interest between the United States and Europe. Certainly, even in the long-term, a united Europe is unlikely to play the kind of role that the USSR played in the Third World and, in particular, in the Middle East region. U.S.-European ideological interests are also identical: both countries are especially fearful of any form of militant ideology, including militant Islam, which could challenge their own. This means that even future U.S.-European rivalry is unlikely to provide the Third World with the kind of opportunities to play off one power against the other for its own gains as the East-West competition did.

Japan, too, despite its problems with the United States and Europe, is unlikely to act as a global counterweight to the United States the way the Soviet Union did. The same applies to China. In fact, given the deep mistrust among China, Japan, Korea, and other East Asian countries, they all welcome a certain U.S. presence and role, including military, in the Pacific region as a balancing factor. The Europeans favor a continued U.S. presence because they see the United States as a counterweight to Germany and also because of uncertainty over

Russia's future, including the possibility of the resurgence of an expansionist Russia.

Because of all these factors, those countries that openly challenge the United States and its vital interests are likely to encounter economic and other pressures and difficulties. And, in the meantime, they are unlikely to get any significant help from other quarters, including Europe or Japan. Because of the commonality of interest among Western powers in regard to the Middle East, this observation will apply especially to this region and to the Islamic parts of the former Soviet Union. Among the Northern Tier countries, Iran—in view of its difficulties with the United States but also with other Western countries—is likely to be most seriously affected by this factor, but a moderation of the Iranian policy and an improvement in U.S.-Iranian relations will ameliorate this negative situation. Nevertheless, because of Iran's inherent potential as a regional power, the West and other major international and regional players will try to prevent it from actualizing this potential, even if Iran should totally abandon its ideological aspirations.

The Emerging System: World Order or Great Power Condominium?

We cannot yet predict the ultimate shape of the international system that will succeed the one that prevailed during the Cold War. There are, however, two basic choices confronting the international community. The first is to seize the opportunities presented by the end of the Cold War to create an international system based on the rule of law and, at least, a modicum of social and economic justice. This could be accomplished by encouraging multilateral action to deal with international economic problems, by strengthening the multilateral institutions, and by a more general rather than selective application of international norms. This choice, needless to say, is the better one, but it is also the one that is more difficult and thus less likely to be adopted.

The other possibility is some kind of unofficial great power condominium, a new version of the nineteenth-century concept of the Concert of Europe, which this time might include a few Asian countries such as China and Japan and perhaps some Third World countries such as India, Brazil, and Egypt. In the long run, this system would be less stable, but in the short-term it would be more appealing to the principal players and hence would have a better chance of being adopted. The trend to this kind of thinking is exemplified in such ideas as the creation of a U.S.-Russian strategic military alliance, as discussed during President Boris Yeltsin's trip to Washington in January 1992, and a change in NATO strategy to enable it to perform military and political functions outside of the traditional sphere of its activity, most notably in the Middle East.[6] Whether such a system will emerge, however, will depend on the following factors:

1. The future of Russia and its relations with the West. Will Russia become an integral part of the Western world, or will it develop competitive relations with the West?[7] If it develops competitive relations with the Western world, what will be the nature, extent, and geographical focus of this competition?

2. The future of Europe and transatlantic relations. Is Europe's interest likely to diverge from that of the United States? If so, in what ways? Is Europe likely to become a global competitor with the United States? If so, what will be the nature of their competition?

3. The future of China and Japan and their relations with the West. Is an Asian pole of power likely to emerge? If so, what will be its likely shape, interest, and aspirations? What are likely to be the ideological underpinnings of such a pole?

4. The evolution of the U.S. domestic scene. Will the American people continue to assume large-scale international burdens? If not, will the United States become mostly a hemispheric power? What are the other systems in which the United States is likely to remain engaged?

It is impossible at this point to provide any clear answers to these questions. What seems clear, however, it that even beyond the current transitional period, it is unlikely that the world will witness the kind of Manichaean competition between the so-called forces of socialism and capitalism that was typical of the Cold War years, incarnating diverging visions of good and evil and light and darkness. Even an eventual confrontation between Islam and the West in the context of a so-called clash of civilizations would apply only to a limited part of the globe and would not have universal impact. Thus the future international system certainly will not be a bipolar one. There will be several poles of power—especially economic—and the competition is likely to be mostly of an economic nature. Political and military disputes are likely to be localized. But the emergence of new competing ideologies and social and economic systems cannot be ruled out. Certainly the gap between the haves and the have-nots and the quest for greater social and economic justice will remain potent political forces potentially capable of mobilizing individuals and nations. Nevertheless, in this new context, again the Third World countries will be mostly the objects of competition, except that this time their leverage over the advanced nations will be even less than in the past. The Northern Tier countries, with the possible exception of Turkey, at least in the short term and depending on the outcome of the Turkish quest to be integrated with the West, will share in this general destiny of Third World nations for the foreseeable future.

Notes

1. On the trade and economic disputes among Western allies see the following: "Fiery Buchanan Attacks 'Unfair' Airbus Subsidies," *Financial Times*, 13 February 1992; and "Troops, Trade Pact Not Linked, Bush Says," *Washington Post*, 12 February 1992. Even more strongly, President Bush accused the European Community of "hiding behind its own iron curtain of protectionism." See "Bush Defends Trip, Warns Against 'Gloomsayers,' " *Washington Post*, 14 January 1992. Also "Genscher Warns Japan on Uruguay Round," *Financial Times*, 14 February 1992.

2. For example, Japan would like to replace Britain as the second most important member of the IMF/World Bank group.

3. See, for instance, "US to Counter Iran in Central Asia," *New York Times*, 6 February 1992.

4. See, for instance, Francis Fukuyama, "Rest Easy. It's Not 1914 Anymore. Nations Break Up as Democracy Grows Up," *New York Times*, 9 February 1992.

5. For example, as was not the case in the past, civil wars in Somalia, Ethiopia, and a number of other countries have received little or no attention despite their heavy human and material costs.

6. See "Bush and Yeltsin Declare Formal End to Cold War; Agree to Exchange Visits," *New York Times*, 2 February 1992. It is reported in this article that during his visit to Washington, Yeltsin suggested that Russia and the United States should develop a global space-based defense against missiles. See also on this theme Fred Ikle, "Living with the Russian Army," *National Interest*, no. 26 (Winter 1991–92).

7. See Charles Krauthammer, "Who Is Losing Russia," *Washington Post*, 19 February 1992.

Contributors ━━━━━━━━━━━━━━━━━

James T. Alexander is a Ph.D. candidate in the Department of Political Science of the University of Illinois at Urbana-Champaign. He has contributed to several review essays on Soviet domestic and foreign policy that have appeared in the German scholarly journal *Osteuropa*.

Gennady Chufrin is deputy director of the Institute of Oriental Studies of the Russian Academy of Sciences. His many publications include *Asia in the 1990s: American and Soviet Perspectives*, coedited with Robert Scalapino (1990); *Science and Technology in ASEAN Countries*, coauthored with Vitaly Kurzanov and Galina Shabalina (1990); and *Foreign Policy of Singapore*, coauthored with Emma Gurevich (1989).

Andre Gunder Frank is professor of development economics and social sciences at the University of Amsterdam. He has published (in twenty-four languages) thirty books in more than one hundred editions and many more printings in a dozen languages; more than three hundred of his articles have been published and reprinted in more than two hundred periodicals. Among his most recent works are *Transforming the Revolution: Social Movements and the World-System*, with S. Amin, G. Arrighi, and I. Wallerstein (1990); and *Resistance in the World System: Capitalist Accumulation, State Policy, Social Movements* (1990), with Marta Fuentes (in German).

Yuri V. Gankovsky is a fellow at the Oriental Institute of the Russian Academy of Sciences. He is vice president of the Scientific Council for the Coordination of Oriental Studies in the Academy and currently heads the Association of Afghanistan Studies and the Association of Friends of Pakistan. He is the author of numerous works including *The Durrany Empire* (1958), *Peoples of Pakistan* (1964), and *Ethnic Movements in Pakistan* (1967).

Anatoly Glinkin is a principal investigator in the Latin American Institute of the Russian Academy of Sciences. He is a member of the editorial board of the journal *América Latina*. He has published numerous books and articles in seven languages, including two in English: *U.S. Policy in Latin America: Postwar to Present* (1983) and *Inter-American Problems: From Bolivar to the Present* (1990), and one in Russian: *The Diplomacy of Simón Bolívar* (1991).

Shireen T. Hunter is deputy director of the Middle East Program at the Center for Strategic and International Studies in Washington. She is the author of *Iran and the World: Continuity in a Revolutionary Decade* (1990), a comprehensive examination of Iranian foreign policy. Her other books include *OPEC and the Third World: Politics of Aid* (1984), and she was editor-contributor of *The Politics of Islamic Revivalism* (1988). Hunter is also the author of many book chapters and numerous articles in leading journals.

Roger E. Kanet is associate vice chancellor for academic affairs, director of international programs and studies, and professor of political science at the University of Illinois at Urbana-Champaign. His recent publications include *Soviet Foreign Policy in Transition,* coedited with Deborah Nutter Miner and Tamara J. Resler (1992); *The Cold War as Cooperation: Superpower Cooperation in Regional Conflict Management,* coedited with Edward A. Kolodziej (1991); and *The Limits of Soviet Power in the Developing World: Thermidor in the Revolutionary Struggle,* coedited with Edward A. Kolodziej (1989).

Mark N. Katz is associate professor of government and politics at George Mason University. He is the author and editor of several books, including *Gorbachev's Military Policy in the Third World* (1989), *Russia and Arabia: Soviet Foreign Policy toward the Arabian Peninsula* (1986), and *Soviet-American Conflict Resolution in the Third World* (editor, 1991); and he has published numerous articles on Soviet foreign and military policy toward the Third World.

Yuri Krasin is a professor at and director of the Center for Social Programs at the International Foundation for Socio-Economic and Political Studies, the Gorbachev Foundation. He is the author of more than four hundred scholarly works on social movements, world politics, and international relations. Among his latest works are *The USSR and the World Community: From Old to New Thinking* (1990) and *Capitalism Today: Paradoxes of Development* (coauthored, 1989).

Viktor A. Kremenyuk is professor and deputy director at the Institute of World Economy and International Relations in Moscow. A leading specialist in Soviet foreign policy, he is the author of numerous books on Soviet–Third World and U.S.-Soviet relations.

Vendulka Kubalkova is professor of international studies at the Graduate School of International Studies, University of Miami. She is director of the Theory of International Relations Program at the University of Miami and codirector of the newly established University of Miami and Florida International University's Inter-University Group on the Transformation of the Soviet bloc. She is the author (with A. A. Cruickshank) of several articles and five books, including *Marxism and International Relations* (1985) and *Thinking New about Soviet "New Thinking"* (1989).

Stephen Neil MacFarlane is professor of political studies at Queen's University and senior fellow at the Center for International Relations. He is the author of several scholarly articles and books, including *Intervention and Regional Security, Superpower Rivalry and Third World Radicalism,* and *Gorbachev's Third World Dilemmas.* He is currently completing a book on Third World security after the Cold War and is working on several projects relating to ethnic and political conflict in the former Soviet Union. He is the coordinator of the American Council of Learned Societies/Russian Academy of Sciences Exchange in problems of international security.

Mohiaddin Mesbahi is associate professor of international relations at Florida International University. He is the author of several articles and book chapters on Soviet-Iranian relations and Central Asian security. His forthcoming works include an edited volume, *Central Asia and the Caucasus after the Soviet Union: Domestic and International Dynamics* (UPF, 1994), and *Moscow and Iran: From the Islamic Revolution to the Collapse of Communism.*

Georgy I. Mirsky is professor at the Institute of International Relations at the Ministry of Foreign Affairs and formerly was head of the Department of Developing Countries at the Institute for World Economy and International Relations. He has lectured at the Warsaw Pact Headquarters in Moscow and the Diplomatic Academy of the Ministry of Foreign Affairs and has undertaken several lecture tours in the Soviet Union for the Knowledge Society. He is the author of several books, including *Asia and Africa—Continents in Movement, Iraq: The Turbulent Period, The Military and Politics in Developing Countries, Class Structure in the Third World,* and *Military and Society in the Third World.*

Vitaly Naumkin is deputy director and head of the Middle East Center, Oriental Institute of the Russian Academy of Sciences. He is also director of the Russian Center for Strategic Research and International Studies. He has been a guest lecturer at numerous institutions, including Columbia University, Johns Hopkins University, and Cairo University. He is the author of many books and articles, including *Contemporary History of the Arab World* (1990) and *The Arab World: Three Decades of Independent Development* (1990).

Alvin Z. Rubinstein is professor of political science at the University of Pennsylvania and a senior fellow of the Foreign Policy Research Institute. Among his major books are *Soviet Foreign Policy since World War II,* 4th edition (1992), and *Moscow's Third World Strategy,* expanded edition (1990), which was awarded the American Association for the Advancement of Slavic Studies' Marshall Shulman prize. His articles have appeared in journals such as *Foreign Affairs, Orbis, Problems of Communism, Pakistan Journal of Social Sciences,* and the *Washington Quarterly.*

Aldo C. Vacs is associate professor of political science at the Department of Government, Skidmore College. He is the author of *Discreet Partners: Argentina and the USSR since 1917* (1984), *The 1980 Grain Embargo Negotiations: The US, Argentina and the USSR* (1988), and numerous articles published in scholarly journals and edited volumes. He is currently studying the diplomatic interactions of the superpowers in the Third World, the political economy of foreign debt in Argentina and Brazil, and the relations between democratization, political and economic developments, and foreign policies in South America.

Elizabeth Kridl Valkenier is resident scholar at the Harriman Institute at Columbia University, where she teaches Soviet relations with the Third World in the political science department. Her publications on various aspects of Soviet policies in the developing countries include *The Soviet Union and the Third World: An Economic Bind* (1985); numerous contributions to edited symposia; more than forty articles for American, English, French, German, Indian, and Mexican scholarly journals; and editorial comments in leading American newspapers.

Irina Zviagelskaya is head of the Research Section at the Institute of Oriental Studies. She is also principal researcher and deputy director of the Russian Center for Strategic Research and International Relations. Among her numerous publications are *The Role of the Israeli Military in States Policy Formation* (1982) and *American Policy toward Conflicts in the Middle East: From the Mid-1970s–1980s* (1990).

Index

410   Index

Sart language, 77, 78
Saudi Arabia, 186, 187, 188, 189, 340;
   Central Asian republics and, 343–44;
   Pakistan and, 383; U.S. and, 210,
   214; USSR and, 333, 338, 351n.13
Schelling, T., 143n.11
Sea lines of communication, 9, 155–56,
   184–85, 240–41. *See also* Law of the
   Sea
Second Cold War, 33–34, 58
The Second Slump (Mandel), 33
Self-identification, 80
Setubal, Olavo, 299–300, 305
77, Group of, 92, 96
Shaba (Zaire), 226
Shamir, Shimon, 86
Shenin, O., 278
Shevardnadze, Eduard: in Africa, 95,
   167; Baker and, 166, 273–74; on Cen-
   tral America, 272, 273–74; in Cuba,
   277; on diplomacy, 166; on "new
   thinking," 131; resignation of, 136,
   198, 202; in South America, 271,
   306; Soviet Chamber of Commerce
   and, 95; Soviet foreign-policy ideology
   and, 133; on Third World conflicts,
   159, 161
Shiites, 213, 362, 366n.21
Shmelov, Nikolai, 97
Shokin, A., 282
Show projects, 90
Shuikov, 326
Siad Barre, Muhammad, 227
Sihanouk, Norodom, 209
Sikhs, 366n.21
Silver, 46
Singapore, 159
Six Day War (1967), 154, 155, 156,
   332
Six, Group of, 305, 306
Slave labor, 25
Slavic republics, 139, 204, 379
Smith, D. and R., 34
Sobchak, Anatoli, 97
Social classes. *See* Class structure
Socialism. *See* Communism
Social sciences, 40n.10, 163
Sokolov, 360
Solidarity (trade union), 55
Sollum (Egypt), 155

Somalia, 165, 227, 229, 231, 233,
   387n.5
Somosa regime, 265
Soto, L., 282
South Africa: vs. Angola, 228, 232; con-
   stitutional reform in, 234; Gorbachev
   regime and, 95, 164–65; military re-
   souces of, 246–47n.9; regional domi-
   nance of, 229, 232
South America, 53, 54, 55, 271, 285–
   324
South Asia, 152
South Atlantic region, 306–7
Southeast Asia, 10, 95, 200, 259–61
Southeast Asia Treaty Organization, 130
Southern Africa, 164–65, 200, 228, 229
Southern countries: economic conditions
   in, 54, 56, 61, 66; "Second World"
   and, 65; USSR and, 89, 103; Western-
   Soviet cooperation in, 92. *See also*
   North-South conflict
South Korea, 251; ASEAN and, 260;
   Russia and, 10, 252, 255–56, 257;
   U.S. and, 259; USSR and, 95; West
   and, 49
South Pacific region, 261
Southwest Asia, 240
South Yemen, 329, 336–37
Soviet Academy of Sciences, 97
Soviet-Argentine Agreement (1953), 287
Soviet Army (40th), 360–61. *See also*
   Red Army
Soviet Chamber of Commerce, 95
Soviet Defense Ministry, 252, 359–60
Soviet Institute of the USA and Canada,
   97
Soviet Institute of World Economy and
   International Relations, 97
Soviet-Iraqi Treaty (1973), 136
Soviet KGB, 279
Soviet Ministry for Foreign Economic
   Relations, 94
Soviet Ministry of Foreign Affairs, 159
Sovietology, 3, 19–44
Soviet Politburo, 149, 161
Soviet successor republics, 51, 61, 216;
   Afghanistan and, 362–64; Persian
   Gulf region and, 341–47; South
   America and, 310–16; Third World
   and, 280–81. *See also* Central Asian